LONGSTREET HIGHROAD GUIDE

— TO THE —

PENNSYLVANIA MOUNTAINS

BY GREG AND KAREN CZARNECKI

LONGSTREET
ATLANTA, GEORGIA

Published by
LONGSTREET PRESS, INC.
a subsidiary of Cox Newspapers,
a subsidiary of Cox Enterprises, Inc.
2140 Newmarket Parkway
Suite 122
Marietta, Georgia 30067

Great efforts have been made to make the information in this book as accurate as possible. However, over time trails are rerouted and signs and landmarks can change. If you find a change has occurred to a trail in the book, please let us know so we can correct future editions.
A word of caution: outdoor recreation by its nature is potentially hazardous. All participants in such activities must resume all responsibility for their own actions and safety. The scope of this book does not cover all potential hazards and risks involved in outdoor recreation activities.

Printed by RR Donnelley & Sons, Harrisonburg, VA

1st printing 1998

Library of Congress Catalog Number 98-87786

ISBN: 1-56352-474-0

Book editing, design, and cartography
by Lenz Design & Communications, Inc., Decatur, Georgia

Cover illustration by Jules Tavernier, *Picturesque America*, 1872

Cover design by Richard J. Lenz, Decatur, Georgia

Illustrations by Danny Woodard, Loganville, Georgia

Climb the mountains and get their good tidings. Nature's peace will flow into you as sunshine flows into trees. The winds will blow their freshness into you, and the storms their energy, while cares will drop off like falling leaves.

—John Muir

Contents

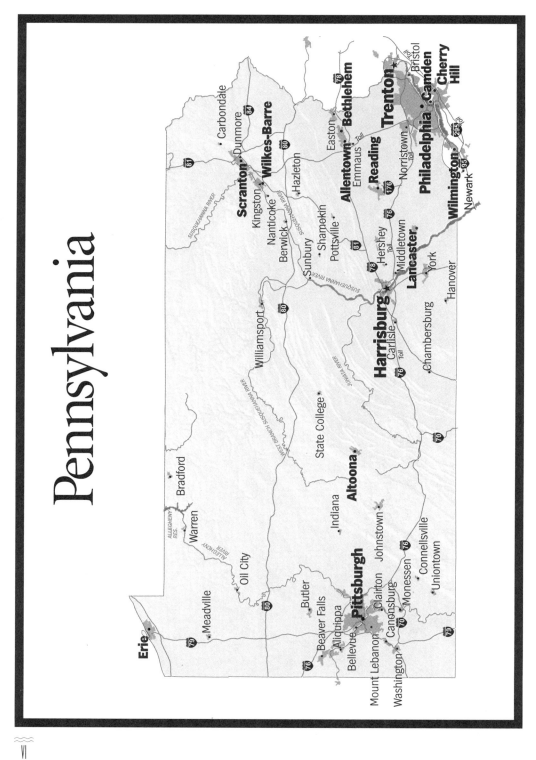

Pennsylvania

How Your Highroad Guide Is Organized

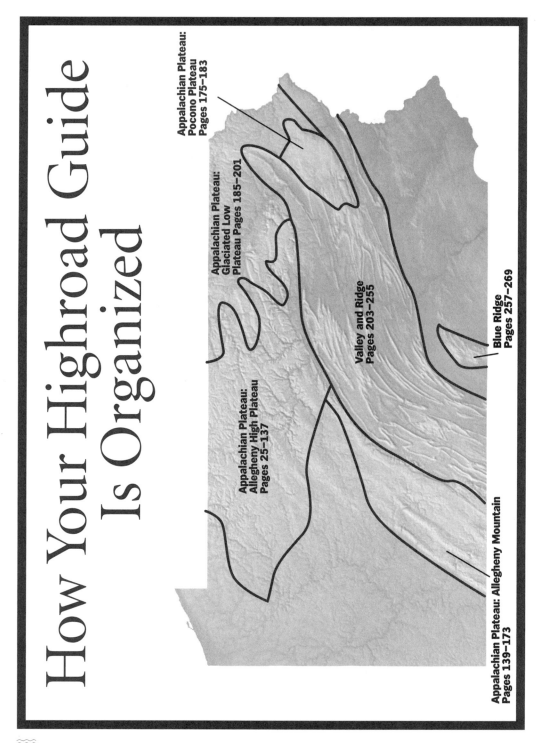

Appalachian Plateau: Pocono Plateau Pages 175–183

Appalachian Plateau: Glaciated Low Plateau Pages 185–201

Appalachian Plateau: Allegheny High Plateau Pages 25–137

Valley and Ridge Pages 203–255

Blue Ridge Pages 257–269

Appalachian Plateau: Allegheny Mountain Pages 139–173

How to Use Your Longstreet Highroad Guide

The *Longstreet Highroad Guide to Pennsylvania* includes a wealth of detailed information about the best of what the Pennsylvania mountains have to offer, including hiking, camping, fishing, canoeing, cross-country skiing, mountain biking, and horseback riding. The *Longstreet Highroad Guide* also presents information on the natural history of the mountains, plus interesting facts about Pennsylvania's flora and fauna, giving the reader a starting point to learn more about what makes the mountains so special.

This book is divided into four major sections using Pennsylvania's main physiographic regions, plus two additional sections. One is an introduction to the natural history of the mountains and the other details long trails.

The maps in the book are keyed by figure numbers and referenced in the text. These maps are intended to help orient both the casual and expert mountains enthusiast. Below is a legend to explain symbols used on the maps. Remember, hiking trails frequently change as they fall into disuse or new trails are created. Serious hikers may want to purchase additional maps from the US Geological Service before they set out on a long hike. Sources are listed on the maps, in the text, and in the appendix. Those wishing to use cabins, pavilions, or campsites at one of Pennsylvania's state parks need to make a reservation by calling the Pennsylvania State Park reservation number: 1-888-PAPARKS.

A word of caution: the mountains can be dangerous. Weather can change suddenly, rocks can be slippery, and wild animals can act in unexpected ways. Use common sense when in the mountains so all your memories will be happy ones.

Legend

Amphitheater	Wheelchair Accessible	Misc. Special Areas
Parking	First Aid Station	Town or City
Telephone	Picnic Shelter	Physiographic Region/ Misc. Boundary
Information	Horse Trail	Appalachian Trail
Picnicking	Horse Stable	Regular Trail
Dumping Station	Shower	State Boundary
Swimming	Biking	70 Interstate
Fishing	Comfort/Rest Station	522 U.S. Route
Interpretive Trail	Cross-country Ski Trail	643 State Highway
Camping	Snowmobile Trail	SR2010 State Route
Bathroom	Park Boundary	T470 Township Road

Map of State Parks

Pennsylvania has 114 state parks. These are mountain state parks featured in this book.

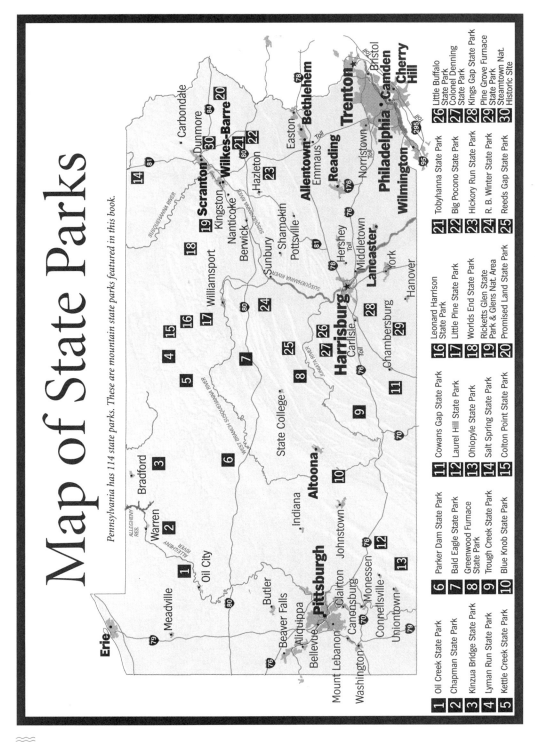

1 Oil Creek State Park	**6** Parker Dam State Park	**11** Cowans Gap State Park	**16** Leonard Harrison State Park	**21** Tobyhanna State Park	**26** Little Buffalo State Park
2 Chapman State Park	**7** Bald Eagle State Park	**12** Laurel Hill State Park	**17** Little Pine State Park	**22** Big Pocono State Park	**27** Colonel Denning State Park
3 Kinzua Bridge State Park	**8** Greenwood Furnace State Park	**13** Ohiopyle State Park	**18** Worlds End State Park	**23** Hickory Run State Park	**28** Kings Gap State Park
4 Lyman Run State Park	**9** Trough Creek State Park	**14** Salt Spring State Park	**19** Ricketts Glen State Park & Glens Nat. Area	**24** R. B. Winter State Park	**29** Pine Grove Furnace State Park
5 Kettle Creek State Park	**10** Blue Knob State Park	**15** Colton Point State Park	**20** Promised Land State Park	**25** Reeds Gap State Park	**30** Steamtown Nat. Historic Site

Preface

When we began to write this book it was our intention to produce a guidebook that would take the reader to all of Pennsylvania's mountainous public lands. We quickly realized that would be impossible, however, because the Commonwealth is blessed with a vast expanse and diversity of publicly owned lands. Instead we have focused on those areas within public lands that have received special protection, that are ecologically or geologically unique, or that offer exceptional recreation opportunities. They may contain a rare or threatened ecosystem, a unique geologic feature, or be home to one or more endangered species. These areas are generally free of development and resource extraction and so present an opportunity to see nature unspoiled.

Hawk Mountain in Berks County

The focal points of this book are state parks, state forests, and federally owned lands with designated wild areas and recreation areas. We have also included three private lands in the book. Bear Run Nature Preserve in southwestern Pennsylvania contains 4,000 acres of pristine woodlands, mountain streams, numerous hiking trails, and the world-famous Fallingwater house designed by Frank Lloyd Wright. Hawk Mountain Sanctuary, located near the eastern end of the state, is widely regarded as the best place in the world to view raptor migrations. Tannersville Cranberry Bog, owned by The Nature Conservancy, is the largest low altitude bog in the eastern United States.

In addition to covering the recreational opportunities and natural aspects of the mountains, we have also woven in the history since the arrival of European settlers. Man has changed the ecology and face of Pennsylvania's mountains. The histories of the two are inextricably intertwined, and you cannot understand one without knowing about the other.

As you read through this book and take it on your travels, please remember that it just scratches the surface of what there is to see and do in Pennsylvania's mountains. The appendices in the back of the book list numerous web sites, addresses, and phone numbers that will lead you to more information about the mountains of our state and the sites covered in this book.

We hope you enjoy using this book as much as we enjoyed writing it. Now use it to help you discover that Pennsylvania memories do last a lifetime.

—Greg & Karen Czarnecki

Acknowledgments

A book isn't just words, it's information and knowledge. While our names appear on the cover, we simply arranged the words. The real credit for this book goes to the foresters, biologists, and land managers of the state, federal, and private resource agencies that provided us with the information and knowledge that fills the pages that follow.

In order to cover the state's forests we worked with the foresters that manage the forests on a day-to-day basis. This book would not have been written without David Williams at Forbes State Forest, Robert Schweitzer at Gallitzin State Forest, Charles Kiehl and John Eastlake at Tiadaghton State Forest, Bob Martin and Jeff Hahn at Elk State Forest, Dave Schiller at Susquehannock State Forest, Ken Barnes at Moshannon State Forest, David Gregg and Bill Bacom at Tioga State Forest, Robert Davey at Sproul State Forest, Ralph Heilig at Rothrock State Forest, Merl Waltz at Buchanan State Forest, Bob Beleski at Tuscarora State Forest, Les Johnson at Bald Eagle State Forest, Anthony Cardwell at Delaware State Forest, Tony Santoli at Lackawanna State Forest, Rick Torsell at Wyoming State Forest, and Gary Zimmerman at Michaux State Forest. We also owe a debt of gratitude to the Bureau of Forestry's endangered plant expert Kathy McKenna, Dan Devlin of the Bureau's Resource Management Division, and its biodiversity coordinator Bob Hill for filling in some of the gaps in our knowledge of rare and endangered species, natural areas, and also for helping us dig up maps on short notice. Thanks also to Gretchen Leslie, communications director for the Pennsylvania Department of Conservation and Natural Resources, for acting as our liaison with the Bureau of Forestry.

Pennsylvania's state parks are managed by an equally well-qualified and dedicated group of professionals. We are indebted to Terry Daltroff at Ricketts Glen State Park, Chris Reese at Black Moshannon State Park, Jerry Frost at Salt Spring State Park, Vicki Paulas at Hickory Run State Park, Ron Dixon at Tobyhanna State Park, Douglas Hoehn and Barbara Drbal at Ohiopyle State Park, Warren Werntz and Audrey Gray at Laurel Hill State Park, Terry Wentz at Trough Creek State Park, Bert Myers at Colonel Denning State Park, Steve Behe at Cowans Gap State Park, John Kaercher at Little Pine State Park, Barry Wolf at Greenwood Furnace State Park, Charles Rea at Reeds Gap State Park, Dennis Laubach at Worlds End State Park, Chip Harrison at Lyman Run State Park, Len Strom at Kinzua Bridge State Park, Scott Streator at Parker Dam State Park, Susan Rensel at Bald Eagle State Park, Mary Herrold at Kettle Creek State Park, Robert Peppel at Chapman State Park, Bob Cross at Little Buffalo State Park, Ed Kautz at R.B. Winter State Park, Jim Davis at Blue Knob State Park, William Williams at Promised Land State Park, and Greg Burkett at Cook Forest State Park. A special thanks also to Wendy Sweger in the bureau's Harrisburg office for helping us locate maps and natural area information, often on very short notice.

It was our good fortune to work with several helpful people at the federal level as well. Among them was Brad Nelson, a wildlife biologist at the Allegheny National Forest and an old friend. Brad provided information on the forest's natural history, management, and the otter and fisher reintroduction projects with which he has been an integral part. Thanks also to Richard Kandare, the forest's historian, and to Lionel Lemery and Gary Kell who reviewed the section covering the Allegheny National Forest. At the other end of the state, Randy Turner provided us with volumes of information about the Delaware Water Gap National Recreation Area.

We'd also like to thank some of the representatives of the private lands included in the book. At the western end of the state, Julie Lalo and Paul Wiegman of the Western Pennsylvania Conservancy provided insight and information about Bear Run Nature Reserve and the Ferncliff Peninsula in Ohiopyle State Park. In eastern Pennsylvania, Roger Spots of The Nature Conservancy provided us with information about the Tannersville Cranberry Bog.

We'd also like to thank our friends Jim Young for contributing the sidebar story about the Bucktail Regiment, and Frank Felbaum of the Wild Resource Conservation Fund for recommending us to Longstreet Press.

Finally, we'd like to thank our publisher, Longstreet Press; Marge McDonald, project director of the Longstreet Highroad series; and series editors, Pam Holliday and Richard Lenz. Marge took a chance on assigning this book to a couple of neophyte book authors and then encouraged us every step of the way. Pam and Richard made sure that our manuscript was readable and organized, and they put up with more than one missed deadline. Thanks again.

—Greg & Karen Czarnecki

Pennsylvania Physiographic Regions

Pennsylvania has seven distinct Physiographic Provinces.

Central Lowland

Allegheny Plateau

Valley & Ridge

New England

Coastal Plain

Piedmont

Blue Ridge

The Natural History of the Pennsylvania Mountains

The surface of the Earth is dynamic. How it looks today is different from how it looked 300 million years ago, or even 100,000 years ago. That's because the Earth's surface is covered with a relatively thin crust of rock floating on a layer of semifluid rock. Rather than one contiguous piece, the Earth's crust is broken into distinct pieces or tectonic plates. These plates bump and grind their way across the Earth's surface, changing shape and size in the process. When two plates collide, one of two things can happen: one can slide over the top of the other, or the edges of each can crinkle like a french fry. In the places where one slides under another, a process called subduction, the descending rock often melts and then bubbles to the surface, creating volcanic mountains such as those seen in the western U.S. When plates collide and the edges crumple, nonvolcanic mountains form. Plates collided to form the Appalachians. The Appalachian Mountain chain extends from Alabama to

[*Above:* Pennsylvania's Grand Canyon from Colton Point State Park, Tioga County]

1

Geologic Time Scale

Era	System & Period	Series & Epoch	Some Distinctive Features	Years Before Present
CENOZOIC	Quaternary	Recent	Modern man.	11,000
		Pleistocene	Early man; northern glaciation.	1/2 to 2 million
	Tertiary	Pliocene	Large carnivores.	13 ± 1 million
		Miocene	First abundant grazing mammals.	25 ± 1 million
		Oligocene	Large running mammals.	36 ± 2 million
		Eocene	Many modern types of mammals.	58 ± 2 million
		Paleocene	First placental mammals.	63 ± 2 million
MESOZOIC	Cretaceous		First flowering plants; climax of dinosaurs and ammonites, followed by Cretaceous-Tertiary extinction.	135 ± 5 million
	Jurassic		First birds, first mammals; dinosaurs and ammonites abundant.	181 ± 5 million
	Triassic		First dinosaurs. Abundant cycads and conifers.	230 ± 10 million
PALEOZOIC	Permian		Extinction of most kinds of marine animals, including trilobites. Southern glaciation.	280 ± 10 million
	Carboniferous	Pennsylvanian	Great coal forests, conifers. First reptiles.	310 ± 10 million
		Mississippian	Sharks and amphibians abundant. Large and numerous scale trees and seed ferns.	345 ± 10 million
	Devonian		First amphibians and ammonites; Fishes abundant.	405 ± 10 million
	Silurian		First terrestrial plants and animals.	425 ± 10 million
	Ordovician		First fishes; invertebrates dominant.	500 ± 10 million
	Cambrian		First abundant record of marine life; trilobites dominant.	600 ± 50 million
	Precambrian		Fossils extremely rare, consisting of primitive aquatic plants. Evidence of glaciation. Oldest date algae, over 2,600 million years; oldest dated meteorites 4,500 million years.	

Newfoundland. In some areas it is less than 100 miles wide, while in others it's almost four times that wide.

Pennsylvania is divided into seven major physiographic provinces, each of which is based on its landform and the type of underlying rocks. Of these, three contain mountainous areas: the Appalachian Plateau, which occupies nearly all of the western portion of the state and its northern tier, the Valley and Ridge province that occupies much of the central part of the state, and the minuscule Blue Ridge province in south-central Pennsylvania. The Pennsylvania portion of the Blue Ridge province is the northern tip of a much larger area that extends southward into Maryland and down to Georgia. The other four physiographic provinces are the Coastal Plain, Piedmont, New England, and Central Lowland.

While the Valley and Ridge province and Appalachian Plateau province together account for nearly all of the state's mountains and most of its landmass, they are very different. The Valley and Ridge province contains very distinct long, narrow ridges separated by broad valleys. From the air the ridges resemble the long tails of some prehistoric dinosaur. The Appalachian Plateau province is composed of rounded hills and high mountains dissected by deep and narrow stream valleys. There is no symmetry to the highlands as there is in the Valley and Ridge province, and from the air the Appalachian Plateau looks hilly.

Orogeny is the term geologists use to describe a mountain-building event. Pennsylvania has experienced four orogenies, and it is the most recent of these, the Alleghenian orogeny, that produced the Appalachian Mountains. Somewhere between 220 and 300 million years ago, Pennsylvania was part of a continent called Laurentia, which was composed of North America and Europe. The rest of the world's landmass, including Africa, South America, Antarctica, India, Australia, and Arabia, comprised the continent of Gondwana. Both of these continents were located on the equator and had a tropical habitat.

The two continents collided and formed one supercontinent called Pangaea. During the collision, Africa ran into the east coast of North America and part of Europe, wrinkling the edge of Laurentia, thus forming the Appalachian Mountains. Areas closest to the collision experienced the most deformation. Geologists believe that's why the Valley and Ridge province, which is closer to what is now the Atlantic Ocean, has very distinct ridges that rise high above the valley floor. Some of the rocks here were bent, while others experienced enough force to break, forming thrust faults. Farther away from the collision, on the Appalachian Plateau, the rocks gently folded, producing much less dramatic topographic relief.

Eventually Pangaea broke apart, with some parts sliding north and others sliding south. North America and Europe slid north and then broke up. Today evidence of Laurentia and the Alleghenian orogeny can be found on both continents. The geologic makeup and age of the Appalachians are identical to those of mountains found in Greenland and Scandinavia, testimony that they were once one contiguous mountain chain.

While Laurentia was on the equator, it teemed with prehistoric life. Like today's tropical rain forest, it was covered with a dense blanket of lush vegetation, and organic matter accumulated in the soil creating a rich humus. At one time the area was also submerged beneath a shallow inland sea that teemed with marine life. During this period, dead and decomposing microorganisms blanketed the surface, creating a rich layer of organic material.

Over the ages the organic material was buried, and through the action of heat and pressure, it was transformed. The carbon that was once a part of the tissues of prehistoric ferns and plants was converted to coal. The bodies of marine organisms were converted into oil and methane, better known as natural gas. These fossil fuels, so-called because they are the remains of ancient creatures, have helped to shape the history and natural complexion of Pennsylvania.

While the Appalachian Plateau was located far enough from the collision with Gondwana to experience only minor folding, a visit to the area today reveals some dramatic topographic relief. Places like Pine Creek Gorge [Fig. 21] in Tioga County, also called the Grand Canyon of Pennsylvania (*see* page 117), and the Youghiogheny River Valley in southwestern Pennsylvania are much different than sites in the Valley and Ridge province. These valleys are deep, narrow, and V-shaped. The valleys on the Appalachian Plateau were created long after the orogeny occurred; they were cut by water.

PEREGRINE FALCON
(Falco peregrinus)
An extremely fast flier, the peregrine falcon feeds on ducks and other water birds.

Moving water can do amazing things to rock. Go to any stream, pick up a rock, and feel it. It's smooth because all of the sharp edges, irregularities, and projections have been worn away. The smoothing process is very gradual and begins with a polishing effect. Over time, however, the cumulative effect can be dramatic.

In the Appalachian Plateau, the innumerable ravines began as low areas between the slightly elevated peaks. Topographic relief was minimal as it is on all plateaus. Over the past couple of hundred million years, however, water flowing off of the gently rolling hills and through the low areas has created a plateau deeply dissected by water.

The effect of water is most dramatic where the largest of streams—the rivers—have cut into the plateau. Ravines so wide that they can rightfully be called valleys are found along the major rivers of the Appalachian Plateau including the Allegheny, Clarion, Monongohela, Youghiogheny, and Ohio rivers.

The cutting effect of rivers is also seen in the Valley and Ridge province. Water gaps, breaks in the ridges produced by the rivers' erosive power, provide some of the most spectacular scenery in the state. Water gaps are found in the central part of the state along the Susquehanna River and its tributary the Juniata River, but the best known water gap in Pennsylvania lies along the state's eastern border. The Delaware water gap was formed by the action of the Delaware River on Kittatinny Ridge, the southernmost of the major ridges in the Valley and Ridge province. It is a part of the Delaware Water Gap National Recreation Area [Fig. 40] (*see* page 205), which lies along both the Pennsylvania and New Jersey sides of the gap and hosts more than 4 million visitors each year.

Water does not have to be liquid to dramatically alter rock. The mountains in the northeastern and northwestern parts of the state have been shaped by frozen water. Pennsylvania has experienced several ice ages, but the most recent ice age, the Wisconsin glaciation, left an important legacy.

The Wisconsin ice sheet covered more than half of North America and was 2 miles thick in places. It was so large and contained so much water that sea levels dropped several hundred feet lower because of it, and the Earth's crust was compressed under its weight. As the ice sheet advanced into Pennsylvania, it scraped the underlying bedrock clean of loose rocks, gravel, and soil, piling it up along the edges and front of the glacier, forming piles called moraines. While not obvious to the untrained eye, these moraines still exist today as wooded hills and ridges. Eventually temperatures warmed and the ice sheet retreated north. Sea levels rose as the ice melted, and the Earth's crust rebounded.

The most significant ecological legacy of the ice ages are wetlands. As the ice melted, water was left behind in small lakes, bogs, and swamps. The number and variety of wetlands found in the state's northeastern and northwestern corners, which were buried beneath the ice, are greater than in any other part of the state.

The Wisconsin glaciation produced effects south of the ice sheet as well. The temperature pattern just south of the ice sheet was similar to that seen on the arctic tundra today. The temperature fluctuated considerably, producing continual freeze-thaw cycles. These cycles produced a great deal of stress on the rocks found along the ridgetops, breaking them into smaller pieces. The rock-strewn talus slopes common in the Valley and Ridge province are believed to have been formed in this way. Where there was a depression or valley surrounded by rocky ridges, the pieces would fall downhill and accumulate in boulder fields like those seen at Hawk Mountain Sanctuary [Fig. 46] (*see* page 253) and Hickory Run State Park [Fig. 3(23)] (*see* page 175).

Pennsylvania's mountains are today a mere shadow of what they were following the Alleghanian orogeny. Geologists believe that in their younger days the Appalachian Mountains were probably higher than the Rockies. While water, ice, and time have worn them down, they are still beautiful to behold and challenging to explore, even in their old age.

Coal, Oil, and Natural Gas

Lying beneath Pennsylvania's mountains is one of the world's richest deposits of fossil fuels. Oil, natural gas, and coal are all that remain of the prehistoric flora and fauna that lived and died here millions of years ago.

Oil and natural gas are found primarily west of the Allegheny Front beneath the Appalachian Plateau. They are often found together because they were both formed from the decayed remains of microscopic sea creatures that were subjected to intense heat and pressure for millions of years.

The world's first commercial oil well was drilled in 1859 at Titusville, in the state's northwestern corner. Oil wells quickly sprang up across much of the Appalachian Plateau. Today, many of the wells are dry, but the rusting pumps, pump houses, and pipelines are still a common site in this part of the state. A significant amount of oil is still being removed, but unlike the oil from Alaska or the Gulf of Mexico that is converted to fuel, Pennsylvania's oil is refined into the world's finest lubricating oil because of its high paraffin content.

While much of the oil has been depleted, natural gas is still found in large quantities. The porous sandstone that lies beneath the plateau allows natural gas to move freely, accumulating in pockets called reservoirs. Reservoirs are often located within anticlines, uplifted folds in the rock produced during the Alleghenian orogeny.

Thousands of wells dot the Appalachian Plateau and can be found in state forests, the Allegheny National Forest, and even in people's backyards. Once a gas reservoir has been pumped dry, its useful life isn't necessarily over. It can also be used for storage. The reservoirs are recharged by pumping natural gas in from other parts of the U.S., as well as Canada, and storing it. Then when the winter heating season arrives, it's pumped back out to heat the homes and businesses of the East Coast. As a result, natural gas pipelines and pumping stations are a common site in many of Pennsylvania's state forests. Much of the natural gas used by the state of Maryland, for example, comes from a reservoir beneath Buchanan State Forest in Bedford County.

As valuable as oil and natural gas are, coal is far and away the most economically important of the three fossil fuels. Pennsylvania and coal are synonymous. In fact, scientists have named the geologic period during which 80 percent of the world's coal supply was produced the Pennsylvanian Epoch. During that time 300 million years ago, the state was blanketed by the prehistoric ferns, plants, and trees that died and

Locomotive 2317, Canadian Pacific and Locomotive 3224, Canadian National team up for one of the Steamtown "double-headed" excursions through the mountains. Coal trains were common and important in Pennsylvania's mountain history.

were compressed into coal.

Not all coal, however, is created equal. The harder it's squeezed, the harder and purer it becomes. The hardest coal in Pennsylvania, therefore, is found along the eastern edge of the mountains, where the collision between North America and Africa created the greatest pressure.

Pound for pound, hard coal, or anthracite, supplies the highest heat value and produces less air pollution than bituminous, or soft coal. Nearly all of the state's anthracite coal is found in the folded rocks of eight northeastern Pennsylvania counties. At the turn of the century, anthracite mines were widespread in this part of the state. The deep, steep mine shafts provided work for thousands of men and supported a major part of the economy in the area. In 1959, however, that all changed when one company extended one of its shafts beneath the floor of the Susquehanna River. The weight of the river above caused the mineshaft to collapse, and the river poured in. Dozens of men drowned and many of the mines around the town of Wilkes-Barre, the center of the anthracite region, were flooded. So cavernous was the hole in the river bottom and so extensive the network of mines, that the river nearly disappeared. The hole was eventually plugged by dropping 30 railroad cars and 400 mine cars into it. That mine disaster forever changed the anthracite industry in Pennsylvania.

Today the anthracite coal industry is only a shadow of what it once was. At its peak in 1917, more than 100 million tons were removed. In 1995, only 8.7 million tons were mined. Most of the anthracite coal removed today is surface mined, or collected from the refuse piles of past mining operations. This process, called remining, is possible because of advances in technology and has led to an increase in the number of tons of anthracite produced over the last couple of years.

The anthracite belt represents only a small portion of the state's coal reserves. The vast majority of Pennsylvania's coal is of the soft or bituminous type. Bituminous coal is found beneath nearly a third of the state, covering most of western Pennsylvania. The coal here is found in relatively flat deposits, called seams, that range from a couple of inches to as much as 8 feet thick. Since coal mining began in Pennsylvania 200 years ago, 10 billion tons of bituminous coal have been removed. That's one of every 4 tons of coal ever mined in the United States. Incredibly, twice that much still lies beneath the surface.

Bituminous coal is mined in 21 southwestern Pennsylvania counties, where it is removed in one of two ways. If the deposit is deep underground, a tunnel or shaft is dug and the coal removed. This process is called deep mining. One of the problems with this type of mining can be subsidence, the land above the shaft sinking. Its not unusual for sinkholes to develop in the middle of roadways or for houses to have cracked foundations and walls as a result.

If the coal is near the surface, as it often is, the surface is peeled back, the coal is scraped out, and the loose material is put back in its place. The barren surface is then planted with grasses and trees. This process is called surface or strip mining, and it drastically changes the landscape. To see what strip mining does to the landscape, take a drive along Interstate 80 through Clearfield County. Here you'll see the native wooded hillsides intermixed with flat-topped hills planted with grasses and little pine trees. These artificial-looking areas are the piles of rock and debris peeled back during

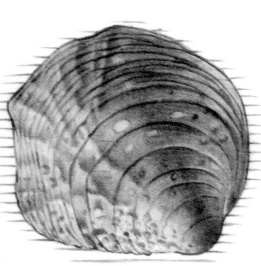

PURPLE WARTYBACK MUSSEL
(Cyclonaias tuberculata)
Because mussels feed by filtering particles from water, they are especially susceptible to pollution and runoff from mining.

the stripping process. There are 550 bituminous strip mines operating in the state today.

Both types of mining are commonly practiced in the state today, and some even occurs on public lands such as state forests. Strip mining and deep mining share some very detrimental environmental side effects. Pyrite is a mineral often found near coal seams. When it's exposed to air and water, as it is during strip mining and underground mining, it breaks down. The iron contained within the mineral is washed away and converted to rust, while the sulfur it contains is leached by the water and converted to sulfuric acid. The release of these two materials produces acid mine drainage.

Acid mine drainage is deadly to nearly all aquatic creatures. It's likely that a trip to the mountains of southwestern Pennsylvania will lead the visitor to at least one stream tainted red with iron and sterilized of life by acid. Regulations today prohibit mining companies from producing acid mine drainage, but the legacy of the past remains. According to the Pennsylvania Department of Environmental Protection, acid mine drainage is the state's largest source of water pollution and has degraded 2,400 miles of the state's streams.

Mountain Ecosystems

For the most part, Pennsylvania's mountains are covered with trees. Trees dominate the valleys, the mountaintops, and the plateaus. But the forest of today is much different than the forest of 300 years ago.

When the first European settlers arrived in Pennsylvania, the entire state was blanketed with trees. In fact, the name Pennsylvania means Penn's Woods. The state was named after its founder, William Penn, who recognized the need to show restraint as the forests were cleared to make room for cities and farms. It was his desire that at least 1 acre of trees be preserved for every 5 acres that were cleared. Unfortunately that's not how things turned out.

As settlers began to spread across the state, they quickly realized that the seemingly endless forest was profit waiting to be taken, and take they did. The vast old-growth white pine and hemlock forests that covered nearly two-thirds of the state were cut. The pines were cut for their wood, much of which was used for shipbuilding, and the hemlock was taken for its bark. The bark was stripped from the trunk and branches, which were left on the ground as waste, and from it tannin and other valuable chemicals were extracted.

Almost every tree was cut, every mountain laid bare. When one mountain was done, the loggers moved onto another. By the turn of the century, Penn's Woods were gone. The entire state, north to south and east to west, had been clear-cut. Then came the fires fueled by the woody debris, called slash, left behind. The fires were so

BLACK CHERRY
(Prunus serotina)
The fallen leaves of the
black cherry are highly
toxic to livestock as
decomposition produces
cyanic acid.

intense that in some areas they even consumed the organic material in the soil, sterilizing it. There are still places in Pennsylvania today where, more than 100 years after the loggers left, not much grows.

Fortunately these areas are relatively small in number, and today Pennsylvania is once again forested. It's estimated that Pennsylvania contains about 17 million acres of forest, covering about 60 percent of the state. The forests of today, however, are much different than the forests of Penn's day. All that remains of the white pine-hemlock forest are small, isolated enclaves that were too remote for the loggers to reach, encompassing about 70,000 acres. They've been replaced with mixed-hardwood (also called northern-hardwood) and mixed-oak forests.

Mixed-hardwood forests account for nearly 40 percent of the state's forest land. The Pennsylvania Bureau of Forestry defines this type of forest as one where sugar maple, beech, and yellow birch account for at least half of the total cubic feet of wood per acre. The balance of the stand can contain any number of species including red maple, hemlock, red oak, white ash, black cherry, white pine, tulip or yellow poplar, black birch, and white birch. Many of the mixed-hardwood forests found on the Appalachian Plateau contain a high population of black cherry, one of the most economically valuable trees in North America because of the fine furniture and veneer produced from it.

Mixed-oak forests are also common in Pennsylvania. These forests are simply defined as those dominated by oaks, and they account for about half of the state's total forested acreage. Often found growing alongside the oaks, making up a significant percentage of the stand, are hickory and maple. This type of forest produces large volumes of nuts, also called mast, which are primary food sources for many of Pennsylvania's game animals including white-tailed deer, black bear, ruffed grouse, and turkey.

Together the mixed-oak and mixed-hardwood forests account for about 90 percent of the state's total. The balance is made up of less common forest types. These include the hemlock cove forest, which is dominated by hemlocks and a complex mixture of hardwoods that grows along stream bottoms. Also unusual is the oak-hard pine forest. These forests are usually found at higher elevations and are dominated by oak, pitch pine, table mountain pine, and Virginia pine. One of the most diverse forest types is the mixed-mesophytic forest. These are found near the southern end of the state and contain dozens of species, none more common than the other.

Logging still occurs in Pennsylvania, but in a sustainable manner so that the growth to removal ratio is greater than 2 to 1. Large scale clear-cutting is no longer practiced, replaced by modern forestry practices. Today, Pennsylvania has the largest hardwood inventory in the United States. According to the Pennsylvania Bureau of Forestry, the economic value of the state's forests is more than $15 billion. While Pennsylvania's forests have suffered greatly and are now much different than those of 300 years ago, the state is once again worthy of the name Penn's Woods.

Flora and Fauna

Some of Pennsylvania's most visible animals are its mammals, which range in size from the tiny pygmy shrew, which weighs only 0.1 ounce, to the black bear, which can weigh as much as 600 pounds. In total the state is home to 63 species of mammals, including 8 shrews, 3 moles, 11 bats, 2 rabbits, 1 hare, 23 rodents (including the beaver and porcupine), 14 carnivores (including the coyote, *Canis latrans*, and bobcat, *Felis rufus*, 2 hoofed mammals, and North America's only marsupial (the Virginia opossum, *Dididelphis virginiana*). Most of these mammals are found within the mountains of Pennsylvania.

As diverse as Pennsylvania's mammal fauna is, many of the largest mammals are no longer found here. They were the victims of over-hunting and habitat loss. Hardest hit were the deep woods species, which lost their homes when the state was clear-cut. Gone are the woods bison (*Bison bison*), gray wolf (*Canis lupus*), wolverine (*Gulo gulo*), moose (*Alces alces*), and mountain lion (*Felis concolor*). On the brighter side, now that the state's forests have regenerated, several woodland species that had disappeared, including the northern river otter (*Lutra canadensisi*), elk (*Cervus elaphus*), and fisher (*Martes pennanti*), have

LEAST SHREW
(*Cryptotis parva*)
This mammal is also known as the "bee" shrew because it sometimes nests in beehives and feeds on bees and their larvae. Pennsylvania and southern New York are the northern-most part of its range.

been successfully reintroduced to Penn's Woods.

Several of the state's mammals are categorized as Species of Special Concern because they are rare, threatened, or endangered in Pennsylvania. Among these are the Allegheny woodrat (*Neotoma magister*), the water shrew (*Sorex palustris*), and two species of bats, the small footed myotis (*Myotis leibii*) and the federally endangered Indiana bat (*Myotis sodalis*). The bats have suffered significant declines because of habitat loss and disruption of the caves in which they hibernate. Cave explorers unknowingly rouse the bats from their winter slumber, causing them to use up the fat reserves they need to survive until the following summer.

LITTLE BROWN BAT
(Myotis lucifugus)
Probably the most abundant bat in North America, this bat is also seen in cities.

It's hard to estimate how many different types of birds are found in Pennsylvania because they're mobile and many of them are migratory. During the spring and fall the number of species increases dramatically, and ornithologists estimate that it reaches nearly 400. There are three distinct migrations that visitors to Pennsylvania's mountains can witness. Each fall, and to a lesser extent each spring, as many as 16 species of hawks, eagles, falcons, and vultures soar along the Appalachian Mountain chain by the tens of thousands. One of the best places to view the migration is Hawk Mountain Sanctuary (*see* page 253).

Less imposing than the raptors, but migrating in greater numbers, are waterfowl. Ranging in size from the diminutive bufflehead (*Bucephala albeola*) to the regal tundra swan (*Olor columbianis*), ducks, geese, and swans by the hundreds of thousands follow the Atlantic Flyway north to their nesting grounds in northern Canada and the Arctic. Unlike the raptors, the waterfowl migration is most easily viewed in the spring because the birds move north gradually, following the warm temperatures and open water. The fall migration occurs much more quickly as the birds rush southward to their wintering grounds. Almost any of the mountain lakes, and even some of the larger rivers, are good places to see large numbers of migrating waterfowl.

The third migration involves much smaller birds. Each spring and fall uncountable numbers of tiny warblers head north from their southern wintering grounds, which for many are the tropical forests of Central and South America. Magnolia warblers (*Dendroica magnolia*), Kentucky warblers (*Oporornis formosus*), chestnut-sided warblers (*Dendroica pensylvanica*), black-throated blue warblers (*Dendroica caerulescens*), and many more spread into the mountains of Pennsylvania and beyond to nest. While the timing of the spring migration varies from one part of the state to another and yearly depending upon the weather, the peak of the migration is usually in May.

Of the 400 or so bird species that migrate through Pennsylvania, about 187 nest in the state. Among them are the endangered osprey (*Pandion haliaetus*), bald eagle (*Haliaeetus leucocephalus*), peregrine falcon (*Falco peregrinus*), and king rail (*Rallus elegans*).

Pennsylvania is also home to 76 species of so-called cold-blooded vertebrates. Reptiles and amphibians aren't really cold-blooded at all. The temperature of their surroundings determines their body temperature, so during the winter they're cold-blooded and during the summer they're hot-blooded. Of the world's 6,000 species of reptiles, 38 are found in Pennsylvania. A like number of the world's 3,000 amphibians are found here as well.

Pennsylvania's mountain-dwelling reptiles include three species of lizards, 10 species of turtles, and 18 species of snakes (two of which are venomous). Two of Pennsylvania's mountain lizards are smooth-skinned, cylindrically shaped animals called skinks. The northern coal skink (*Eumeces anthracinus*) and the five-lined skink (*Eumeces fasciatus*) are active during the day, when they can be found rummaging through the leaf litter on the forest floor looking for insects and other invertebrates. The other mountain-dwelling lizard, the northern fence lizard (*Sceloporus undulatus*), is also active during the day and is a member of the iguana family.

Among Pennsylvania's turtles, the snapping turtle (*Chelydra serpentina*) is the largest and one of the best known. This omnivorous turtle, which eats everything from aquatic plants to ducklings, is found throughout Pennsylvania. Less common is the stinkpot turtle (*Sternotherus odoratus*) which is the state's only musk turtle and is so named because of a pair of glands that emit an objectionable odor. Other turtles include the common midland painted turtle (*Chrysemys picta*), the endangered bog turtle (*Clemmys muhlenbergii*), and the wood turtle (*Clemmys insculpta*), which spends most of its time on the forest floor rather than in a pond or stream.

GARTER SNAKE
(*Thamnophis sirtalis*)
Garter snakes have three stripes, one on back and one on each side. They're often found near water.

All of Pennsylvania's nonvenomous snakes belong to the family Colubridae, whose members have heads that are somewhat tubular and not distinct from the rest of their body (unlike the venomous species, which have spade-shaped heads). These snakes include the well-known Eastern garter snake (*Thamnophis sirtalis*), the

HELLBENDER
(*Cryptobranchus alleganiensis*)
The hellbender grows to
29 inches.

ill-tempered northern water snake (*Nerodia sipedon*), and the beautiful and reportedly docile Eastern smooth green snake (*Opheodrys vernalis*).

All three of Pennsylvania's venomous snakes belong to the pit viper family and two of them are found in the mountains. The copperhead (*Agkistrodon contortrix*) is a relatively shy animal that likes rocky, wooded hillsides throughout the southern two-thirds of the state. The timber rattlesnake (*Crotalus horridus*) is a mountain species that inhabits the central two-thirds of the state. While both snakes are poisonous, and medical attention should be sought immediately after any bite, the snakes can withhold their venom, which is designed to paralyze their prey when they make a defensive strike.

Pennsylvania's amphibians include frogs, toads, and salamanders. While frogs and toads are the most numerous amphibians worldwide, including about 3,500 species, there are only 16 found in Pennsylvania. Among them are three toads, seven tree frogs (which have sticky toe pads that allow them to climb about in trees and shrubs), and six true frogs, including the well-known bullfrog (*Rana catesbeiana*).

Penn's Woods contain 22 species of salamanders ranging in size from the gargantuan 2-foot-long Eastern hellbender (*Cryptobranchus alleganiensis*) to the diminutive four-toed salamander (*Hemidactylium scutatum*) that may be no more than 2 inches long. These smooth-skinned amphibians live in many mountain habitats and include totally aquatic species such as the mudpuppy (*Necturus maculosus*), mole salamanders that spend most of their lives underground such as the Eastern tiger salamander (*Ambystoma tigrinum*), woodlands species such as the northern dusky salamander (*Desmognathus fuscus*), and the threatened green salamander (*Aneides aeneus*) whose Pennsylvania range is limited to sandstone outcroppings in Fayette County.

Pennsylvania's waterways are home to 159 species of fish, including warm-water species such as bass, pike, perch, and panfish, and cold-water species such as trout. Only one of the state's four trout, the brook trout (*Salvelinus fontinalis*), is a native of Pennsylvania. More than a dozen species of fish are on the Species of Special Concern list. Many of them are darters, members of the minnow family that require pristine mountain streams, which are today subjected to siltation, agricultural pollution, and acid mine drainage.

Among Pennsylvania's least understood and least appreciated wildlife are the invertebrates. Invertebrates are animals without backbones, and worldwide they account for 97 percent of all animal species. Insects, worms, freshwater clams, spiders, and many others make up Pennsylvania's invertebrate population. Experts estimate there are at least 15,000 invertebrate species in Pennsylvania, dwarfing all of the other taxonomic groups. Of these, three have been designated Species of Special Concern. The regal fritillary (*Speyeria idalia*) is a large orange and black butterfly found in wet meadows, bogs, and marshes where it feeds on the nectar of violets, thistles, and milkweeds. The other two endangered invertebrates, the northern riffleshell (*Epioblasma* torulosa) and clubshell mussel (*Pleurobema clava*), are fresh-water clams found in the Allegheny River watershed. Freshwater clams are among the most endangered animals in North America. At one time Pennsylvania's streams, rivers, and lakes contained 65 species of clams. Today that number has declined to 47, and many of those are now declining rapidly. The clams are particularly vulnerable because they require very clean water and because they aren't able to migrate to new areas when conditions deteriorate. Additionally, larval clams live as parasites on the gills of fish, so any decline in the fish population results in a decline in the clam population.

While not often thought of as wildlife, plants form the foundation of every food chain and provide shelter and living space for all of the animals found within the mountains of Pennsylvania. Plants are an incredibly diverse group of organisms, living on the soil, in the soil, in the water, and even on other plants. Pennsylvania has 2,076 species of native vascular plants—trees, wildflowers, and grasses—but the state also contains a wide variety of other plant types. When mosses, liverworts, and algae are considered, the number jumps to several thousand. Pennsylvania's flora includes more than 200 species that are considered endangered and many more are classified as threatened.

Pennsylvania is home to more than 60 species of native trees, which due to wise management by the state's natural resource agencies and landowners, now blanket 60 percent of the state. Wildflowers occur in nearly all of the mountain ecosystems, from woodland to field to rocky outcrops. Because most of these small plants require a significant amount of sun, many of the woodland species bloom in the spring before the trees leaf out. Trillium (*Trillium* spp.), spring beauty (*Claytonia virginica*), common wood sorrel (*Oxalis montana*), bloodroot (*Sanguinaria canadensis*), and mayapple (*Podophyllum peltatum*) are just a few of the spring wildflowers found blooming in the state's mountains. Wildflowers growing in open areas, on the other hand, can be found in bloom from spring to fall and include the oxeye daisy (*Chrysanthemum leucanthemum*) and wild lupine (*Lupinus perennis*), which grow in fields and along roads; the threatened jeweled shooting-star (*Dodecatheon ametystinum*), which is found only on limestone outcrops and river bluffs; and even the prickly pear cactus (*Opuntia humifusa*) which grows in open rocky sites.

Forest Pests

Pennsylvania's forests have suffered from more than man's onslaught. Trees are good food for many creatures, and usually that's not a problem because nature maintains a balance and most trees survive. Occasionally, however, nature's control mechanisms aren't enough and pests become a problem.

Pests come in all shapes, sizes, and life-forms. They're not always insects. In fact, the worst pest ever faced by Pennsylvania's forests was, and is, a fungus. *Cyphonectria parasitica*, the cause of chestnut blight, forever changed the complexion of the state's forests.

The American chestnut was one of the most common trees in Pennsylvania at the turn of the century, when biologists estimate that it accounted for 25 percent of the state's timber. The first case of chestnut blight in Pennsylvania was reported in 1912, and by 1950 the tree had been eliminated from the state. Foresters consider the blight more catastrophic than the massive clear-cutting of the last century because the forests have recovered from the cutting, but the American chestnut has not returned. All that remains are occasional short-lived stump sprouts growing from the root systems of trees that died more than a half century ago.

The oak has replaced the chestnut as the dominant tree. Pennsylvania's forests contain more oaks today than at probably any time in the past, opening the door for oak-loving pests like the gypsy moth. The gypsy moth, a native of Asia, was accidentally released by silk growers trying to increase the productivity of their silk moths. The moths, so named because the caterpillars migrate each night from the leaves to the base of the trunk, are now found throughout the state. Their populations aren't usually large enough to do much damage, but like many pests they periodically undergo population explosions.

When the population is high, they can defoliate thousands of acres, eating almost anything with leaves or needles. Anyone who has walked through a forest experiencing a heavy gypsy moth infestation won't soon forget it. Even on a cloudless day there's the sound of light rain, but the rain isn't water, it's caterpillar droppings.

When a tree looses its leaves, it looses its ability to produce the sugar it uses as food. However, defoliation is not always a death sentence. If a tree looses its leaves late in the growing season, after it has flowered and produced seed, it will probably survive and produce leaves again the following year. But if the caterpillars attack early in the growing season or if the tree is already stressed, perhaps from defoliation the year before, it may not survive.

The gypsy moth isn't the only moth to wreak havoc on Pennsylvania's oak forests. Two small moths experience population cycles similar to the gypsy moth, and since they often occur together, they can do significant damage. The oak leaftier (*Croesia semipurpurana*) and the oak leaf roller (*Archips semiferana*) are early season caterpillars with a taste for young leaves and unopened buds. The oak leaftier is a small, yellow moth about 0.5 inch long, while the oak leaf roller is similar in size but mottled brown in color. These two moths did extensive damage to the state's forests in the late 60s and early 70s. Periodic outbreaks have been reported since, the most recent in 1997 in Cameron, Elk, Clearfield, Warren, Clinton, and Cambria counties.

Not all of the pests threatening Pennsylvania's forests are small. One of the state's most sought after game animals also has a taste for trees. The white-tailed deer has increased in number over the past several decades, and its taste for seedlings has nearly halted forest regeneration in some areas. A hike through many of the state's northern tier forests reveals only two things growing beneath the canopy of mature trees, ferns and black cherry seedlings. These are two of the few plants that the deer find unpalatable.

The Bureau of Forestry is actively engaged in research and replanting efforts geared toward restoring forest diversity.

The loss of the chestnut tree to an exotic blight forever changed the ecosystem of the Appalachian Mountains. Providing food and shelter, the chestnut was an important tree to man and wildlife. The chestnut was a canopy species, rising to heights of more than 100 feet, and the tree ranged from southern Maine to central Mississippi. The annual mast crop, usually with the nuts from hickories and oaks, inundated the forest floor every fall, providing an easy bounty for Appalachian wildlife. A popular material for furniture, the chestnut's lumber is rot-resistant and was said to shelter a man "from cradle to grave." A blight imported on exotic plants in the early 1900s spread from New England to wipe out the chestnut. Today, saplings are found in the forest sprouting from rootstock, but the tree can't survive long before falling victim to the blight. Groups such as the American Chestnut Foundation continue to look for a "cure" and restore the chestnut to its former glory.

Trees are planted inside protective plastic tubes that let sun in but keep deer out. Some areas are now even being surrounded by high fences to keep the deer out.

Waterways and Wetlands

Next to forests, the most visible ecosystems of Pennsylvania's mountains are its waterways and wetlands. The mountains of Pennsylvania fall within three watersheds. The western part of the state is drained by the Ohio River and its major tributaries the Allegheny, Clarion, Monongohela, and Youghiogheny rivers. The central part of the state is drained by the Susquehanna River and its tributaries the Juniata River and the West Branch Susquehanna River. The Susquehanna is the largest tributary of the Chesapeake Bay. In fact, the Chesapeake Bay is the ancient river floodplain of the Susquehanna River. The mountains within the eastern part of the state are drained by the Delaware River, which forms the boundary between Pennsylvania and New Jersey. The river and its tributaries, including the Schuylkill and Lehigh rivers, supply the Delaware Bay.

The Pennsylvania Department of Environmental Protection has established water quality designations to protect the state's highest quality streams. The most pristine waters are classified as Exceptional Value Waters. These waterways lie within a designated natural area in a state forest or state park, are protected within national parks, have outstanding geology, or contain endangered or threatened species. Less pristine waterways are designated as High Quality Waters. To receive this designation a stream must exceed the levels necessary to support the propagation of fish, shellfish, wildlife, and recreation, in and on the water. Both Exceptional Value and High Quality waters are protected by regulations promulgated by state agencies. A stream can also be designated a Wild Trout Stream. This is a designation assigned by the Pennsylvania Fish and Boat Commission to streams that support reproducing populations of native trout.

One of the reasons that Pennsylvania has so many High Quality and Exceptional Value waterways is that much of the precipitation and groundwater that feeds them passes through nature's filtering system, wetlands. A wide variety of wetlands are found within the mountains; however, they are not evenly distributed. Wetlands are far more common in the northeastern and northwestern corners of the state, which were covered with ice during the last ice age. Also common in these formerly glaciated areas are small lakes. This is clearly seen in the Poconos, where there seems to be a lake every mile or two.

There are many different types of wetlands, but four are most common within the mountains: swamps, marshes, wet meadows, and bogs. The wetlands differ from one another primarily in the amount of water they hold and the types of plants that live within them.

Marshes are wetlands dominated by herbaceous plants such as rushes, sedges, and cattails. Marsh plants are specially adapted to grow in saturated soil with their roots and lower stems submerged. Marshes can have as little as an inch or two of water to as much as a couple of feet. As the water depth increases, floating aquatic plants such as spatterdock (*Nuphar advena*) and pond lily (*Nuphar microphyllum*) replace the rushes and sedges. Water levels can vary seasonally as well. It's not uncommon for a marsh to contain a foot or two of water in the spring and be nearly dry by summer.

Marshes are among the most biologically diverse of all ecosystems. Beneath the surface is a rich assemblage of invertebrates including the aquatic larva of dragonflies, damselflies, and mosquitoes. Once the insects emerge from their watery incubator and into their adult terrestrial world, they serve as food for birds, such as the tree swallow (*Iridoprocne bicolor*) and marsh wren (*Cistothorus* spp.), as well as flying mammals such as the little brown bat (*Myotis lucifigus*) and the big brown bat (*Eptesicus fuscus*).

The marsh plants also serve as food. Canada geese and puddle ducks, such as the mallard, nest here and feed on the succulent shoots of pickerel weed and duck potato. They in turn attract predators. Some, such as the coyote, are general predators that feed here and in the nearby forests. Other predators, such as the mink (*Mustela vison*), are tied to wetlands because their primary prey, the muskrat (*Ondatra zibethicus*), is found only in wetlands.

Another common mountain wetland is the swamp, which is dominated by woody vegetation. Venture into a swamp and you'll see not cattails and pond lilies but trees and shrubs. As in marshes, water levels in swamps can vary. Some contain a couple of inches of water, while others may contain a couple of feet, and the level can vary seasonally as well. Common swamp trees include red maple (*Acer rubrum*) and green ash

GOLDEN CLUB
(*Orontium aquaticum*)
With waxy leaves that repel water, the golden club is also called neverwet.

(*Fraxinus pennsylvanica*). Growing in the understory and around the periphery of the forested areas are shrubs such as highbush blueberry, buttonbush, and alder.

Both swamps and marshes are easily recognized by the standing water they contain for most if not all of the year and also by the distinctive plants that grow there. Not as recognizable is the wet meadow. This type of wetland generally contains standing water only during the wettest times of the year, usually in the spring. Unlike a swamp or marsh, you could walk through this wetland during the summer and not even get your feet wet.

Wet meadows contain plants that can grow in inundated soil for only part of the year. To survive they also need a dry period as well. The plants commonly found here include herbaceous species such as soft rush (*Juncus effusus*) and tear-thumb, and shrubs such as arrowwood (*Viburnum* sp.) and red-osier dogwood (*Cornus stolonifera*).

The most unusual of the state's wetlands is the bog, an artifact of the last ice age. As the glaciers retreated, pools of meltwater were trapped in basins underlain by impermeable rock or clay. These small lakes, almost all of which were at high elevations, were eventually colonized by a floating plant called sphagnum moss. Over time the moss completely covered the lake forming a mat so thick that plants can take root. The plants that grow here, however, are highly specialized because a bog is a very inhospitable place to live.

Bogs are highly acidic environments that prohibit the growth of bacteria necessary for decomposition. As a result, the plants that grow here must contend with high acid, low nutrient conditions. Bog plants are so highly adapted to this unusual habitat that they are found nowhere else. Pennsylvania's bogs are home to small carnivorous plants such as the sundew and pitcher plant, thick-leafed shrubs such as Labrador tea and cranberry, and trees like the black spruce and tamarack. This type of wetland and the plants found there are generally associated with the colder climate of southern Canada. Here in Pennsylvania bogs are uncommon, so many of them are protected as natural areas.

Pennsylvania's State Forests

The Pennsylvania Bureau of Forestry and its sister agency, the Pennsylvania Bureau of State Parks comprise the Pennsylvania Department of Conservation and Natural Resources. This cabinet-level agency was created in 1995, and its high position in the state government hierarchy is an indication of the significance of the state's vast public lands.

The Bureau of Forestry had humble beginnings. In response to the massive clear-cutting of the state's forests at the end of the nineteenth century, the Department of Agriculture formed the Division of Forestry. Its primary goal was to see to the rebirth of Pennsylvania's once magnificent forests.

Once the logging companies had cleared an area, they quickly sold it because it was a tax liability rather than a resource. Much of the land often sold for as little as $1 or $2 per acre. The Division of Forestry took advantage of these low prices and made its first purchase of land in Clinton County along Young Woman's Creek in what is today Sproul State Forest. The purchases continued and still do today, albeit at a much slower rate. Today the state forest system includes 20 state forests encompassing more than 2 million acres in 48 counties. This represents about 10 percent of all the forested land in the state.

EASTERN WHITE PINE
(Pinus strobus)

Pennsylvania's state forests are managed for multiple uses. According to state law, their purpose is "to provide a continuous supply of timber, lumber, and wood, and other forest products, to protect the watersheds, conserve the water, and regulate the flow of rivers and streams of the state and to furnish opportunities for healthful recreation of the public." In addition to timber harvesting, oil and gas are also extracted from state forests. Balancing conservation, recreation, and commercial resource extraction is not an easy task.

The Bureau of Forestry has achieved its multiple-use mandate by writing management plans for each of the state forests. As part of the process, ecologically significant areas were identified and given special protection as natural areas. The Pennsylvania Bureau of Forestry identifies a natural area as one of unique scenic, historic, geologic, or ecological value which will be maintained in a natural condition by allowing physical and biological processes to operate, usually without direct human intervention. These areas are set aside to provide locations for scientific observation of natural systems, to protect examples of typical and unique plant and animal communities, and to protect outstanding examples of natural interest and beauty.

There are 61 natural areas encompassing about 69,000 acres within the Pennsylvania state forest system. In order to ensure their protection, the Bureau of Forestry has set the following guidelines for state forest natural areas:

—Only primitive backpack camping is allowed and only in designated areas.

—No motorized vehicles or boats are allowed.

—Logging is prohibited. Trees are only removed to ensure public safety.

—Mineral development is prohibited. Subsurface oil and gas rights will be leased only when no surface disturbance is required.

The Bureau of Forestry has also designated some parts of the state forest system as wild areas. These are extensive areas which the general public is permitted to see, use, and enjoy for such activities as hiking, hunting, fishing, and the pursuit of peace and solitude. Wild areas usually encompass at least 3,000 acres but not more than 15,000 acres. There are 14 officially designated wild areas encompassing more than 110,000 acres within the state forest system.

Wild areas are subject to most of the same limitations that apply to natural areas, with one exception. Timber harvesting is permitted but is limited to sanitation, salvage, and wildlife improvement cuts.

Recreational facilities abound within the state forest system, including 2,600 miles of roads and 2,500 miles of hiking trails. Visitors can fish, hike, cross-country ski, and, on designated trails, ride horses, all terrain vehicles (ATVs), and snowmobiles. Additionally, there are numerous state forest picnic areas with tables, fireplaces, potable water, and parking.

Pennsylvania's State Parks

Pennsylvanians are blessed with one of the most diverse and extensive state park systems in the nation. From the founding of the first state park at Valley Forge in 1893, the system has grown to include 114 parks. Pennsylvania's state parks serve a different function than its state forests. Their mission "is to provide opportunities for enjoying healthful outdoor recreation and to serve as outdoor classrooms for environmental education."

Today no Pennsylvanian has to travel more than 25 miles to get to the nearest state park. The parks range in size from the tiny 3-acre Sand Bridge State Park in southeastern Pennsylvania's Union County, to the sprawling Pymatuning State Park, which encompasses more than 21,000 acres in Crawford County in northwestern Pennsylvania. State parks include a wide variety of ecosystems and historical sites including spectacular waterfalls, rare wetland ecosystems such as bogs, national natural landmarks, rare and endangered wildlife, high quality streams, mountain lakes, old-growth forests, gristmills, and lighthouses. The parks are heavily used. Presque Isle State Park, a 3,200-acre peninsula on the south shore of Lake Erie is the most popular. With 4 million visitors a year, it's more heavily used than Yellowstone National Park.

The Bureau of State Parks has designated areas of particular ecological significance, those with unique plant and animal communities or outstanding examples of natural interest or beauty, as natural areas. In order to preserve the natural character of the areas, restrictions are placed on the activities that can occur there, and natural physical and biological processes are allowed to occur without human interference. Construction, timber cutting, and other modifications occur only if they are necessary to preserve the natural character of the area or are in the interest of public safety. There are currently 22 natural areas encompassing more than 11,000 acres. The natural areas program is an active one, however, and new areas are still being added.

Since outdoor recreation is one of the primary charters of the state park system, each park offers a wide range of recreational opportunities. Since each park is unique, having a different combination of natural features, not all parks offer the same types of recreation. Some types of recreation, such as hiking and camping, are found in many of the parks, while others, such as whitewater rafting and rock climbing that require specific natural features, are only found in a few of the parks. Most of the activities, including the many environmental education programs, are free. Camping, however, does entail a fee, which varies depending upon whether you are pitching a tent or using a cabin. To get more information on camping fees or to make a reservation call 1-888-PA-PARKS.

CHESTNUT OAK
(Quercus prinus)
This is also called rock oak because of its
preference for a rocky habitat.

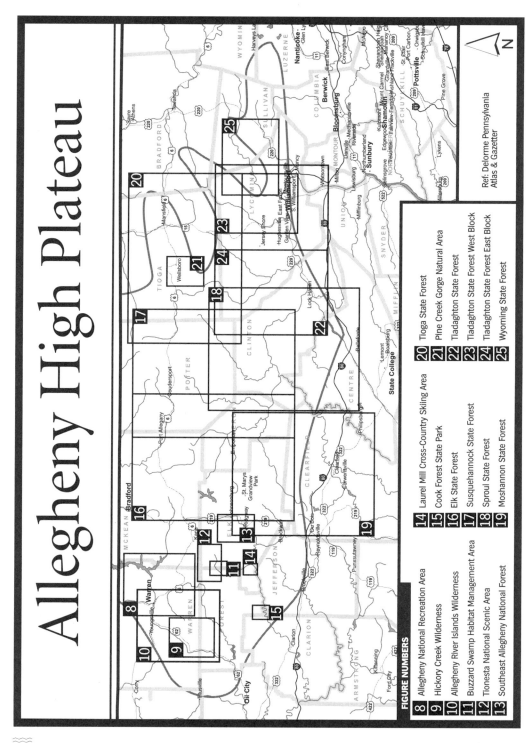

Allegheny High Plateau

Ref: Delorme Pennsylvania
Atlas & Gazetter

FIGURE NUMBERS

8 Allegheny National Recreation Area
9 Hickory Creek Wilderness
10 Allegheny River Islands Wilderness
11 Buzzard Swamp Habitat Management Area
12 Tionesta National Scenic Area
13 Southeast Allegheny National Forest

14 Laurel Mill Cross-Country Skiing Area
15 Cook Forest State Park
16 Elk State Forest
17 Susquehannock State Forest
18 Sproul State Forest
19 Moshannon State Forest

20 Tioga State Forest
21 Pine Creek Gorge Natural Area
22 Tiadaghton State Forest
23 Tiadaghton State Forest West Block
24 Tiadaghton State Forest East Block
25 Wyoming State Forest

Appalachian Plateau:
the Allegheny High Plateau

T he Appalachian Plateau province is the largest of Pennsylvania's eight physiographic provinces and includes about 60 percent of the state. It covers all of western Pennsylvania, the state's northern tier, and its northeast corner. All or part of 44 of the state's 67 counties are located within the province, which also extends into Ohio and New York.

The Appalachian Plateau is divided into six sections: Pittsburgh Plateau, Allegheny Mountain, Allegheny High Plateau, Pocono Plateau, Glaciated Low Plateau, and Glaciated. Two of these, the Pittsburgh Plateau and Glaciated sections, do not fall within the mountains of Pennsylvania and so are not covered in this book.

While the province is called a plateau, visitors might think it's misnamed. Numerous streams and rivers have dissected the Appalachian Plateau over the past 200 million years creating deep valleys and gorges. The topographic relief has been

[*Above:* Rim Rock Overlook in the Allegheny National Forest in Warren County]

accentuated by the different rates at which the underlying sandstone, limestone, and shale erode.

As Pennsylvania was being settled during the late eighteenth and early nineteenth centuries, long before there were highways or railroads, rivers served as the primary routes of travel. Several of the state's major rivers lie on the Appalachian Plateau. On the western part of the plateau at Pittsburgh, the Ohio River is formed by the meeting of the Allegheny and Monongohela rivers. These two rivers are fed by the Clarion, Conemaugh, Casselman, and Youghiogheny rivers. On the eastern part of the plateau lie the headwaters of the Susquehanna River, its tributary the Lackawanna River, and the Lehigh and Lackawaxen rivers, which are tributaries of the Delaware River.

In western Pennsylvania elevations on the plateau increase from west to east. Elevations on the western half of the plateau range from 1,400 feet near the Ohio border to around 2,400 feet along the Allegheny Front, a steep escarpment which marks the border with the Valley and Ridge physiographic province. Just to the west of the escarpment near the Pennsylvania/Maryland border are a series of parallel ridges known as the Laurel Highlands. The highest point in the state, 3,213-foot-high Mount Davis, is located on one of these ridges.

Plateau elevations in the northeastern corner of the state average 1,600–2,000 feet. Two escarpments are found in this corner of the Appalachian Plateau. One is located where the plateau borders the Delaware River, and the other marks the western boundary with the Valley and Ridge Province.

At one time, about 320 million years ago during the Pennsylvanian Period, much of this physiographic province was covered by vast swamps and a shallow inland sea. The climate was tropical because the North American continent had not yet drifted north from the equator, and the shallow sea was full of microscopic organisms encased in calcium carbonate shells. The shells accumulated on the bottom of the sea over millions of years, and as the continent slid north, heat and pressure transformed the tiny creatures' remains into the limestone that is common across the plateau today.

The plants that inhabited the swamps have also left their legacy on the Appalachian Plateau. As their remains accumulated in the bottom of the swamp, they decomposed, and over time and under heat and pressure, they were transformed into fossil fuels. The Appalachian Plateau contains some of the world's largest coal deposits and natural gas reservoirs. It was also the site of the world's first commercial oil well, which was drilled at Titusville in 1859.

Coal mining has left many scars on the plateau. Abandoned strip mines and piles of rock removed from deep mines are commonplace. Groundwater and precipitation flowing through these sites pick up heavy metals and become highly acidic. The result is 2,400 miles of Pennsylvania streams that are highly polluted.

Fossil fuels have also had a positive impact on Pennsylvania. Pittsburgh, for example, became the steel-making center of the world because of its close proximity to the vast bituminous coal fields of southwestern Pennsylvania. The coal was converted to coke, which is a critical element in the conversion of iron to steel.

Today most of the plateau is blanketed with the second-growth forests that grew after the area had been clear-cut in the late nineteenth and early twentieth centuries. Logging is still an important industry today, but now it is guided by the principles of sustained forestry.

The Appalachian Plateau is a major recreation and tourism area. It contains the Allegheny National Forest, 41 state parks, and 12 state forests.

Allegheny High Plateau Section

The Allegheny High Plateau is the highest section within Pennsylvania's Appalachian Plateau. Most of the area is heavily forested and sparsely populated. St. Marys and Warren, with populations less than 30,000, are the largest towns. All or part of Warren, Forest, Venango, Clarion, Jefferson, Elk, McKean, Cameron, Clearfield, Centre, Clinton, Potter, Tioga, and Lycoming counties are in this section.

The Allegheny High Plateau borders the Valley and Ridge province along the Allegheny Front, a well-defined escarpment known locally as Allegheny Mountain. To the north lies New York State, to the east the Glaciated Low Plateau, and to the south and west the Glaciated and Low Pittsburgh plateaus.

The gently rolling hills, made primarily of sandstone and shale, have been deeply dissected by numerous streams, most of them tributaries of the Allegheny River, Tioga River, and West Branch of the Susquehanna River. As a result, visitors to the area might find it hard to believe that this is a plateau. The deepest stream cuts are in the western portion of the high plateau, where melting glaciers poured vast amounts of water through the waterways and intensified the erosion.

The highest point on the Allegheny High Plateau, at 2,560 feet in Potter County, is unusual because it is a triple divide. The meeting place of three watersheds, rain falling here flows either to the Atlantic Ocean, the Gulf of Mexico, or the Great Lakes.

The geologic history of the area has shaped its human history. Deep within the sandstone are pockets of oil and gas, by-products of prehistoric plant decomposition. Man has been tapping into those pockets for more than 130 years, and even today most of the state's active oil and gas wells are found here. In fact, some of the largest gas fields in the eastern United States and the world, the Benzetter and Leidy fields, are located in this part of northern Pennsylvania.

Major east-west roadways within the area include US Route 6, which runs from Warren to Mansfield, and PA Route 120, which provides a scenic drive from Emporium to Lock Haven. North-south routes include US Routes 62 and 15, and PA Route 219. One of the most scenic routes in Pennsylvania is the section of Pennsylvania Route 44 from Jersey Shore to Coudersport. Along this stretch are numerous scenic vistas overlooking uplands, lowlands, and Kettle Creek and Slate Run gorges.

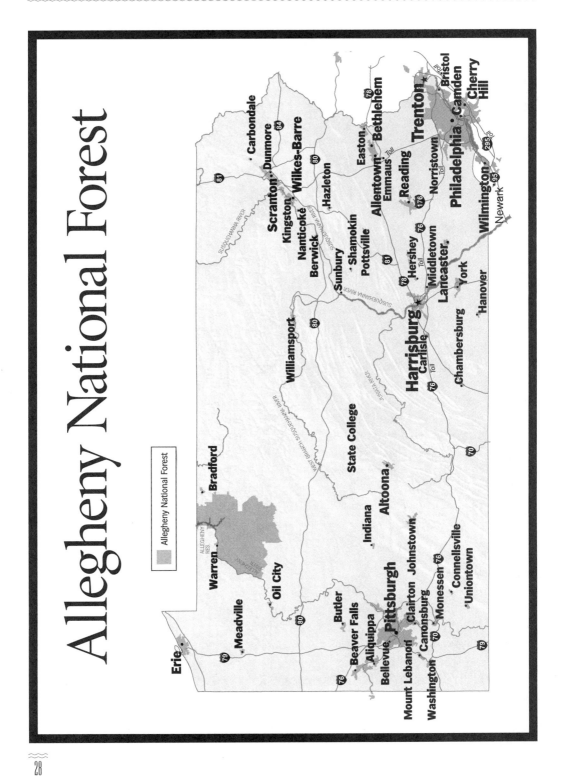

Allegheny National Forest

Allegheny National Forest

[Fig. 7] Created in 1923 by President Calvin Coolidge, the Allegheny National Forest encompasses about 513,000 acres of woodland in Elk, McKean, Forest, and Warren counties. The only national forest in Pennsylvania, Allegheny is a very different place today than it was when the Europeans arrived.

The first inhabitants of the forest area are thought to have been ice-age hunters known as Paleo-Indians. They lived in the bottomlands where travel was made easy by more than 700 miles of streams and rivers and where game animals such as white-tailed deer (*Odocoileus virginianus*), turkey (*Melagris gallopavo*), elk (*Cervus elaphus*), and even wood bison (*Bison bison*) were plentiful.

By 300 A.D. individual Native American cultures began to occupy the area. One of the earliest was the Hopewell culture, which colonized much of the Allegheny River as it established its trading network. The Hopewell are well known for their burial mounds, some of which are still located in the Buckaloons area at the forest's northwest corner.

As time progressed, the Allegheny River corridor was partitioned by more and more native cultures. Not unexpectedly, conflicts developed, and tribal wars became common. By the time Europeans began to explore this part of Pennsylvania, the native cultures coalesced into what was known as the Seneca Nation of the Iroquois Confederacy. The Seneca Nation tolerated Europeans but allowed them to travel no further up the Allegheny River than what is today Franklin in Venango County.

With the onset of the Revolutionary War, the Senecas sided with the British against the colonists. The war was waged to the south and east, but the Continental Army destroyed the Seneca village at Buckaloons in 1779 in retaliation. Historians consider this to be the only Revolutionary War battle fought in northwestern Pennsylvania.

Peace was made between the Senecas and the colonists, and Chief Cornplanter, leader of the Seneca Indian tribe at this time, was rewarded for his part in the peace-making process with a private land grant. In addition, land just north of the Allegheny National Forest in southern New York was deeded to the Senecas and is today the Allegany Indian Reservation.

After the Revolutionary War, the fledgling United States embarked on a westward expansion, and before the age of planes and trains, waterways were highways. It was the age of sail, when tall ships were the primary vehicle for man and cargo, and the growing country was hungry for timber, especially tall, straight trees to be used as masts. The tree of choice was the white pine (*Pinus strobus*), and what is today the Allegheny National Forest was then a sea of white pine and hemlock (*Tsuga canadensis*), with scattered enclaves of hardwoods.

From 1800 until the Civil War, logging of white pine was the economic mainstay of much of northern Pennsylvania. By the middle of the eighteenth century, however, nearly all of the white pine had been cut and rafted down the Allegheny River to markets from Pittsburgh to New Orleans. The forest was changing, but even more drastic changes were yet to come.

Two events occurred in western Pennsylvania, within five years of one another, which would forever change the landscape of the Allegheny National Forest and would alter the course of history. The first occurred in 1859 when Colonel William Drake drilled the first oil well at Titusville only 40 miles from the forest, ushering in the Industrial Revolution. Oil drilling spread across northwestern Pennsylvania, giving rise to boomtowns like Gusher City and Balltown that came and went in the blink of an eye.

While the towns are gone now, hundreds of small oil wells are still producing. Pennsylvania crude oil isn't used to produce fuel, but it is considered among the world's finest lubricating oils because of its high paraffin content. The oil legacy is apparent in the forest where rusting pumps of a hundred years ago, as well as producing wells (much of the mineral rights in the forest are privately owned), are common. The national forest today contains 6,000 producing wells on about 5,000 of its half million acres.

Five years after the discovery of oil another technological advance occurred: the railroad. Located on the Allegheny High Plateau, the Allegheny National Forest is characterized by deep stream cuts, resulting in elevations ranging from 1,046 to 2,263 feet. The bottomlands along rivers and streams had been cut over, but the more rugged uplands had been left relatively untouched. In 1864 the first railroad was built along the Allegheny Plateau. Now that there was a way to move the logs out of the uplands, the stage was set for the deforestation of the remainder of northern Pennsylvania.

With the uplands open for exploitation and the white pine gone, hemlock became the tree of choice. Previously used just for its bark, called Tanbark because the tannin it contained was used in leather tanneries, new uses for hemlock were found. Shingle mills, sawmills, and hardwood distillation plants popped up all over the Allegheny Plateau. The Twin Lakes Recreation Area is the former site of a wood alcohol factory town.

The period of railroad logging, which was at its peak from 1890 to 1930, was the final part of an era of intense exploitation that began with the cutting of the first white pine. The virgin white pine and hemlock forests that blanketed the mountains and valleys of the Allegheny National Forest were gone, leaving slash (leftover dead wood, such as branches and limbs) and a smattering of less desirable hardwoods. Slash-fed wildfires were common toward the end of the period. One of the worst was the Owl's Nest Fire, which affected 23,000 acres. So intense was the fire that parts of the area still support only stunted vegetation more than 70 years later.

The Allegheny National Forest of today is dominated by northern hardwoods like black cherry (*Prunus serotina*), yellow poplar (*Liriodendron tulipifera*), white ash

(*Fraxinus americana*), and red (*Acer rubrum*) and sugar maple (*Acer saccharum*). Although white pine and hemlock are still found in the forest, they are in the minority, and the large stands of virgin conifers have been reduced to a handful of small enclaves. The forest is different ecologically than it was 200 years ago, but its wild character, vast tracts of unbroken canopy, and functioning deep woods ecosystems have returned.

Man has played almost as large a role in the forest's return as he played in its demise. Once Allegheny was established as a national forest, protecting it from further widespread exploitation, attention was turned to remediation. This remediation phase occurred from 1933 to 1942 when the Civilian Conservation Corps, better known as the CCC, was put to work

TULIPTREE OR YELLOW-POPLAR
(Liriodendron tulipifera)
Of eastern broadleaved trees, the tuliptree is one of the straightest and tallest and has one of the largest diameter tree trunks. Wind-borne seeds of the tulip poplar make their way into the openings in mountain forests to take over in areas denuded by heavy logging or disease.

restoring the nation's natural resources and building a recreational infrastructure that remains today.

Fourteen CCC camps were built in the forest. From these bases of operation, corps members built roads and cabins, developed recreation areas (including the Loleta and Twin Lakes areas), and planted more than 20,000 acres of pine trees to reduce the severe stream and hillside erosion and to try to restore the forest's original character.

Today the forest has 16 developed campgrounds, many the products of the CCC. Some of these recreation areas have unique histories of their own. The Loleta Recreation Area, for example, was the site of a logging boomtown from 1889 to 1913. The

Buckaloons Recreation Area sits on the site of an Indian village, and the Red Bridge Recreation Area is near the site of a CCC camp that was used as a German prisoner-of-war camp during World War II.

Today the Allegheny National Forest, like all national forests, is managed for multiple sustained uses, as mandated by Congress. The employment figures for the area in and around the forest illustrate what those multiple uses are. Timber production in the forest accounts for 700 to 1,000 jobs, oil and gas production provides about 900 jobs, and recreation employs 1,600 people.

What only 100 years ago was some of the most heavily logged land in the world, today supports vast stands of economically valuable maple and cherry. Logging occurs throughout most of the forest and millions of board feet are cut every year, half of it used as pulpwood and much of the rest used for furniture and veneers. It's estimated that one-third of the world's available supply of black cherry is growing in the Allegheny National Forest.

Most people, however, visit the forest not because it is an economic resource but because it's a recreational resource. It's a place to enjoy activities tied to the outdoors and nature and a place to leave society behind and enjoy solitude as their ancestors did. The forest offers a multitude of recreational opportunities. It contains 54 miles of cross-country ski trails, 360 miles of snowmobile trails, 185 miles of hiking trails, and 106 miles of ATV trails.

The most notable recreational feature is the Allegheny Reservoir. Formed in 1965 when the Kinzua Dam was built to flood 27 miles of the upper Allegheny River Valley, the reservoir encompasses 12,000 acres. Ten of the forest's 16 campgrounds are located on the reservoir, and five of them can be reached only by boat or on foot. While camping is allowed throughout much of the forest, visitors should be aware that camping is prohibited on the shores of the reservoir or within 1,500 feet of the timberline.

Of the forest's half million acres, about 9,000 have been designated wilderness area. The Hickory Creek [Fig. 9] and Allegheny River Islands [Fig. 10] wilderness areas were designated by Congress as areas "where the earth and its community of life are untrammeled by man, where man himself is a visitor who does not remain." These areas are managed to protect the area for future generations. Specific regulations apply, such as the prohibition of motorized vehicles and horseback riding.

A visitor to the forest will find many of the plant and animal species typical of a northern hardwood forest. Black bear (*Ursus americanus*), turkey (*Meleagris gallopavo silvestris*), ruffed grouse (*Bonasa umbellus*), and porcupine (*Erethizon dorsatum*) are all relatively common. Among the less common animals are two members of the weasel family: the river otter (*Lutra canadensis*) and its porcupine-eating cousin the fisher (*Martes pennanti*) have both been reintroduced to the Allegheny National Forest. In all there are more than 300 species of wildlife found in the forest, including approximately 150 species of songbirds.

As you walk through many areas of the forest, you'll be struck by the lush green undergrowth of ferns that blankets the forest floor. If you look closer, you'll see that very few plants other than ferns are growing there. Missing are the wildflowers, shrubs like the American yew (*Taxus canadensis*) and elderberry (*Sambucus canadensis*), and perhaps most importantly, seedlings of the trees forming the canopy above your head.

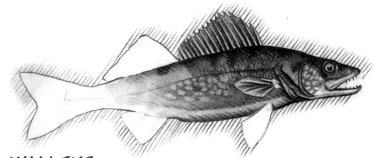

WALLEYE
(*Stizostedion vitreum*)
With a common name stemming from its large eye, the walleye is sometimes erroneously called a "walleyed pike." Walleye can grow to 2 feet long and up to 20 pounds.

This lack of diversity is due to an animal so influential and so common that it shapes the composition, and consequently the future, of the forest. White-tailed deer (*Odocoileus virginianus*) eat nearly everything but the ferns and black cherry, which they don't have a taste for. In order to learn what effect the deer have on forest diversity, several deer-free study areas have been established behind high fences. After a number of years, these enclosed areas contain a dense understory of trees, wildflowers, and shrubs. Visitors to the Hearts Content National Scenic Area [Fig. 10(1)] can see a small-scale example of this dramatic growth in a small deer exclosure along the main trail.

Deer are among 37 species which are hunted or trapped throughout the Allegheny National Forest. Hunters should be familiar with the various seasons established by the Pennsylvania Game Commission and be aware that licenses are required by Pennsylvania residents and nonresidents as well.

With 700 miles of streams and several reservoirs, fishing is a popular sport. Muskellunge (*Esox masquinongy*), yellow perch (*Perca flavescens*), channel catfish (*Ictalurus punctatus*), and rainbow (*Oncorhynchus mykus*), brown (*Salmo trutta*), brook (*Salvelinus fontinalis*), and lake trout (*Salvelinus namaycush*) are among the 70 species found in the forest's warm- and cold-water fisheries. The state-record northern pike (*Esox lucius*) (22 pounds, 8 ounces, 45.5 inches) and walleye (*Stizostedion vitreum*) (17 pounds, 36.25 inches) were caught here. A Pennsylvania fishing license is required for both residents and nonresidents, and seasons vary from species to species.

Most of the forest is what biologists call second growth: virgin forest was cut and the next generation of trees now dominates. While little of the virgin, old-growth

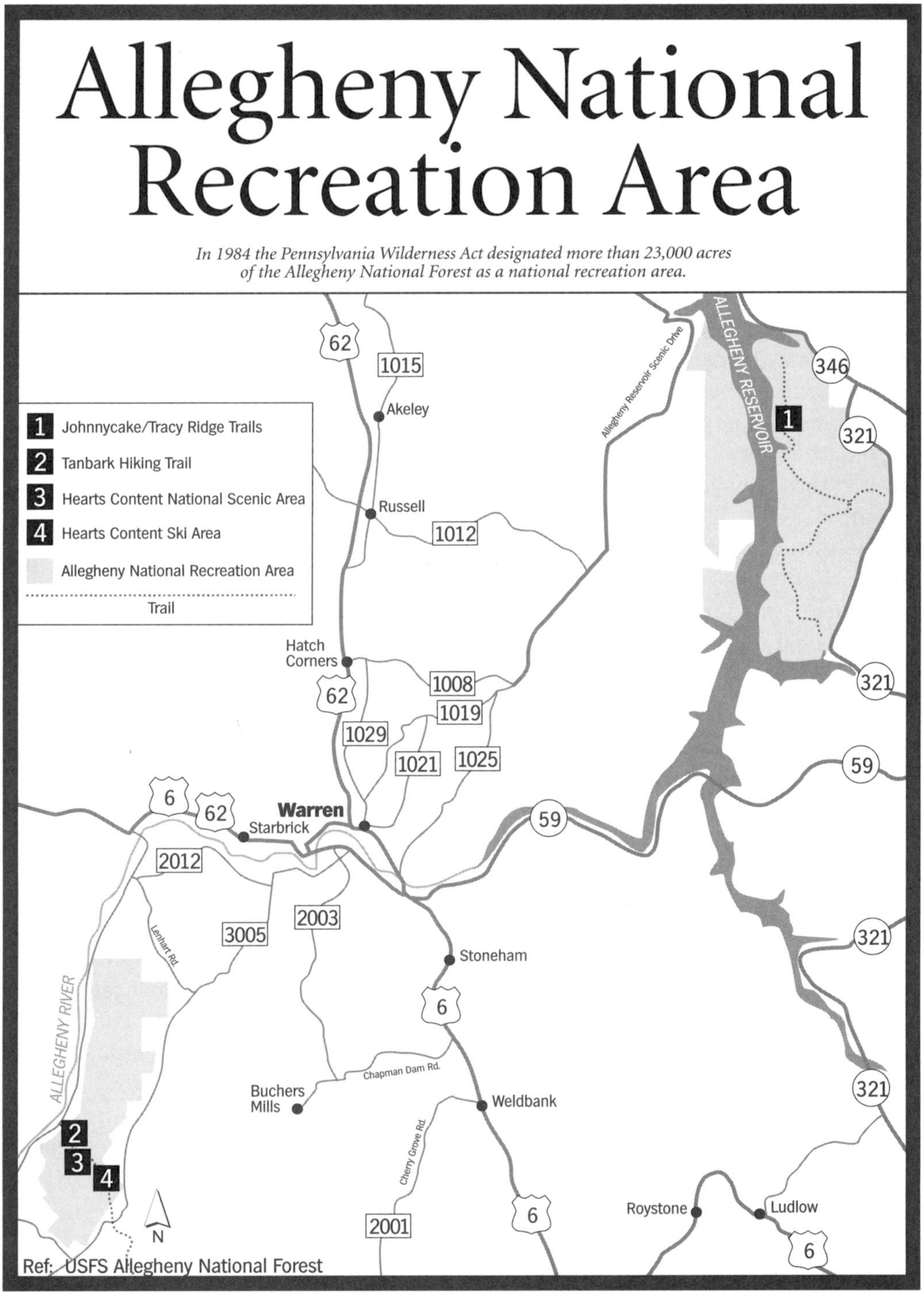

Allegheny National Recreation Area

In 1984 the Pennsylvania Wilderness Act designated more than 23,000 acres of the Allegheny National Forest as a national recreation area.

1 Johnnycake/Tracy Ridge Trails
2 Tanbark Hiking Trail
3 Hearts Content National Scenic Area
4 Hearts Content Ski Area
Allegheny National Recreation Area
Trail

62
1015
Akeley
346
321
Russell
1012
Hatch Corners
62
1008
1019
1029
1021
1025
6
62
Warren
Starbrick
59
2012
2003
3005
Lenhart Rd.
Stoneham
6
ALLEGHENY RIVER
Chapman Dam Rd.
Buchers Mills
Weldbank
Cherry Grove Rd.
2
3 **4**
2001
6
Roystone
Ludlow
6
N
321
59
321
321
Allegheny Reservoir Scenic Drive
ALLEGHENY RESERVOIR
1

Ref: USFS Allegheny National Forest

forest remains, foresters say that portions of the second growth are maturing into old growth. There are several areas within the forest that are now dominated by trees more than 110 years old and that have a significant amount of dead wood and woody material on the ground, both characteristics of an old-growth forest. While the old-growth forest of today is much different than the old-growth forest which was home to Chief Cornplanter, conservation efforts of the past 100 years are beginning to erase the excesses of the century before.

ALLEGHENY NATIONAL RECREATION AREA

[Fig. 8] In 1984 the Pennsylvania Wilderness Act designated more than 23,000 acres of the Allegheny National Forest as a national recreation area to preserve and protect its natural features, and to ensure that the area is available for recreation. The Allegheny National Recreation Area is actually two separate tracts of land, one in the northern part of the forest lying along both sides of the Allegheny Reservoir and another along the forest's western edge on the east shore of the Allegheny River.

The northernmost segment, the larger of the two, stretches from the New York state line to Sugar Bay and contains five campgrounds and several boat launches. The North Country National Scenic Trail passes through the area, connecting with the Johnnycake/Tracy Ridge Trails (*see* page 37).

The smaller portion of the Allegheny National Recreation Area is located southwest of Warren and northwest of the Hickory Creek Wilderness Area [Fig. 9]. This area contains some of the least-developed land in the Allegheny National Forest and is adjacent to three of the islands in the Allegheny River Islands Wilderness [Fig. 10]. The primary trail running through the area is the Tanbark Trail (*see* below).

Directions: Northern Portion: Take the Allegheny River Scenic Drive north from Warren for 7 miles.

Southern Portion: From Tidioute cross the Allegheny River and follow US Route 62 north for 4 miles to the entrance of the Tanbark Trail.

Activities: Hunting, fishing, cross-country skiing, canoeing, and boating. Mountain biking, biking, and horseback riding but not on hiking trails.

Facilities: Campgrounds, boat launches, picnic areas, hiking trails, bike trails.

Dates: Open year-round.

Closest town: Tidioute in the south and Warren in north.

For more information: Allegheny National Forest, PO Box 847, Warren, PA 16365. Phone (814) 723-5150.

TANBARK HIKING TRAIL

[Fig. 8(2)] The Tanbark Hiking Trail runs from US Route 62 north of Tidioute in the Allegheny National Recreation Area to the North Country National Scenic Trail at Dunham Siding (*see* page 276). Along its 8.8-mile course, the trail is marked with off-white markers and informational signs. Most of the trail passes through second-growth

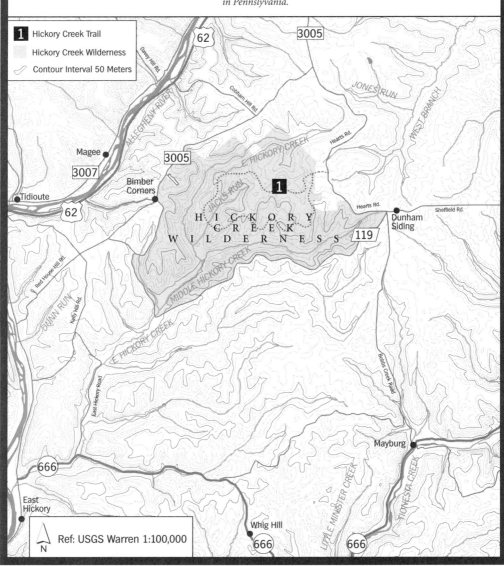

Hickory Creek Wilderness

Hickory Creek Wilderness is the only Congressionally designated wilderness in Pennslyvania.

1 Hickory Creek Trail

Hickory Creek Wilderness

Contour Interval 50 Meters

Ref: USGS Warren 1:100,000

hardwoods on the Allegheny Plateau, crossing Slater Run and Hickory Creek along the way. The trail connects with the Hickory Creek Trail (*see* page 39) and passes through a small portion of the Hickory Creek Wilderness Area. It offers varying degrees of difficulty but includes a precipitous drop from the plateau down to the Allegheny River that is best suited for hikers in good physical condition.

Trail: 8.8 miles one-way.

Elevation: 1,200–1,900 feet.

Degree of difficulty: Varies from difficult as it climbs from the river up to the plateau, to easy along the plateau.

Surface and blaze: Unpaved with off-white markers.

JOHNNYCAKE/TRACY RIDGE TRAILS

[Fig. 8(1)] Named after streams, the Johnnycake/Tracy Ridge Trails form two sides of a triangular trail loop that runs from the Tracy Ridge Recreation Area to the Allegheny Reservoir and back. The third side is formed by a 2.4-mile segment of the North Country National Scenic Trail. Together the three make for a day-long hike of varying difficulty and scenery. Along the way the hiker climbs relatively steep slopes and passes rocky outcrops, hemlock-lined stream channels, and broad expanses of second-growth oak (*Quercus* spp.) forests. In addition to the normal national forest regulations, hikers on these trails should be aware that campfires are permitted only within fire rings and camping is permitted away from the trail only.

Directions: To reach the trailhead from Bradford, follow PA Route 346 west for about 13.5 miles. Turn left onto PA Route 321 and drive 2.6 miles to the parking area and trailhead, which are marked by a sign.

Trail: 6.3-mile section of a 8.7-mile triangular loop (for the additional 2.4 miles *see* North Country Scenic Trail, page 276)

Elevation: From 1,328 feet along the Allegheny Reservoir to 2,245 feet at the Tracy Ridge Recreation Area.

Degree of difficulty: Strenuous.

Surface and blaze: Unpaved with off-white markers.

HICKORY CREEK WILDERNESS

[Fig. 9] Tucked in between the Allegheny River and the Hearts Content National Scenic Area is the Hickory Creek Wilderness. Encompassing 8,663 acres in the west-central part of the Allegheny National Forest, the wilderness provides visitors with a remote, deep-woods experience. The terrain is moderate with no steep slopes. Elevations range from 1,273 feet along East Hickory Creek to 1,900 feet on the plateau.

From 1840 to 1940 the wilderness was owned by the Wheeler and Dusenburg logging company. Most logging companies of that era cut all of the trees in an area and then moved on, a process sometimes referred to as "cut out and get out logging." Wheeler and Dusenburg operated differently. They practiced a form of sustainable

Small Whorled Pogonia

The small whorled pogonia (*Isotria medeoloides*) is the rarest orchid in Pennsylvania, with only three known populations in the state. The single or paired greenish-yellow flowers sit atop a stalk about 10 inches high and are surrounded by a whorl of leaves, giving the flower its name. In Pennsylvania the flowers are found on dry, rocky hillsides within second-growth mixed oak forests. The small whorled pogonia experiences long periods of dormancy. After a plant blooms, it remains dormant underground for 10 years or more before sprouting and blooming again. Historically, the pogonia occurred from southern Ontario to Georgia, but today it is restricted to only 52 isolated populations. It has been listed as a federally endangered species since 1982.

forestry that allowed them to utilize the land for 100 years, long enough that they eventually harvested the second-growth forest that replaced the original forest they had cut years before. Today the area is unique because it contains third-growth forest.

Visitors to the Hickory Creek Wilderness may still come across remnants of old Wheeler and Dusenburg logging camps. The company was also largely responsible for building the nearby town of Endeavor, where many of the original buildings are still in use. Pennsylvania's oldest operating sawmill is located there as well.

Within the wilderness there are a number of different ecosystems, determined primarily by elevation and drainage patterns. The wilderness encompasses most of the East Hickory Creek and Middle Hickory Creek watersheds.

A hike through the Hickory Creek Wilderness Area will take you through streams, wet meadows, and bogs. Here you'll encounter wetland species such as green darners (*Anax junius*), snapping turtles (*Chelydra serpentina*), wood ducks (*Aix sponsa*), and native brook trout. Also found here is a species whose capability to change its environment is rivaled only by man. North America's largest rodent, the beaver (*Castor canadensis*), has created wetlands as it floods areas in search of food and building materials.

A word of caution—while all of the waterways within the Hickory Creek Wilderness are high quality, hikers and campers are advised to boil water for at least five minutes before drinking it. Beaver commonly have a protozoan called *Giardia* within their digestive systems, and any water which they inhabit is likely to contain it also. Pity the poor outdoorsman who drinks *Giardia*-contaminated water. He'll spend much of his outing in intestinal distress rather than enjoying himself.

As hikers leave the creek and wetlands behind, they move through wet valleys dominated by birch (*Betula* spp.) and hemlock. Ruffed grouse, black bear, and assorted salamanders call these valleys home.

Along the top of the plateau the forest changes again. Oak and hickory (*Carya ovata*) dominate the landscape, shaping the animal community with their yearly production of mast. White-tailed deer and turkey feed on the nuts and in turn are fed on by bobcat (*Felis rufus*) and coyote (*Canis latrans*).

While no rare or endangered species have been confirmed within the wilderness, the area has been identified as potential nesting habitat for the bald eagle (*Haliaeetus leucocephalus*). U.S. Forest Service biologists also suspect that the small whorled pogonia (*Isotria medioloides*), a delicate member of the orchid family that thrives in rocky, acidic soil, might grow here.

Many common but seldom-seen animals live here as well. Little brown bats (*Myctis lucifigus*) and big brown bats (*Eptescus fuscus*) are common, and biologists have found that the area contains a particularly large population of barred owls (*Strix varia*). Showy woodland flowers such as trillium (*Trillium* spp.), wood sorrel (*Oxalis montana*), and trout lily (*Erythonium americanum*) are also well represented. Wildflower enthusiasts should plan a spring excursion in the wilderness because the colorful blooms disappear once the canopy of leaves choke the sunlight from the forest floor.

The abundance of wildlife makes this a prime hunting area, and visitors are advised to wear fluorescent orange during the big game season, October through December, and during the spring turkey season, April through May.

Directions: From the Mohawk Exit of US Route 6 near Warren, follow Pleasant Drive south for 11 miles. At the hard curve, turn left onto the gravel road and go south 4 miles. Park at the Hearts Content National Scenic Area.

Activities: Hunting, fishing, hiking, camping.

Facilities: Hickory Creek Trail.

Fees: None.

Dates: Open year-round.

Closest town: Tidioute, 5 miles.

For more information: Allegheny National Forest, PO Box 847, Warren, PA 16365. Phone (814) 723-5150

HICKORY CREEK TRAIL

[Fig. 9(1)] The Hickory Creek Trail is the only major hiking trail in the Hickory Creek Wilderness Area. It forms an 11.1-mile loop, and the trail is maintained in a relatively primitive condition, making it somewhat challenging. The trailhead is located at the Hearts Content National Scenic Area parking lot. As with the rest of the Hickory Creek Wilderness, no mechanized or motorized devices are allowed, including mountain bikes.

Trail: 11.1-mile loop.

Elevation: It varies as the trail crosses the plateau and climbs into and out of stream valleys; however, there are no steep slopes.

Degree of difficulty: Moderate.

Surface and blaze: Unpaved with minimal maintenance. Yellow-paint tree blazes currently being changed to unpainted tree blazes.

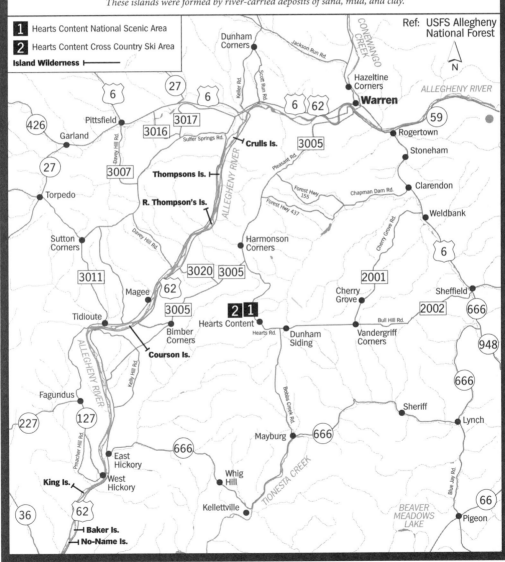

Allegheny River Islands Wilderness

*Seven of the islands in the Allegheny River are part of the Allegheny River Islands Wilderness.
These islands were formed by river-carried deposits of sand, mud, and clay.*

1 Hearts Content National Scenic Area
2 Hearts Content Cross Country Ski Area
Island Wilderness ⊢━━━┤

Ref: USFS Allegheny
National Forest

N

CONEWANGO CREEK

ALLEGHENY RIVER

Dunham Corners
Jackson Run Rd.

Hazeltine Corners
Warren
6 62

27
6 6
59

Keller Rd.
Scott Run Rd.

Pittsfield
426
Garland
3017
3016
Sulfer Springs Rd.
Crulls Is.
Rogertown
Stoneham

27
3007
Davey Hill Rd.
Thompsons Is. ⊢
3005
Pleasant Rd.

Torpedo
R. Thompson's Is.
ALLEGHENY RIVER
Forest Hwy 155
Chapman Dam Rd.
Clarendon

Cherry Grove Rd.

Forest Hwy 437
Weldbank

Davey Hill Rd.
Sutton Corners
Harmonson Corners
6

3011
3020 **3005**
2001

Magee
62
Cherry Grove
Sheffield
3005
2002
666

Tidioute
Bimber Corners
2 **1**
Hearts Content
Bull Hill Rd.
Vandergriff Corners
666

Hearts Rd.
Dunham Siding
948

Kelly Hill Rd.
Courson Is.

ALLEGHENY RIVER
666

Fagundus
Bobbs Creek Rd.
Sheriff
Lynch

227
127
Mayburg
666

Preacher Hill Rd.
East Hickory
666

King Is.
West Hickory
Whig Hill
TIONESTA CREEK

Blue Jay Rd.

36
62
Kellettville
BEAVER MEADOWS LAKE
66
Pigeon

⊢ **Baker Is.**
⊢ **No-Name Is.**

ALLEGHENY RIVER ISLANDS WILDERNESS

[Fig. 10] Officially listed as the smallest designated wilderness area in the United States, the Allegheny River Islands Wilderness is composed of seven small islands encompassing only 368 acres. The islands are what geologists call alluvial deposits, formed when the river slows and drops its load of sediment, gravel, and rocks.

Hiking and camping are allowed on all of the Allegheny River islands managed by the U.S. Forest Service, ranging in size from the 10-acre No Name Island to the 96-acre Crull's Island. Be advised, however, that many of the islands located in this stretch of the Allegheny River are privately owned, so obtain permission before entering.

One of the wilderness islands, Baker Island, was directly in the path of a tornado which struck in 1985. Most of the trees on the 67-acre island were blown over in the storm, and the effects can still be seen today.

This riverine ecosystem is worth exploring because the islands contain the only sycamore (*Platanus occidentatalis*) forest in the Allegheny National Forest. The sycamore is to the eastern forest what the redwood is to the western forest. The trees can grow up to 11 feet in diameter and were used by Native Americans to build dugout canoes. Modern-day canoers visiting the islands will find Indian plantain (*Cacalia atriplicifolia*), star flower (*Trientalis borealis*), foamflower (*Tiarella cordifolia*), wild leek (*Allium tricoccum*), garlic mustard (*Alliaria officinalis*), painted trillium (*Tillium undulatum*), and other pseudo-wetland plants growing beneath the towering sycamores.

These islands weren't always so wild. At one time this was Native American farmland. The Seneca Indians knew that the Allegheny River could rise rapidly, making the islands an unsuitable place to live, but they also knew that with every flood came a new layer of nutrient-rich sediment, making the islands ideal cropland.

It was on one of these agricultural islands, Thompsons Island, that an unusual historical event occurred. In 1779, General Sullivan of the Continental Army sent a detachment of soldiers to the area to punish the Senecas for their support of the English during the Revolutionary War. The soldiers destroyed the village at Buckaloons and then attacked the Senecas who were tending their crops on the island. This fight was the only Revolutionary War battle fought in northwestern Pennsylvania.

Some of the other islands have unusual histories as well. Crull's Island contained a tavern from the 1820s to the 1850s during the era of the white pine lumber boom. Tidioute Island was the site of the world's first offshore oil well, which was drilled in the 1860s. Eventually most of the islands were tapped for their oil. Today all traces of the farm fields, tavern, and oil wells have long since been erased by the river.

Found around these islands and throughout the upper reaches of the Allegheny River and its tributaries are the only known federally endangered invertebrates in Pennsylvania. The clubshell mussel (*Pleurobema clava*) and the northern riffleshell (*Epioblasma rangiana*), like many freshwater clams, have suffered because of poor

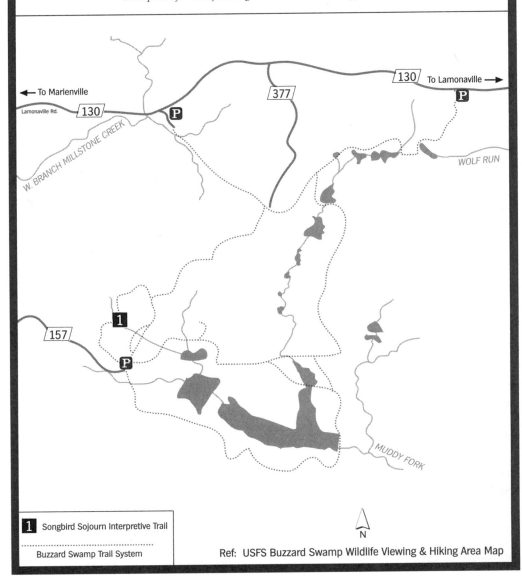

Buzzard Swamp Habitat Management Area

Fifteen man-made ponds were constructed in the early 1960s in the Buzzard Swamp Area for wildlife management and recreational opportunities.

← To Marienville

Lamonaville Rd.   130

130   To Lamonaville →

377

W. BRANCH MILLSTONE CREEK

WOLF RUN

157

1

MUDDY FORK

1 Songbird Sojourn Interpretive Trail

Buzzard Swamp Trail System

Ref: USFS Buzzard Swamp Wildlife Viewing & Hiking Area Map

N

water quality and declines in populations of the fish they parasitize as larva. Both clams are believed to have occurred throughout the Ohio River drainage basin. It is also possible that they may have occurred within the larger riverine systems that flow into the Mississippi River. Since these animals have not been extensively studied, and the information that is available is widely scattered and sporadic, it's difficult to make any definitive statements about their historic distribution.

The presence of these two clams is a testament to the quality and unspoiled nature of this waterway.

Directions: To reach the northern islands, launch from the Buckaloons Recreation Area boat launch 15 miles west of Warren on US 6. To reach the middle islands use the boat launch at Tidioute along US 127. To reach the southern islands use the boat ramp along US 62 just across the river from the village of West Hickory.

Activities: Hiking, hunting, fishing, camping.

Facilities: None.

Dates: Open year-round.

Fees: None.

Closest town: Tidioute.

For more information: Allegheny National Forest, PO Box 847, Warren, PA 16365. Phone (814) 725-5150.

BUZZARD SWAMP HABITAT MANAGEMENT AREA

[Fig. 11] Buzzard Swamp is cooperatively managed by the U.S. Forest Service and the Pennsylvania Game Commission for the benefit of wildlife, particularly waterfowl. Located on the Atlantic flyway, the swamp supports at least 25 species of waterfowl during the spring migration.

Fifteen man-made ponds constructed by the Pennsylvania Game Commission during the 1960s are home to a bounty of panfish and bass, and fishing and boating are permitted. Only those boats without motors are allowed, and they must be carried from the trailhead, which is 1 mile from the nearest lake.

The only portion of Buzzard Swamp closed to visitors is the 40-acre propagation area, which is managed for nesting waterfowl. Binoculars and spotting scopes will allow the visitor to view bald eagle, osprey, waterfowl, and other wildlife here and throughout the area.

Directions: From PA Route 66 in Marienville, follow Loleta Road south 1 mile to Forest Road 157. Turn left and drive about 1 mile to parking area.

Activities: Hiking, cross-country skiing, mountain biking, fishing, wildlife viewing, nonmotorized boating.

Facilities: Trails. Restrooms scheduled to open in fall 1998.

Dates: Open year-round.

Fees: None.

Closest town: Marienville, 2 miles.

Tionesta Scenic Area

The Twin Lakes Trail begins at the Black Cherry National Recreation Interpretive Trail and runs west to join with the North Country National Scenic Trail.

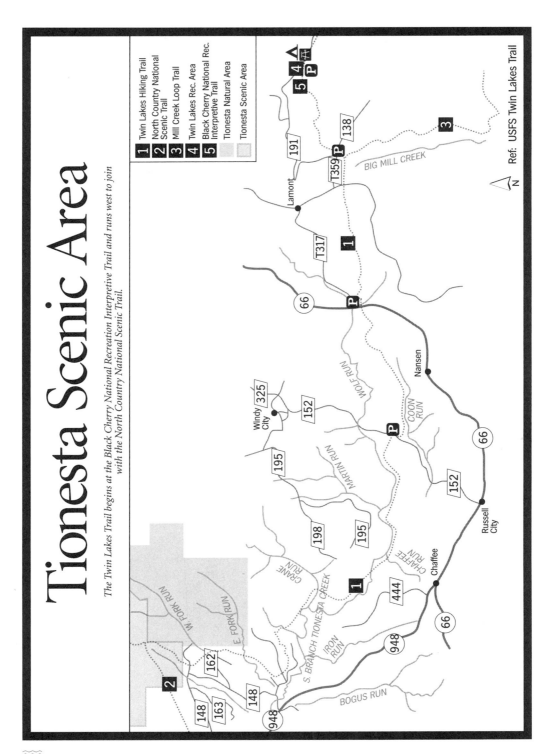

1	Twin Lakes Hiking Trail
2	North Country National Scenic Trail
3	Mill Creek Loop Trail
4	Twin Lakes Rec. Area
5	Black Cherry National Rec. Interpretive Trail
	Tionesta Natural Area
	Tionesta Scenic Area

Ref: USFS Twin Lakes Trail

For more information: Allegheny National Forest, PO Box 847, Warren, PA 16365. Phone (814) 725-5150.

BUZZARD SWAMP TRAIL SYSTEM

[Fig. 11] Running through the Buzzard Swamp Wildlife Viewing Area is the 11-mile Buzzard Swamp Trail System. In this exceptional wildlife viewing area, you can see waterfowl, songbirds, deer, and, if you're lucky, perhaps even a black bear. A portion of the trail system is a self-guided interpretive trail. The Songbird Sojourn Interpretive Trail [Fig. 11(1)] begins at Forest Road 157 and extends for 1.5 miles. Pamphlets identifying various sites along the way are available at the trailhead.

The interconnecting trails are open to hiking, mountain biking, and cross-country skiing, but they are off-limits to all motorized devices. The trails are relatively flat and easy to walk, but since only a portion of the trail system is marked with gray diamonds, the hiker should pay close attention to the periodic trail signs.

Trail: 11-mile system of interconnecting trails.

Elevation: 1,660–1,760 feet.

Degree of difficulty: Easy.

Surface and blaze: Unpaved. Most of the trails are not marked, so watch for informational signs for directions.

TIONESTA NATIONAL SCENIC AREA

[Fig. 12] This 2,000-acre tract gives the visitor a glimpse of what Pennsylvania's Allegheny Plateau looked like before settlers moved in and clear-cut the area. Two hundred years ago this type of beech, hemlock, and maple forest covered 6 million acres.

The Tionesta Scenic Area, which contains 300- to 400-year-old trees, is a secluded, nearly roadless tract of forest that was added to the National Registry of Natural Landmarks because of its old-growth characteristics. These large old-growth trees are home to fishers, which are large members of the weasel family, brown creepers (*Certhia familiaris*), blackburnian warblers (*Dendroica fusca*), and other deep woods species.

FISHER (*Martes pennanti*)
A boreal species, the shy fisher is an adept climber and swimmer that eats porcupines and snowshoe hares.

With gently rolling uplands and relatively steep-sided stream valleys, the area is typical of many on the Allegheny High Plateau. Elevations range from 1,500 feet along the stream bottoms to 1,960 feet on the plateau. The northern half of the area was affected by a series of tornadoes that devastated many parts of northwestern Pennsylvania in 1985. An adjacent 2,000-acre parcel, now known as the Tionesta Research Natural Area, is being studied to evaluate forest regeneration and ecological changes that occur in hemlock and hardwood forests after a tornado.

The North Country National Scenic Trail [Fig. 12(2)] passes through the Tionesta Scenic Area, where it intersects with the Twin Lakes Hiking Trail (*see* below). In addition to the other named trails that run through the area, there are two short hiking trails near the parking lot. Both trails, one that is 1 mile long and takes about one hour to hike and the other that is about 0.25 mile long and takes about 15 minutes to walk, pass through virgin hemlock forest and past a viewing platform that allows the visitor to look out over the wide swath of a tornado blowdown.

In order to preserve the natural character of the area, some recreational activities are prohibited. Overnight camping and campfires are not allowed, and mountain bikes and motorized vehicles are limited to open road use.

Directions: From US Route 6 in Ludlow, take Forest Road 133 south approximately 6 miles. Signs along the road will direct you to the parking area.

Activities: Hiking, hunting, and fishing. Mountain biking is permitted on the roads only.

Facilities: Trails.

Dates: Open year-round.

Fees: None.

Closest town: Ludlow, 6 miles.

For more information: Allegheny National Forest, PO Box 847, Warren, PA 16365. Phone (814) 723-5150.

TWIN LAKES HIKING TRAIL

[Fig. 12(1)] This 14.7-mile trail passes through an ecologically and topographically diverse area as it connects the Twin Lakes Recreation Area [Fig. 12(4)] in the east to the 3,200-mile North Country National Scenic Trail in the Tionesta Scenic Area (*see* page 45). The west end of the trail can be reached from the North Country Scenic Trail as it passes through the Tionesta Scenic Area. There are two parking and access areas along the middle of the trail. Additionally, the east end begins at the Twin Lakes Recreation Area [Fig. 12(4)], where there is a parking area, picnic ground, and campground. To reach the Twin Lakes Recreation Area follow PA Route 321 north from Wilcox for about 2.2 miles. Turn left onto Forest Route 191 and drive 2 miles to the parking area, which is on the left.

From the Twin Lakes Recreation Area, the trail takes the hiker across Hoffman Run, up onto the Allegheny Plateau, and then down again into the Wolf Run and

Tionesta Creek lowlands. Since the trail crosses several creeks and the associated lowlands, hikers should expect to encounter wet spots. Native brook trout and brown trout can be caught in Wolf Run and Tionesta Creek, as well as Crane Run which is an officially designated wilderness trout stream.

The Twin Lakes Trail is the second longest trail in the Allegheny National Forest, and it passes through active oil and gas fields. Caution should be exercised around pumping equipment because some wells are on timers and could begin operating without notice.

Since the trail rises in and out of stream cuts in the plateau, some parts of the hike are more challenging than others. Only hikers in good physical condition should attempt the entire trail.

Trail: 14.7 miles.
Elevation: 1,730–2,020 feet.
Degree of difficulty: Moderate to strenuous.
Surface and blaze: Unpaved with off-white markers.

HEARTS CONTENT NATIONAL SCENIC AREA

[Fig. 8(3), Fig. 10(1)] While diminutive in size at only 122 acres, the Hearts Content National Scenic Area contains some of the Allegheny National Forest's biggest attractions. Living here are massive white pine, hemlock, and beech (*Fagus* spp.) trees which began life as seedlings 300 to 400 years ago.

A walk along the Hearts Content Scenic Interpretive Trail, which has both a 0.25-mile and a 1-mile loop beginning at the Hearts Content National Scenic Area 15 miles southwest of Warren, takes the visitor into a forest like the one encountered by the first Europeans to enter this area in the 1700s.

There are, however, some differences between the forest of yesterday and the forest of today. You'll notice that the ground is covered with a lush carpet of ferns and that very few tree seedlings are present. White-tailed deer are common here, as they are throughout the state of Pennsylvania, and their large population eats the tasty seedlings and leaves behind the unpalatable ferns. The ferns look beautiful, but the situation does not bode well for the future of the forest.

You'll also notice that most of the beech trees appear to be dying. If you look closely at the smooth bark you may notice tiny white spots. These are the scales of beech bark disease. Foresters estimate that within 20 years all of the beech trees within the Hearts Content National Scenic Area will be dead, but their massive skeletons will continue to support numerous species of wildlife for decades to come.

If you want to learn more about the Hearts

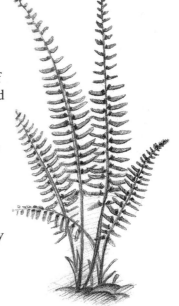

CHRISTMAS FERN
(Polystichum acrostichoides)

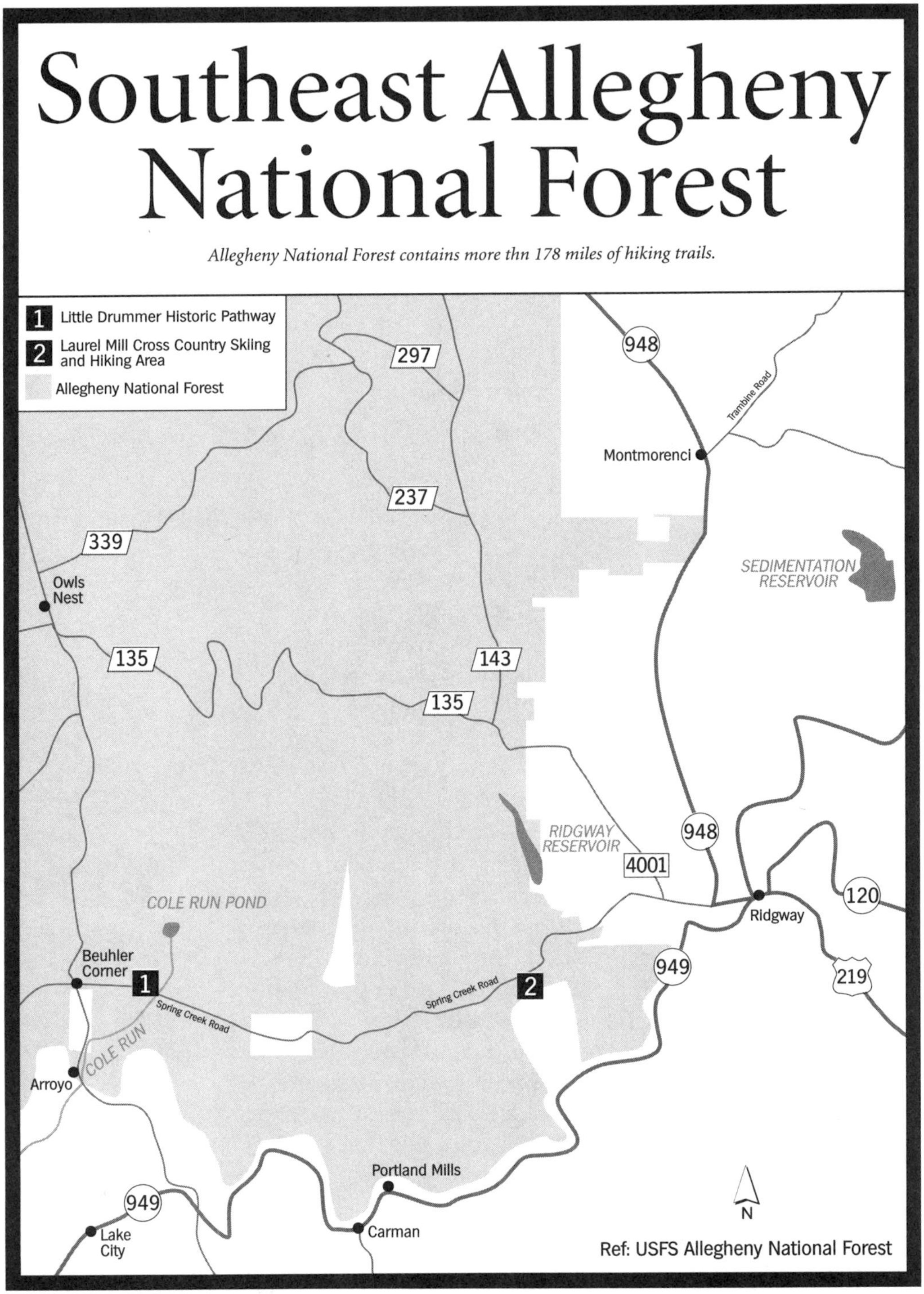

Southeast Allegheny National Forest

Allegheny National Forest contains more thn 178 miles of hiking trails.

1 Little Drummer Historic Pathway
2 Laurel Mill Cross Country Skiing and Hiking Area
Allegheny National Forest

948

297

Trambue Road

Montmorenci

237

339

Owls Nest

SEDIMENTATION RESERVOIR

135

143

135

RIDGWAY RESERVOIR

4001

948

COLE RUN POND

120

Beuhler Corner **1**

Spring Creek Road **2**

Spring Creek Road

949

Ridgway

219

COLE RUN

Arroyo

949

Portland Mills

N

Lake City

Carman

Ref: USFS Allegheny National Forest

Content National Scenic Area before exploring on your own, stop at the Hearts Content Campground across the road from the trailhead and check out an audio tape. The Hearts Content National Scenic Area shares a parking area with the Hickory Creek Wilderness (*see* page 37), which lies just on the other side of Pleasant Drive.

Directions: From the Mohawk Exit of US Route 6 near Warren, follow Pleasant Drive south for 11 miles. At the hard curve, turn left onto the gravel road and go south 4 miles.

Activities: Hiking.

Facilities: Campground, cross-country ski trail, restrooms, and picnic area are adjacent to the Hearts Content Scenic Interpretive Trail.

Dates: Open year-round.

Fees: None.

Closest town: Tidioute, 4.5 miles.

For more information: Allegheny National Forest, PO Box 847, Warren, PA 16365. Phone (814) 723-5150.

HEARTS CONTENT CROSS-COUNTRY SKI AREA

[Fig. 8(4), Fig. 10(2)] The Hearts Content Cross-Country Ski Area provides skiers with ungroomed trails which follow roads, old railroad grades, and existing trails. The trail system is composed of three loops. The Wheeler Loop, which begins and ends at the Hearts Content National Scenic Area parking lot, extends 1.3-miles and loops around Wheeler fire tower. The Tom's Run Loop begins at the Hearts Content picnic area on Hearts Content Road, 10 miles north of Sheffield, and is 3.2 miles long. It follows Tom's Run up a gradual rise to the plateau, eventually meeting up with the Ironwood Loop. This loop, which runs for 3.3 miles, is the least used and can be reached from the Dunham Siding intersection along Hearts Content Road.

Trail: 6.5 miles in 3 loops.

Elevation: 1,800–1,900 feet.

Degree of difficulty: Easy.

Blaze: Blue diamonds.

▓ LAUREL MILL CROSS-COUNTRY SKI/HIKING AREA

[Fig. 14, Fig. 13(2)] The Laurel Mill Cross-Country Ski/Hiking Area is an 11.6-mile trail system located at the extreme southeastern corner of the Allegheny National Forest between the Clarion River and the Ridgway Reservoir. This relatively new trail system, which was completed in 1986, is composed of a series of loops that will challenge beginning skiers and experienced skiers alike. The loops, most of which are groomed, range in length from 0.65 mile to 3.2 miles and have benches for the weary skier or hiker who needs to stop and rest or just enjoy the solitude.

Three of the loops are located north of Spring Creek Road. The 1-mile Elk Loop is a good choice for novice skiers, while the adjacent 1.2-mile Scout Loop is somewhat

Laurel Mill Cross-Country Skiing Area

In 1984 the Pennsylvania Wilderness Act designated more than 23,000 acres of the Allegheny National Forest as a national recreation area.

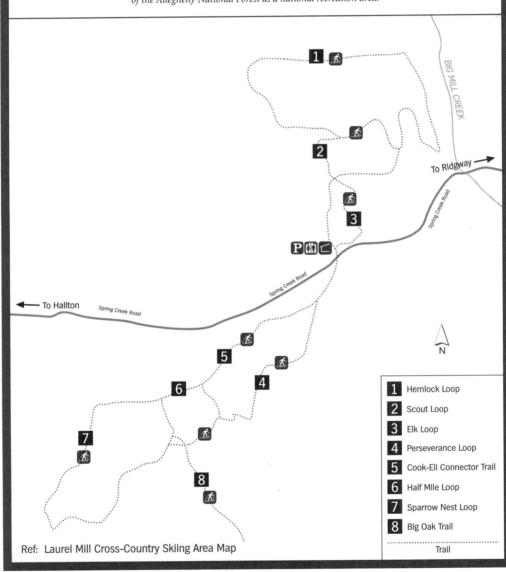

1 Hemlock Loop
2 Scout Loop
3 Elk Loop
4 Perseverance Loop
5 Cook-Eli Connector Trail
6 Half Mile Loop
7 Sparrow Nest Loop
8 Big Oak Trail

········ Trail

Ref: Laurel Mill Cross-Country Skiing Area Map

more challenging because it has a few small hills. Both trails serve as a good warm-up for more experienced skiers on their way to Hemlock Loop, which is attached to the north end of the Scout Loop. The Hemlock Loop, which at 3.2 miles is the longest loop in the system, provides some scenic views of Big Mill Creek and the Ridgway Reservoir. It is more difficult because it climbs and descends some hills and contains a few more turns.

There are also three loops south of Spring Creek Road. The 1.25-mile Perseverance Loop and 1.1-mile Half Mile Loop are both rated as easy and are well suited to beginning skiers. Adjacent to the southern end of the Half Mile Loop is the challenging Sparrow Nest Loop. Located in what is called the Clarion River Undeveloped Area, this 1.8-mile loop lies in the most secluded part of the trail system and is recommended for experienced skiers only.

Hikers, fishermen, and hunters also use the trails. During the spring, wildflowers bloom throughout the area, and it is possible that the endangered small-whorled pogonia (*Isotria medeoloides*) may be found in the Clarion River Undeveloped Area. Anglers will find good fishing in Big Mill Creek in the northern part of the area and in the Clarion River in the southern portion. Hunting is good throughout the area,

WILD TURKEY
(Meleagris gallopavo)
A popular game bird in Pennsylvania, turkeys can fly well for short distances but prefer to run. Ben Franklin thought the turkey should be the national emblem for the United States instead of the Bald Eagle.

with bear, turkey, white-tailed deer, and small game present.

A trail brochure that contains a detailed map of the Laurel Mill Cross-Country Ski/Hiking Area is available from the Ridgway Ranger District, Rural Delivery #1, State 948 North, Ridgway, PA 15853. Phone (814) 776-6172.

To reach the trailhead follow Township Road 307 (Spring Creek Road) west from Ridgway for 3 miles to the trailhead parking area on the right.

Trail: 11.6-mile system of loops.

Elevation: 500 feet.

Degree of difficulty: Easy to difficult.

Surface and blaze: Unpaved, blue diamonds.

▨ LITTLE DRUMMER HISTORICAL PATHWAY

[Fig. 13(1)] Located about 8 miles west of Ridgway in Elk County, on Township Road 307, also called Spring Creek Road, is a unique double-loop trail that offers hikers a look at habitat management in the Allegheny National Forest. The Little Drummer Historical Pathway is an interpretive trail located within the Owl's Nest Ecosystem Demonstration Area. The trail takes its name from the male ruffed grouse, whose habit of beating its wings during the breeding season is called drumming, and from the old railroad grade and oil well equipment found along the trail, which date back to an earlier era.

The trail is broken up into two loops: a 1-mile loop north of Spring Creek Road that goes to Cole Run Pond and a loop 2.1 miles long that is attached to the northern end of the shorter loop and goes around Cole Run Pond. Portions of the area are managed to maintain a mature hardwood forest. The wildlife found here includes turkey, black bear, and cavity-nesting species such as pileated woodpeckers and flying squirrels. Other parts of the area are managed to provide younger forest habitats. Ruffed grouse, woodcock, and many species of warblers call these areas home. The trail is moderately challenging and often wet in spots. A color brochure that details all of the trail's highlights is available from the forest office. Camping is permitted along the trail.

RED-BELLIED WOODPECKER
(Melanerpes carolinus)
Despite its name, the red patch on the woodpecker's belly is faint, in contrast to its bright red crown.

Along the shorter loop, hikers will walk through pine plantations planted before World War II, and through areas where trees have been cut to provide sun for fruit-bearing shrubs used by wildlife for food. In another area, mature aspen trees have been cut to make room for a

SOUTHERN FLYING SQUIRREL

(Glaucomys volans) This squirrel doesn't fly but glides.

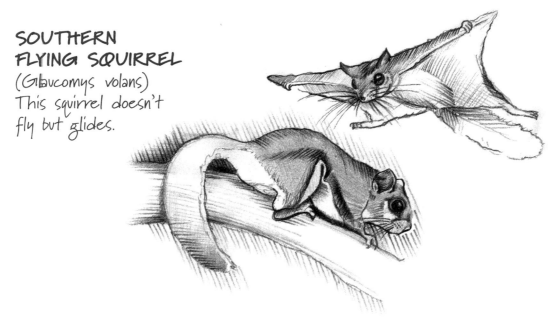

young stand of quaking aspen, a preferred habitat of ruffed grouse. The younger trees didn't grow from seeds, but rather from the roots of the trees that were cut. The return leg of the loop follows the former pathway of the Tionesta Valley Railroad, which hauled logs during the early part of the twentieth century.

The longer loop of the trail begins on an old skid trail, so named because horses were used to drag or skid logs along it to collection areas called landings. The site of an old landing can also be seen. It's a field where the soil has been so compacted that trees still won't grow there. Soil compaction is a common problem in areas being logged today as well because of the heavy equipment used to cut and skid the logs. Horses are being used more and more often today by landowners that want to minimize environmental damage when harvesting timber from their woodlots.

The trail also passes several different types of wetlands. Riparian (streamside) wetlands containing sphagnum moss and Juneberry (*Amelanchier* sp.) are found along Cole Run, which passes through the center of the loop. The stream feeds Cole Run Pond, which was built during the 1960s to provide waterfowl habitat. Another type of wetland, beaver ponds, can be seen to the south of the trail.

Hikers will also see several uncommon types of conifers. Cedar shrubs have been planted recently to provide winter cover for turkeys. Before World War II, the Work Projects Administration planted larch, a non-native tree that naturally occurs much farther north.

Trail: Two loops, 3.1-miles.

Elevation: 500 feet.

Degree of difficulty: Moderate.

Surface and blaze: Unpaved, off-white diamonds.

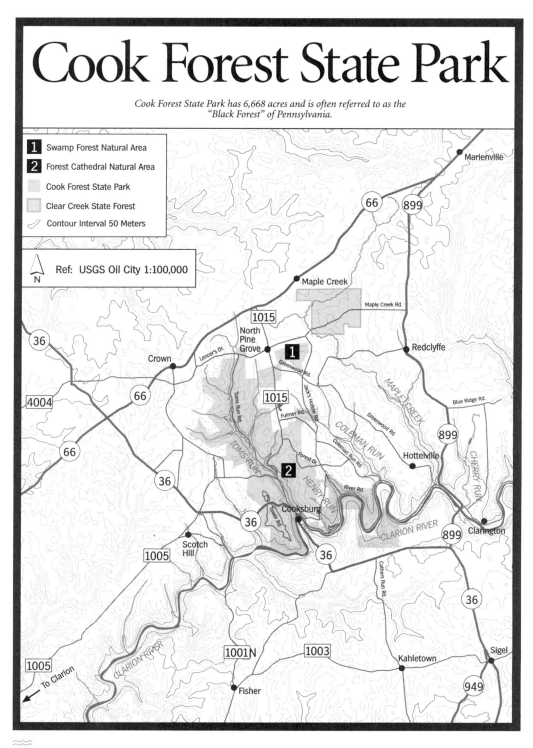

Cook Forest State Park

Cook Forest State Park has 6,668 acres and is often referred to as the "Black Forest" of Pennsylvania.

1 Swamp Forest Natural Area

2 Forest Cathedral Natural Area

Cook Forest State Park

Clear Creek State Forest

Contour Interval 50 Meters

Ref: USGS Oil City 1:100,000

N

Marienville

66 899

Maple Creek

Maple Creek Rd.

1015

36

North Pine Grove

Redclyffe

Crown

Lencers Dr.

Greenwood Rd.

66

4004

Toms Run Rd.

1015

Jack's Hollow Rd.

Fulmer Rd.

Greenwood Rd.

Blue Ridge Rd.

66

COLEMAN RUN

899

MAPLE CREEK

36

Forest Dr.

Coleman Run Rd.

Hottelville

CHERRY RUN

2

HENRY RUN

River Rd.

Tower Rd.

Cooksburg

36

36

CLARION RIVER

899 Clarington

Scotch Hill

36

Cathers Run Rd.

1005

36

1005

To Clarion

CLARION RIVER

1001N

1003

Kahletown

Sigel

Fisher

949

State Parks

▦ COOK FOREST STATE PARK

[Fig. 15] Cook Forest State Park provides a unique combination of old-growth forest and a multitude of recreational opportunities in an area small enough to enjoy both in the same day. Like most of the parks on the Allegheny Plateau, Cook Forest is a product of geology, ecology, and man's influence.

Magnificent white pine and hemlock greeted John Cook when he arrived here in 1826 to determine if an east-west canal could be built off of the Clarion River. While the canal was never built, Cook decided to stay and built a sawmill at the mouth of Tom's Run at what is today Cooksburg. Over the next 100 years, his descendants expanded the logging operations and the family landholdings to include several sawmills, a flour mill, and a small village.

In 1927, approximately 6,055 acres of old-growth forest were purchased from the A. Cook Sons Company by a newly formed private conservation group called the Cook Forest Association. Eventually the land came under the ownership of the state of Pennsylvania and today forms the nucleus of the 6,668-acre Cook Forest State Park.

Sometimes referred to as the Black Forest of Pennsylvania because the towering pines and hemlocks prevented sunlight from reaching the forest floor, Cook Forest State Park is located along the west shore of the Clarion River in Clarion, Forest, and Jefferson counties. Unlike much of northwestern Pennsylvania, this area was not subject to glacial activity during the last ice age because high elevations in McKean and Potter counties to the northeast blocked the movement of glaciers as they moved south.

Because of the old-growth white pine and hemlock here, the park was designated a National Natural Landmark in 1969. There are three main areas of old-growth forest within Cook Forest, the Swamp Forest Natural Area in the northeast, the Forest Cathedral Natural Area near the center of the park, and the Seneca Area just south of the park office.

There are ample opportunities to explore the old-growth forest on the 27-mile trail system comprised of 16 marked trails ranging from 0.6 to 3 miles in length. Hikers should be aware that the Indian and Seneca trails are relatively steep and not recommended for visitors with heart conditions. Additionally, hikers should be aware that there are two marked trails which are very long. The Baker Trail runs for 140 miles from Freeport to the Allegheny National Forest, and the North Country Scenic Trail runs from New York to North Dakota.

Cook Forest State Park is a year-round recreational facility. In addition to the hiking trails, many of which are also suitable for cross-country skiing, there are 20 miles of snowmobile trails, 10 acres of sledding slopes, and a lighted ice-skating pond. There is a 226-site campground open throughout the year.

The Clarion River is one of the park's most prominent features. Named in 1817 by land surveyor Daniel Standard who thought "the ripple of the river sound[ed] like a distant clarion," the Clarion is a wide, relatively slow-moving river ideal for floating logs. During the heyday of logging, logs were tied together in rafts and floated down the Clarion to the Allegheny River, where they made their way to Pittsburgh for sale. The logs were tied together in an area flooded by the damming of Tom's Run. A walk today along Tom's Run reveals some of the stone and earthen foundations of the bracket dams used to flood the area for the log rafts.

Today, instead of logs floating down the river past the park, you'll see canoes. The Clarion is ideal for canoeing, and canoes can be rented at the park. A canoe launch area is located in the north end of the park, and there are several landing areas downstream in the southern portions of the park. Other recreational opportunities within the park include trout fishing, horseback riding on 4.5 miles of designated trails, hunting, swimming, and camping.

Directions: Take Exit 13 off of Interstate 80 and follow PA Route 36 north to Cooksburg.

Activities: Hiking and fishing are allowed throughout the park. Hunting, camping, snowmobiling, swimming, ice skating, and horseback riding are permitted in designated areas.

Facilities: Trails, cabins, campgrounds, visitors center, pool, scenic overlooks, picnic areas.

Dates: The park is open year-round, but some of the facilities, such as the pool, the back section of the campground, and cabins, are closed during the winter months.

Fees: There is a charge for the cabins and campgrounds.

Closest town: Cooksburg, less than 1 mile.

For more information: Cook Forest State Park, PO Box 120, Cooksburg, PA 16217. Phone (814) 744-8407.

FOREST CATHEDRAL AND SWAMP FOREST NATURAL AREA

[Fig. 15(1), Fig. 15(2)] Two of the three old-growth stands within Cook Forest State Park have been designated natural areas by the Pennsylvania Bureau of State Parks in order to preserve their natural character. One is a wetland and the other a hillside upland.

Located in the northeastern corner of the park is a good example of a wetland dominated by old-growth trees. The 246-acre Swamp Forest Natural Area is dominated by hemlock and is located in one of the most remote parts of the park. The only trail in the area is the Baker Trail, which in Cook Forest State Park is also a part of the North Country Scenic Trail. Be aware, however, that the Baker Trail extends far beyond the boundaries of the park.

Unlike the remote Swamp Forest Natural Area, the 555-acre Forest Cathedral

Natural Area is one of the most accessible old-growth forests in the state. The Forest Cathedral Natural Area is located close behind the Log Cabin Visitor's Center, which was built in the 1930s by the Civilian Conservation Corps and today houses logging exhibits and is used for environmental education programs.

A short walk along the Longfellow Trail, which begins at the visitor's center, takes the hiker to some of the largest white pines and hemlocks in Pennsylvania. Ecologists believe that many of these 200-foot-tall trees began life after a severe drought and forest fire in 1644.

While only 1.2 miles long, the Longfellow Trail serves as a good access point for other trails that travel deeper into the forest. From it you can connect to the 1.1-mile Birch Trail, named for the trees. You can also connect to the relatively steep Indian Trail, which passes through a second-growth white pine forest, and the Joyce Kilmer Trail, which takes you through 1.5 miles of virgin pine and hemlock. Each of these trails also connects with the Rhododendron Trail which passes through the center of the Forest Cathedral Natural Area and includes a swinging bridge over Tom's Run. Cross-country skiing is not recommended within the natural area due to the steep terrain.

Directions: To reach the Forest Cathedral Natural Area take Exit 13 off of Interstate 80 and follow PA Route 36 north to Cooksburg. Signs will direct you to the park office and visitor's center, both of which are adjacent to trailheads leading into the Forest Cathedral Natural Area. To reach the Swamp Forest Natural Area follow PA Route 36 north from Cooksburg for approximately 1 mile. At the Y in the road bear right onto Vowinckel Road. Follow Vowinckel Road for approximately 3 miles to a small parking area marked with a sign for the North Country National Scenic Trail.

EASTERN HEMLOCK
(Tsuga canadensis)
Long-lived hemlocks develop slowly in the shade. Their bark was once a commercial source of tannin in the production of leather.

Hike the North Country National Scenic Trail north to the Swamp Forest Natural Area.

Activities: Hiking, fishing.

Facilities: Trails.

Dates: Open year-round.

Fees: None.

Closest town: Cooksburg, less than 1 mile.

For more information: Cook Forest State Park, PO Box 120, Cooksburg, PA 16217. Phone (814) 744-8407.

OIL CREEK STATE PARK

[Fig. 3(1)] In 1859, Colonel Edwin Drake drilled the world's first successful oil well along a small, quiet stream in northwestern Pennsylvania. Drake chose this spot along Oil Creek because oil occurred naturally on the surface of the ground along the creek. He struck oil just 69 feet below the surface, setting off an oil boom that lasted less than 20 years but changed this part of the state and the rest of the world forever.

Drake's well was located just south of the town of Titusville in Venango County. Word quickly spread of the discovery, and oil wells began popping up all over. Oil boom towns appeared just as fast, turning previously remote areas into bustling centers of activity. Up and down the quiet little stream, towns and wells seemed to be everywhere. But by the mid-1870s the wells began to dry up, the towns died, and people moved on. The site of Drake's well is now a museum and historic park that lies just north of Oil Creek State Park.

While the oil boom days are gone, oil is still one of the main industries in this part of the state. A drive through any of the nearby towns of Rouseville, Titusville, or Oil City takes you past large oil refineries operated by Quaker State, Pennzoil, and numerous smaller oil companies. Similarly, a drive down any of the backcountry roads reveals innumerable small oil wells that are still pumping away. They don't produce the volumes of the 1800s, but the oil they do produce is considered the finest lubricating oil in the world because of its high paraffin content. Just north of Oil City is McClintock No. 1, an oil well now owned by Quaker State that has been producing oil since 1861.

Today, 13.5 miles of that scenic stream valley that changed history are part of Oil Creek State Park. This sprawling 7,075-acre park is devoted to preserving the history of the oil boom. To look at the park today, it's hard to imagine what it must have been like 140 years ago. The towns and nearly all of the wells are gone, and all that remains are the rusting pumps, wellheads, and pipes. Nature has reclaimed the land, and once again it is lush, forested, and green. The combination of history and nature, along with a very well-developed trail system and recreational facilities, make this one of the most unique and interesting of Pennsylvania's state parks.

A good place to begin a visit to the park is at Petroleum Centre, one of the old boomtowns. This quiet area, which now contains rusting oil equipment overgrown by trees and brush, picnic pavilions, trails, and restrooms, was home to 3,000 people in 1863. It is near the park office, visitor center, concession areas, and trailheads.

Petroleum Centre is also a good place to begin an excursion on the Oil Creek State Park Trail. This 8.5-foot-wide asphalt bike trail runs from Petroleum Centre north to the Drake Well Museum. A trail guide is available from the park office. The trail begins on the east side of Oil Creek, then crosses to the west side about 1 mile north of Petroleum Centre. It passes quite a few historical areas, including old oil fields, the boomtown of Pioneer, and Miller Farm. Miller Farm was the end of the line for the Oil Creek Railroad, which transported oil out of the valley. Located here was the world's first oil pipeline, which extended 5.5 miles to the town of Pithole, the largest of the oil boomtowns.

From end-to-end, the Oil Creek State Park Bike Trail extends for 9.7 miles, but it encounters only a few rolling hills, so it's an easy ride. There are restrooms, interpretive signs, picnic areas, and rain shelters along the trail. Bike rentals are available at the southern trailhead at Petroleum Centre. To make the ride more interesting, consider riding one way and then hopping on to the Oil Creek and Titusville Railroad for the ride back. This excursion train runs between the museum and Petroleum Centre and will carry your bike for only a little bit more than the standard passenger fare. The Oil Creek State Park Trail is very popular, so you can expect a little traffic on nice days.

The trail isn't just used during nice weather. It's also a popular cross-country ski spot during the winter and is especially good for novice skiers. There's also a 10-mile network of trails along the east rim of the Oil Creek gorge, primarily made up of old logging and oil lease roads. Park personnel set the tracks so skiers have an established trail, making the going a little easier. The ski area has a parking lot and warming hut, complete with a fireplace, restrooms, ski maps, and information. Skiers will enjoy scenic vistas of the Oil Creek Valley and will see evidence of tornadoes that came through here in 1985.

Located near Petroleum Centre, along SR 1007 that runs through the southern end of the park, is Wildcat Hollow. The hollow was named long before the oil boom, but its name is now part of the oilman's dictionary. Once Drake made his discovery, entrepreneurs quickly claimed nearly all of the land along the creek. Those who were late on the scene found that the only place left to drill was the untested Wildcat Hollow. Even now, drilling for oil in an uncertain location is called wildcatting. Today, Wildcat Hollow is an outdoor education area that includes picnic facilities and 4 theme trails: a 1-mile geology trail, a 0.25-mile forestry trail, a 0.25-mile oil history trail, and a 1-mile wetland trail. School programs are held throughout the year at Wildcat Hollow.

There are more than 73 miles of hiking trails within the park, some of which are short and easy and others that are long and difficult. The main trail within the park

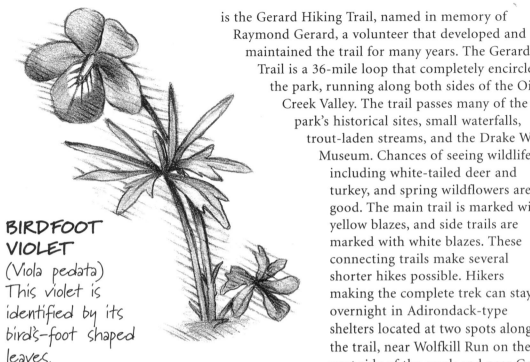

BIRDFOOT VIOLET

(Viola pedata) This violet is identified by its bird's-foot shaped leaves.

is the Gerard Hiking Trail, named in memory of Raymond Gerard, a volunteer that developed and maintained the trail for many years. The Gerard Trail is a 36-mile loop that completely encircles the park, running along both sides of the Oil Creek Valley. The trail passes many of the park's historical sites, small waterfalls, trout-laden streams, and the Drake Well Museum. Chances of seeing wildlife, including white-tailed deer and turkey, and spring wildflowers are good. The main trail is marked with yellow blazes, and side trails are marked with white blazes. These connecting trails make several shorter hikes possible. Hikers making the complete trek can stay overnight in Adirondack-type shelters located at two spots along the trail, near Wolfkill Run on the west side of the creek and near Cow Run on the east side. Reservations must be made ahead of time and there is a nominal charge.

One of the park's best hikes is the Petroleum Centre Loop, which begins behind the park office. This 6-mile-long trail, which follows the Gerard Hiking Trail and some of its connectors along much of its path, offers a glimpse of many of the park's ecosystems. Mixed-oak and hardwood forests, with their complement of wild geranium (*Geranium maculatum*), violets, and Canada mayflower (*Maianthemum canadense*), lie along the upland portions of the trail, while the stream bottoms are dominated by hemlocks and contain red trillium, spring beauty (*Claytonia virginica*), and bedstraw (*Galium* sp.). Since the trail climbs hillsides and descends into the Hemlock Run and Oil Creek valleys, hikers should be prepared for a somewhat strenuous hike. Also along the trail are scenic views of the Oil Creek Valley and an area that was heavily damaged by the 1985 tornadoes.

Oil Creek is one of the largest trout streams in Pennsylvania, and many of its tributaries contain brook trout, making the park a favorite with trout fishermen. The creek also contains sizable populations of bass. Flies and other trout-fishing equipment can be purchased at the bike rental concession located at Petroleum Centre. Anglers should be aware that the 1.5-mile stretch of stream from the Petroleum Centre Bridge to the Oil Creek and Titusville railroad bridge is a delayed harvest-artificial lure area.

Pennsylvania's Wild Trout

Pennsylvania's state fish, the brook trout (*Salvelinus fontinalus*), is also the state's only native trout. The brookie, as anglers often call it, has lived in Pennsylvania's streams since before the ice ages. Brookies were so common at the turn of the century that the daily creel limit was 40 fish, and 20-inch fish were not uncommon. But as the number of roads increased so did the number of anglers fishing the cold, remote mountain streams. This coupled with competition from stocked fish and degraded water quality has decreased the size and distribution of native, wild brook trout.

Pennsylvania's streams are also home to two introduced trout—the brown trout (*Salmo trutta*) and the rainbow trout (*Oncorhynchus mykiss*). The brown trout was introduced to Pennsylvania waterways in the 1880s. This fish is a native of Europe and has proved to be a serious competitor of the native brookie. The rainbow trout is a native of the cold-water streams along the Pacific Coast. While this fish was introduced to the state at the same time as the brown trout, it has not been as successful so its wild populations are not as widespread.

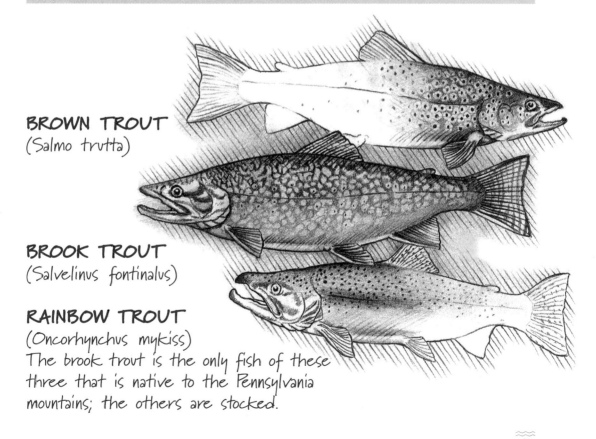

BROWN TROUT
(Salmo trutta)

BROOK TROUT
(Salvelinus fontinalus)

RAINBOW TROUT
(Oncorhynchus mykiss)
The brook trout is the only fish of these three that is native to the Pennsylvania mountains; the others are stocked.

Most of the time Oil Creek is slow moving, so it's good for canoeing in the spring. There are canoe launch areas near Drake Well Museum and also near Petroleum Centre, with take-out points at Petroleum Centre and Rynd Farm, a historical site near the park's southern entrance. Call the park office for information on creek levels.

Directions: From the stoplight in Rouseville follow PA Route 8 north for 1 mile to the park entrance, which is on the right.

Activities: Hiking, biking, canoeing, fishing, hunting, picnicking, cross-country skiing, train excursion.

Facilities: Trails, bike rental concession, tackle shop, visitor center, scenic overlooks, picnic areas, historic sites, canoe launches, train station.

Dates: Open year-round.

Fees: There is a charge for camping along the Gerard Trail and for picnic pavilions for groups.

Closest town: Rouseville, 1 mile.

For more information: Oil Creek State Park, RR 1, Box 207, Oil City, PA 16301. Phone (814) 676-5915.

LYMAN RUN STATE PARK

[Fig. 3(4)] Lyman Run State Park encompasses 595 acres of mixed hardwoods nestled within the Susquehannock State Forest in Potter County. The park's most conspicuous feature is 45-acre Lyman Lake, which was built in 1950 for flood control by damming Lyman Run. Surrounding the lake is a northern hardwood forest dominated primarily by maple and black cherry. This lush forest stands in stark contrast to the way the area looked in 1900, when loggers had clear-cut the area and all that remained were bare hillsides. In the 1930s, the civilian Conservation Corps set up a camp in the park and planted the trees that today blanket the park.

Lyman Lake is the focal point of much of the park's recreational facilities. A guarded swimming beach is open from Memorial Day to Labor Day, and there are bathhouses, a food concession, and picnic areas adjacent. For those who want to go canoeing there's also a boat rental concession nearby. During the winter both ice skaters and ice fishermen use the lake. Caution should be exercised, however, because the park does not monitor ice thickness or conditions.

The park contains two campgrounds with a total of 42 campsites. One of the campgrounds is located near Lyman Run Road near the southern end of the park, and the other is north of the lake near one of its tributaries, Daggett Hollow Run. Both campgrounds can accommodate tents and trailers and are open from the second Friday of April until the close of antlerless deer season in December. The lower campground is primitive, but the upper one has electrical hook-ups.

Lyman Run Trail is a relatively easy, 2-mile hike that provides opportunities for viewing wildlife. The trail begins near the spillway below the dam and follows the southern shore of the lake. During the spring and fall migration, waterfowl congregate on the lake and in the marshes at its western end. Eagles and osprey are common visitors to the lake as well, frequently perching at the top of the tall spruce trees along the shoreline. Woodland songbirds, white-tailed deer, and even black bears may be seen along the trail as well. The park has four or five resident bears that are routinely seen during the daytime and in the campground looking for an easy meal. The trail continues into the Susquehannock State Forest, passing a beaver pond before it meets up with the Susquehannock Trail System (*see* page 99).

A much more difficult trail is the Beehive Trail, which begins at the Daggett Run Campground and climbs a steep hill as it passes out of the park and into state forest land. The trail, which extends 3 miles to Rock Run Road, passes through a mixed hardwood forest that is home to turkey, white-tailed deer, and woodland songbirds. The steep and difficult Losey Trail and moderately challenging Spur Line Trail pass through similar habitats. A map showing the location of all trails and trailheads is available from the park office.

The Susquehannock State Forest contains a 43-mile long network of snowmobile and ATV trails, and Lyman Run State Park is a popular point of departure. A large parking area and restrooms are located near a snowmobile/ATV trailhead within the park, just off of Lyman Run Road north of the spillway below the dam.

Sportsmen will find many opportunities in the park and adjacent state forest lands. The lake is stocked with rainbow trout. Anglers can fish from shore or from electric motor boats (i.e. those without internal combustion engines). Additionally, a 3-mile section of Lyman Run, upstream from the lake on state forest land, has been designated a selective harvest program area. This pristine stream contains native brown trout and brook trout and is well known among trout fishermen. Hunters have more than 500 acres of the park open to them as well as all of the extensive Susquehannock State Forest. The most common game species in the park are turkey, white-tailed deer, and bear.

Directions: From Galeton follow Lyman Run Road north for about 6 miles into the park.

Activities: Hiking, fishing, hunting, swimming, boating, picnicking, camping, snowmobiling, ice skating.

Facilities: Trails, campground, picnic areas and a pavilion that can be reserved, boat launch, guarded beach.

Dates: Open year-round.

Fees: There is a charge for camping, for boats not registered in Pennsylvania, and for reserving the picnic pavilion.

Closest town: Galeton, 6 miles.

For more information: Lyman Run State Park, 454 Lyman Run Road, Galeton, PA 16922. Phone (814) 435-5010.

🏞 KETTLE CREEK STATE PARK

[Fig. 3(5)] During the 1930s the Civilian Conservation Corps built a dam across Kettle Creek just south of Summerson Run to produce Kettle Creek Lake. They then built camping facilities along the shoreline and Kettle Creek State Park was born. In 1962 the U.S. Army Corps of Engineers constructed the Alvin R. Bush Dam across Kettle Creek about 2 miles north of the original dam built by the CCC. This was one of four dams built as part of the flood control project for the West Branch of the Susquehanna River. The resulting Kettle Creek Reservoir encompasses 160 acres and has about 4.5 miles of shoreline. Surrounding it are 1,783 acres of woodland that make up the bulk of today's Kettle Creek State Park.

Kettle Creek State Park is located in Kettle Creek Valley in western Clinton County. The original parkland surrounding Kettle Creek Lake encompasses only about 10 acres and serves primarily as a campground. Nonmotorized boats are permitted on the lake, but there is no developed boat launch facility. While there aren't any trails within this small section of the park, there is a trailhead for the Donut Hole Trail (*see* page 109) across the road from the campground.

Most of the park lies within the northern parcel, which surrounds Kettle Creek Reservoir and a 4-mile stretch of Kettle Creek. PA Route 4001 passes through the entire length of the park, and there is a scenic vista along the road near the dam that offers a nice view of the reservoir. The park welcomes 40,000 to 50,000 visitors each year and is busiest during the beginning of trout season in the spring, during the peak of fall foliage in October, and during the summer holidays.

Kettle Creek Reservoir is a popular fishing spot and is well known for its bass and trout. Anglers fish from both the shore and from nonmotorized (i.e. those without internal combustion engines) or electric boats. Additionally, all of the reservoir's tributaries contain native trout.

The fish attract more than fishermen. Bald eagles and osprey, both of which feed almost exclusively on fish, are common here during the summer. While these two large birds-of-prey have similar diets, they have distinctly different ways of catching their dinner. The eagle soars above the reservoir waiting for a fish to swim close to the surface. Once he sees one, he swoops down over the water and catches the unsuspecting fish in his talons. The osprey, on the other hand, takes a more direct approach. He hovers, searching for a fish, and then dives headlong into the water, completely submerging himself. He then uses his 6-foot wing span to take off from the reservoir, while at the same time shaking off the water like a dog that just escaped from the bathtub.

Located along the western shore of the reservoir is a small camping area (71 sites) that can accommodate trailers or tents. At the lower campground near Kettle Creek Lake, there are 44 sites. There are no water or sewer hook-ups available, but there are electricity hook-ups. Adjacent to the campground is a playground. Along the upper campground (27 sites) is the nature trail, an easy 30-minute hike that loops through a mixed hardwood forest and across Butler Hollow and Sugar Camp Run. The trail is a good place to see spring wildflowers and can be used to reach Butler Trail, which continues on into the Sproul State Forest (*see* page 103). Somewhat more difficult is the Bearfield Run Trail. This old logging road, which is also used by bikers, snowmobiles, horseback riders, and cross-country skiers, climbs a forested hillside and also continues into the Sproul State Forest. This trail is especially good for birding. A map showing the location of all the trails and trailheads is available at the park office.

While there's no guarantee, park visitors may be lucky enough to see the area's newest wildlife attraction. Kettle Creek State Park is only a few miles from the area where elk were released within the Sproul State Forest. The elk, which were released in 1998, have been seen several times at Kettle Creek State Park, most often on the softball field.

Directions: From Westport follow PA Route 4001 north for about 7 miles into the park.

Activities: Hiking, camping, swimming, hunting, fishing, ice skating, cross-country skiing, snowmobiling, boating, biking, picnicking, softball.

Facilities: Trails, campground, playgrounds, guarded beach, boat mooring, picnic areas, softball field.

Dates: Open year-round.

Fees: There is a charge for camping and group picnic area.

Closest town: Westport, 7 miles.

For more information: Kettle Creek State Park, HCR 62, Box 96, Renovo, PA 17764. Phone (717) 923-6004.

NORTHERN CARDINAL
(Cardinalis cardinalis)
A favorite among birdwatchers because of the male's bright coloring, the cardinal is a southern bird whose habitat has spread northward in the past century.

🦅 BALD EAGLE STATE PARK

[Fig. 3(7)] Up until the early 1700s central Pennsylvania was home to the Leni-Lenape Indian Nation. In 1720, however, the Leni-Lenape were conquered by, and absorbed into, the Iroquois Nation. Their last chief was named *Wapelanewack*, which in English means "bald eagle." It is after him that this state park, the valley in which it lies, and the stream that flows through it are named.

Bald Eagle State Park encompasses 5,900 acres within Centre County and has as its focal point Foster Joseph Sayers Lake. The lake is named after a World War II hero

TIGER SWALLOWTAIL
(*Papilio glaucus*)
This butterfly takes its name from its yellow wings with black tigerlike stripes. The female's wings are brownish-black in its dark phase.

that won two Congressional Medals of Honor and lived in the town of Howard, which lies along the park's southeastern border. The lake that bears his name was constructed in 1969 for flood control by building a dam across Bald Eagle Creek. As part of the flood control process, it is drawn down in November to ensure that there's enough volume to contain spring precipitation and snowmelt. During drawdown the lake level falls 20 feet, exposing the original Bald Eagle Creek stream channel and fossils that can't be seen at any other time of the year. The water level rises enough by mid-May to permit all of the lake's water-related recreational activities. When full, the lake is 8 miles long, encompasses 1,730 acres, and has 23 miles of shoreline.

Located on the north side of the lake, not far from the dam, is the main recreation area. The 1,200-foot-long guarded beach that is open from Memorial Day to Labor Day is one of the most popular attractions in the park. Visitors will also find shower and changing facilities, a concession stand, and the wooded Schenck's Grove Picnic Area here. Just north of the beach is the Skyline Picnic Area, another shaded grove with playgrounds, volleyball courts, and horseshoe pits.

The lake supports a warm-water fishery that includes panfish, bass, yellow perch, walleye, and muskie. Powerboats are permitted on the lake, and there are six boat launches and a marina with 368 mooring slips available to rent on a seasonal basis. Three of the boat launches, Bald Eagle, Lower Greens Run, and Hunter Run West, are open 24 hours a day to provide access to night fishermen.

Located near the marina is a boat rental concession. Unlike many of the concessions found in Pennsylvania state parks, which are limited to nonmotorized boats, this one rents nearly every type of watercraft. Rowboats, canoes, small motorboats, pontoon boats, and even personal watercraft are available. Additionally, boaters can buy fuel, parts, fishing and boating supplies, and even have their boats serviced here.

The main campground in the park is the Russell P. Letterman Campground, which is within walking distance of the beach and marina and contains 101 campsites. Of these four can accommodate visitors with disabilities. Since the park and campground are popular, reservations are recommended.

Bald Eagle State Park is a year-round recreational facility and has much to offer the winter visitor. Near the summer/winter boat launch, 3.5 acres of the lake's surface are set aside for ice skating. A much larger area, 630 acres, is open to ice fishing and ice boating. For those who prefer to stay on shore, cross-country skiing and sledding are popular. Located a short distance north of Schenck's Grove Picnic Area, along Skyline Drive, about 5 acres of hillside have been set aside for sledding and tobogganing. Nearly 12 miles of the park's hiking trails, both within the main recreational area and north of PA Route 150, are used for cross-country skiing. Skiers can contact the park office for trail conditions and a map.

While mixed hardwoods cover some parts of the park, most of the park's acreage is dominated by old farms that have reverted to grasslands. Because most of Pennsylvania's native grasslands and fields have been lost to development, the Bureau of State Parks intends to maintain these old farmlands as grasslands and prevent them from evolving back into forests.

To educate visitors about the value of grasslands and other aspects of the park, there is an environmental education specialist who conducts programs year-round, including nature hikes, lectures, and the Youth Environmental Learning Series. Park visitors can participate in scheduled programs, while organizations and schools can contact the park office to schedule special activities for their group.

The best way to see the park's grasslands and forests is to hike the trails. For those who want an easy, sunny hike, the Butterfly Trail is a good choice. This 1.25-mile trail, which originally was a fitness trail, winds through a series of 14 gardens that have been planted specifically for butterflies. There are nectar-rich flowers that provide food for the adults, whose tubelike mouthparts are designed specifically to suck this sugar-rich liquid. Also growing here are host plants, whose leaves are eaten by the butterfly's immature life stage, the

BUTTERFLY WEED
(Asclepias tuberosa)
This plant is often found in home gardens because its bright orange, star-shaped flowers attract butterflies. The plant's roots have been used in India as a cure for pleurisy and for other pulmonary ailments.

caterpillar. For a shadier hike, try the Lakeside Trail, which runs through a hardwood forest along the southern shore of the lake. This 2-mile-long trail is relatively level but very rocky, so be sure to wear a good pair of hiking shoes. Another popular hiking area lies across PA Route 150. The Hunter Run Trail is composed of two loops that total 4 miles in length, and it is so named because the eastern loop crosses Hunter Run. Each loop passes through both forested areas and fields.

The longest hike in the park incorporates the Butterfly Trail and many of the short, unnamed trails within the main recreation area. This 7.5-mile walk connects the beach, Russell P. Letterman Campground, Hunter Run West boat launch, and the marina, and it passes through all of the park habitats. Along the route hikers will see open grasslands, fields dotted with Virginia pine (the first trees to invade the grassland), young forests dominated by aspen, and the final stage of succession, a hardwood forest. A map showing the location of all the trails and trailheads is available at the park office.

Directions: From Interstate 80 Exit 23 follow PA Route 50 north for 10 miles to the park.

Activities: Hiking, fishing, hunting, swimming, boating, camping, ice skating, cross-country skiing, sledding, ice boating, ice fishing.

Facilities: Multi-purpose trails, picnic areas, campgrounds, marina, boat launches, playgrounds, boat rental, beach, sledding area, ice skating area.

Dates: Open year-round.

Fees: There is a charge for camping.

Closest town: Howard.

For more information: Bald Eagle State Park, 149 Main Park Road, Howard, PA 16841. Phone (814) 625-2775.

PARKER DAM STATE PARK

[Fig. 3(6)] Parker Dam is a 968-acre state park nestled on the Allegheny Plateau within the Moshannon State Forest. William Parker, the park's namesake, was a logger who worked in this area during the 1870s, and as was the practice at the time, he built a log slide to transport the trees down the hillside. Once he had the logs along the banks of Laurel Run, which runs through the center of the park, he then had to move them downstream. To accomplish this he built a dam across the creek and floated the logs in the water that built up behind it. By opening the dam, he sent the water, and all of the logs, downstream. Five of these splash dams were built along the creek, each operated by a different logger. While the original splash dam is gone, a dam built by the Civilian Conservation Corps in the 1930s now stands in its place. Also found in the park is an authentic re-creation of the logslide, the only one of its kind in the eastern United States.

Parker Dam State Park, like nearly all of Pennsylvania's forestland, was clear-cut during the 1800s. Since that time the forest has regrown and the park is almost completely forested by mixed hardwoods and oak. Until recently, a small area of virgin, old-growth hardwoods stood on the hillside just northeast of the lake. Foresters believe the trees survived the logger's axe because the sugar maple and ash trees that grew here were, at that time, considered undesirable species. Unfortunately, these ancient giants met their match in May of 1985. A massive tornado cut a swath through Moshannon State Forest and directly through the center of Parker Dam State Park. Campers within the park never saw the funnel cloud, just a massive black cloud that seemed to skirt along the hillside. At the north end of the park, five campers were inside one of the cabins built by the CCC 50 years before. As they huddled inside the doorway, hanging on to one another, the tornado tore the roof from the cabin, but the campers, and the cabin, survived.

AMERICAN MOUNTAIN-ASH
(Sorbus americana)
Found along swamp borders as well as on mountainsides, the mountain-ash produces clusters of orange-red fruit for birds and rodents.

What didn't survive, however, was the stand of old-growth trees. A hiking trail, the Trail of Giants, which passed through the old growth, was littered with the remains of the trees. Today the trail has been renamed the Trail of New Giants. Hikers will find a couple of old-growth trees along the trail, but the effects of the tornado are still evident. While the second-growth trees on the east side of Mud Run Road were salvaged for their timber value, the trees on the west side of the road, where the trail is located, were not. While the trail is level, hikers still must climb over downed trees, making the 1-mile hike a difficult one.

There are many recreational facilities within the park, most of them centered around the lake. On the west side of the lake, near the bridge that carries Mud Run Road, is a small guarded beach. Swimmers will also find a concession stand, picnic pavilions, and a boat launch nearby. Only nonmotorized boats (i.e. those without internal combustion engines) are permitted on the lake. On the opposite side of the lake is a campground complete with a shower house, playground, and the log slide display.

The lake is also a popular fishing spot. Brook trout are stocked here, and fishermen will find bass, panfish, and catfish as well. Trout are also stocked for the winter ice fishing season. Anglers share the lake with ice skaters, who have a designated area near the swimming beach that is plowed and groomed.

In addition to recreational opportunities, the park has educational opportunities as well. Located near the dam is a log cabin that houses a Civilian Conservation Corps visitor center. Inside the cabin, visitors will find displays that highlight the CCC's accomplishments and show what it was like to work and live as a Corps member during the Depression. Located near the beach is a nature center. This small visitor center contains displays that highlight the wildlife and ecosystems of the park as well as the park's logging history.

Because of its location, Parker Dam State Park is a popular point of departure for hikers, skiers, and snowmobilers heading into the Moshannon State Forest. Many of the park's trails begin at the recreation areas near the lake and radiate out into the state forest like the spokes of a wheel. One of these is the Beaver Trail, a relatively easy, 2.3-mile loop. The trail follows an old logging tram road and passes by several beaver dams on Mud Run. The Souders Trail is a self-guiding nature trail that takes about one hour to hike. A brochure is available for this moderately challenging, 0.75-mile trail. The Logslide Trail passes the log slide, which sits in the same spot that William Parker's did 120 years ago. At the trailhead, hikers can see logging tools and learn more about the logging industry of the last century. The 0.5-mile-long trail, which extends into the state forest, takes about 30 minutes to hike and is moderately challenging. Another short trail, the Stumpfield Trail, is worth a hike. This 0.5-mile trail passes through an area that experienced severe fires after it was logged. The fires consumed the organic material in the soil, and the area is just now beginning to mature into forest again. The trail is relatively easy and takes about 30 minutes to hike.

The 74-mile-long Quehanna Trail (*see* page 112) passes through the park. Parker Dam has the distinction of having the westernmost trailhead on this lengthy trail. Hikers heading south can get on the trail at the Log Slide Trail trailhead, while those heading north follow Fairview Road, which is a hiking and snowmobiling trail, into the state forest. A map showing the locations of the trails and trailheads is available at the park office.

Directions: From Penfield follow PA Route 153 south for 2.3 miles. Turn left onto Mud Run Road and follow it for about 2 miles into the park.

Activities: Hiking, fishing, hunting, camping, boating, swimming, snowmobiling, ice skating, sledding, cross-country skiing, picnicking.

Facilities: Campground, boat launch, guarded beach, picnic area, amphitheater, cabins, concession stand, CCC interpretive center, visitor center, trails, ball field, logslide display.

Dates: Open year-round.

Fees: There is a charge for camping.

Closest town: Penfield, 5 miles.

For more information: Parker Dam State Park, RD 1, Box 165, Penfield, PA 15849. Phone (814) 765-0630.

LITTLE PINE STATE PARK

[Fig. 23, Fig. 3(17)] Little Pine State Park encompasses a 2,158-acre mountain valley within the Tiadaghton State Forest in Lycoming County. Running through the center of the park is Little Pine Creek, a tributary of Big Pine Creek, which flows into the Susquehanna River. Little Pine Creek was a major transportation route for logs during the lumbering era of the last century, and the park, like the state forest, was completely cut at that time. Today the park is almost entirely wooded with oaks dominating the mixed hardwood forest.

The park began as a picnic area built by the Civilian Conservation Corps during the 1930s. In 1950 a dam was built across the stream to form the 94-acre Little Pine Lake, which serves as both a recreational facility and a flood control device. In 1972, the dam was put to the test when the worst rainstorm ever recorded in central Pennsylvania came in the form of Hurricane Agnes. The water rose and began to flow over the spillway. The lake grew from 94 to 634 acres and a wall of water 4.5 feet high flowed over the spillway for 6 hours. The dam held, but many of the park's recreational facilities were destroyed and had to be rebuilt. Hurricane Agnes was the only time water has ever flowed over the spillway.

Today the park is a popular recreational facility with the lake as the focus. Swimmers will find a small guarded beach located on the western shore of the lake. Located near the beach, which is open from Memorial Day to Labor Day, is a picnic area, playgrounds, and a volleyball court. Also located on this section of the lake is a boat rental and mooring area where park visitors can rent canoes and paddleboats. Only electric motorized boats are permitted on Little Pine Lake.

Anglers will find plenty of good fishing spots on the lake. For those who don't have a boat, there are 3.3 miles of shoreline, as well as more than 4 miles of Little Pine Creek upstream from the lake. Four species of trout—brook, rainbow, palomino, and brown—are stocked each year. Both the lake and creek also contain warmwater species such as bass, pike, panfish, and catfish. A portion of the stream near the northern end of the park has been designated an artificial lure only area.

This is also a popular recreation area during the winter. A portion of the lake near the beach is plowed and groomed for ice skaters and there are even goals provided for hockey players. Additionally, there are 2 acres of slopes that are used for sledding and tobogganing near the bathhouse.

Another recreational area is located near the southern end of the park below the dam. A campground that can accommodate 104 tents or trailers (33 sites with electrical hook-ups) is found here and is open from April 1 to the end of antlerless deer season in November. Playgrounds, the park office, and an amphitheater used for environmental education programs, are also found in this area. Snowmobilers venturing into the Tiadaghton State Forest will find a parking area down the road from the campground along English Run Road, which is a snowmobile trail that leads into the forest.

Another area worth mentioning is the lower picnic area, which is located about 1.5 miles south of the park along SR 4001. This 5-acre site sits along Little Pine Creek among white pine, maple, and river birch, and has picnic tables, grills, restrooms, potable water, and a small footbridge.

Within the park there are several nice hiking trails providing a variety of lengths and difficulties. The shortest and easiest trail is the Carsontown Trail, which is a loop 0.88 mile long. The trail is level and well suited for families, who will see many woodland wildflowers including columbine (*Aquilegia canadensis*), blue-eyed grass (*Sisyrinchium angustifolium*), wood anemone (*Anemone quinquefolia*), and jack-in-the-pulpit (*Arisaema triphyllum*). The Carsontown Trail is located in the northern end of the park along Little Pine Creek.

Another relatively easy trail runs along the eastern shore of the lake and up along Little Pine Creek. The Lakeshore Trail is a 5-mile-long loop that provides the hiker with a variety of habitats and wildlife. The trail begins in an area that was once farmland but is now fields and meadows. Deer and groundhogs are frequently seen along this section of the trail, and occasionally osprey and bald eagles are seen along the lakeshore. Once the trail crosses Naval Run it enters a mixed hardwood forest. Attentive hikers may see wood ducks (*Aix sponsa*), deer, wild turkey, and maybe even a bear.

Three of the parks more challenging trails are the Spike Buck Trail, Love Run Trail, and Panther Run Trail. The Spike Buck Trail is the second steepest in the park. It is 2.7 miles long and offers outcroppings of rock and flagstone and beautiful vistas. The Love Run Trail is a 3.1-mile-long wooded hike that passes through an area with large hemlocks and mountain springs. The trail begins on Love Run Road, not far from the swimming beach, and ends at the Panther Run Trail. At the intersection of the two trails, hikers will come across an old flagstone quarry that was in operation until the 1930s. The stone quarried here was used to build fireplace hearths and interior floors. The Panther Run Trail, which runs for 2.7 miles to SR 4001, is considered by many to be the most scenic trail in the park, offering vistas of the park and creek below and passing rock outcrops. Hikers should be aware, however, that some sections are very steep. The 189-mile-long Mid State Trail (*see* page 275) passes through the southern end of the park. Along the way it shares its path with some of

JACK-IN-THE-PULPIT
(*Arisaema triphyllum*)
This common biennial grows to 3 feet tall and produces bright red clusters of berries.

Hurricane Agnes

On June 19, 1972 an early season hurricane came ashore in Florida and then proceeded northward through Georgia, the Carolinas, Virginia, Maryland, and into Pennsylvania and New York. Shortly after moving over land, the hurricane was downgraded to a tropical storm, but the greatest damage was yet to be done. By the time it reached Pennsylvania on June 23, the storm was sucking water out of the Atlantic Ocean and dumping it across central and eastern Pennsylvania.

The storm dropped 18 inches of rain, sending almost every stream and river in the state out of its banks. Fifty Pennsylvanians lost their lives and damages totaled $2.3 billion. Hardest hit was the Susquehanna watershed. In Harrisburg the river climbed out of its banks and flooded the first floor of the governor's mansion. Even worse hit were the towns of Scranton and Wilkes-Barre, both of which were protected by levees. More than 100,000 people were evacuated before the levees were breached. The water level in downtown Wilkes-Barre reached 9 feet in spots.

By the time the storm passed out into the northern Atlantic, more than 210,000 people had been forced from their homes nationwide and 122 had lost their lives. The flood records set by Tropical Storm Agnes in Pennsylvania have not been broken.

the park's trails, including the Love Run Trail. It is the only trail in the park where overnight camping is permitted. A map showing the locations of trails and trailheads is available from the park office.

Bear, white-tailed deer, turkey, and grouse are among the game species common in the park and adjacent state forest. Hunting is permitted within 1,700 acres of the park and all of the state forest. Hunters needing to hone their marksmanship skills or sight in their rifle will find separate archery and shooting ranges at the northern end of the park off of SR 4001.

Directions: From PA Route 44 in Waterville follow SR 4001 north for 4 miles into the park.

Activities: Hiking, fishing, hunting, camping, swimming, boating, picnicking, cross-country skiing, tobogganing, ice skating, snowmobiling.

Facilities: Trails, campground, amphitheater, picnic areas, playgrounds, boat launch, guarded beach.

Dates: Park is open year-round. Beach is open Memorial Day–Labor Day. Camping is open Apr. 1–early Dec.

Fees: There is a charge for camping.

Closest town: Waterville, 4 miles.

For more information: Little Pine State Park, HC 63, Box 100, Waterville, PA 17776. Phone (717) 753-6000.

WORLDS END STATE PARK

[Fig. 3(18)] Worlds End State Park lies within the deep gorge of Loyalsock Creek as it meanders in an S shape through the Wyoming State Forest (*see* page 133). Steep forested hillsides rise from the creek, offering challenging trails and scenic overlooks. As the creek rushes through the park it tumbles over sandstone boulders, rocks, and small waterfalls, creating whitewater that beckons kayakers during early spring and late fall.

Early visitors to the area named the park. The only route through the valley was a road high on the steep mountainside, giving them the feeling that they were at the end of the world. The 780-acre park was purchased by the state in the 1930s after it, like the state forest around it, had been clear-cut. Today the park is dominated by mixed hardwoods, with hemlocks common along the stream. The Civilian Conservation Corps built most of the park's recreational facilities and infrastructure during the 1930s.

Many of the park's trails radiate into the Wyoming State Forest, making this a popular starting point for hikers, cross-country skiers, and snowmobilers. For those who wish to stay in the park, there are several camping options. For organized groups there is a tent camping area that can accommodate up to 100 people. There is also a campground along PA Route 154 that can accommodate tents and trailers. The most luxurious of all the accommodations are the 19 cabins, which are furnished and have appliances and a fireplace. Advanced reservations are required for all of these camping facilities.

Loyalsock Creek is the focal point of recreation in the park. Kayakers can take advantage of any part of the creek within the park except the area near the dam. Since the water level is only high enough for safe whitewater boating as few as six days a year, whitewater enthusiasts should check with the park office before setting out. Fishermen use the river too, which is stocked with trout each year by the Pennsylvania Fish and Boat Commission. Swimmers looking for a place to immerse in the cold mountain water will find a small guarded beach located near the dam.

Small portions along the periphery of the park are open to hunting. When combined with the vast acreage of the surrounding Wyoming State Forest, hunters will find many opportunities to pursue white-tailed deer, turkey, ruffed grouse, and black bear.

There are a number of good hiking trails within the park. One of these is the Canyon Vista Trail, a moderately challenging trail that takes about three hours to hike. This 3.5-mile, blue-blazed loop takes the hiker from Loyalsock Creek up the mountainside, past a talus slope, and to Canyon Rock Vista, which provides a view of the park and valley below. Another trail that offers a good view of the valley is the High Rock Trail. This 1-mile-long trail takes about one hour to hike because it is quite steep and rocky. The trail, which is marked with yellow blazes, rises from the park office to High Rock Vista and High Rock Falls and then descends to PA Route 154. Many of the trails are suitable for cross-country skiing and some of the roads are also open to snowmobiles.

The 59-mile-long Loyalsock Trail (*see* page 136) passes through the western end of the park. Along its route here it passes several waterfalls and scenic vistas.

Several of the park's trails continue into the Wyoming State Forest. One of these is the Worlds End Trail, which extends 3.25 miles from the park office to the Loyalsock Trail in the state forest. This rugged, red-blazed trail, which passes an old coal mine, takes about five hours to hike out and back. A longer option, however, is to return to the park via the Loyalsock Trail, making a 10.5-mile round-trip hike. Another park trail that hooks up with the Loyalsock Trail within the state forest is the rugged Link Trail. This trail, which is marked with yellow circles containing a red X, is 8.5 miles long and passes Canyon Vista and Double Run along its route. The shortest and easiest trail within the park is the Double Run Nature Trail. This 1.2-mile loop extends into the state forest, passing

POISON SUMAC
(*Toxicodendron vernix*)
Poison sumac is a shrub or a tree with 7–13 oval leaves on red stalks.

Cottonwood Falls and crossing Double Run. The trail is marked with white rectangles with green stripes and only takes about one hour to hike.

A map showing the locations of the park's trails and trailheads is available at the park office.

Directions: From Forksville follow PA Route 154 south for about 1.5 miles into the park

Activities: Hiking, camping, fishing, swimming, whitewater boating, fishing, hunting, picnicking, snowmobiling, cross-country skiing, horseback riding.

Facilities: Trails, guarded beach, picnic areas, campground, cabins, scenic vistas, outdoor chapel.

Dates: Open year-round. Beach open Memorial Day–Labor Day. Campground open early spring through mid-Dec. Cabins open year-round.

Fees: There is a charge for camping.

Closest town: Forksville, 2 miles.

For more information: Worlds End State Park, PO Box 62, Forksville, PA 18616. Phone (717) 924-3287.

CHAPMAN STATE PARK

[Fig. 3(2)] Chapman State Park has many of the same natural features and recreational facilities found in many of Pennsylvania's state parks. What sets it apart from the rest is that many of the facilities have been designed to accommodate the disabled. So extensive are these facilities that people come from all over Pennsylvania and beyond to enjoy the park, resulting in more than a quarter of a million visitors annually.

The park encompasses 805 acres, including a 68-acre lake on the West Branch of Tionesta Creek. Chapman State Park is predominantly forested, dominated by mixed hardwoods, and is part of a much larger public land complex that includes the Allegheny National Forest (*see* page 29) and state game lands, both of which are adjacent. Because of its proximity to these other public lands and a trail system that radiates out from the park, Chapman serves as a good starting point for backpacking, skiing, and snowmobiling trips.

The lake is a popular recreation spot year-round. Fishermen can pursue both cold-water species, such as trout, and warm-water species, such as bass, from nonmotorized boats, from shore, or from the two handicapped-accessible fishing piers. There is also good trout fishing in the creek, both within the park and in the adjacent Allegheny National Forest. Swimmers will find a large, guarded, sandy beach on the lake's eastern shore. Located here is a specially designed ramp that allows handicapped visitors to enter the water, either with or without a wheelchair.

Many of the park's other recreational facilities are accessible to the handicapped as well. Picnic tables are designed to accommodate wheelchairs and sit on paved surfaces with paved walks leading up to them. Restrooms, an amphitheater (used for nondenominational religious services), and even some of the campsites, in which the fire ring, picnic table, and camping pad can be reached by wheelchairs, are all designed for the disabled. To further increase access, park maintenance and access roads that are closed to the public can be used by handicapped visitors to reach some of the park's recreational facilities.

Chapman State Park is popular during the winter as well. During the first weekend in February, the park holds a winter carnival that includes one of the largest sled dog races in Pennsylvania. As long as temperatures are cold enough, 3 acres of ice on the lake are plowed for ice skating, and the remainder of the lake is open for ice fishing and ice boating. For those who prefer to stay on solid ground, there is a lighted

BLUETS
(Houstonia lanceolata)
White to purple flowers.

tobogganing hill just down the road from the park office.

There are 12 miles of hiking trails within the park. The newest trail in the park is 0.5 mile long and is wheelchair accessible. Constructed in 1998, the trail is covered with crushed limestone and will eventually become an interpretive trail. Adjacent to the trailhead is a handicapped-accessible picnic area. Adams Run Trail is a 2.9-mile-long trail that meanders through the park's southwestern corner and along Adams Run. There are two scenic overlooks along this trail, which is moderately challenging. The shortest trail in the park is the Lowlands Trail. This 0.2-mile pathway crosses the West Branch of Tionesta Creek near the southern end of the lake and is the easiest way to get around the lake.

Visitors interested in an educational hike will want to try out the Nature Trail. This self-guided trail has two loops, an easy one that is 0.7 mile long and a slightly more difficult 1-mile loop. A brochure is available at the park office. Another easy, but significantly longer hike can be made along the Game Lands Trail. The trail begins near the boat mooring area and follows the access road into the game lands. It then returns to park along an old railroad grade, ending at the camping area. The trail can be made into a loop by using the Lowlands Trail for a 2.3-mile round trip, or by using park roads around the lake for a 4-mile loop.

More difficult is the Penny Run Trail. This 1.4-mile trail climbs uphill into the Allegheny National Forest before returning to the park. A small portion of the Lumber Trail, which runs from the town of Marienville to Kinzua Dam on the Allegheny Reservoir, lies within the park as well. This snowmobile trail is suitable for hiking as well.

Several of the park's trails are suitable for cross-country skiing, including the Adams Run Trail and Penny Run Trail. The only trail in the park open to bikes is the Lowlands Trail. Using this trail and park roads, bikers can make a complete loop around the lake, a ride which takes them through most of the park's recreational areas. A map showing the locations of all trails and trailheads is available at the park office.

Directions: From PA Route 6 in Clarendon turn south onto Railroad Street at the light. Follow Railroad Street for 5 miles into the park.

Activities: Hiking, swimming, hunting, fishing, sledding, ice skating, ice boating, ice fishing, cross-country skiing, biking, camping, picnicking.

Facilities: Campground (with electrical facilities), guarded beach, trails, amphitheater, fishing pier, playground, picnic area, boat rental, food concession. Many facilities are accessible to the handicapped.

Dates: Open year-round.

Fees: There is a charge for camping.

Closest town: Clarendon, 5 miles.

For more information: Chapman State Park, RR2, Box 1610, Clarendon, PA 16313. Phone (814) 723-0250.

⬚ KINZUA BRIDGE STATE PARK

[Fig. 3(3)] Kinzua Bridge State Park is a small park with a very big attraction. The focal point of this 316-acre park is the 2,053-foot-long Kinzua Viaduct, a railroad bridge that was built to transport oil, timber, and coal, out of McKean County. The bridge was built in 1882 and then completely rebuilt in 1900 to accommodate heavier trains. Towering 301 feet above the Kinzua Creek Valley, the steel bridge weighs nearly 7 million pounds. As impressive as the bridge is to look at, perhaps the most impressive thing about it is the length of time it took to build it. At the turn of the century, long before modern construction technology and heavy-lifting helicopters, 150 men built the bridge in a little over three months.

The 2,053-foot-long Kinzua Viaduct is a railroad bridge that towers 301 feet above the Kinzua Creek Valley. The steel bridge weighs nearly 7 million pounds and was built in a little over three months by 150 men.

As the great era of railroads began to decline, so did the number of trains that crossed Kinzua Viaduct. The last freight train passed over the bridge in 1959. In 1986, however, the Knox, Kane, Kinzua Railroad was formed and now runs an excursion train from Marienville to the Kinzua Bridge State Park. The round-trip excursion is 97 miles, but there is no boarding in the park. The nearest boarding point is in Kane, about 16 miles away. To learn more about this steam train, which winds its way through the Allegheny National Forest from June until October, call the Knox, Kinzua, Kane Railroad at (814) 927-6621. While park visitors are allowed to walk across the bridge, they should listen for the approaching train and stay off of the bridge as it crosses.

Kinzua State Park opened in 1970, and the viaduct was added to the National Register of Historic Civil Engineering Landmarks in 1977. Two things draw people to the park: one is the bridge and the other is spectacular fall foliage, which peaks during the first two weeks of October. Both can be appreciated from the southern end of the bridge where the park's recreational facilities are located. There is a scenic lookout, a picnic pavilion, an interpretive kiosk, and a group tent camping area that can be reserved by organized groups. The bridge, overlook, restrooms, and some of the picnic tables, are accessible to the handicapped.

There is only one trail within the park. The Aspen Trail runs from the overlook at the southern end of the bridge, 300 feet down into the Kinzua Creek Gorge, and up the other side to the northern end of the bridge. The trail provides many good views of the bridge and passes old oil field equipment, another vestige of a past era. As the trail passes through the northern hardwood forest, hikers have a good chance of seeing deer, turkey, and, if they're lucky,

SUGAR MAPLE
(Acer saccharum)
Sugar maple's sap is the source of maple syrup and sugar.

a black bear. At the bottom of the gorge, the trail crosses Kinzua Creek over a foot-bridge. Trout fishing is good in the stream, with stocked fish found west of the bridge and native trout found to the east in the creek and its tributaries. This 1.6-mile-long trail is relatively difficult. The southern end of the trail follows an old logging road and is somewhat steep, but the northern side is considerably steeper and quite rocky.

Directions: From PA Route 6 in Mount Jewett follow SR 3011 north for 4 miles to the park.

Activities: Hiking, picnicking.

Facilities: Picnic area, hiking trail, handicapped-accessible scenic overlook.

Dates: Open year-round.

Fees: None.

Closest town: Mount Jewett, 4 miles.

For more information: Kinzua Bridge State Park, c/o Bendigo State Park, Box A, Johnsonburg, PA 15845. Phone (814) 965-2646.

▨ LEONARD HARRISON AND COLTON POINT STATE PARKS

[Fig. 3(16), Fig. 3(15), Fig. 20(1), Fig. 20(2), Fig. 21(1), Fig. 21(2)] Located on opposite sides of the Pine Creek Gorge, these easily accessible state parks provide some of the best

The view of Pine Creek Gorge, Pennsylvania's Grand Canyon, from Leonard Harrison State Park

views of Pennsylvania's Grand Canyon. The parks are surrounded by the Pine Creek Gorge Natural Area but are a part of the Pennsylvania state park system and not the state forest. In their entirety, they are also designated as natural areas.

Leonard Harrison State Park, which is named after the businessman who donated the area to the state in 1922, is located on the east rim of the canyon. Picnic areas, campgrounds, restrooms, and a nature center are open from mid-April to mid-October.

Several trails are worth exploring in this 585-acre park. To appreciate the gorge from the bottom as well as the top, hike the 1-mile Turkey Path Trail which takes the hiker down to the creek, passing a waterfall on Little Four-Mile Run along the way. The trail has steps, hand rails, and observation decks for catching your breath and enjoying the view.

Situated on 368 acres on the opposite side of the creek, Colton Point State Park was named after a well-known lumberman. The park, which is a good access point for the West Rim Trail (*see* page 119), is registered as a National Historic Landmark Park in tribute to the Civilian Conservation Corps, which helped develop many of the facilities within Pennsylvania's public lands.

Directions: To get to Leonard Harrison State Park, take PA Route 660 west from Wellsboro to its terminus, a distance of about 10 miles. To get to Colton Point State Park, take Colton Road south from Ansonia for 5 miles.

Activities: Camping, hiking, fishing, hunting.

Facilities: Campgrounds, nature center (Leonard Harrison State Park only), trails, picnic areas, reservable pavillion, playground.

Dates: Visitor center and campgrounds open mid-April to mid-October. Trails open year-round (weather permitting).

Fees: None, except for overnight camping and reserving the pavillion.

Closest town: Ansonia, 10 miles from Leonard Harrison and 5 miles from Colton Point.

For more information: Leonard Harrison State Park, RR 6, PO Box 199, Wellsboro, PA 16901. Phone (717) 724-3061.

🏞 RICKETTS GLEN STATE PARK

[Fig. 3(19)] Ricketts Glen State Park encompasses 13,050 acres in Sullivan, Columbia, and Luzerne counties. The park is named after Colonel Robert Ricketts, a veteran of the Battle of Gettysburg and previous owner of the area. Ricketts' heirs had planned to sell the land to the federal government to be used as a national park, but World War II ended that plan and the Commonwealth of Pennsylvania purchased it in 1942.

The park is located along the edge of the Allegheny Front, a steep escarpment formed by a series of mountain ridges on the edge of the Appalachian Plateau. Ricketts Glen is located on two of these ridges, North Mountain and Red Rock Mountain. Streams that flow from the plateau, down the Allegheny Front, and into the Valley and Ridge Province below often do so in dramatic fashion, splashing over waterfalls in their descent. This is especially true of Kitchen Creek, which descends 1,000 feet in a little over 2 miles. The creek and its numerous waterfalls are the focal point of the Glens Natural Area (*see* page 83).

Logging became a major industry in the area when the railroad moved in, and from 1890–1913 much of the area was clear-cut. During that period the logging town of Ricketts sprung up and was home to more than 1,000 people and the largest sawmill in this part of the country. Nothing remains today of either the town or the mill.

Another legacy of that era are the two artificial lakes constructed within the park to facilitate the movement of logs. The larger of these is Lake Jean, which is located in the northwestern corner of the park. Today it's a recreational lake, but it once contained hundreds of thousands of board feet of hemlock and hardwood logs. This 245-acre lake is fed by Ganoga Lake, which is a spring-fed lake located just north of the park. Ganoga Lake has the distinction of being the highest natural lake east of the Rocky Mountains.

Toward the eastern end of the park lies the smaller Mountain Spring Lake, which was formed by building a dam across Bowman Creek. While the lake was built to serve the lumber industry, it spawned a second industry. The lake's high elevation along the edge of the Allegheny Front produces prolonged periods of subfreezing weather, and consequently ice.

Ice was a valuable commodity in the days before the modern electric refrigerator, so men that cut trees during the summer cut ice during the winter. After clearing the snow from the surface of the frozen lake, giant chunks of ice 55 feet wide and 80 feet long were hewn from the frozen surface. They were then floated to a sawmill, cut into smaller pieces, and stored in large wooden barns known as icehouses. As many as 150 men quarried ice from the lake during the winter. During the summer 20 men were employed full-time loading the ice into railroad cars bound for New York City and eastern Pennsylvania.

The ice industry came to an end when the railroad pulled out in 1948. Seven years later the town of Mountain Springs, which appeared with the ice industry, disappeared with the closing of its post office. Today the 40-acre Mountain Springs Lake

Numerous waterfalls are found on Kitchen Creek.

and the land to the east are owned and managed by the Pennsylvania Fish and Boat Commission. The only men found on the lake today are fishermen pursuing not ice but gamefish, panfish, and trout.

Ricketts Glen State Park contains 26 miles of hiking trails including the Grand View Trail. This 1.9-mile loop traverses three counties in the southwestern corner of the park. Along the trail lies a scenic overlook along the edge of the Allegheny Front. The overlook sits on the highest point on Red Rock Mountain, 2,449 feet above sea level, and from here you can see 11 counties in three states. Stretching to the west and east lies the Allegheny Front, to the north is the Appalachian Plateau, and to the south, 1,200 feet below, lies the Wyoming Valley. The trail, which is used by snowmobiles during the winter, provides a moderately difficult hike and is marked with blue blazes.

In addition to hiking, there are numerous other recreational opportunities in the park. At Lake Jean visitors can picnic, swim, fish for gamefish and panfish, or ply the waters in a non-motorized boat. Many of the park's trails and campgrounds are also found here. In addition to the hiking trails, many of which are also used by snowmobilers and cross-country skiers during the winter, there are also 9 miles of equestrian trails.

Hunting is another popular park activity. Nine thousand of the park's 13,050 acres are open to hunters. In combination with the 83,000 acres of adjacent state game lands, most of which was also purchased from the Ricketts family, hunters have access to 145 square miles of forestland. The most common quarry are white-tailed deer, black bear, turkey, and small game.

Directions: From the town of Red Rock follow PA Route 487 north for about 3.5 miles to Lake Jean. The road is quite steep, so visitors towing heavy trailers are advised to follow PA Route 487 south from the town of Dushore, a distance of about 19 miles.

Activities: Hiking, camping, fishing, hunting, horseback riding, snowmobiling, cross-country skiing, ice skating, swimming, boating.

Facilities: Trails, picnic area, guarded beach, boat rental.

Dates: Open year-round.

Fees: Fees charged for camping.

Closest town: Red Rock, 3.5 miles.

For more information: Ricketts Glen State Park, RR 2, PO Box 130, Benton, PA 17814. Phone (717) 477-5675.

GLENS NATURAL AREA

[Fig. 3(19)] The most outstanding natural feature of the Glens Natural Area are its waterfalls. Kitchen Creek and its tributaries flow from Lake Jean to points south, descending the Allegheny Front along the way. The stream passes over sandstone and shale that erode at different rates thereby producing the waterfalls. Many of the trees here are more than 500 years old and over 100 feet high. Ring counts on dead trees have even revealed trees as old as 900 years. The combination of old-growth trees and more than 22 waterfalls led to the area being designated a National Natural Landmark.

Kettle Creek begins as two separate branches, one draining Lake Jean and the other draining forested areas to the east. The Lake Jean branch passes through a deep ravine called Ganoga Glen, while the other branch passes through Glen Leigh. The two branches join at Waters Meet, and then flow through Ricketts Glen. Waterfalls are found in all three stream valleys. The largest is Ganoga Falls, a 94-foot-high waterfall in Ganoga Glen.

Black Bear

The black bear (*Ursus americanus*) is Pennsylvania's only bear and is the state's biggest carnivore. An adult male can tip the scales at 600 pounds. While the bear is relatively common in the northern, mountainous parts of the state, hikers are more likely to come across signs of the animals, such as droppings, their 9-inch long hindprints, or trees with claw marks, tooth marks, or fur from rubbing.

This large carnivore spends much of its time eating plant material. The pursuit of berries, fruits, nuts, roots, and seeds occupies a large part of its time. When it does eat meat, it's usually insects, fish, bird eggs, carrion, or small mammals, rather than larger prey. Bears are, of course, also quite fond of human food and are frequent visitors to garage dumps and campgrounds.

Contrary to popular belief bears do not hibernate, which is a state of greatly reduced respiration, heartbeat, and a near cessation of other metabolic processes. Instead they become dormant and go into a deep sleep. After engorging in the fall to develop a thick layer of fat, bears climb into their winter sleeping quarters, which are chambers beneath a tree, a rock, or within a log that a bear has lined with grass and moss. It is within this winter den, while the sow (a female bear) is asleep, that her cubs are born. The young bears will stay with her for the next year or so until they set up their own home territory.

All of the waterfalls are accessible by the Falls Trail, although the hike is a difficult one. Portions of this trail system are more than 100 years old, having been constructed when Colonel Ricketts owned the land. The trail is an unblazed trail system composed of four segments. The Ganoga Glen and Glen Leigh segments are both 1.4 miles long. The segment which runs through Ricketts Glen, from PA Route 118 to Waters Meet, is 1.8 miles long. The fourth part of the trail, runs 1.2 miles from Ganoga Glen to Glen Leigh.

Those who prefer a short, easy hike should consider the Evergreen Trail. The trail begins across PA Route 118 from the Falls Trail, about 1.75 miles west of Red Rock, and extends 1 mile through a hemlock and white pine forest. This unblazed trail passes 36-foot high Adams Falls.

This remote area is also unique for another reason. Man has influenced Pennsylvania's ecosystems in many ways, one of which has been the introduction of exotic species. It sometimes occurs intentionally, as it did with the dandelion which was imported from the far east as an ornamental flower, and sometimes it occurs accidentally, such as it did with the recently introduced zebra mussel. The glens in Ricketts Glen State Park are primarily free of introduced species and is believed to represent the forests that existed at the time Christopher Columbus discovered the New World. Also found along the cliffs and behind the waterfalls are a wide diversity of mosses, lichens, and liverworts.

Directions: From the Ricketts Glen State Park entrance road off of PA Route 487 take the 1st road to the right and follow it to the Falls Trail trailhead.

Activities: Hiking, fishing.

Facilities: Hiking trails.

Dates: Open year-round.

Fees: None.

Closest town: Red Rock, 3.5 miles.

For more information: Ricketts Glenn State Park, RR 2, PO Box 130, Benton, PA 17814. Phone (717) 477-5675.

BLACK MOSHANNON STATE PARK

[Fig. 19(1)] During the late 1800s, one of the primary methods of long distance travel in Pennsylvania was the stagecoach, which often traveled on toll roads called turnpikes. One of these was the Erie Turnpike, which connected Philadelphia with the Great Lakes' city of Erie in the northwestern corner of the state. At the halfway point, the stagecoaches had to climb a steep escarpment called the Allegheny Front. Located atop the front was the small town of Antes, a stagecoach stop. The area where the town once stood is today the 3,394-acre Black Moshannon State Park. The only thing that remains of Antes is a one-room schoolhouse.

At about the same time that stagecoaches were passing through the park, timber companies began clear-cutting the vast stands of white pine and hemlock that blanketed the area. To make the logs easier to handle and move, they built a splash dam near a series of beaver ponds to form a large mill pond. In the 1930s, long after the loggers had left, the Civilian Conservation Corps rebuilt the dam to form Black Moshannon Lake.

Today this 250-acre lake forms the recreational center of Black Moshannon State Park. The lake contains warm-water gamefish and panfish as well as native brook trout. Trout are also found in the streams that flow into the lake and Black Moshan-

RUFOUS-SIDED TOWHEE
(Pipilo erythrophthalmus)
A loud "drink-your-tea" song coming from underbrush or thicket identifies the towhee.

non Creek, which flows out of it. Only nonmotorized boats are permitted on the lake. During the winter the lake is used for ice skating, ice fishing, and ice boating.

In addition to the lake, wetlands are the most prominent natural feature of Black Moshannon State Park. Bogs, swamps, and marshes are common and cover a significant portion of the park. Because of its high altitude, species not ordinarily found this far south live here. Birds such as the Canada warbler (*Wilsonia canadensis*) and northern waterthrush (*Seiurus noveboracensis*) don't just pass through during migration, they nest here as well. Also found here are northern wetland plants such as Arctic cottongrass (*Eriophorum* sp.), mountain holly (*Ilex montana*), leatherleaf (*Chamaedaphne calyculata*), and snowberry (*Symphoricarpos albus*).

There are 16 miles of trails running through the park, several of which continue into the Moshannon State Forest. A good choice for a short hike is the Bog Trail. The trail is a 0.5-mile boardwalk that crosses a bog, allowing hikers to see wetland plants such as blueberries, lilies, and carnivorous sundews at close range. This trail can be reached from the boat launch #3 parking area along West Side Road. Follow PA Route 504 west from the visitor's center to West Side Road, a distance of a couple hundred feet.

The Hay Road Trail can also be reached from this parking area. This trail is so named because farmers once traveled this route to harvest marsh grasses, which they used as bedding material for their livestock. Today hikers follow this 1.1-mile grassy trail to experience a mixed-oak forest or to connect with several of the park's other trails.

In addition to hiking trails, there are 12 miles of cross-country ski trails, 2 miles of mountain bike trails, and a snowmobile trail that connects to a much larger system in the Moshannon State Forest.

Directions: From Philipsburg Follow PA Route 504 east for about 10 miles.

Activities: Hiking, camping, hunting, fishing, swimming, cross-country skiing, mountain biking, snowmobiling, skating, ice fishing, ice boating.

Facilities: Hiking trails, biking trails, guarded beach, visitor's center, snowmobile trails, campsites, cabins, boat launches, boat rental.

Dates: Park open year-round. Some camping facilities closed during winter.

Fees: There is a charge for camping and boat rentals.

Closest town: Philipsburg, 10 miles.

For more information: Black Moshannon State Park, RD 2, Box 183, Philipsburg, PA 16866. Phone (814) 342-5960.

BOG NATURAL AREA

[Fig. 19(2)] Located near the southern end of Black Moshannon Lake is the Bog Natural Area. Only about half of this 1,592-acre area is actually bog. The rest is primarily other types of wetlands, such as scrub/shrub and wooded wetlands, with small areas of mixed-oak forest mixed in.

The bog is an exceptional place to view wildflowers. All three of Pennsylvania's carnivorous plants—the sundew, pitcher plant, and bladderwort (*Uticularia* sp.)—can be seen here. Also found here are 11 species of orchids, including the purple-fringed orchid (*Habenaria fimbriata*) and ladies tresses (*Spiranthea* sp.). While the orchid family is one of the largest in the plant kingdom, containing more than 20,000 species, most orchids are tropical, and they are rarely found in large numbers. Nearly all the orchids found in North America grow only in acidic wetlands such as this bog.

The best way to visit the Bog Natural Area is by the Moss-Hanne Trail. This 7.4-mile trail passes through mixed-oak forests, spruce and hemlock groves, and several types of wetlands. Two portions of the trail are boardwalks, one passing through a

EASTERN REDCEDAR

(Juniperus virginiana)
Cedar chests are made from the fragrant wood of this tree.

marsh and the other passing through an alder (*Alnus* sp.) swamp. The trail covers gentle slopes and so is a relatively easy hike, but hikers should wear waterproof footwear because portions adjacent to wetlands are often wet. The trail is marked with orange blazes. The Moss-Hanne trailhead is located at the overlook at the southern end of West Side Road. The only other trail passing through the natural area is a small portion of the 1-mile-long Indian Ridge Trail, which runs from PA Route 504 in the north, about 0.8 mile west of the park's visitor's center, to the Hay Road Trail in the south.

Directions: From PA Route 504 follow West Side Road to its terminus, a distance of about 1 mile.

Activities: Hiking, cross-country skiing.

Facilities: Trails.

Dates: Open year-round.

Fees: None.

Closest town: Philipsburg, 10 miles.

For more information: Black Moshannon State Park, RR 1, PO Box 183, Philipsburg, PA 16866. Phone (814) 342-5960.

WHITE-TAILED DEER

(*Odocoileus virginianus*) The white-tailed deer may be the most popular wild animal in the U.S. When alarmed, the whitetail raises its tail, alerting other deer to possible danger.

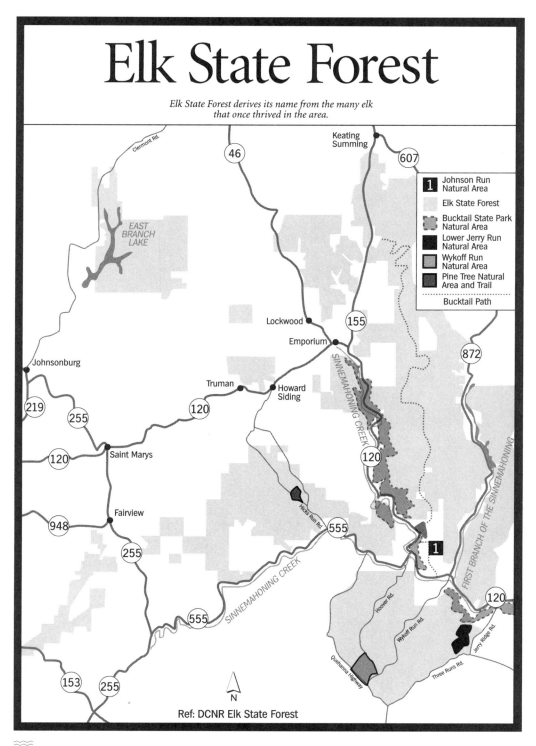

Elk State Forest

*Elk State Forest derives its name from the many elk
that once thrived in the area.*

Clermont Rd.

46

Keating
Summing

607

1 Johnson Run
Natural Area

Elk State Forest

Bucktail State Park
Natural Area

Lower Jerry Run
Natural Area

Wykoff Run
Natural Area

Pine Tree Natural
Area and Trail

Bucktail Path

EAST
BRANCH
LAKE

Lockwood

155

Emporium

872

Johnsonburg

SINNEMAHONING CREEK

Truman

Howard
Siding

219

255

120

120

120

Saint Marys

Hicks Run Rd.

FIRST BRANCH OF THE SINNEMAHONING

Fairview

555

1

948

555

120

255

SINNEMAHONING CREEK

Hoover Rd.

Wykoff Run Rd.

Jerry Ridge Rd.

153

255

Quehanna Highway

Three Runs Rd.

N

Ref: DCNR Elk State Forest

State Forests

Elk State Forest

[Fig. 16] The area now known as the Elk State Forest shares a legacy common to many of the public lands found on Pennsylvania's Allegheny Plateau. Extensive logging followed by wildfires fueled by the limbs and waste wood on the ground left the area barren and treeless.

The forest has returned, but the original pine and hemlock forest supported a different animal community than is found here today. Elk State Forest takes its name from one early inhabitant.

The elk, a large cousin to the now-common white-tailed deer, was once found throughout Pennsylvania. By the middle of the nineteenth century, however, Pennsylvania's elk population, like its forests, was shrinking. In 1867 the state's last known native elk was killed near Ridgway in Elk County. But as the forest has rebounded, so has the elk, albeit in a much smaller way and only with man's help.

In 1913 the Pennsylvania Game Commission restocked Pennsylvania with 177 Rocky Mountain elk, establishing the easternmost herd in the United States. While the elk population has fluctuated over the past 65 years, reaching a low of 35 in the early 1970s, today the elk number more than 250.

The site of a half-ton bull elk and his harem is not uncommon today in southwestern Cameron County or southeastern Elk County. Usually found in a 70-square-mile area stretching from Benzette in the west to the Hicks Run watershed in the east, the animals are often seen from the roads. A good place to begin looking for elk is at the elk viewing area located 3.5 miles north of the Benezette Hotel along Winslow Hill Road. During the rutting season, you may even be lucky enough to hear a bugling bull. The Elk State Forest was born in 1900 when the state purchased 3,487 acres of land along Middle Jerry Run with the intent of regenerating the forest. Since that time the forest has grown to encompass about 200,000 acres of northern Elk and southern Cameron counties, as well as small portions of Potter, Clinton, and McKean counties. The forest is part of a large state forest complex, bounded on the south by Moshannon State Forest, on the east by Sproul State Forest, and on the north by Susquehannock State Forest. The boundaries of the forest are marked with metal tags and white paint on trees.

Elevations vary from a low of 740 feet where the Sinnemahoning Creek has cut into the plateau, to as high as 2,380 feet at the summit of Wildwood Mountain in Elk County. Another prominent topographic feature is the Continental Divide. Running from Saint Mary's to Boone Mountain, the divide marks the boundary between the Atlantic and Gulf of Mexico drainage basins. Rain falling on the west side of the divide travels to the Mississippi River via the Allegheny River and then on to the Gulf

NORTHERN RED OAK

(Quercus rubra)
Red oaks can be identified by tiny bristles on the tip of each leaf.

of Mexico. Water falling on the east side of the divide flows to the Susquehanna River and then on to the Atlantic Ocean through the Chesapeake Bay.

Like many of Pennsylvania's state forests, most of the facilities found within the Elk State Forest are the product of the Civilian Conservation Corps of the late 1930s and early 1940s. CCC members also helped fight some of the post-logging wildfires. A monument to eight CCC firefighters killed in a 1938 wildfire and a picnic area can be found 3 miles south of Emporium along PA Route 120.

The forest contains six primary trails and over 100 miles of maintained roads that are open to public travel. Many miles of timber sale roads are closed to all vehicles but can be used by hikers, bikers, and horseback riders. Snowmobiles are allowed only on designated trails. Primitive camping is permitted throughout the forest.

Directions: To reach the forest's headquarters, follow PA Route 155 approximately 0.25 mile north of Emporium.

Activities: Hiking, snowmobile riding, camping, hunting, fishing.

Facilities: Hiking trails, snowmobile trails, picnic area, camping area.

Dates: Open year-round.

Fees: None.

Closest town: Emporium.

For more information: Elk State Forest, Forest District Headquarters, PO Box 327, Emporium, PA 15834. Phone (814) 486-3353.

JOHNSON RUN NATURAL AREA

[Fig. 16(1)] The Johnson Run Natural Area was designated because it is a relic of the forest that existed when the first European settlers moved into the area. Located here are 200-year-old white pines that escaped the logger's ax, hemlocks not stripped of their bark for the tannery, and assorted old-growth hardwoods.

The 216-acre area lies along Johnson Run and adjacent to a portion of the Bucktail State Park Natural Area at the southern end of Elk State Forest. There are no developed recreational facilities within the area, and the primary activities are hunting and hiking. Finding a place to park can be difficult due to limited parking alongside PA Route 120.

The only trail passing through the area is the Bucktail Path. While only 0.5 mile of the path passes through the Johnson Run Natural Area, the Bucktail Path is one of the longest hiking trails in Elk State Forest. Extending 30 miles from Sinnemahoning near the southeastern corner of Cameron County to near Sizerville State Park in Potter County, the trail passes through northern hardwood forests and forests dominated by oak and hickory.

In addition to a variety of forest types, a hike along the Bucktail Path presents elevations ranging from 850 to 2,200 feet. Some areas will appeal to the beginning hiker, while others are best reserved for the more advanced hiker. There is no parking area or trailhead for the Bucktail Path within the Johnson Run Natural Area.

Directions: Follow PA Route 120 west from the town of Sinnemahoning for about 4 miles. The natural area can be reached on foot by following either Johnson Run or the natural gas pipeline north for about 0.25 mile. The area's boundaries are not marked.

Activities: Hiking, hunting.

Facilities: Bucktail Path.

Dates: Open year-round.

Fees: None.

Closest town: Driftwood, 1 mile.

For more information: Elk State Forest, Forest District Headquarters, PO Box 327, Emporium, PA 15834. Phone (814) 486-3353.

▓ LOWER JERRY RUN NATURAL AREA

[Fig. 16] The Lower Jerry Run Natural Area encompasses 892 acres of the Lower Jerry Run stream valley in southeastern Cameron and southwestern Clinton counties. The area is steep and rocky, and it has no maintained or designated trails. This remote area contains no developed recreation facilities and hunting is the primary form of recreation enjoyed here.

Located near the southern end of the area is a remnant stand of old-growth pine, hemlock, and hardwoods. Mixed hardwoods, a lack of development, topographic variability, and clear mountain streams make the area significant for many types of reptiles and amphibians, so the Pennsylvania Bureau of Forestry has designated this a special protection area for these types of animals. This designation means that any type of disturbance of these creatures, including hunting, is prohibited.

A visitor to this area could encounter the rarely seen northern coal skink (*Eumeces anthracinus*) or the more common wood frog (*Rana sylvatica*).

SPRING PEEPER
(Hyla crucifer)
This treefrog is identified
by an X on its back.

RED SALAMANDER
(Pseudotriton ruber)

Woodland-dependent species such as the wood turtle (*Clemmys insculpta*), with its sculptured shell and unusual climbing abilities, and the mountain dusky salamander (*Desmognathus ochrophaeus*) are also found here. Snakes, including the common northern water snake (*Nerodia sipedon sipedon*) and the much maligned timber rattlesnake (*Crotalus insculpta*), also rely on wooded, protected areas such as this one.

Directions: From Sinnemahoning travel 0.6 mile on PA Route 120. Turn right onto Wykoff Run Road and then left on Jerry Run Road just after you cross the creek. Drive approximately 7 miles to Three Runs Road. Turn left, and go approximately 1 mile to Jerry Ridge Road, which is an Old Woods Road on the left. From this point you'll have to hike down the trail. About 0.8 mile down the trail turn right onto an unmarked branch of the trail. This leads into the natural area.

Activities: Hunting.
Facilities: None.
Dates: Open year-round.
Fees: None.
Closest town: Sinnemahoning, 4.5 miles.
For more information: Elk State Forest, Forest District Headquarters, PO Box 327, Emporium, PA 15834. Phone (814) 486-3353.

PINE TREE NATURAL AREA AND PINE TREE TRAIL

[Fig. 16] The Pine Tree Natural Area encompasses 276 acres and is unusual in that it contains an area of old field white pine. The area where the white pine now stand was cleared out of the virgin pine forest by a farmer in the mid-1800s. When the farmer abandoned his field, white pine seedlings sprouted once again from seeds blown in from the surrounding forest. Eventually, the surrounding forest was clear-cut, leaving only the white pine seedlings in the abandoned field. As time passed the field pines grew, shading out all of the other species, while the surrounding area developed into a second-growth hardwood forest.

The remnants of the old farm and the field pines are located along the Pine Tree Trail that follows the road used by the original settler. In fact, remnants of the farmhouse foundation can still be seen. This 2-mile interpretive trail can be reached from the Hicks Run Camping Area at one end or from the parking area at the other end along East Branch Hicks Run Road. The trail is marked with blue paint blazes, and points of interest are marked with white numbers.

Directions: From Benzette travel east along PA Route 555, 7 to 8 miles. Turn left onto Hicks Run Road and travel about 2 miles. Turn left onto West Branch Hicks Run Road, and the trailhead is on the right across the road from the Hicks Run Camping Area. To reach the other end of the trail, take the East Branch Hicks Run Road for approximately 1 mile. The trail entrance is on the left side of the road, just across a small bridge over Hicks Run.

Activities: Hiking, hunting.

Facilities: Trail. Camping area is adjacent.

Dates: Open year-round.

Fees: None.

Closest town: Dents Run, 3 miles.

For more information: Elk State Forest, Forest District Headquarters, PO Box 327, Emporium, PA 15834. Phone (814) 486-3353.

🐾 WYKOFF RUN NATURAL AREA

[Fig. 16] Wykoff Run is a 1,252-acre tract of land located within the Elk Forest section of the Quehanna Wild Area. Like most of the Allegheny High Plateau, the Wykoff Run Natural Area was subjected to clear-cutting and oil and gas removal. More recently, however, from the mid-1950s to the mid-1960s, parts of it were used by the Curtiss Wright Corporation for jet engine development and nuclear research. As a result, visitors can still see large treeless areas and remnants of industrial activity.

Today the area is used primarily for hunting, hiking, and cross-country skiing. Two streams, Wykoff Run and Red Run, drain the area and contribute to a number of different habitat types, including wetlands and moist hemlock woodlands. Most of Wykoff Run, however, is dominated by northern hardwoods and white birch. Like the Lower Jerry Run Natural Area (*see* page 91), which also lies within the Elk State Forest, this natural area has been designated a special protection area for reptiles and amphibians. These animals may not be disturbed in any way, and hunting seasons permitted elsewhere in the state for various species of frogs, turtles, and snakes do not apply here. The Old Hoover Trail (sometimes labeled the Quehanna Cross-country Ski Trail) is the only trail within the Wykoff Run Natural Area. The trailhead is located at the intersection of Wykoff Run Road and the Quehanna Highway.

Directions: Follow Wykoff Run Road south from PA Route 120 east of Sinnemahoning a distance of about 8 miles.

INDIAN CUCUMBERRROOT
(Medeola virginiana)
This is identified by two whorls of leaves; greenish yellow flowers droop from the top whorl.

Activities: Hiking, hunting, fishing, cross-country skiing.
Facilities: Trails, roads.
Dates: Open year-round.
Fees: None.
Closest town: Sinnemahoning, 8 miles.
For more information: Elk State Forest, Forest District Headquarters, PO Box 327, Emporium, PA 15834. Phone (814) 486-3353.

BUCKTAIL STATE PARK NATURAL AREA

[Fig. 16] "The said park shall be called and known as the 'Bucktail State Park,' in commemoration of the Bucktail Regiment which embarked from Driftwood, in Cameron County, in April 1861 upon rafts of their own construction to hasten their arrival at the imperiled state capitol." These were the words and wishes of the Pennsylvania legislature in 1933 as it created what is today the Bucktail State Park Natural Area within the Elk and Sproul state forests.

The Bucktail Regiment for which the park is named consisted of mountain men from McKean, Elk, and Cameron counties who voluntarily traveled to the southeastern part of the state to fight in the Civil War. The area now encompassed by the Bucktail State Park Natural Area and the adjacent private lands is known locally as the Bucktail Canyon in their memory.

The canyon's history goes back even farther than the Civil War, however. It was reportedly used by Native Americans as a route to the Eastern Continental Divide, which separates the Atlantic Ocean and Mississippi River drainage basins. The Native Americans called it the Sinnemahoning Trail.

The Bucktail State Park Natural Area is unusual in that it includes of a series of fragmented government-owned parcels with numerous private inholdings, roughly paralleling a 75-mile stretch of PA Route 120 from Emporium to Lock Haven. The state forest natural area encompasses a total of 16,433 acres along the Sinnemahoning Creek and along the west branch of the Susquehanna River.

Other than the three towns of Renovo, Emporium, and Lock Haven and a few small villages, the 75-mile stretch is almost completely forested, making it one of the most scenic drives in the state, especially during the fall.

Directions: The area lies along PA Route 120 from Emporium to Lock Haven.
Activities: Scenic drive.
Facilities: Wayside Memorial Picnic Area, 3 miles south of Emporium.
Dates: Open year-round.
Fees: None.
Closest town: Emporium, Renovo, Lock Haven.
For more information: Elk State Forest, PO Box 327, Emporium, PA 15834. Phone (814) 486-3353.

The Bucktail Regiment

In 1861 President Lincoln called on state governors for 75,000 volunteers to serve in the Union Army. One of the Pennsylvania volunteers, a recruit from Smethport serving under Colonel Kane, put a piece of deer hide in his cap and called himself a "bucktail." The name stuck and the rest of Kane's recruits from north central Pennsylvania followed suit. Consequently, they were one of the few Federal regiments that was immediately recognized by friend or foe.

Upon arriving in Harrisburg the Bucktails were informed that Pennsylvania had already met its quota of troops. Governor Curtin decided to take the extra troops and establish the Pennsylvania Reserve Volunteer Corps to guard the state's southern border and provide additional federal troops if needed. Due to early rebel victories, it became evident that they were needed immediately.

Coming from all walks of life, but mainly from the lumber and farming communities of the mountains of Pennsylvania, they were experienced riflemen and became well known on the field of battle. They fought in most of the campaigns of the Eastern Theater including, Second Bull Run, Seven Days Battle (Peninsula Campaign), Antietam, Fredericksburg, Gettysburg, Spotsylvania, and Cold Harbor. Of the over 1,200 men that formed the original Pennsylvania Bucktail Regiment, fewer than 400 made it through to see the surrender of Lee's forces at Appomattox.

GREAT LAUREL
(Rhododendron maximum)
With evergreen leaves and clusters of white to pink flowers, this rhododendron grows on moist slopes or swamps.

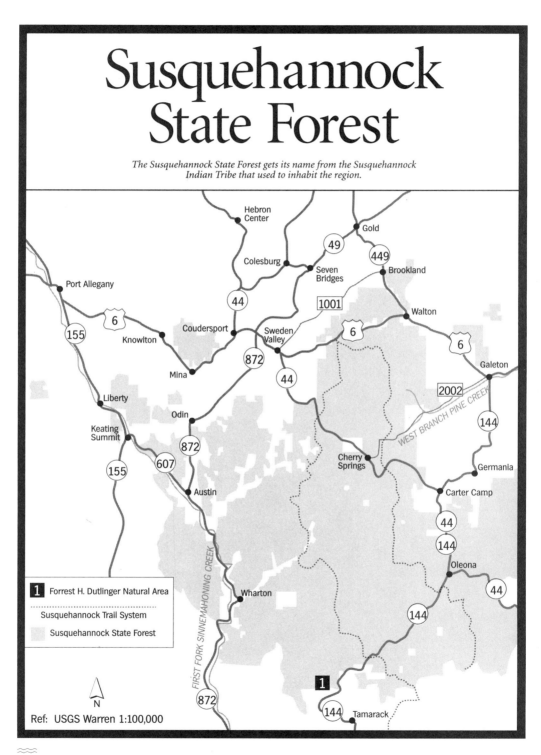

Susquehannock State Forest

The Susquehannock State Forest gets its name from the Susquehannock Indian Tribe that used to inhabit the region.

1 Forrest H. Dutlinger Natural Area

Susquehannock Trail System

Susquehannock State Forest

N

Ref: USGS Warren 1:100,000

Susquehannock State Forest

[Fig. 17] The Susquehannock State Forest is named after the Indian tribe that once inhabited this part of north central Pennsylvania. Located primarily within Potter County, this 262,000-acre forest also occupies a small portion of Clinton and McKean counties. The forest is located in a sparsely populated part of the Allegheny High Plateau, and it is bounded on the east by the Tioga and Tiadaghton state forests and on the south by the Sproul and Elk state forests.

In addition to forests, the Susquehannock contains numerous streams and wet-lands, including marshes that are dominated by emergent aquatic plants like cattails, shrub dominated swamps, and wet meadows.

Susquehannock is unique among Pennsylvania's state forests in that it lies within three major watersheds. Since the Continental Divide runs through the center of the Susquehannock, rain falling in the eastern part of the forest flows to the Atlantic Ocean via the Susquehanna River and the Chesapeake Bay. Precipitation falling in the western portions of the forest flow to the Gulf of Mexico through the Allegheny River and then the Mississippi River. The third drainage area is in the northeast corner of Potter County. Rain and melting snow in this area drain into the Genesee River, which flows into Lake Ontario, making this part of the Great Lakes drainage basin.

Like the rest of the Allegheny High Plateau, the forest was clear-cut during the late 1800s and early 1900s. The original pine and hemlock have been replaced by second-growth northern hardwoods such as beech, maple, and black cherry. White pine and hemlock can still be found in some of the wet ravines, and scattered oak forests occur near the southern edge of the forest. Many of the oak forests, however, have been defoliated by the oak-loving caterpillar called the oak leaf roller.

Logging of the northern hardwoods growing here today still plays an important role in the area's economy. But unlike the past, when large logging companies owned the land and cut any tree in sight, the Pennsylvania Bureau of Forestry manages the forest for multiple purposes, including recreation, wildlife habitat, and the sustained yield of timber.

Those interested in the history of logging in Pennsylvania should stop by the Pennsylvania Lumber Museum. The museum, which is located along PA Route 6 between Coudersport and Galeton, is operated by the Pennsylvania Historical and Museum Commission and contains a full-size sawmill and logging camp.

Timber is not the only valuable commodity found in the forest. This part of Pennsylvania was part of a vast, shallow inland sea during the Devonian Period. At about the same time that the first winged insects appeared, well before the age of the dinosaurs, the area was rich in plant life. As the water level in the sea fluctuated, the plants died and were covered with sediment. Eventually, time, heat, and pressure worked together to convert the sediment to sandstone and the plants into natural gas.

The deepest gas well in the Appalachian Basin, 18,834 feet below the surface, is

The white-tailed deer is so numerous in parts of the state that it is considered a pest.

found here. Three natural gas storage fields are also located within the forest. These storage areas are impervious pockets within the sandstone where gas companies store natural gas for future use.

There are many recreational opportunities within the forest. There are 89 miles of maintained foot trails, including part of the Susquehannock Trail System. Access to the area is made easy by 180 miles of state forest roads, and the Coudersport–Jersey Shore Pike, a portion of PA Route 44 that cuts through the heart of the forest which has been designated a scenic highway. While there are currently no special protection areas within the forest, the Hammersley watershed is listed as a proposed wild area. This topographically diverse area, with its deep stream cuts and native trout, has not been officially named a wild area because the gas, oil, and mineral rights are privately owned.

Three state parks are located within the boundaries of the Susquehannock State Forest: Denton Hill, Lyman Run, and Ole Bull.

Directions: From Coudersport follow US Route 6 east for approximately 8 miles. The forest's district headquarters are located on the right.

Activities: Hiking, ATV/snowmobile riding, hunting, fishing.

Facilities: Hiking trails, ATV/snowmobile trail, lumber museum.

Dates: Open year-round.

Fees: None.

Closest town: Coudersport, approximately 8 miles.

For more information: Susquehannock State Forest, PO Box 673, 3150 E. Second Street, Coudersport, PA 16915. Phone (814) 274-8474.

SUSQUEHANNOCK TRAIL SYSTEM

[Fig. 17] The Susquehannock Trail System is an 85-mile loop that traverses the eastern portion of the Susquehannock State Forest. The trail is composed of old logging roads, railroad grades leftover from the era of railroad logging, and trails built by the Civilian Conservation Corps in the late 1930s and early 1940s. Near its southern end, in Clinton County just below the Potter County line, the Susquehannock Trail System connects with the Donut Hole Trail (*see* page 109) in two places along the boundary of the Susquehannock and Sproul state forests.

A hike along the Susquehannock Trail System takes the hiker through second-growth forests atop the Allegheny High Plateau. The path rises and falls as it climbs in and out of stream channels eroded into the sedimentary rock. The clear and clean streams support native trout, but hikers should carry potable water or boil the stream water before drinking to avoid giardiasis. It will take 7 to 10 days to hike the entire trail, and overnight camping and campfires are permitted.

Since the trail is composed of old roads and railroad grades, it is a relatively easy hike, with only a few steep areas along the stream cuts. Hikers might be surprised to find parts of the trail running along cleared natural gas pipeline rights-of-way. The pipes are transporting gas from the Leidy gas field, one of the largest subterranean pools of natural gas in the world.

There are numerous points of access along the trail as it crosses state forest roads and secondary state highways. The northern end of the trail is located on PA Route 6 about 10 miles east of Coudersport at the Susquehannock State Forest District Office. The southern trailhead is located at the Forest headquarters along PA Route 44, 8 miles southeast of Oleona. The village of Cross Fork, which has a grocery store, restaurant, and motels, lies at about the halfway point along Kettle Creek. Also located near Cross Fork is the state forest headquarters. The trail is maintained by the Susquehannock Trail Club, which also has a detailed map.

Trail: 85-mile loop.

Elevation: 1,100–2,500 feet.

Degree of difficulty: Moderate.

Surface and blaze: Unpaved. Orange paint blazes.

For more information: Susquehannock Trail Club, PO Box 643, Coudersport, PA 16915.

BEE BALM
(Monarda didyma)
Used to produce a medicinal tea by Native Americans, bee balm is seldom visited by bees, but instead is usually pollinated by hummingbirds.

FORREST H. DUTLINGER NATURAL AREA

[Fig. 17(1)] The Forrest H. Dutlinger Natural Area is a remote, 1,521-acre chunk of forest located at the southern edge of the Susquehannock State Forest. The area contains a portion of Hammersley Fork Run and one of its tributaries, Peach Bottom Run. The natural area is named after a state forester who worked for the Department of Forests and Waters, the predecessor of the present day Bureau of Forestry, for 50 years.

There is only one trail running into the Forrest H. Dutlinger Natural Area. The Peach Bottom Trail begins at the mouth of Peach Bottom Run where it empties into Hammersley Fork on the area's eastern boundary. The trail climbs up the narrow ravine carved by the stream, passing a small waterfall where it spills into Hammersley Fork. The moderately challenging trail passes through a mixed hardwood forest for about 0.75 mile before reaching a stand of trees responsible for the natural area designation.

A 158-acre stand of old-growth timber lies along the stream, a vestige of the forest that once grew here. When loggers first moved into this area during the eighteenth century, they only removed white pine and then moved on. Eventually the loggers returned, but they never cut the trees in this small section of the ravine. It's speculated that a land dispute led to the preservation of this old-growth forest.

While hemlocks are the dominant species, there are also some old-growth red oak, white pine, beech, maple, and gum. Scattered among the giant hemlocks, some of which are 3.5 feet in diameter and over 100 feet tall, are the stumps of the virgin white pine that were cut during the last century.

The rest of the Forrest H. Dutlinger Natural Area, which is located on a plateau 1,140 feet above the trailhead, is a mixed-oak forest. The only signs of man's presence in this remote area are a natural gas pipeline, an old logging road, and a gas exploration road. A brochure describing the natural area and showing the trail and trailhead are available from the forest office.

Directions: From the village of Cross Forks follow PA Route 144 south for 4.6 miles. Turn

EASTERN CHIPMUNK
(Tamias striatus)
Chipmunks live in underground burrows up to 12 feet long.

right onto Hammersley Road (a dirt road) and follow it until vehicle access is prohibited. Hike across the suspension bridge and follow the road for about 0.5 mile to the trailhead.

Activities: Hiking, hunting, fishing.

Facilities: Hiking trail.

Dates: Open year-round.

Fees: None.

Closest town: Cross Forks, 5.5 miles.

For more information: Susquehannock State Forest, PO Box 673, Coudersport, PA 16915. Phone (814) 274-3600.

YELLOW BIRCH (Betula alleghaniensis)

This is one of the most valuable birches and also one of the largest hardwoods in northeastern North America growing up to 100 feet tall with a 2½-foot trunk. Its curly, shiny bark is flammable when wet, so prized by campers needing tinder for starting a campfire. In Autumn, the leaves turn bright yellow.

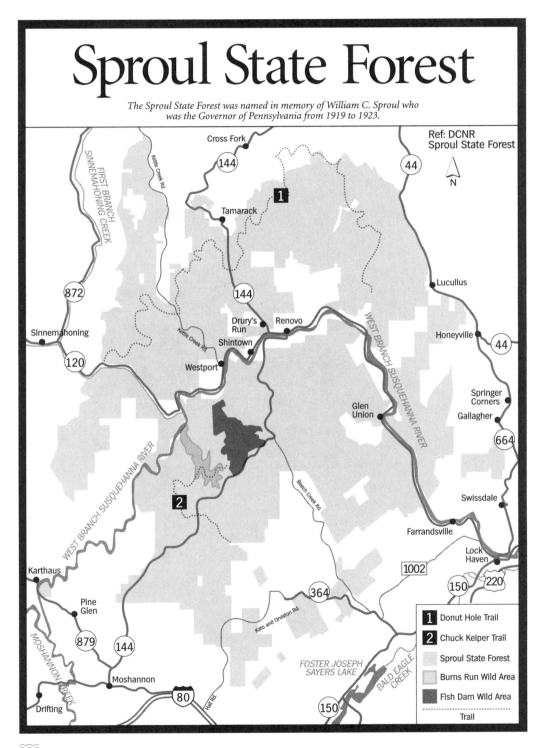

Sproul State Forest

The Sproul State Forest was named in memory of William C. Sproul who was the Governor of Pennsylvania from 1919 to 1923.

Ref: DCNR
Sproul State Forest

N

Cross Fork

144

1

44

Tamarack

Lucullus

144

Drury's Run   Renovo

Shintown

Honeyville

44

Westport

FIRST BRANCH SINNEMAHONING CREEK

Kettle Creek Rd.

872

Sinnemahoning

120

Kettle Creek Rd.

WEST BRANCH SUSQUEHANNA RIVER

Glen Union

Springer Corners

Gallagher

664

Swissdale

WEST BRANCH SUSQUEHANNA RIVER

2

Beech Creek Rd.

Farrandsville

Lock Haven

1002

150   220

Karthaus

Pine Glen

364

Kato and Orviston Rd.

150

MOSHANNON CREEK

879   144

Moshannon

80

Hall Rd.

FOSTER JOSEPH SAYERS LAKE

BALD EAGLE CREEK

150

Drifting

Legend:

1 Donut Hole Trail

2 Chuck Keiper Trail

Sproul State Forest

Burns Run Wild Area

Fish Dam Wild Area

Trail

Sproul State Forest

[Fig. 18] The 290,000-acre Sproul State Forest, Pennsylvania's largest, was born in 1898 when the first tract of land was purchased. It was the beginning of both the forest, and what would become a 2.1-million-acre state forest system.

The forest is located in western Clinton and northern Centre counties, on the Allegheny High Plateau. Two hundred years ago the area was an unbroken sea of white pine and hemlock. That all changed during the latter half of the nineteenth century when the pines were cut for their lumber and the hemlocks were cut for the tannin in their bark, which was needed by the leather industry.

The forest has grown back, but it's a different forest, one dominated by mixed oaks and hardwoods. The Sproul State Forest is one of the most rugged and remote Pennsylvania state forests. Black bear, white-tailed deer, turkey, and bobcat range across the plateau and down into the deep stream valleys etched into the sandstone.

The forest has seen many natural disasters. After it was clear-cut, much of the land experienced massive forest fires, fueled by the dead wood and branches left behind by loggers. Once the second-growth forest was established, fungal blights and insect infestations, including pests such as gypsy moths and oak leaf rollers, defoliated vast tracts within the forest. Even the weather hasn't been kind. Massive flooding occurred during Hurricane Agnes in 1972, and in 1985 a tornado destroyed more than 10,000 acres of trees and 76 miles of hiking trails.

Beneath the sandstone throughout much of this part of Pennsylvania are subterranean pools of natural gas. A 40,000-acre portion of the Sproul State Forest is currently utilized for underground natural gas storage and, to a lesser extent, natural gas exploration. The Leidy gas storage area, a natural subterranean pocket located in Clinton and Potter counties, is one of the world's largest underground storage areas.

Also lying below the surface is coal. During the early 1900s, numerous mines operated in the area, removing the bituminous coal needed to sustain the Industrial Revolution.

The major waterway within the Sproul State Forest is the West Branch of the Susquehanna River. Canoeing on the river is popular, primarily during the spring when the water level is high. A canoe launch is located on PA Route 879, south of Karthaus. Another popular aquatic pastime is trout fishing in the forest's 400 miles of cold-water streams. Twelve of the streams contain native trout and have been designated wilderness trout streams.

Hunting is also a major activity in the forest. All of the popular big game species, such as white-tailed deer and black bear, are hunted here, as well as game birds, such as turkey and Pennsylvania's state bird, the ruffed grouse (*Bonasa umbellus*). Given the rough terrain and vastness of the forest, hunters and other recreational users of the forest are advised to bring their compass, map, and orienteering skills.

The forest is crisscrossed by two hard-surfaced roads, dirt roads, state forest roads,

Elk

When the first Europeans arrived, elk (*Cervus elaphus*) were relatively common in the mountains of Pennsylvania. By the middle part of the nineteenth century, however, the *wapiti*, as they were called by the Shawnee Indians, were gone from the state because of over-hunting and habitat loss.

In the hopes of establishing the only elk herd east of the Mississippi, the Pennsylvania Game Commission trapped 177 elk in Yellowstone National Park between 1913 and 1926 and transported them from South Dakota to north-central Pennsylvania. The herd still exists today and contains 300 to 400 animals, most of them found within a 227 square mile area within Elk and Cameron counties. In early 1998, 16 of the elk were trapped and moved from this area to the Sproul State Forest in Clinton County. Plans call for eventually moving up to 100 elk to establish a second herd and also to reduce crop damage being caused in Elk and Cameron counties. The range of the original elk herd is expanding into farmland and the elk are eating the crops. The animals that are eating the crops are being trapped and transferred, thereby reducing crop damage.

Elk are large animals, with cows weighing up to 500 pounds and bulls up to 800 pounds, and they can be aggressive, particularly during the mating season. To provide the public with a place to watch the animals from a safe distance, an elk viewing area was constructed on state game lands in 1995. To reach the elk viewing area follow Winslow Hill Road north from the town of Benzette for about 3.5 miles. The best time to see the animals is at dawn and dusk during the mating season in September and October. The viewing area is well marked and has parking.

powerlines, and pipeline rights-of-way. Some of these have been designated for specific recreational activities such as snowmobiling, ATV riding, and horseback riding.

Located near the north end of the forest, just east of Kettle Creek State Park, is a designated ATV trail. This trail is the only area in the forest open to ATVs, and it takes riders through old strip mines (some of which have been revegetated), old woods roads, and forest trails. During the winter these trails can be used by snowmobiles. Also located near Kettle Creek State Park is a 15-mile-long equestrian trail.

The Hiding Bear Ski Trail is located on Hyner Mountain near the northeast corner of the forest. The 14-mile loop trail varies in difficulty and is recommended for people with at least some cross-country skiing experience. Two parking areas, one on PA Route 44, 3.8 miles north of Haneyville and the other at the intersection of Ritchie Road and Hyner Mountain Township Road about 1 mile west of the village of Lucullus, serve as points of access to the trail.

There are three small areas within the forest that have been designated natural areas because they are, or were, high mountain bogs. The 164-acre Cranberry Swamp

Natural Area is located in Clinton County at the headwaters of Cranberry Run and at one time was a bog. Over time the bog was colonized by white pine, through the natural process of succession, and it evolved into a forest. During the great logging period of the nineteenth century, the pine were all cut and then forest fires ravaged the area. These factors, combined with beaver activity in the area, have turned 64 acres of the pine forest back into a wetland. The East Branch Swamp Natural Area is a similar area with a similar history. This 182-acre natural area, which is located on the east side of PA Route 144 near Bark Camp and the Fish Dam Wild Area, has the added distinction of containing a 10-acre stand of virgin hemlock. Tamarack Swamp Natural Area still contains a high mountain bog. This natural area encompasses 124 acres and is also located along PA Route 144 near the village of Tamarack.

Directions: From Renovo follow PA Route 120 approximately 3 miles west to Shintown. The forest's headquarters are located on the left side of the road.

Activities: Hiking, horseback riding, cross-country skiing, snowmobile and ATV riding, hunting, fishing.

Facilities: Hiking trails, equestrian trails, snowmobile and ATV trails, picnic areas.

Dates: Open year-round.

Fees: None.

Closest town: Renovo, less than 1 mile.

For more information: Sproul State Forest, HCR 62, Box 90, Renovo, PA 17764. Phone (717) 923-6011.

FISH DAM WILD AREA

[Fig. 18] The Fish Dam Wild Area encompasses the 5,000-acre watershed of Fish Dam Run and its tributaries. The streams within the area, which support native brook trout, have been designated as exceptional value streams because of their high water quality. The area is bounded on the southeast by PA Route 144 (there are two scenic vistas along this road which overlook the wild area) and on the northwest by a portion of the Bucktail State Park Natural Area. The only maintained trail within the area is a portion of the Chuck Keiper Trail (*see* page 107), which passes through the southeastern portion.

The Fish Dam Wild Area was the victim of a major tornado in 1985 that killed nearly a quarter of the trees. In the blowdown area, visitors can still see the effects of the tornado.

When the dense conifer stands of the last century disappeared (*see* Sproul State Forest, page 103), so did many of the animals that depended on them. Among those animals that disappeared was a large member of the weasel family. Known by names such as fisher cat and fisher weasel, and occasionally misidentified as a black panther because of its color and tree-climbing abilities, the last native fisher confirmed in Pennsylvania was in Clinton County in 1901. But fishers have been reintroduced and are making a comeback.

Fisher

Two hundred years ago Pennsylvania was forested from border to border. For an animal like the fisher (*Martes pennanti*), which likes to spend much of its time in the trees and often travels without setting a foot on the ground, this was an ideal place. The dense woods also held an ample supply of the fisher's favorite foods: small mammals, such as red squirrels, snowshoe hares, and porcupines.

This black-brown member of the weasel family has a home range that can be as large as 150 square miles. As the logging companies began to clear-cut their way across the state, the fisher began to disappear along with the trees. Also, the fisher was and is one of the most sought after furbearers. Even though they're not trapped in Pennsylvania today, because they're so rare, they are trapped in the states where they are common, such as New York and some of the New England states. By the turn of the century, the fisher was thought to be extirpated from Pennsylvania. There were periodic reports of possible fisher sightings, but none that could be confirmed. If any still did exist, they were few and far between.

Capitalizing on their success with introducing another large weasel to Pennsylvania, the river otter, Penn State University and the Pennsylvania Game Commission decided to undertake a fisher reintroduction program. As of December 1997, 47 fishers have been released in Pennsylvania within the Allegheny National Forest along Tionesta Creek and its tributary Upper Sheriff Run. The Allegheny was chosen because of its large unbroken tracts of forest and relative remoteness. As you hike through the remote woodlands of the Allegheny National Forest, don't expect to see a fisher. These animals are primarily nocturnal, and when they are out during the day, as they sometimes are, they are very secretive and keep their distance from people.

While fishers prefer conifers, they will live in dense, second-growth, deciduous woods as well. The area must be totally forested and have a closed canopy. The Fish Dam Wild Area meets those criteria, and so it was chosen as one of a handful of reintroduction sites by the Pennsylvania Game Commission and Penn State University. Additionally, the area is large enough to support a population of these animals. Each animal requires 16 square miles of forest to hunt for porcupines, squirrels, and other small mammals.

Directions: Take PA Route 144 south from South Renovo for approximately 7 miles.

Activities: Hunting, hiking, fishing.

Facilities: Chuck Keiper Trail.

Dates: Open year-round.

Fees: None.

Closest town: South Renovo, 7 miles.

For more information: Sproul State Forest, HCR 62, Box 90, Renovo, PA 17764. Phone (717) 923-6011.

BURNS RUN WILD AREA

[Fig. 18] The Burns Run Wild Area contains the watershed of Burns Run and its tributaries—2,000 of the most rugged and wild acres in the state of Pennsylvania. Typical of many streams on the Allegheny High Plateau, Burns Run has engraved an 800-foot-deep canyon into the underlying rock, creating a steep escarpment on either side of the stream. The stream and its tributaries have been classified as wilderness trout streams because of their exceptional water quality and native trout population. Fishermen in canoes can reach the mouth of Burns Run where it flows into the West Branch of the Susquehanna River near its confluence with Sinnemahoning Creek. The upper reaches of the stream, and the eastern portions of the Burns Run Wild Area, can be reached from either Jew's Run Road or Fischer Fire Road. Be aware, though, that the descent to the creek is steep and rocky.

The only trail running through the wild area is a small portion of the Chuck Keiper Trail (*see* below), which passes through the eastern end of the area, paralleling Owl and Burns runs.

Directions: Take PA Route 144 south from South Renovo for approximately 11 miles. Turn right on Jew's Run Road. The Chuck Keiper Trail crosses Jew's Run Road about 1 mile from the intersection. The trail crossing is marked with a post, but there is no parking area. The wild area is a short hike south along the trail.

Activities: Hiking, fishing, hunting.

Facilities: A portion of the Chuck Keiper Trail passes through, but there is no trailhead.

Dates: Open year-round.

Fees: None.

Closest town: South Renovo, 11 miles.

For more information: Sproul State Forest, HCR 62, Box 90, Renovo, PA 17764. Phone (717) 923-6011.

CHUCK KEIPER TRAIL

[Fig. 18(2)] If you're looking for a backwoods hike where you're not likely to encounter anyone else, this is the trail for you. The 50-mile-long Chuck Keiper Trail travels through the southern portion of the Sproul State Forest, south of the West Branch of the Susquehanna River. As it winds its way through the forest, this trail passes through the Fish Dam and Burns Run wild areas, rising and falling through the deep cuts generated by these streams over hundreds of thousands of years.

Constructed from an assemblage of old railroad grades, old woods roads, and fire trails constructed by the Civilian Conservation Corps more than 50 years ago, the trail is two, 25-mile loops with numerous scenic vistas scattered along its course. The trail crosses several forest roads and PA Route 144, making access easy. One of the easiest places to get on the trail is at the State Camp parking area about 10 miles south of Renovo. The trailhead is clearly marked.

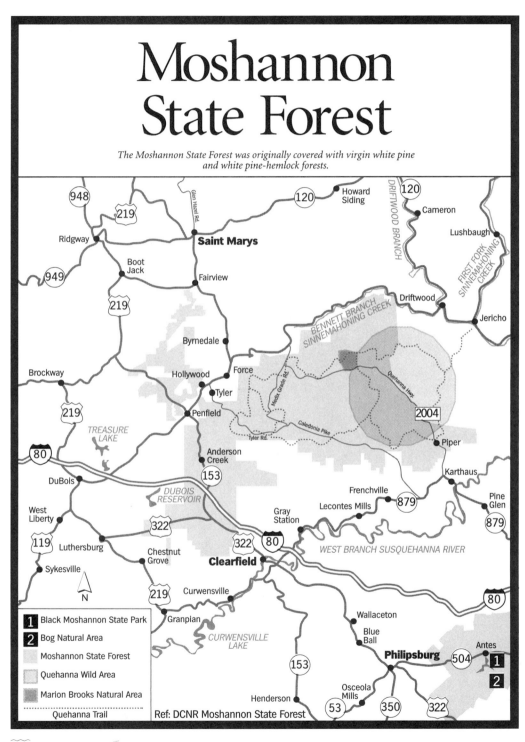

Moshannon State Forest

The Moshannon State Forest was originally covered with virgin white pine and white pine-hemlock forests.

Ref: DCNR Moshannon State Forest

Trail: 2, 25-mile loops.
Elevation: 1,000–2,200 feet.
Degree of difficulty: Moderate to strenuous in spots.
Surface and blaze: Unpaved and marked with rectangular, orange paint blazes.

🟫 DONUT HOLE TRAIL

[Fig. 18(1)] Created by knitting a series of fire trails constructed by the Civilian Conservation Corps together with old railroad grades and woods roads, the Donut Hole Trail stretches 90 miles from Jericho to near Farrandsville. As it winds its way through the Sproul State Forest, the Donut Hole Trail crosses numerous streams, including Kettle Creek, Womans Creek, and Hyner and Bull runs. These watercourses have been eating into the native sandstone for hundreds of thousands of years, resulting in stream valleys as deep as 800 feet. Hikers should be prepared for challenging terrain.

Along its path, the trail passes through several private inholdings, and it joins up with the Susquehannock Trail System to pass from northern Clinton County into southern Potter County and then back again. There are several designated scenic vistas along the trail, and portions pass through the Bucktail State Park Natural Area, affording a magnificent view of the Susquehanna River Valley.

To reach the eastern end of the trail follow Farrandsville Road north from Farrandsville to the parking area on State Game Land 89, a distance of about 1 mile. Trailheads are also located at Hyner Run State Park, about 2 miles north of Hyner on Hyner Run Road, along PA Route 144 approximately 5.5 miles north of Renovo, in Kettle Creek State Park, and on PA Route 120 near Jericho.

Trail: 52 miles.
Elevation: 800–2,200 feet.
Degree of difficulty: Moderate to strenuous.
Surface and blaze: Unpaved, red blazes being changed to orange.

Moshannon State Forest

[Fig. 19] The Moshannon State Forest encompasses nearly 190,000 acres of forest land, most of it in Clearfield, Elk, and Centre counties. Formed by knitting together several smaller state forests, Moshannon sits within three physiographic sections: the Allegheny High Plateau, the Pittsburgh Plateau, and the Allegheny Mountain Section.

The highest and lowest points in the forest are both in Clearfield County, at 2,405 feet and 800 feet respectively. Most of the forest is drained by the West Branch of the Susquehanna River, but a small portion near DuBois lies in the Allegheny River drainage basin.

Today's Moshannon State Forest, like many of the forests in Pennsylvania, has been shaped by man. The original pine, hemlock, and northern hardwood forests were completely cut during the last century. The first to go were the white pines, which were moved from the uplands to the West Branch of the Susquehanna by a process called splashing. A series of dams, called splash dams, were constructed along the river's small tributaries. After the logs were stacked behind one of the splash dams, the gate was closed to flood the area. When the gate was opened, the trees flowed, or splashed, to the dam below. The process was repeated until the logs reached the river.

About the time the white pines disappeared, the logging railroads appeared, and the remaining forests were cut. Many areas then experienced severe, ground-searing wildfires that nearly sterilized the soil. There are still areas today where the stumps of the original white pine and hemlock, skeletons from an era gone by, stand on soil able only to support ferns.

Like all state forests, Moshannon is managed for multiple uses. Nearly 132,000 acres are classified as commercial forest land, meaning that controlled cutting of the second-growth northern hardwoods and oaks is permitted. Gas wells are also very common. Many of the more remote areas of the forest have been made accessible by roads constructed when the large Boone Mountain and Benzetter gas fields were discovered. Even with these consumptive activities taking place, there are numerous recreational opportunities in the Moshannon.

There are three state parks located within this state forest. Parker Dam State Park is located 17 miles north of Clearfield and can be reached by taking PA Route 153 north from Interstate 80 (Exit 18) to Mud Run Road. The park contains a campground, cabins, a picnic area, and a 20-acre lake, and it can be used as an access point to the Quehanna Trail (*see* page 112).

Located alongside Interstate 80 at Exit 18 is S.B. Elliot State Park. The park is primarily a large, wooded picnic area with associated cabins and campsites that are rented on a weekly basis during the summer. Advance registration is necessary.

Black Moshannon State Park is located south of Interstate 80, between Philipsburg and Unionville along PA Route 504. The focal point of the 3,394-acre park is a 250-acre, spring-fed lake. The park contains numerous recreation areas including a beach, picnic grounds, camping area, and downhill skiing area.

Many of the facilities found in the forest are the products of the Civilian Conservation Corps.

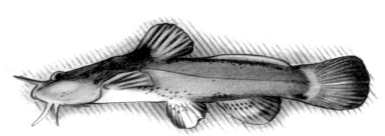

MOUNTAIN MADTOM (*Noturus eleutherus*) Adults grow up to 5 inches in length. Found in the Ohio, Cumberland, and Tennessee river drainages.

During the late 1930s and early 1940s, the CCC built roads, planted trees, and built recreational facilities, including many of those found at Black Moshannon, S.B. Elliott, and Parker Dam state parks. The forest also contains 53 hiking trails and two cross-country ski trails.

One of the most noticeable features of the forest is the abundance of streams. The name Moshannon comes from the Indian word *Moss-hanne*, which means "moose stream." There are 103 miles of major trout streams in the Moshannon that contain both native and stocked trout. Sportsmen also fish in Black Moshannon Lake, which contains bass, muskellunge, walleye, and panfish.

Hunting is permitted throughout the forest. Since hunting is a popular activity, visitors are advised to wear fluorescent orange during the fall and spring hunting seasons. Once the antlerless deer hunting season ends, a snowmobile trail system is opened. The system is composed of groomed trails and forest roads, most of which are closed to all other forms of vehicular traffic during the winter months. Snowmobile trailheads are located within all three of the state parks located in the forest.

Directions: From PA Route 879, 1.5 miles west of Karthaus, follow the Quehanna Highway north for approximately 4.5 miles. The unmanned forest headquarters is on the right. The manned district office is located off I-80 at Exit 18.

Activities: Hiking, cross-country skiing, hunting, fishing, snowmobiling, downhill skiing.

Facilities: Hiking trails, cross-country ski trails, picnic areas, snowmobile trail system, downhill skiing area, horseback riding, scenic driving.

Dates: Open year-round.

Fees: None.

For more information: Moshannon State Forest, PO Box 952, Clearfield, PA 16830. Phone (814) 765-0821.

QUEHANNA WILD AREA

[Fig. 19] The Quehanna Wild Area is a vast, 48,000-acre area located within both Moshannon and Elk state forests. The area provides an excellent opportunity to enjoy a large, relatively undeveloped second-growth forest typical of the Allegheny High Plateau.

While the wild area designation prevents permanent development, the area did see development in the past. From 1955 to 1963, the Curtis Wright Corporation leased or purchased 50,000 acres within what is today state forest land, including most of the Quehanna Wild Area. The company operated a nuclear reactor and plastic manufacturing operation, and it developed and tested jet and atomic engines. The only active remnant of this former activity is the 100-acre Quehanna Industrial Complex, which houses several industrial tenants.

A wide variety of habitats are found within the area, from oak and hardwood forests to turf in the old industrial areas. Many of the forested areas show the effects of the oak leaf roller (*Archips semiferana*). This voracious caterpillar defoliates oak trees, killing the weaker ones, most of which are weak because they were defoliated in previous years.

Hunters and fishermen use the Quehanna Wild Area throughout the year. Trout are found in many of the streams, including Mosquito Run and Upper Three Runs. White-tailed deer, bear, turkey, grouse, and waterfowl are found throughout the area and are hunted during the designated seasons. Also found here are elk, which expanded their range into the Quehanna Wild Area in the early 1990s. Hunters should be aware that there is no hunting season for elk in Pennsylvania.

Unlike most Pennsylvania state forest wild areas, Quehanna contains a road system. The Quehanna Highway runs through the heart of the area, connecting with Wykoff Run Road, which runs north to the West Branch of the Susquehanna River, and Reactor Road, which leads to the remaining industrial complex. These and other roads make nearly all of this vast area accessible.

While all of the Quehanna Wild Area is open to public recreation, snowmobiles, off-road vehicles, and vehicular camping are prohibited.

Directions: From PA Route 555 east of Sinnemahoning, take Wykoff Road south for 3.5 miles.

Activities: Hiking, biking, hunting, fishing.

Facilities: Trails.

Dates: Open year-round.

Fees: None.

Closest town: Sinnemahoning, 3.5 miles.

For more information: Moshannon State Forest, PO Box 952, Clearfield, PA 16830. Phone (814) 765-0821.

QUEHANNA TRAIL

[Fig. 19] The Quehanna Trail is a 73-mile loop which runs through Elk and Moshannon state forests. The trail crosses some of the roughest and most remote terrain in Pennsylvania. Elevations range from 2,100 feet along the Allegheny Plateau to 1,000 feet in some of the stream valleys.

The trail passes through the Quehanna Wild Area and Marion Brooks Natural Area. A wide range of ecosystems lie along the trail, including wetlands, northern hardwoods, oaks along the plateau, and riverine ecosystems in the gorges. Black bear, white-tailed deer, turkey, elk, fisher, and even rattlesnakes could be encountered along the trail.

While hiking the entire trail is a long, strenuous proposition, there are numerous trailheads located along its length, making shorter hikes possible. Additionally, there are spurs which connect the Quehanna Trail with the Donut Hole Trail (*see* page 109) and Bucktail Path (*see* page 91). One of the best places to get on the trail is at the trailhead about 0.75 mile north of the forest's headquarters on the Quehanna Highway (*see* directions to Moshannon State Forest, page 111). There is a parking area and gate on the right side of the road, and maps are available there as well.

The trail is marked with orange blazes. Blue blazes are used to mark connector trails that can shorten the loop, and to mark a series of cross-country ski trails along the eastern portion of the Quehanna Trail.

Trail: 73-mile loop.

Elevation: 1,000–2,100 feet.

Degree of difficulty: Moderate to strenuous.

Surface and blaze: Unpaved with orange blazes. Connectors and cross-country ski trails have blue blazes.

For more information: Moshannon State Forest, PO Box 952, Clearfield, PA 16830. Phone (814) 765-0821.

MARION BROOKS NATURAL AREA

[Fig. 19] The Marion Brooks Natural Area is the only designated natural area within the Moshannon State Forest. The area encompasses slightly less than 1,000 acres of oak forest in the middle of the Quehanna Wild Area along the Quehanna Highway. Within the oak forest are two small but unusual ecosystems.

At the southeastern corner of the area is a small bog. Bogs are acidic wetlands which formed when glacial ice or meltwater was left behind after the last ice age. These nutrient-poor habitats often contain carnivorous plants, and this one is no exception. The sundew plant grows here, supplementing the food it makes, through the process of photosynthesis, with insects that become trapped on its sticky leaves.

Another unusual ecosystem found here is dominated by white birch (*Betula papyrifera*), also called paper birch. Not common in this area, biologists believe this 22-acre stand developed after the intense post-logging fires destroyed all the organic material in the soil. The white birch grow in a pure stand because they exude a toxin into the soil which prevents any other trees from growing, a phenomenon which scientists call allelopathy. The trees' reign is coming to an end, however, because they are nearing the end of their 80-year life span.

The area is easily accessible by car, because of its close proximity to the Quehanna Highway, or by foot. The Quehanna Trail runs through the center of the natural area, and since the Marion Brooks portion is relatively level, it is frequently used by cross-country skiers.

Directions: From the village of Medix Run, follow the Quehanna Highway south approximately 6 miles to the parking area.

Activities: Hiking, hunting, cross-country skiing.

Facilities: Quehanna Trail.

Dates: Open year-round.

Fees: None.

Closest town: Medix Run, 6 miles.

For more information: Moshannon State Forest, PO Box 952, Clearfield, PA 16830. Phone (814) 765-0821.

Tioga State Forest

Tioga State Forest is named after the Tyoga tribe of the Seneca Indians and is 160,000 acres.

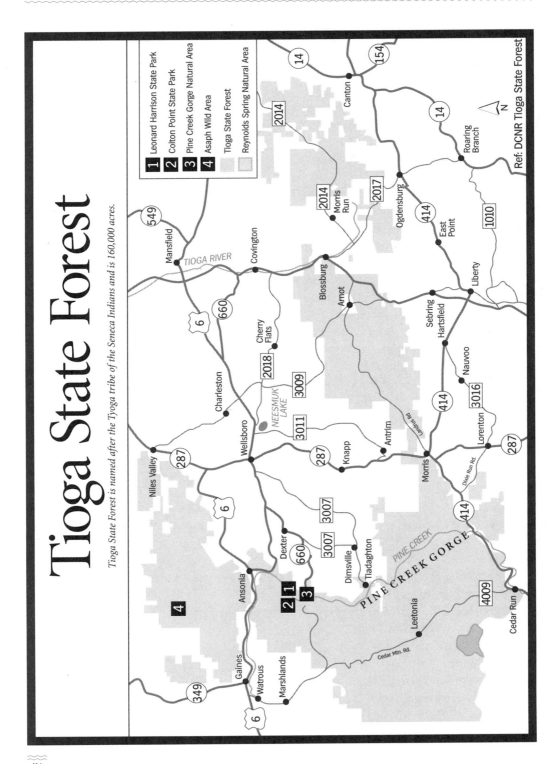

Ref: DCNR Tioga State Forest

Legend:
1 Leonard Harrison State Park
2 Colton Point State Park
3 Pine Creek Gorge Natural Area
4 Asaph Wild Area
Tioga State Forest
Reynolds Spring Natural Area

Tioga State Forest

[Fig. 20] Named after the Seneca Indian tribe that once inhabited the area, the Tioga State Forest contains 160,000 acres in north central Pennsylvania's Bradford and Tioga counties. It includes arguably the most spectacular natural feature in Pennsylvania, a section of the Pine Creek Gorge known officially as the Pine Creek Gorge Natural Area but more commonly called the Grand Canyon of Pennsylvania.

The forest is a topographically diverse area, ranging in elevation from more than 2,500 feet along the ridgetops to 780 feet where Pine Creek passes out of the southern edge of the forest. While mountains and valleys are often formed by geologic processes such as folding and faulting, the topography of the Tioga State Forest is due to the action of water flowing over rock. Over the past 10 million years, streams like Pine Creek and Cedar Run have etched themselves into the landscape, producing numerous waterfalls, including one in the eastern part of the forest at Falls Brook and another on Campbells Run north of Tiadaghton.

When the first European settlers arrived here, the most common trees were white pine, hemlock, chestnut, and red maple, with other hardwoods and oaks scattered throughout. Those forests disappeared during the latter half of the eighteenth century when large logging companies clear-cut the area trying to satisfy the nation's insatiable appetite for lumber. Since the land wasn't worth much once the trees were gone, the state was able to purchase the area, piece by piece, from 1900 to 1955, at low cost.

Today the forest contains two different forest communities, one dominated by white pine and the other by northern hardwoods such as beech, black cherry, sugar maple, and yellow birch (*Betula alleghaniensis*). For a short period during the 1940s, the latter was harvested and processed by birch mills that extracted birch oil from the tree's bark for use in the fragrance industry. Today all of the Tioga State Forest, excluding the natural areas, wild areas, and state parks, is considered commercial forest and is therefore open to logging.

Lumber isn't the only natural resource that has been extracted from the forest. One of the state's first coal mines was located near Blossburg, just outside the state forest. Coal has played a major role in the development of this part of the state, and many parts of the forest have been strip-mined to reach the bituminous coal that lies beneath the surface.

Numerous recreational opportunities exist within the forest. There are 7 miles of cross-country ski trails, three developed hiking trails, and 175 miles of snowmobile routes. There are also three state forest picnic areas. The Asaph Picnic Area is located along Asaph Run adjacent to the Asaph Wild Area. Near the eastern edge of the forest, in eastern Tioga County, is the County Bridge Picnic Area. The Bradley Wales Picnic Area is located within the Pine Creek Gorge Natural Area, just across the ravine from Tiadaghton.

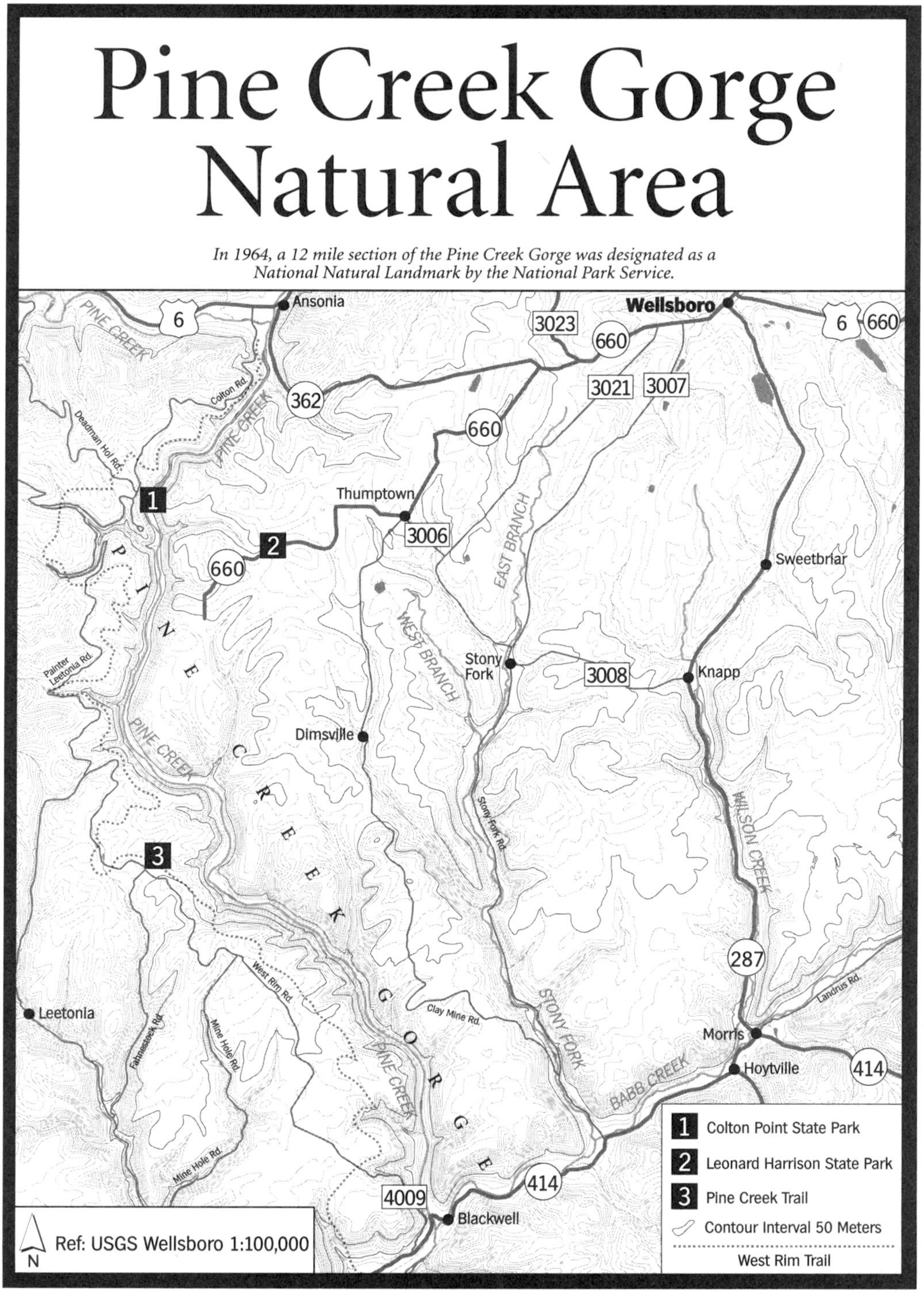

Pine Creek Gorge Natural Area
In 1964, a 12 mile section of the Pine Creek Gorge was designated as a National Natural Landmark by the National Park Service.
Ansonia
Wellsboro
6
3023
660
6
660
362
3021
3007
Colton Rd.
PINE CREEK
Deadman Hol Rd.
Thumptown
3006
EAST BRANCH
Sweetbriar
WEST BRANCH
Stony Fork
3008
Knapp
Painter Leetonia Rd.
Dimsville
P I N E C R E E K G O R G E
Stony Fork Rd.
WILSON CREEK
287
Landrus Rd.
West Rim Rd.
Clay Mine Rd.
STONY FORK
Leetonia
Fahnestock Rd.
Mine Hole Rd.
Morris
Hoytville
414
BABB CREEK
4009
Blackwell
N
Ref: USGS Wellsboro 1:100,000
1 Colton Point State Park
2 Leonard Harrison State Park
3 Pine Creek Trail
Contour Interval 50 Meters
West Rim Trail

Directions: From the intersection of PA Route 6 and PA Route 362 east of Ansonia, follow PA Route 362 east for about 1 mile to Pine Creek Gorge Natural Area.

Activities: Hiking, biking, cross-country skiing, hunting, fishing, snowmobiling.

Facilities: Hiking trails, cross-country ski trails, bike trails, camping areas, picnic areas, snowmobile routes.

Dates: Open year-round.

Fees: None.

Closest town: Ansonia, 0.5 mile.

For more information: Tioga State Forest, One Nessmuk Lane, PA Route 287 South, Wellsboro, PA 16901. Phone (717) 724-2868.

PINE CREEK GORGE NATURAL AREA

[Fig. 21, Fig. 20(3)] Better known as the Grand Canyon of Pennsylvania, the Pine Creek Gorge Natural Area runs along both sides of Pine Creek for about 18 miles, from Ansonia to Blackwell. The gorge, which is up to 1,000 feet deep and 1 mile wide in spots, formed when a glacier blocked Pine Creek, reversing the water flow from north to south. When the glacier retreated, it left behind a pile of gravel, clay, and sand (called a moraine) that permanently reversed the flow of Pine Creek.

The 12,163-acre natural area was designated a National Natural Landmark by Congress in 1968 because of its unique character and scenic beauty. Two of the best places to view the gorge are Leonard Harrison [Fig. 3(16)] and Colton Point [Fig. 3(15)] state parks, which lie across the gorge from one another. These parks offer numerous recreational opportunities and serve as a good point of departure for a trip along one of the trails which run through the natural area.

Wildflower enthusiasts will want to visit the area during the springtime. More than 50 species of wildflowers bloom here in April and May, fading in number where the oak-dominated canopy throws the forest floor into semidarkness.

Spring is also a good time for observing wildlife. Some species, such as the fish-eating osprey (*Pandion haliaetus*), are migrating, some, such as black bears, are venturing forth with their young for the first time, and others, like the bald eagle (*Haliaeetus leucocephalius*), are nesting.

Bald eagles have been known to nest north of Blackwell for the last six years. They have nested in a remote area of the gorge where the only people likely to see them are those rafting down Pine Creek. Visitors have been more likely to see eagles during the winter before the creek freezes over. Several of the birds have wintered here until the ice prevented them from reaching the fish that make up the bulk of their diet.

There are many scenic vistas and picnic areas located along the west side of the gorge. These are best reached by taking the West Rim Trail from Colton Point State Park (*see* page 80).

Those who want to explore the canyon at the stream level can walk or bike along the Pine Tree Trail on the canyon's east side. This trail is relatively flat and covered with crushed limestone, making it ideal for hiking, biking, and cross-country skiing in the winter. On the popular 19-mile trail users will pass waterfalls, cross numerous small bridges, and probably encounter many other hikers and bikers. Trail hours are from one-half hour before sunrise to one-half hour after sunset. There are numerous marked access points along the trail with parking areas. One of the most used access points is the Turkey Path Trail in Leonard Harrison State Park (*see* page 80).

Directions: To go to Leonard Harrison State Park from Wellsboro, follow PA Route 660 to its terminus, a distance of about 10 miles. To get to Colton Point State Park, take Colton Road south from Ansonia for 5 miles.

Activities: Hiking, hunting, fishing, wildlife watching, rafting, biking, cross-country skiing, overnight camping.

Facilities: Trails, picnic areas, scenic vistas.

Dates: Open year-round.

Fees: None.

Closest town: Ansonia, less than 1 mile.

For more information: Tioga State Forest, One Nessmuk Lane, PA Route 287 South, Wellsboro, PA 16901. Phone (717) 724-2868.

PINE CREEK TRAIL

[Fig. 21(3)] In 1988 Consolidated Rail Corporation, better known as Conrail, decided to do away with its Corning Secondary Track, which ran through Pine Creek Gorge in Tioga and Lycoming counties. Once the rails and ties were removed, the broad, level bed seemed tailor made for a trail. The Department of Environmental Protection, the predecessor of the current Department of Conservation and Natural Resources, negotiated with Conrail and secured the rights to construct a trail on the old railroad bed.

The Pine Creek Trail is being built in segments, and the first segment opened in August 1996. Already this is one of the busiest and most popular trails in north central Pennsylvania. Once the trail is complete, it will stretch from the Tioga State Forest (*see* page 115) near Wellsboro Junction, through the Tiadaghton State Forest (*see* page 123), to Jersey Shore, a distance of 62 miles.

The 19-mile section that is now open begins on the west side of the Pine Creek Gorge about 1 mile south of Ansonia, and runs south to Rattlesnake Rock, where it shares a parking area with the West Rim Trail (*see* page 119). The old railroad bed has been covered with crushed limestone, providing a good surface for hikers, bikers, and cross-country skiers in the winter. Horses are not permitted on the covered surface, but there is a parallel equestrian trail alongside portions of the Pine Creek Trail.

As the trail runs downstream it passes through state forest land, state park land, and private land as well. For most of its length the trail remains close to Pine Creek, offering good views of both slow-moving stretches of water and rapids. Portions of the trail pass through wooded areas, but for the most part the trail is open and quite sunny. About 3 miles south of the northern trailhead, the Turkey Path descends the gorge's eastern rim from the Leonard Harrison State Park Natural Area (*see* page 80). This is a popular point of access to the Pine Creek Trail, especially for day hikers. Camping is permitted on state forest land with a permit, but hikers need to make sure they're in the state forest and not on private land.

To reach the northern trailhead follow PA Route 6 east from Ansonia to PA Route 362. Follow PA Route 362 south for about 0.25 mile and turn right onto Darling Run Road, which leads to the trailhead. To reach the southern trailhead follow PA Route 414 south from Blackwell for 2 miles to the parking area.

Trail: 19 miles.

Elevation: Varies by only 300 feet.

Degree of difficulty: Easy.

Surface and blaze: Crushed limestone.

WEST RIM TRAIL

[Fig. 21] The West Rim Trail traverses the west rim of the Pine Creek Gorge for 30 miles from Ansonia to Blackwell. Hiking this trail provides some of the most spectacular views in Pennsylvania, but the hiker should be prepared for a strenuous, multiday hike. The trail has been named one of the best trails in Pennsylvania by *Outside Magazine*.

The trail takes the hiker through oak forests and northern hardwoods along the Allegheny Plateau, down into deep ravines cut by streams flowing into Pine Creek, and across wet meadows. The trail contains ten scenic vistas and passes through the Bradley Wales Picnic Area. Parking is located at the northern trailhead, which is just across Colton Road from the forest's headquarters, and at the southern trailhead along PA Route 414 just west of Blackwell. Both trailheads are well marked. In addition, there are several side branches or connecting trails. The trail is limited to foot traffic only; no bikes or motorized vehicles are allowed. Adjoining the northern end of the trail is the Bee Tree Ski Trail. Maps are available from the Tioga State Forest office.

Trail: 30 miles one-way.

Elevation: 900–2,000 feet.

Degree of difficulty: Strenuous.

Surface and blaze: Unpaved with orange blazes. Connecting trails have blue blazes.

REYNOLDS SPRING NATURAL AREA

[Fig. 20] This remote, 1,302-acre area was designated a natural area by the Bureau of Forestry because it contains a diversity of ecosystems. There are stands of oak, aspen, and northern hardwoods and a unique type of wetland called a bog. Sometimes referred to as pine swamps because of the black spruce and tamarack trees that grow along their edge, bogs are acidic wetlands in which decomposition is retarded. The result is a nutrient-poor habitat where plants have to find different sources of nitrogen. Two of the plants in Reynolds Spring find nitrogen in insects. These plants have become carnivorous. One is the northern pitcher plant (*Sarracenia purpurea*), so named because its colorful leaves are vase-shaped. Insects enter the leaves, attracted by the color, but they cannot escape because of the recurved hairs which line the inside of the "pitcher." Exhausted from the fight, the insect falls into the rainwater that has collected inside the bottom of the leaf and drowns.

Slowly, through the action of enzymes secreted by the plant and by bacterial decomposition, the insect is reduced to the elements and nutrients that form it. The pitcher plant then absorbs the nutrients (especially the nitrogen-containing compounds) from the insect soup, thus overcoming the low-nutrient environment of the bog.

The sundew (*Drosera* sp.), another carnivorous plant, takes a slightly different approach to insects. Sticky droplets and hairs cover the stems and leaves of the sundew. Insects careless enough to brush against the plant are trapped. Enzymes within the plant then break down the insect, and the nutrients are absorbed.

These carnivorous plants, and their better-known counterpart the Venus flytrap (*Dionaea mucipula*) that lives in nutrient-poor pinelands in the Carolinas, pay a price for these adaptations. The plants are so specifically designed for this habitat that they can grow nowhere else. And since bogs are rare, so are the plants.

The only developed trail within the area is the Little Morris Trail, a portion of which parallels Morris Run. Hikers on this moderately difficult trail will pass through 1.75 miles of mixed oak forest with a dense understory of mountain laurel. Elevations vary from 1,800 to 2,100 feet. To reach the marked trailhead, follow Gamble Run Road for 6 miles from PA Route 414, 2 miles south of Cedar Run.

Directions: From Cedar Run, take PA Route 414 south for 1 mile to Gamble Run Road and turn right. Drive 7 to 6 miles to the trailhead along Little Morris Run.

Activities: Hiking, hunting, fishing.

Facilities: Trail.

Dates: Open year-round.

Fees: None.

Closest town: Cedar Run, 7.5 miles.

For more information: Tioga State Forest, One Nessmuk Lane, Wellsboro, PA 16901. Phone (717) 724-2868.

ASAPH WILD AREA

[Fig. 20(4)] The Asaph Wild Area is located in the northwestern corner of the Tioga State Forest, about 2.5 miles northwest of Asaph. It has been designated a wild area because of its size—2,070 acres—and its roadless, undeveloped state. Second-growth northern hardwoods and oak have replaced the pine and hemlock forest of the past.

The area contains an interconnected system of maintained trails marked with blue blazes. The trail system, which is composed of old logging roads, runs throughout the Asaph Wild Area and passes around the periphery of its two most prominent features, Cranberry Swamp and Black Ash Swamp.

Cranberry Swamp is a misnomer since the wetland doesn't contain any cranberries although it's likely they were once found there. What it does contain, however, are some wetland plants whose future is in question.

One of the most common groups of hydrophytes, water-loving plants that grow in wetlands, are the sedges. Sedges are easy to identify because they have triangular stems, hence the old adage "Sedges have edges". While most species of sedge are common, biologists with Pennsylvania's Natural Diversity Inventory have designated some of the sedges in Cranberry Swamp as Species of Special Concern. This designation means the sedges are either rare, endangered, or scientists haven't encountered them enough to know how common they are.

Located at the northern end of the Asaph Wild Area is the Black Ash Swamp Natural Area. The swamp is the product of an animal whose ability to modify its habitat is rivaled only by man. The wetland was formed when beaver moved into the area around the headwaters of Right Asaph Run and flooded the area to make it easier to move tree limbs back to their lodge. Eventually the beaver moved on, leaving the newly created wetland behind.

Over time the flooded area began to dry out and parts of the wetland began to develop into a meadow. This process, where one ecosystem evolves into another, is called succession. This successional beaver meadow was one of the reasons that the Black Ash Swamp was designated a natural area. Recently, however, beaver have moved back into the area, and the area is once again a wetland. A hike along the Cross Trail takes the visitor below the beaver dam and along the periphery of Cranberry Swamp. To reach the trailhead, travel north on Asaph Road from the village of Asaph and bear right onto Right Asaph Road. The trailhead is located 0.5 to 0.75 mile north of the intersection with Sand Road.

While remote, the Aspah Wild Area is user friendly. Located just a few minutes by car from the village of Ansonia and Pennsylvania's Grand Canyon, there is a state forest picnic area adjacent to the wild area. The Middle Ridge Trail, a 3-mile-long trail, begins at the picnic area and ends at the Cross Trail near the edge of Black Ash Swamp.

Directions: From US Route 6 in Ansonia travel 2 miles north to Aspah. From there take Asaph Road to the picnic area.

Activities: Hiking, hunting, fishing.

Facilities: Trails, picnic and camping area adjacent.

Dates: Open year-round.

Fees: None.

Closest town: Aspah, 2 miles.

For more information: Tioga State Forest, One Nessmuk Lane, PA Route 287 South, Wellsboro, PA 16901. Phone (717) 724-2868.

Tiadaghton State Forest

Tiadaghton State Forest is made up of three blocks: South Block, West Block, and East Block.

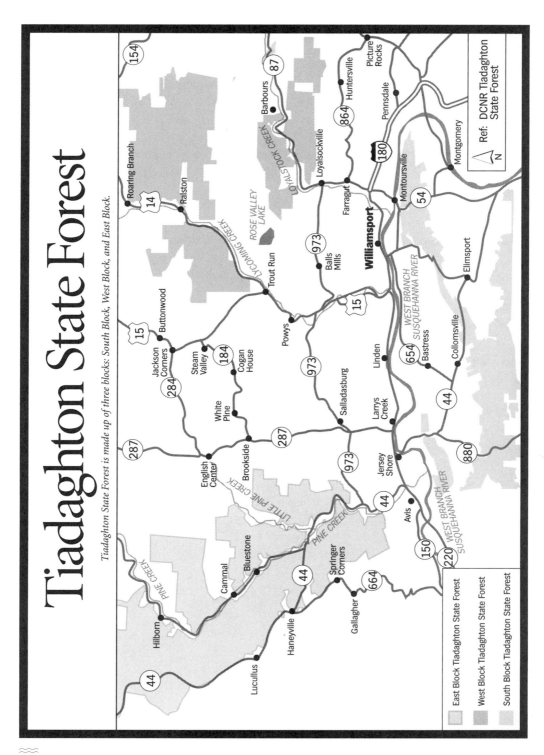

Tiadaghton State Forest

[Fig. 22] Tiadaghton State Forest contains 214,973 acres of woodland located primarily in Lycoming County. The forest is broken into three distinct tracts of land: the East and West blocks which lie on the Allegheny High Plateau and the South Block which lies within the Valley and Ridge physiographic province.

The West Block, which is the largest of the three, lies along both sides of Pine Creek Valley. Pine Creek, which the Iroquois Indians called Tiadaghton, is the largest tributary of the West Branch of the Susquehanna River. This West Block is part of an area once known as the Black Forest of Pennsylvania, which was 750,000 acres of pine and hemlock forest. Today it is dominated by second-growth oak forests mixed with small stands of northern hardwoods.

Located at the northwest corner of Lycoming County, the West Block contains some of the most remote and rugged forestland in Pennsylvania. Special protection areas include the Wolf Run Wild Area, Algerine Wild Area, Algerine Swamp Natural Area, Miller Run Natural Area, and the Bark Cabin Natural Area. The latter has been designated a natural area to preserve a 7-acre tract of old-growth hemlock. Also found here are Upper Pine Bottom and Little Pine state parks.

The forest's East Block is also located on the Allegheny High Plateau. European settlers in this part of Lycoming County were greeted by a northern hardwood forest, dominated by beech, birch, and maple. Today the forest is composed primarily of second-growth northern hardwoods in the north and oak in the south. Like most of the Allegheny Plateau, the East Block is a rolling plateau with deeply cut stream channels.

Numerous hiking and cross-country ski trails run through the East Block. Two special protection areas, the McIntyre Wild Area and the Devils Elbow Natural Area, are found here. The two major waterways are Loyalsock Creek, which is paralleled by PA Route 87, and Lycoming Creek, which is paralleled by PA Route 14.

The Devil's Elbow Natural Area is a 403-acre tract of land located in the northeastern corner of the Tiadaghton State Forest. The parcel was designated a natural area because it contains a bog. Found here are pitcher plants, round-leaved sundew, cottongrass, and other plants adapted to life in this acidic, nutrient-poor wetland. There are no trails within the area, but the Sand Spring Trail, a loop of the Hawkeye Cross Country Ski Trails, circles around it. For information on these trails, contact the state forest office.

Since it is located in the Valley and Ridge province, the South Block of the forest is very different geologically from the other two blocks. The Valley and Ridge province is composed of parallel, tree-covered ridges interspersed with valleys containing farms and towns. This part of the Tiadaghton State Forest is composed of portions of White Deer Ridge and Bald Eagle Mountain. Given their close proximity to developed areas, these ridges see heavy recreational use. This area was originally a pine-hemlock forest, but today it is primarily a mixed-oak ecosystem.

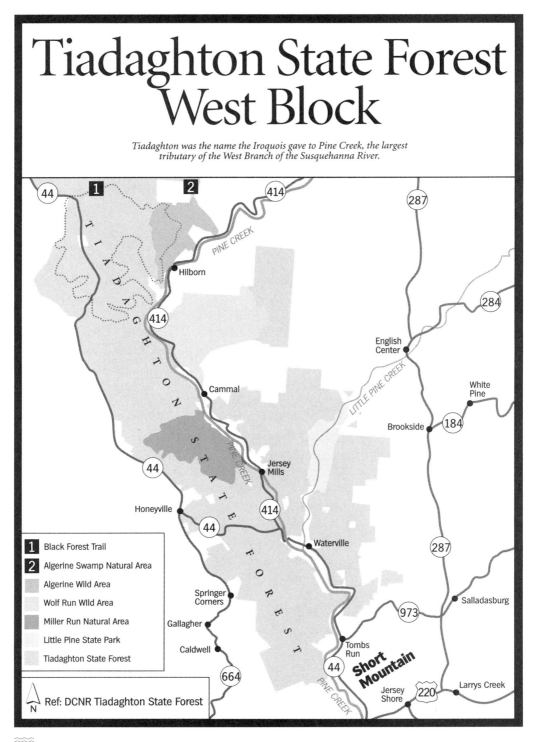

Tiadaghton State Forest West Block

Tiadaghton was the name the Iroquois gave to Pine Creek, the largest tributary of the West Branch of the Susquehanna River.

1 Black Forest Trail
2 Algerine Swamp Natural Area
Algerine Wild Area
Wolf Run Wild Area
Miller Run Natural Area
Little Pine State Park
Tiadaghton State Forest

N
Ref: DCNR Tiadaghton State Forest

There are several scenic vistas within the South Block. One that is especially breath-taking is located on PA Route 15 about 2 miles south of Williamsport. From this vantage point on Bald Eagle Mountain, you look down on the towns of Williamsport and Mon-toursville and across the West Branch of the Susquehanna River. In the distance you can see the East Block of the Tiadaghton State Forest on the Allegheny High Plateau.

As with many of Pennsylvania's state forests, the land which is now the Tiadagh-ton was purchased in pieces from big lumber companies after they had clear-cut the area. Fires were widespread during the 1890s and early 1900s, primarily due to all of the dead wood and slash left behind by loggers. About 25 percent of today's Tiadagh-ton is considered noncommercial forest, due either to inaccessible terrain or poor soil fertility resulting from the fires of nearly 100 years ago.

The Tiadaghton State Forest contains 100 miles of trails and 330 miles of state forest roads. Most of these facilities, as well as numerous picnic and camping areas, were constructed by the Civilian Conservation Corps during the late 1930s and early 1940s. The forest is managed for multiple uses, mainly logging and recreation. In recent years, the recreational opportunities have been expanding with the develop-ment of new trails and the designation of 17,000 acres of wild areas and 4,500 acres of natural areas.

Directions: On Route 15 South in Williamsport, cross the Susquehanna River. Go to the second traffic light, turn east and go 4 blocks. The forest office is on the north side of the road.

Activities: Hiking, cross-country skiing, hunting, fishing.

Facilities: Hiking trails, cross-country ski trails.

Dates: Open year-round.

Fees: None.

Closest town: South Williamsport, 1 mile.

For more information: Tiadaghton State Forest, 423 E. Central Avenue, South Williamsport, PA 17701. Phone (717) 327-3450.

West Block of Tiadaghton State Forest

▒ ALGERINE WILD AREA

[Fig. 23] The Algerine Wild Area encompasses 3,700 acres of topographically diverse woodland. The area is located in the north end of the West Block, and it borders Pine Creek in several places. Elevations vary from 2,000 feet on the plateau to 900 feet where Gamble Run flows into Pine Creek. Several small trails pass through the area, including the Jack Herrit, Red Ridge, Putt Hollow, Algerine, and Huckleber-ry trails. The largest trail to pass through the area is a portion of the Black Forest Trail (*see* page 126). Many of these trails are suitable for cross-country skiing.

In addition to hiking and cross-country skiing, hunting and fishing are popular activities. Native brook, rainbow, and brown trout can be caught in Slate Run, which is restricted to fly-fishing.

Directions: Take PA Route 44 north from US Route 220 west of Jersey Shore. At the junction with PA Route 414, travel north on PA 414 for approximately 15 miles.

Activities: Hiking, hunting, fishing, cross-country skiing.

Facilities: Trails.

Dates: Open year-round.

Fees: None.

Closest town: Slate Run, less than 0.25 mile.

For more information: Tiadaghton State Forest, 423 E. Central Avenue, South Williamsport, PA 17701. Phone (717) 327-3450.

BLACK FOREST TRAIL

[Fig. 23(1)] Old railroad grades and roads, a legacy of the logging era, have been combined to form the Black Forest Trail. The 42-mile loop begins and ends in the Algerine Wild Area, rising and falling as it climbs in and out of stream valleys cut into the Allegheny Plateau. The trail is named after the vast pine and hemlock forest that grew here before the area was clear-cut during the last half of the eighteenth century.

There are several scenic vistas along the path, and there are side loops suitable for cross-country skiing or hiking that serve as connections with the Susquehannock Trail System (*see* page 99). While the trail is challenging and steep in areas, it is heavily used, and hikers are not likely to be alone. The trailhead is located adjacent to a forest road just across Pine Creek from Slate Run. Trail maps and patches are available from the Tiadaghton Forest Fighters Association.

Trail: 42-mile loop.

Elevation: 900–2,000 feet.

Degree of difficulty: Moderate to strenuous.

Surface and blaze: Unpaved. Orange circles.

For more information: Tiadaghton Forest Fighters Association, PO Box 5091, S. Williamsport, PA 17701.

TEABERRY

(Gaultheria procumbens)
Because of its wintergreen flavor, this is used in teas, candies, medicines, and chewing gum.

ALGERINE SWAMP NATURAL AREA

[Fig. 23(2)] The Algerine Swamp Natural Area is located north of the Algerine Wild Area, and it encompasses 84 acres of land on both sides of the Lycoming County/ Tioga County border. The focal point of the area is a glacial bog.

Glacial bogs were formed during the last ice age when retreating glaciers left chunks of ice and meltwater behind in deep depressions. These wetlands can be thought of as giant puddles of icy-cold water that are covered with a lid of peat, which is partially decomposed sphagnum moss. In most places the peat is several feet thick, and as you walk across the bog, the ground seems to tremble or quake, hence the common name, quaking bog.

The Algerine bog, like all bogs, is a nutrient-poor environment due to its high acidity and arrested decomposition. The plants that grow here are adapted to these conditions and aren't found in any other habitats. Here you'll see carnivorous plants, like sundew and pitcher plants, and Labrador tea (*Ledum groenlandicum*), a shrub with thick leathery leaves. Growing near the edges of the bog are black spruce and balsam fir. Beware of the open water areas where you'll find rushes and sedges growing. The peat blanket here is thin, and you could fall through into the icy-cold water below. A portion of the bog is on private land, and visitors are encouraged to stay within the state forest's boundaries.

Directions: From the intersection of US Route 220 and PA Route 44, just west of Jersey Shore, follow PA 44 north through the Pine Creek Gorge for about 12 miles to Gamble Run Road. Turn left on Gamble Run Road and drive about 2.5 miles. The Algerine Swamp Natural Area is on the left.

Activities: Hiking, hunting, fishing.

Facilities: Trails.

Dates: Open year-round.

Fees: None.

Closest town: Slate Run, 4.5 miles.

For more information: Tiadaghton State Forest, 423 E. Central Avenue, South Williamsport, PA 17701. Phone (717) 327-3450.

MILLER RUN NATURAL AREA

[Fig. 23] The Miller Run Natural Area is an oak and northern hardwood forest encompassing 4,000 acres to the west of Pine Creek. While it was designated a natural area because it is remote, secluded, and roadless, it still offers some recreational opportunities.

Five streams, tributaries of Pine Creek, flow through the area. Over the centuries the streams have cut deep valleys within the plateau, making for spectacular scenery. Two scenic vistas look over deep stream cuts. At the southern end of the natural area is a vista which looks over the McClure Run stream valley. To reach the vista, turn left on Sinking Springs Road from PA Route 414 about 3 miles north of the intersection of PA Routes 44 and 414 (*see* directions to Algerine Wild Area, page 126). Travel about 2 miles to Sinking Springs Spur Road. The vista is at the end of this marked road, and parking is available. At the northern end of the forest along Lebo Road is a vista which gives a spectacular view of the Pine Creek valley. Travel 3 to 3.5 miles north of Haneyville on PA Route 44, and follow Lebo Road to its terminus.

These streams are home to native trout. Trout fishermen are drawn to Solomon Run, which is home to large native brook trout. The easiest way to reach the stream is from the Solomon Run Trail. This steep trail has a trailhead on Browns Run Road.

In addition to fishing, hiking and hunting are popular within the Miller Run Natural Area. Hikers and hunters can gain access to the area via seven trails: McClure Run, McClure, Shanty Point, Solomon, Green, Twin Pines, and Sam Carson. Additionally, a portion of the Pitch Pine Trail runs through the area. This trail is used by experienced cross-country skiers and can be accessed from PA Route 44, which runs along the western border of the natural area.

Directions: From Lock Haven travel north along PA Route 664 for approximately 16 miles to Browns Run Road. Turn right onto Browns Run Road. There are two access points off of this road.

Activities: Hiking, hunting, fishing.

Facilities: Trails, scenic vistas.

Dates: Open year-round.

Fees: None.

Closest town: Haneyville, 2 miles.

For more information: Tiadaghton State Forest, 423 E. Central Avenue, South Williamsport, PA 17701. Phone (717) 327-3450.

WOODCHUCK

(Marmota monax)
Also known as the groundhog, the woodchuck hibernates in its burrow until late winter, and usually does not emerge on February 2, as popularly believed, to look for its shadow.

▨ WOLF RUN WILD AREA

[Fig. 23] One of the most remote areas within the Tiadaghton State Forest, the Wolf Run Wild Area contains 6,900 acres of rugged woodland. From its highest point at 2,000 feet, the land drops to 800 feet along Pine Creek which borders the west end of the area.

The entire area is open to hunting, within the seasonal limitations set by the Pennsylvania Game Commission. Fishermen will find native trout in Wolf Run, Mill Run, and Bonnell Run. Hunters, fishermen, and hikers can gain access to the forest through a series of short, unnamed, interconnected trails with trailheads along Silver Springs and Barrens roads. Another point of access is the Cammal Trail, with a trailhead along PA Route 414 just north of the village of Cammal. Two major trails also pass through the area. A portion of the Mid State Trail, which is 171 miles long, passes through the eastern part of the Wolf Run Wild Area (see Mid State Trail, page 275). The most popular trail in the western half of the area is the Golden Eagle Trail.

The Golden Eagle Trail is one of the most beautiful day hikes in Pennsylvania. The trail, which is marked with orange paint blazes, is an 8.6-mile loop that begins at a parking area along PA Route 414. Along its course it offers scenic views of Wolf Run and Pine Creek. It travels into deep stream cuts, past a waterfall, and into a state gameland managed by the Pennsylvania Game Commission. The Golden Eagle Trail traverses rugged terrain, and its entire length should only be tackled by hikers in good physical condition.

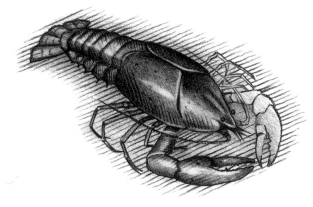

EASTERN CRAYFISH
(Cambarus bartonii)

Directions: To reach the Golden Eagle Trail, take PA Route 44 north from US Route 220 west of Jersey Shore. At the junction with PA Route 414, travel north on PA 414 for approximately 8 miles. A parking area and sign are located about 2 miles north of Cammal.

Activities: Hiking, hunting, fishing.

Facilities: Trails.

Dates: Open year-round.

Fees: None.

Closest town: Cammal, less than 1 mile.

For more information: Tiadaghton State Forest, 423 E. Central Avenue, South Williamsport, PA 17701. Phone (717) 327-3450.

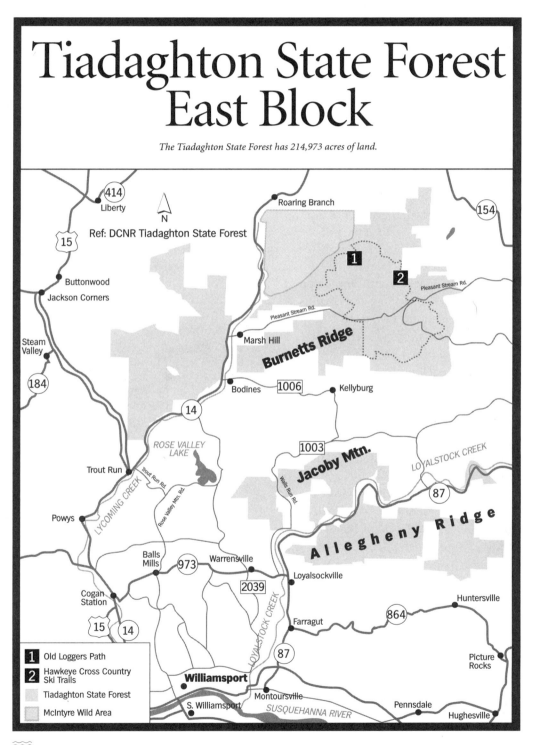

Tiadaghton State Forest East Block

The Tiadaghton State Forest has 214,973 acres of land.

Ref: DCNR Tiadaghton State Forest

N

414 Liberty

154

15

Roaring Branch

1 (Old Loggers Path)

2

Pleasant Stream Rd.

Buttonwood

Jackson Corners

Pleasant Stream Rd.

Marsh Hill

Burnetts Ridge

Steam Valley

184

Bodines 1006 Kellyburg

14

ROSE VALLEY LAKE

1003

Jacoby Mtn.

LOYALSTOCK CREEK

Trout Run

Trout Run Rd.

Rose Valley Mtn. Rd.

Wells Run Rd.

87

Powys

Allegheny Ridge

Balls Mills 973 Warrensville

Loyalsockville

2039

Cogan Station

LOYALSTOCK CREEK

Farragut

864

Huntersville

15 14

87

Picture Rocks

Williamsport

Montoursville

Pennsdale

S. Williamsport

SUSQUEHANNA RIVER

Hughesville

1 Old Loggers Path
2 Hawkeye Cross Country Ski Trails
 Tiadaghton State Forest
 McIntyre Wild Area

East Block of Tiadaghton State Forest

MCINTYRE WILD AREA

[Fig. 24] The McIntyre Wild Area is a 7,500-acre woodland tract located in northeastern Lycoming County, east of Ralston, along PA Route 14. Designated a wild area because of its size and remoteness, hunting, fishing, and hiking are the primary recreational uses for this area. The area contains an abundance of streams that begin as wetlands on the plateau and slice their way through the rock as they journey to Lycoming Creek. Waterfalls are common throughout the area. One of the streams, Rock Run, is stocked with trout every year by the Pennsylvania Fish and Boat Commission.

In addition to peace, solitude, and magnificent scenery, hikers will also find remnants of a nineteenth-century coal mining town. There is a series of interconnected, unnamed trails which run through a portion of the McIntyre Wild Area.

Directions: From the intersection of US Route 15 and PA Route 14, follow Route 14 north to Ralston. Turn right onto Rock Run Road and cross Lycoming Creek. Turn left onto McIntyre Road, which leads into the wild area.

Activities: Hiking, hunting, fishing.

Facilities: Trails.

Dates: Open year-round.

Fees: None.

Closest town: Ralston, 1 mile.

For more information: Tiadaghton State Forest, 423 E. Central Avenue, South Williamsport, PA 17701. Phone (717) 327-3450.

OLD LOGGERS PATH AND HAWKEYE CROSS-COUNTRY SKI TRAILS

[Fig. 24(1), Fig. 24(2)] The Old Loggers Path is an assemblage of old logging trails and railroad grades constructed by the Central Pennsylvania Lumber Company during the logging boom of the 1800s. The path is a 27-mile trail with a series of attached loops and connectors that make up the Hawkeye Cross-Country Ski Trail System. The trails pass through the valleys of Rock Run and Pleasant Stream and are primarily wooded. There are several vistas along the path which look over stream valleys, adjacent private lands, and the McIntyre Wild Area.

While there are several parking areas with access to the trail, the only winter access is just past the stop sign in Masten, a logging ghost town that today is home to private hunting clubs.

Trail: 27-mile loop.

Elevation: 1,400–2,000 feet.

Degree of difficulty: Moderate.

Surface and blaze: Unpaved. Old Loggers Path and ski trails marked with orange rectangles. Connector trails marked with blue blazes.

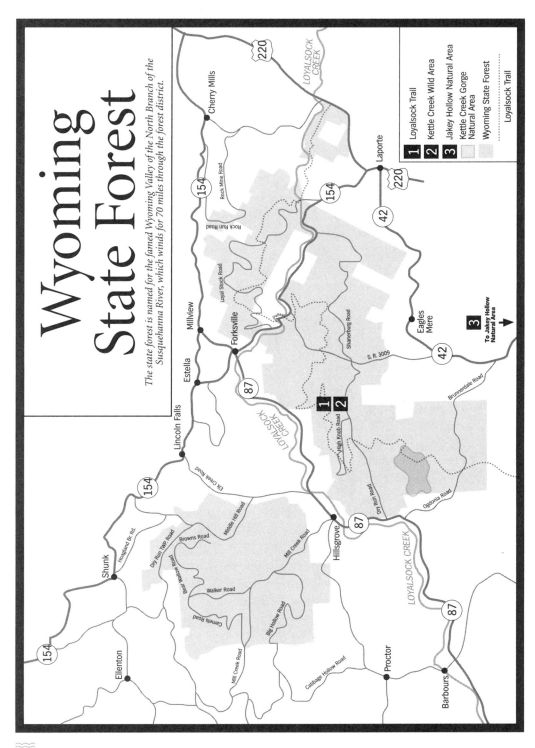

Wyoming State Forest

The state forest is named for the famed Wyoming Valley of the North Branch of the Susquehanna River, which winds for 70 miles through the forest district.

Legend
1 Loyalsock Trail
2 Kettle Creek Wild Area
3 Jakey Hollow Natural Area
Kettle Creek Gorge Natural Area
Wyoming State Forest
Loyalsock Trail

Wyoming State Forest

[Fig. 25] The Wyoming State Forest encompasses 42,000 acres of mixed hardwoods in an area known as the Endless Mountains of northeastern Pennsylvania. The forest is almost completely contained within western Sullivan County, and it contains high plateaus and ridges dissected by deep stream valleys. Slicing through the center of the forest is Loyalsock Creek, a tributary of the North Branch of the Susquehanna River.

One hundred years ago this part of the Allegheny High Plateau was blanketed with a dense forest dominated by white pine and hemlock intermixed with smaller numbers of sugar maple, birch, and beech. During the early part of the twentieth century this untapped economic resource caught the eye of lumber companies, and by the mid-1920s nearly every tree was gone. Shortly thereafter the state of Pennsylvania began purchasing the land, including nearly 37,000 acres from the Central Pennsylvania Lumber Company, to form the Wyoming State Forest.

Today the forest contains a mixture of even-aged northern hardwoods including maple, cherry, ash, and beech. A large component of the forest is black cherry, the most economically valuable tree growing in Pennsylvania. Because black cherry is shade intolerant, it couldn't grow beneath the dense pine canopy. This mainstay of today's Pennsylvania lumber industry, therefore, is a direct result of the clear-cutting of 70 years ago.

This vast tract of relatively undeveloped forestland is a sportsman's paradise. Loyalsock Creek and its tributaries provide more than 50 miles of trout streams, and four of the tributaries, Ketchum Run, Kettle Creek, Noon Branch, and Shanerburg Run, are all designated Exceptional Value Streams because of their pristine water quality. There are also two mountaintop ponds that have been designated by the Pennsylvania Fish and Boat Commission as State Forest Fishing Areas. Sones Pond and Bear Wallow Pond both feature a gravel boat ramp and have restrooms and picnic areas. Sones Pond can be reached by following PA Route 154 north from Laporte for about 2 miles to Rock Run Road. Turn right and watch for the sign. To reach Bear Wallow Pond follow Mill Creek Road north from Hillsgrove for 3.3 miles. Turn right onto Camels Road and follow it for about 1.3 miles to Bear Wallow Road. Turn right and watch for the sign. The entire forest is also open to hunting, and white-tailed deer, turkey, and black bear are all common here.

There are four special management areas located within the Wyoming State Forest. Near the southwestern corner of the forest are the Kettle Creek Wild Area and Kettle Creek Gorge Natural Area (see page 134), which contain a remote stretch of the Kettle Creek Gorge. South of the state forest is a small, isolated tract of land called Jakey Hollow Natural Area (see page 136), which contains a stand of old-growth trees.

The newest natural area within the Wyoming State Forest is the Tamarack Run Natural Area. This 234-acre parcel is located along Loyalsock Road about 8 miles northeast of Worlds End State Park (see page 74). Found within the natural area is a complex of boreal conifer wetlands, better known as bogs, which are more typical of areas much farther north in Canada. There are no designated trails within the natural area, but the Sones Trail and Rock Run Trail, both with trailheads along Rock Run Road, border it. Since the area contains several rare wetland plant species, and also because the bog habitat is very fragile, visitors to the area are asked to stay on the dry upland areas.

The Wyoming State Forest contains an extensive trail network. There are 40 hiking trails traversing 75 miles, 20 miles of cross-country ski trails, and 55 miles of roads that have been designated as joint-use areas for automobiles and snowmobiles. While there are trailheads throughout the forest, one of the most popular starting points is located near the intersection of High Knob Road and State Route 3009, about 3 miles north of Eagles Mere. Located here is a parking area, restrooms, and trailheads for snowmobiling, hiking, cross-country skiing, and horseback riding.

One of the forests's most popular hiking trails begins here. The Fern Rock Nature Trail is a 2-mile-long interpretive trail that only takes about two hours to hike. There are 31 numbered stations along the trail that indicate interesting natural features. Picking up a trail brochure from the forest office will help you identify these natural features. The trail passes a swamp and beaver dams and crosses old logging roads. At the north end of the loop, the trail runs along a small stretch of Ketchum Run, a native trout stream. For those not wanting to hike the entire loop, there is a shortcut that cuts the hike in half. The trail, which is marked with orange circles containing the letters FR, is rough in spots and so is moderately challenging.

About 4 miles to the west of the parking area along High Knob Road is the park's best-known scenic vista, High Knob. From here visitors can look over the Loyalsock Creek valley and portions of Sullivan and Lycoming counties. Running from High Knob down to the forest headquarters building is the High Knob Trail. This steep, rocky trail passes through a mixed hardwood forest that is home to turkey, white-tailed deer, and black bear.

Directions: Follow PA Route 87 south from Hillsgrove for about 1.6 miles. Turn left onto Dry Run Road and the forest headquarters is on the right.

Activities: Hiking, hunting, fishing, horseback riding, snowmobiling, cross-country skiing. Primitive camping permitted with permit from forest headquarters.

Facilities: Trails, scenic overlooks, boat launching possible for fishing.

Dates: Open year-round.

Fees: None.

Closest town: Hillsgrove, 1.6 miles.

For more information: Wyoming State Forest, RR 2, Box 47, Bloomsburg, PA 17815. Phone (717) 387-4255.

▓ KETTLE CREEK WILD AREA AND KETTLE CREEK GORGE NATURAL AREA

[Fig. 25(2)] The Kettle Creek Wild Area is a remote 2,582-acre woodland centered around Kettle Creek valley about 3 miles southeast of Hillsgrove. It has been designated a wild area because of its vast, roadless, undeveloped nature. The forest is primarily second-growth northern hardwood, but there are small enclaves of oak and aspen found on the south-facing slopes. The most prominent natural features are Kettle Creek and the Kettle Creek Gorge with its cliffs and talus slopes. There are several hiking trails that lead into the area, including the Loyalsock Trail (*see* page 136). About 3.25 miles of this 59-mile trail winds through the wild area.

The Loyalsock Trail also passes through the Kettle Creek Gorge Natural Area. The natural area encompasses 754 acres of the Kettle Creek Wild Area and includes a 1.5-mile stretch of the gorge. It has been designated a natural area to ensure that this pristine Wilderness Trout Stream and associated watershed retain their remote, unspoiled character. The cliffs and rocky slopes along the 900-foot-deep gorge are known to be home to the rare timber rattlesnake and are suspected to contain the endangered Allegheny woodrat. The natural area has also been designated a special protection area for reptiles and amphibians. Other than the Loyalsock Trail, there are no trails within the natural area.

Directions: To get to the Kettle Creek Gorge Natural Area follow Dry Run Road east from the park for about 3 miles to the Loyalsock Trail. Hike the trail south for about 2 miles into the natural area.

Activities: Hiking, hunting, stream fishing.

Dates: Open year-round.

Fees: None.

Closest town: Hillsgrove, 4.6 miles.

For more information: Wyoming State Forest, RR 2, Box 47, Bloomsburg, PA 17815. Phone (717) 387-4255.

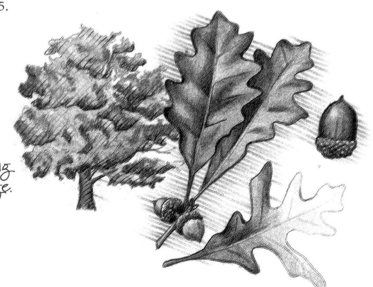

WHITE OAK
(Quercus alba)
The leaves on a single oak tree may have different shapes, making identification a challenge. White oak leaves have deep or shallow clefts between lobes.

▨ JAKEY HOLLOW NATURAL AREA

[Fig. 25(3)] Tucked away along a small, unnamed tributary of Little Fishing Creek in Columbia County, is an isolated piece of the Wyoming State Forest called the Jakey Hollow Natural Area. The Commonwealth of Pennsylvania purchased this 58-acre parcel of land in 1990 for a little more than $1,000 per acre, a small price to pay for such a special place. The lower part of the hollow contains a second-growth forest dominated by assorted hardwoods, oaks, and hemlock. Near the upper end, however, lies one of the most unique stands of virgin trees in Pennsylvania. While nearly all of the surviving enclaves of virgin timber in the state contain only white pine and hemlock, Jakey Hollow also contains virgin beech, cherry, gum, and maple. The young trees in this diminutive 10-acre stand are already a century old. The oldest are estimated to be more than 300 years old and tower more than 125 feet above the forest floor. There are no trails within the Jakey Hollow Natural Area.

Directions: To reach Jakey Hollow follow PA Route 42 north from Exit 34 off Interstate 80 for about 3 miles. A sign on the right marks the natural area.

Activities: Hiking.

Facilities: None.

Dates: Open year-round.

Fees: None.

Closest town: Bloomsburg, 4 miles.

For more information: Wyoming State Forest, RR 2, Box 47, Bloomsburg, PA 17815. Phone (717) 387-4255.

LOYALSOCK TRAIL

[Fig. 25(1)] The Loyalsock Trail is a rugged wilderness trail that parallels Loyalsock Creek as it winds its way from the Wyoming State Forest in Sullivan County to the Tiadaghton State Forest in Lycoming County. The trail is 59.3 miles long, but there is road access every 4 to 10 miles, making day hikes possible. Backpackers tackling the entire trail can camp on state forest land but should first obtain a camping permit.

The trail begins in the west near Montoursville, about 10 miles north of the point

RIVER OTTER (Lutra canadensis)
Sociable animals, river otters wrestle, play tag, and roll around riverbanks and in water. Their streamlined bodies, webbed toes, and eyes and ears that can be closed underwater make them well suited for life in and around water.

Reintroduction of the River Otter

At one time the river otter (*Lutra canadensis*), Pennsylvania's largest member of the weasel family, was found throughout the mountains of Pennsylvania. By the turn of the century, however, it was nearly gone, a victim of habitat loss, trapping, and water pollution. In 1983, when the Pennsylvania Game Commission began a reintroduction program, the otter's Pennsylvania range was limited to the Pocono Plateau. A total of 105 otters were released across the state. In western Pennsylvania they are now found in Tionesta Creek, the Allegheny River, and the Youghiogheny River. In the north-central and northeastern part of the state they have been released in Kettle Creek, Pine Creek, and Loyalsock Creek.

The otter is supremely adapted to its aquatic habitat with its webbed feet and a large muscular tail that acts as a rudder and propels it through the water. As it paddles its way through its riverine environment it feeds on fish, frogs, crayfish, and assorted aquatic invertebrates. Contrary to what many anglers may think, they don't routinely eat gamefish, preferring the easier-to-catch minnows and suckers. River otters are social animals and the family lives together year-round. Because they are large animals, weighing as much as 25 pounds, they have relatively large territories. Each adult otter requires about 5 miles of stream.

where Loyalsock Creek flows into the Susquehanna River. The trail serpentines its way through the southern portion of the Tiadaghton State Forest before turning north into Sullivan County and into the Wyoming State Forest. It is the only trail passing through the Kettle Creek Gorge Natural Area (*see* page 134), and it also passes near High Knob before entering the Worlds End State Park (*see* page 74). The trail reaches its eastern terminus along Route 220 north of Laporte.

Along much of its route the trail follows footpaths, old logging roads, and former railroad grades within the Loyalsock Creek watershed. The trail varies in difficulty from level wooded stretches to steep rocky areas that pass along cliffs and crevasses. Just as varied are the ecosystems it passes through, from deep hardwood forests, to rhododendron thickets, to rocky slopes.

To reach the western trailhead follow PA Route 220 north from Laporte for about 3 miles to the trailhead, which is on the left. The eastern trailhead can be reached by following PA Route 87 north for 10 miles from Montoursville. A sign marks the trailhead. There is also a trailhead within Worlds End State Park (*see* page 74). A pocket-size trail guide and maps are available from the Williamsport Alpine Club, PO Box 501, Williamsport, PA 17703.

Trail: 59 miles one-way.

Degree of difficulty: Easy to difficult.

Surface and blaze: Unpaved, yellow rectangles with horizontal red stripe.

Allegheny Mountain, Glaciated Low, & Pocono Plateaus

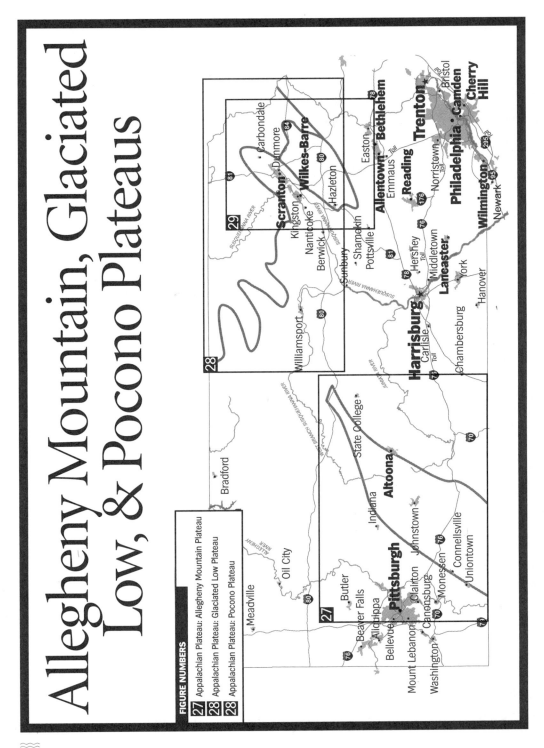

FIGURE NUMBERS

27 Appalachian Plateau: Allegheny Mountain Plateau
28 Appalachian Plateau: Glaciated Low Plateau
28 Appalachian Plateau: Pocono Plateau

Appalachian Plateau: Allegheny Mountain, Glaciated Low, & Pocono Plateaus

The Allegheny Mountain Section is a broad plateau that rises in elevation from west to east. The section is bounded on the west by the Pittsburgh Plateau Section, on the east by the Valley and Ridge province, and on the south by West Virginia and Maryland. While the largest town within the section is Johnstown, with a population of less than 30,000, many of the public lands within the section are heavily used by residents of Pittsburgh, less than 20 miles away. All or part of Centre, Blair, Clearfield, Cambria, Indiana, Westmoreland, Somerset, and Fayette counties are located here.

The Allegheny Mountain Section is crossed by innumerable small streams that feed three rivers which cross the plateau: the Youghiogheny River, the Conemaugh River, and the Casselman River. As each of these rivers flow to the Ohio River they have cut deep gorges into the underlying sandstone. Where they cross the higher

[*Above:* Ohiopyle Falls in Ohiopyle State Park in Fayette County]

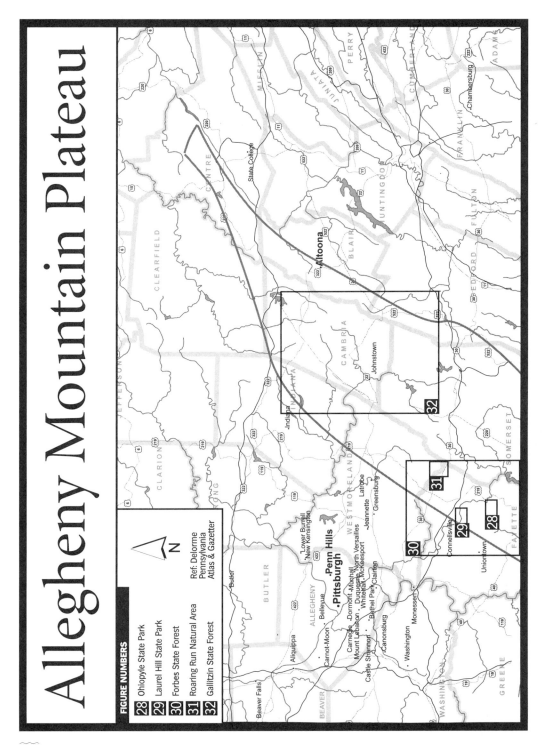

Allegheny Mountain Plateau

FIGURE NUMBERS

28 Ohiopyle State Park
29 Laurel Hill State Park
30 Forbes State Forest
31 Roaring Run Natural Area
32 Gallitzin State Forest

Ref: Delorme
Pennsylvania
Atlas & Gazetter

N

ridges at the east end of the province, spectacular water gaps, some nearly 1,000 feet deep, have developed. Many of the streams and rivers pass through areas of mixed sandstone and shale, which erode at different rates. The result is numerous waterfalls and rapids.

There are several prominent topographic features within the section. The eastern border of the Allegheny Mountain Section forms the boundary between the Allegheny Plateau province and the Valley and Ridge province. A steep escarpment of 2,395 feet to 2,887 feet called the Allegheny Front marks the boundary. The front reaches its highest point in Bedford County at Blue Knob with an elevation of 3,150 feet, the second highest point in Pennsylvania.

Lying to the west of the Allegheny Front are three parallel ridges running southwest/northeast. Closest to the front lies Negro Mountain, which reaches an elevation of 3,213 feet at Mount Davis, the highest point in Pennsylvania. Laurel Ridge lies west of Negro Mountain and rises to 2,799 feet. The westernmost ridge is Chestnut Ridge rising to 2,779 feet.

As with most of Pennsylvania, the Allegheny Mountain Section was completely logged from the late 1800s to the early 1900s. Coal mining has also shaped the area. Both activities continue today.

The major east-west roadways within the Allegheny Mountain Section are US Route 22 and Interstate 76. The latter is better known as the Pennsylvania Turnpike, the oldest toll road in the United States. The only major north-south roadway in this section is US Route 219.

MAYFLY
(Order Ephemeroptera)
The translation of the mayfly's Latin name is "living a day." Adult mayflies metamorphized from naiads, emerging from the water to mate in mid-air.

Females lay eggs within the hour. All adult mayflies lack mouthparts to feed and as a result die soon after mating.

Ohiopyle State Park

Located primarily in Fayette County, Ohiopyle State Park encompasses approximately 19,046 acres of rugged natural beauty and serves as the gateway to the Laurel Mountains.

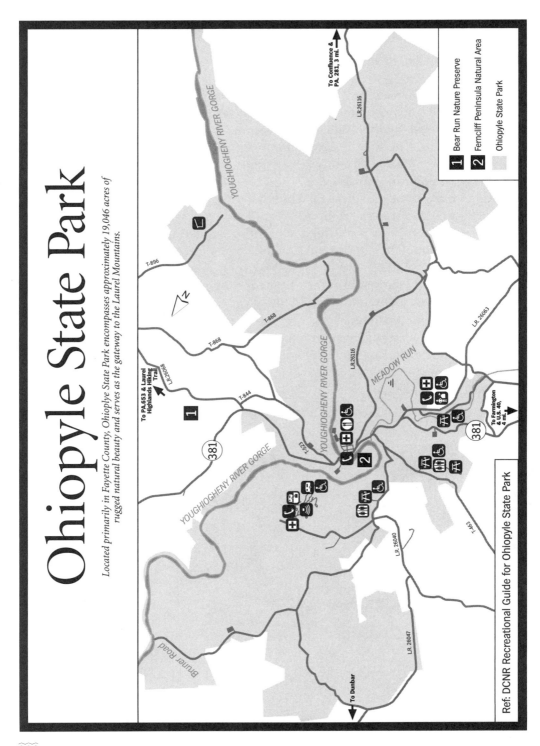

Legend:
1 Bear Run Nature Preserve
2 Ferncliff Peninsula Natural Area
Ohiopyle State Park

YOUGHIOGHENY RIVER GORGE

MEADOW RUN

To Confluence & PA. 281, 3 mi.

To Farmington & U.S. 40, 4 mi.

To Dunbar

To PA.653 & Laurel Highlands Hiking Trail

Bruner Road

Ref: DCNR Recreational Guide for Ohiopyle State Park

State Parks

▓ OHIOPYLE STATE PARK

The year was 1754. Two European countries were vying for the land that is today Canada and the United States. The British had a stronghold on the eastern part of the U.S., from New England through Virginia and points south. The French held much of eastern Canada.

A great treasure lay to the west, stretching from western Pennsylvania to the Pacific Coast. The French decided that the best way to prevent British expansion to the west was a line of forts stretching from Canada to southwestern Pennsylvania. Key among these was Fort Duquesne, which stood at the confluence of the Monongahela and Allegheny rivers at what is today Pittsburgh. Where these two rivers met, a mighty third river, the Ohio, was born. The Ohio River was the gateway to the entire Mississippi River drainage basin, and the country that controlled this waterway held the key to the west.

Recognizing this, a British expeditionary force led by 21-year-old George Washington traveled from Virginia to capture Fort Duquesne. Washington decided to take his force up the Youghiogheny River (pronounced yock-a-gainey), which meets the Monongahela River a short distance south of Pittsburgh. His river journey ended when he encountered the Youghiogheny's Ohiopyle Falls.

Washington then took his forces over land and continued on to Fort Duquesne. His attempt to capture the fort was unsuccessful and marked one of the earliest battles of the French and Indian War.

Today, Ohiopyle Falls is the focal point of Ohiopyle State Park, which encompasses approximately 19,000 acres along both sides of the Youghiogheny River Gorge in Fayette County. The gorge was cut as water flowed across an uplifted fold of rock called the Laurel Hill anticline, but more commonly called Laurel Ridge. The ridge is composed primarily of shale and sandstone, which erode at different rates. Consequently, there are numerous dips in the river channel where the less resistant shale has eroded more quickly than sandstone, producing waterfalls, rapids, and some of the most turbulent and best-known whitewater rafting areas in the eastern United States. The river's name comes from the Native American word *Ohiopehle* meaning "frothy white water."

In addition to its unique geology, Ohiopyle State Park offers a wide range of recreational opportunities, including hiking, biking, rafting, snowmobiling, skiing, hunting, and fishing. The park contains 80 miles of day-hiking trails as well as the southern end of the 70-mile-long Laurel Highlands Hiking Trail. The trails vary in difficulty from relatively easy, flat trails to those that are steep, difficult, and somewhat dangerous in spots. Short spurs connect many of the trails. A list of marked trails follows:

International Scale of River Difficulty

The following designations are used to describe the difficulty of navigating a watercraft down a freshwater stream:

Class I: Moving water with a few riffles and small waves. Few or no obstructions.

Class II: Easy rapids with waves up to 3 feet, and wide, clear channels that are obvious without scouting. Some maneuvering is required.

Class III: Rapids with high, irregular waves often capable of swamping an open canoe. Narrow passages that often require complex maneuvering. May require scouting from shore.

Class IV: Long, difficult rapids with constricted passages that often require precise maneuvering in very turbulent waters. Scouting from shore is often necessary, and conditions make rescue difficult. Generally not possible for open canoes. Boaters in covered canoes and kayaks should be able to Eskimo roll.

Class V: Extremely difficult, long, and very violent rapids with highly congested routes which nearly always must be scouted from shore. Rescue conditions are difficult and there is significant hazard to life in event of a mishap. Ability to Eskimo roll is essential for kayaks and canoes.

Class VI: Difficulties of Class V carried to the extreme of navigability. Nearly impossible and very dangerous. For teams of experts only, after close study and with all precautions taken.

Great Gorge Trail: This trail, which is marked with green blazes, extends 2.5 miles from the Cucumber Run Picnic Area to the Kentuck Trail. It parallels Cucumber Run, passes Cucumber Falls, and then continues along the Youghiogheny River. Elevations range from 1,000–1,400 feet. To reach the Cucumber Run Picnic Area follow PA Route 381 from the town of Ohiopyle south for about 0.5 mile and turn right into LR 26071. Travel about 0.3 mile and turn left onto T-463. Drive approximately 0.7 mile and turn left onto the picnic area access road.

Kentuck Trail: Extending more than 4 miles from the Tharp Knob Picnic Area to the Mitchell Place Trail, this trail is marked with pink blazes and ranges in elevation from 1,100–1,650 feet. To reach the Tharp Knob Picnic Area follow PA Route 381 from the town of Ohiopyle south for about 0.5 mile and turn right into LR26071. Travel about 1.1 miles and turn right onto the picnic area access road.

Sproul Trail: This 3.5-mile trail, which begins at the Kentuck Campground, is composed of a series of loops, several of which are also used by cross-country skiers. The trail is marked with purple blazes and ranges from 1,500–1,700 feet in elevation. To reach the Kentuck Campground follow PA Route 381 from the town of Ohiopyle south for about 0.5 mile and turn right into LR26071. Travel about 1.3 miles to a 4-way intersection. Turn right onto T-976 and travel 1.3 miles to the campground access road on the right.

Beech Trail: This moderate to difficult trail extends 2.7 miles from the

Kentuck Campground to the bicycle trail. Portions of the trail are steep and narrow, dropping from 1,590–1,240 feet in a relatively short distance. The trail is marked with white blazes. To reach the Kentuck Campground follow PA Route 381 from the town of Ohiopyle south for about 0.5 mile and turn right into LR26071. Travel about 1.3 miles to a 4-way intersection. Turn right onto T-976 and travel 1.3 miles to the campground access road on the right.

Johnathan Run Trail: This 1.5-mile trail is marked with blue blazes and follows Johnathan Run from Brunner Run Road, at an elevation of 1,380 feet, down to the bike path, at an elevation of 1,100 feet. To reach the trailhead parking area follow PA Route 381 from the town of Ohiopyle south for about 0.5 mile and turn right into LR26071. Travel about 1.3 miles to a 4-way intersection. Continue straight through the intersection, the parking area is located about 1.5 miles down the road on the right.

Mitchell Trail: This is a 1.8-mile loop with a trailhead at the Old Mitchell Place parking lot. The trail is marked with red blazes and ranges in elevation from 1,580–1,700 feet. To reach the trailhead parking area follow PA Route 381 from the town of Ohiopyle south for about 0.5 mile and turn right into LR26071. Travel about 1.3 miles to a 4-way intersection. Continue straight through this intersection and travel about 2 miles to a 3-way intersection and turn right onto Brunner Run Road. The parking area is about 1.1 miles down the road on the right.

Meadow Run Trail: This gradually sloping trail extends for 3 miles from the trailhead to its terminus at Cucumber Run. Highlights include access to the natural water slides on Meadow Run and scenic views of the river rapids. Elevations range from 1,040–1,660 feet, and the trail is marked with yellow blazes. To reach the trailhead parking area follow PA Route 381 from the town of Ohiopyle south for about 1 mile to the parking area access road on the left.

Sugarloaf Trail: Running from the bike path parking lot to the mountain bike trails, this 3.8-mile path presents a moderate climb and is marked with orange blazes and ranges in elevation from 1,220–2,020 feet. From the town of Ohiopyle follow LR 26116 southeast for about 2.8 miles to a 4-way intersection. Turn left and travel about 1.1 miles. The parking area is located on the right.

Baughman Trail: This trail also runs from the bike path parking lot to the mountain bike trail, but it is considerably more difficult than the Sugarloaf Trail. The trail is rocky, narrow, and twisting. Elevations range from 1,220–2,160 feet, and the trail is marked with red blazes.

Those who prefer biking to hiking can use the Youghiogheny River Trail that parallels the river. Created by paving 28 miles of abandoned railroad grade, the trail is relatively flat and easy, making it ideal for joggers and hikers as well. For the more adventurous bikers, a mountain bike trail system is available. This 9.5-mile trail system is located in the southern end of the park on Sugarloaf Knob (elevation 2,640 feet) and is composed of a series of six interconnected loops. This set of trails is designated for snowmobile use during the winter months. The park's other popular

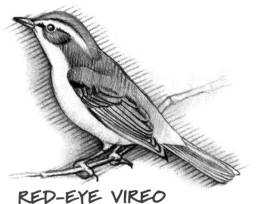

RED-EYE VIREO
(*Vireo olivaceus*)
This vireo is identified by its
white stripe above red eyes and
by its persistent singing.

winter activities include tobogganing and cross-country skiing on 30 miles of designated trails.

Sportsmen can also take advantage of the park. Fishermen will find good trout fishing within the Youghiogheny, which is stocked each year by the Pennsylvania Fish and Boat Commission, and in the much calmer Meadow Run. Hunting and trapping are also permitted in 18,000 of the park's 19,000 acres.

Ohiopyle State Park's best-known recreational activity, however, is whitewater boating. Two separate segments of the river are used. The area above Ohiopyle Falls near the town of Confluence, known as the "Middle Yough," stretches for 9 miles and contains Class I and II rapids. The area below the falls, the "Lower Yough," is a 7.5-mile stretch containing Class III and IV rapids.

Park visitors can attempt these rapids on their own, using privately owned or rented kayaks and inflatable rafts, or join guided river tours. These areas can be dangerous, especially the Lower Yough, and visitors should be familiar with the river, wear safety equipment, and have a good working knowledge of whitewater rafting. Since the Lower Yough is one of the most heavily used stretches of river in the U.S., the number of people allowed on it at any one time is limited. Visitors must sign in on weekdays and obtain launch permits on weekends and holidays. Additionally, there are established launch times.

See appendix D for companies that are permitted to operate whitewater tours within the boundaries of the park.

Directions: From the Pennsylvania Turnpike take Exit 9 at Donegal. Travel east on PA Route 31 to PA Route 381. Travel south on PA Route 381 to Ohiopyle.

Activities: Whitewater boating, hiking, biking, camping, fishing, hunting, snowmobiling, tobogganing, cross-country skiing.

Facilities: Trails, picnic areas, boat launches, playgrounds, 237 campsites with modern plumbing.

Dates: Open year-round. Campsites: Mar.–last day of antlerless deer season in Dec.; reservations are recommended.

Fees: None.

Closest town: Ohiopyle, within the park.

For more information: Ohiopyle State Park, PO Box 105, Ohiopyle, PA 15470. Phone (724) 329-8591.

FERNCLIFF PENINSULA NATURAL AREA

As the Youghiogheny meanders through the park it runs into a tongue of Pottsville sandstone. Over the years it has cut into the softer shale around the edge of the sandstone creating a horseshoe bend in the river, and consequently, the Ferncliff Peninsula. The 100-acre peninsula has been a popular tourist destination for more than 100 years. In the late 1800s, steam trains carried Pittsburghers here by the droves for weekend holidays. The small peninsula held a hotel, tennis court, bowling alley, and dance hall.

Today the Ferncliff Peninsula is officially classified as a natural area by the Pennsylvania Bureau of State Parks and has been designated a National Natural Landmark by the U.S. Department of the Interior. Other than 4 miles of easy hiking trails, the area no longer contains any structures. It is left alone to let natural processes take place.

Before flowing through southwestern Pennsylvania on its way to a rendezvous with the Monongohela River, the Youghiogheny first passes through West Virginia and Maryland. Along the way it picks up the seeds of southern wildflowers not normally found in Pennsylvania. As the river passes around the horseshoe curve along the Ferncliff Peninsula, the water slows and the seeds are deposited on the shore. Since the gorge is deep and sheltered from the wind, the year-round average temperature is slightly warmer than the rest of the area. This combination of southern seed, warmer climate, and rich river soil has produced a pocket of southern wildflowers, many of which are not found this far north anywhere else. Among them are Carolina tassle-rue (*Trautvetteria caroliniensis*) and the large-flowered marshallia (*Marshallia grandiflora*). Also found here is the umbrella magnolia (*Magnolia tripetala*), a threatened tree.

There are five trails on the peninsula that form a series of interconnected loops. The main loop, from which all of the other trails can be reached, is the 1.7-mile-long Ferncliff Trail. This trail parallels the river and takes about an hour to walk. The trail system contains several scenic vistas and offers close-up views of the rapids.

Directions: From the Pennsylvania Turnpike take Exit 9 at Donegal. Travel east on PA Route 31 to PA Route 381. Travel south on PA Route 381 to the parking area located on the right just before the bridge across the Youghiogheny River. The trailhead is adjacent to the parking lot.

Activities: Hiking, fishing.

Facilities: Trails.

Dates: Open year-round.

Fees: None.

Closest town: Ohiopyle, adjacent.

For more information: Ohiopyle State Park, PO Box 105, Ohiopyle, PA 15470. Phone (724) 329-8591.

DUTCHMAN'S BREECHES
(Dicentra cucullaria)
White, waxy petals shaped like baggy trousers give this plant its humorous name.

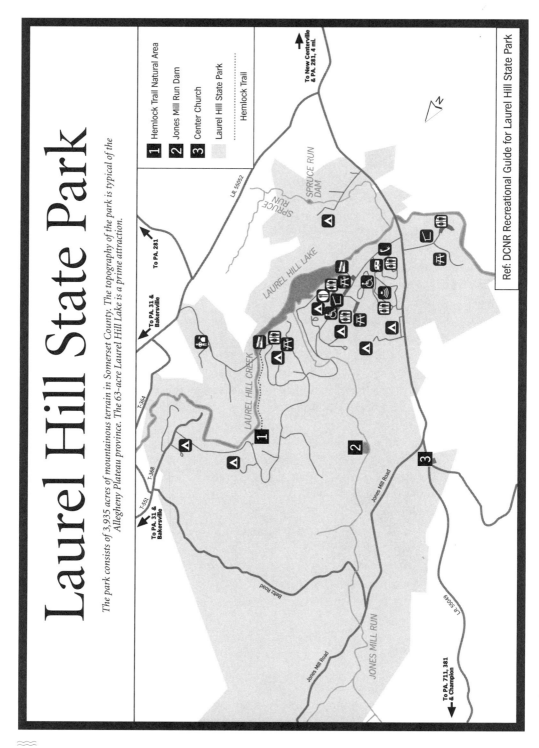

Laurel Hill State Park

The park consists of 3,935 acres of mountainous terrain in Somerset County. The topography of the park is typical of the Allegheny Plateau province. The 63-acre Laurel Hill Lake is a prime attraction.

1 Hemlock Trail Natural Area
2 Jones Mill Run Dam
3 Center Church
  Laurel Hill State Park
  .... Hemlock Trail

Ref: DCNR Recreational Guide for Laurel Hill State Park

🪨 LAUREL HILL STATE PARK

In the late 1790s, Secretary of the Treasury Alexander Hamilton convinced the Continental Congress to levy an excise tax on whiskey to help pay off the debt incurred during the Revolution. Among those effected were the Scotch-Irish of western Pennsylvania, who were well known for their rye whiskey. An independent lot, they refused to pay, and so began the Whiskey Rebellion of 1791–1794.

In response, George Washington sent the Continental Army to quell the uprising. The army set up camp in what is today Laurel Hill State Park. The rebellion ended without bloodshed when Washington made a deal with the whiskey makers. They were offered free land in a part of Virginia that is today Kentucky. The settlers had to agree to grow corn, which they did, promptly converting it to corn whiskey, the forerunner of today's bourbon. The world famous Kentucky Bourbon, therefore, has its roots in the Laurel Highlands of Pennsylvania.

MOUNTAIN LAUREL
(*Kalmia latifolia*)

Laurel Hill State Park encompasses 3,935 acres of woodland on the east side of Laurel Ridge. The park is located within Somerset County, which is part of a five county area known as the Laurel Highlands. The park is dominated by mixed hardwoods such as tulip poplar, oak, black cherry, and birch with an understory of rhododendron and mountain laurel (*Kalmia latifolia*), Pennsylvania's state flower. Fifteen miles of spring-fed mountain streams run through the park, emptying into Laurel Hill Lake. The 63-acre lake, formed by a dam across Laurel Hill Creek, is the focal point of the park.

Numerous recreational facilities, most of them built by the Civilian Conservation Corps in the late 1930s and early 1940s, are located along the lake's western shore. There are four picnic areas within the park containing horseshoe pits, playgrounds, a ballfield, and more than 500 picnic tables. For overnight visitors there is a tent-and-trailer camping area with 264 sites, some with electricity, as well as cabins and a group tent-camping area.

There are 12 miles of hiking trails within the park, listed from the least to the most challenging.

Pump House Trail: This is the easiest trail in the park, climbing gradually uphill for about 1 mile from the trailhead to its terminus along the Martz Trail. From the visitor's center follow the main park road north for about 1-mile to the parking area on the left.

Tram Road Trail: This fairly level trail follows an old logging road. Be prepared—it crosses Jones Mill Run in several places and there are no bridges. From the visitor's center follow the main park road north for about .9 mile to the trailhead on the left.

Pennsylvania's State Flower—The Mountain Laurel

Sharing many of the characteristics of its well-known cousin the rhododendron, the mountain laurel was named the state flower of Pennsylvania in 1933. The mountain laurel is an evergreen shrub that likes both dry and wet acidic soil, and it is found throughout all but the northwestern corner of the state.

The shrub, which can grow as tall as 20 feet and sometimes looks more like a tree, often grows in very dense thickets called "heath balds." These thickets are ideal cover areas for wildlife, and while the plants are poisonous to livestock, white-tailed deer and ruffed grouse commonly eat the leaves and buds.

The mountain laurel has large white and pink flowers that bloom in the spring, making it one of the most beautiful of all native shrubs. While most people have probably not seen a blooming heath bald, many have seen the mountain laurel because it, like the rhododendron, is commonly used as an ornamental shrub.

Martz Trail: This is a level, grassy trail that stretches for 1.2 miles and is often wet. From the visitor's center follow the main park road north for about 1.2 miles to the intersection with Buck Run Road. Turn left and travel about 0.5 mile then turn left again. The trailhead is located at the end of the road.

Waterline Trail: This is a short, 0.5-mile trail with a moderate uphill climb. The trail begins at the same parking area as the Pump House Trail.

Ridge Trail: While most of this 1.5-mile trail presents a moderate uphill climb, hikers should be aware that the beginning of the trail is very steep. From the visitor's center follow the main park road north for about 0.8 mile to the trailhead on the left.

Bobcat Trail: This is the steepest trail in the park. To make it easier begin at the end on Beltz Road and walk downhill to the end on Buck Run Road. To reach the trailhead follow Beltz Road east from the intersection of Jones Mill Road for 0.7 mile.

Lake Trail: This trail runs along the undeveloped, east side of Laurel Hill Lake. The trail is not recommended for most visitors because it is steep, slippery, narrow, and dangerous in spots. From the visitor's center follow the main park road north for about 1.75 miles to the trailhead on the right.

Several of these trails, including Martz, Pump House, and Water Line, are open to snowmobiles during the winter. Along with several of the park roads, they make up a 10-mile-long snowmobile trail system that connects with a 60-mile system in the adjacent Forbes State Forest. Snowmobiling is permitted after antlerless deer season in December. Other winter sports in the park include ice skating, ice fishing, and ice boating on Laurel Hill Lake.

Sportsmen use the park year-round. Roughly half of the park is open to hunting, with upland game birds such as turkey and grouse, small game such as rabbits and squirrels, and white-tailed deer being the most common quarry. Fishermen will find bass, catfish, and panfish in the lake, as well as trout in Laurel Hill Creek and its tributary, Jones Mill Run. Nonmotorized boats (i.e. those without internal combustion engines) are permitted, and canoes and paddleboats can be rented at the guarded beach.

Directions: From the Pennsylvania Turnpike take Exit 10 (Somerset Exit), drive west on PA Route 31 from Somerset for 10 miles. Turn left on the unnumbered route and follow the sign to the park.

Activities: Hiking, camping, hunting, fishing, snowmobiling, ice skating, ice fishing, ice boating.

Facilities: Trails, campgrounds (reservations required, call 888-PA-PARKS), picnic areas.

Dates: Open year-round.

Fees: None.

Closest town: Bakersville, 2 miles.

For more information: Laurel Hill State Park, 1454 Laurel Hill Park Rd., Somerset, PA 15501. Phone (814) 445-7725.

HEMLOCK TRAIL NATURAL AREA

The Hemlock Trail Natural Area is a 6-acre stand of virgin hemlock located along the western side of Laurel Hill Creek. The trees escaped the loggers ax and today remain as an example of the bottomland forest that once grew throughout the stream valley. The forest floor is dark, covered with a thick blanket of needles, and the only undergrowth are young hemlocks. In an attempt to enlarge the hemlock stand, state park managers are transplanting hemlock seedlings in the adjacent second-growth deciduous forest. The hemlocks, which are shade tolerant, grow well under the deciduous canopy and will eventually shade out the hardwoods and replace them.

Passing through the natural area and stretching from Laurel Hill Lake to Buck Run Road is the Hemlock Trail. Hikers along the trail will experience a variety of habitats, ranging from virgin forests dating back to the days of William Penn, to second-growth forests that have grown since loggers clear-cut the area.

As the trail climbs out of the lowlands it passes through a second-growth, mixed-hardwood forest. Unlike in the hemlock forest, sunlight is abundant, allowing plants to grow beneath the canopy. This is also a much drier forest, with rain and snowmelt running rapidly downhill to the bottomlands. The understory here contains wildflowers such as trillium and shrubs such as rhododendron. The Hemlock Trail presents the hiker with a moderate, uphill climb. The entire trail is 1.5 miles long, but the hike to the virgin hemlock stand is only 0.5 mile.

Directions: From the main entrance to the park on LR 55052 follow the paved road about 0.5 mile. A parking area and trailhead are located just across the bridge over Laurel Hill Creek.

Activities: Hiking, fishing.
Facilities: Trail.
Dates: Open year-round.
Fees: None.
Closest town: Bakersville, 2 miles.
For more information: Laurel Hill State Park, 1454 Laurel Hill Park Rd., Somerset, PA 15501. Phone (814) 445-7725.

🔲 BLUE KNOB STATE PARK

Just to the east of the Allegheny Front in the Valley and Ridge province lies Blue Knob, the second highest point in Pennsylvania. At an elevation of 3,146 feet above sea level, Blue Knob is just 67 feet lower than Mount Davis, the state's highest point. The peak is composed of quartzite, an impervious type of sandstone made almost completely of quartz.

Blue Knob State Park, which is located atop the mountain, is among the largest of Pennsylvania's state parks, encompassing 5,614 acres. Despite its size it's not heavily used, receiving only about 150,000 visitors each year. Even on busy days the park seems empty because its numerous recreational facilities are widely spaced and isolated from one another, due to the varied topography.

The park was originally developed by the National Park Service as one of several prototype parks built near urban areas. With the help of the Civilian Conservation Corps, the park service built many of the recreational facilities to provide outdoor recreation for the citizens of Johnstown and the surrounding communities. In 1945 the federal government turned it over to Pennsylvania and it became Blue Knob State Park.

If it's mountainous recreation you're looking for, Blue Knob is the park for you. For visitors who want to spend the night, there are several camping areas within the park, including the highest campground in the state. Tent and trailer camping are both available, but all of the campgrounds are primitive and lack utilities. The campgrounds are all remote and offer a secluded, wilderness camping experience.

Hunting and fishing are both popular activities. With more than 5,000 acres of the park open to hunting, along with 12,000 additional acres of adjacent game lands, hunters have a vast area where they can pursue white-tailed deer, grouse, turkey, and black bear. Many of the streams contain native brook trout and are stocked as well. One of the best fishing areas is Bob's Creek, which runs through the eastern portion of the park, roughly paralleling Monument Road.

Numerous trails run through the park, many of them multi-use trails. Among the most challenging is the Mountain View Trail. This trail is a 5-mile-long loop that climbs to the top of the mountain. The trail is remote, rocky, and steep, providing a deep wilderness hike. Hikers on this path routinely see wildlife but rarely see other park visitors. Among the trail's highlights are two scenic vistas. The Pavia Overlook faces west and offers a dramatic view of the Allegheny Front and the Appalachian Plateau. The Queen Overlook offers a spectacular view in the opposite direction, looking east over the Valley and Ridge province.

Another trail that provides some exceptional views is the Three Springs Trail. This 5-mile-long trail runs along the face of the mountain and is an especially good place to see wildlife, including deer and bear. The trail presents a moderately challenging hike and has some steep sections.

The Saw Mill Trail intersects the park running from a trailhead in the southern end of the park to a trailhead located along Knob Road about

The Hemlock— Pennsylvania's State Tree

"If Pennsylvania were to select one tree as characteristic of our state, nothing would be better than the hemlock." So said Dr. Joseph Rothrock, considered by many the father of forestry in Pennsylvania, in the late 1800s. Eventually the state took his advice and made the hemlock the official state tree. Unfortunately, by then the hemlock forest was nearly gone.

Once the hemlock blanketed Pennsylvania from edge to edge. Today it is still common, but rarely is it found in the vast stands that it was when the first Europeans arrived. Even more rare are the virgin, old-growth trees. The trees can live a very long time; the record for an Eastern hemlock is 988 years.

Hemlocks are evergreens that can grow to 70 feet high and are most commonly found in moist valleys and lowlands, as well as on rocky outcrops. Their most distinguishing characteristic is their needles, which are flat and have two fine white lines underneath. About a third of the needles fall each year and form a dense mat on the forest floor. The high level of tannin in the needles on the ground, combined with the near total shade resulting from the dense canopy of needles above, prevents other plants from growing, resulting in nearly pure stands of hemlock with no undergrowth.

2.5 miles north of the park office. As it runs along the toe of the mountain, it passes through a variety of terrains and is relatively isolated. This 3.5-mile trail is moderately challenging.

Trout fishermen might want to consider a hike along the Rock'N'Ridge Trail. About half of this 2.8-mile loop follows Pavia Run, which contains native brook trout. About halfway along the trail the topography changes from level to a series of small ridges radiating from the base of the mountain. Since hikers must climb up and down these ridges, the trail is moderately challenging.

Nearly all of the park's trails connect with one or more others as well as with park roads. As a result there are a seemingly unlimited number of hikes, varying in length, difficulty, and the type of ecosystem and topography thorough which they traverse.

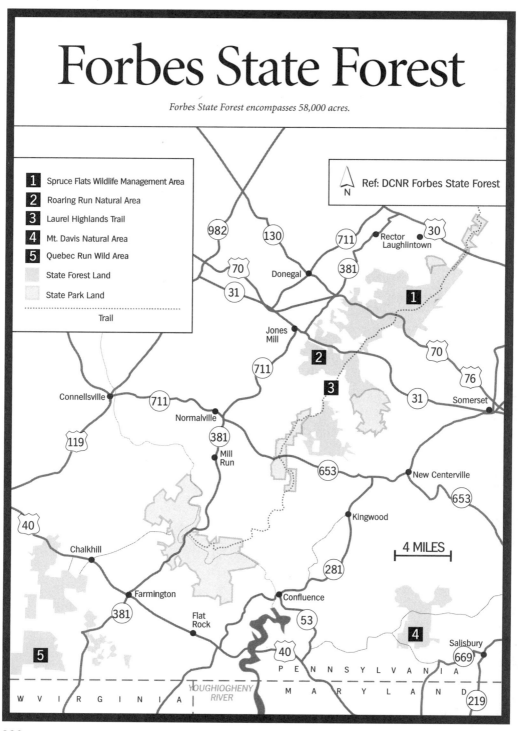

Forbes State Forest

Forbes State Forest encompasses 58,000 acres.

1 Spruce Flats Wildlife Management Area
2 Roaring Run Natural Area
3 Laurel Highlands Trail
4 Mt. Davis Natural Area
5 Quebec Run Wild Area

State Forest Land

State Park Land

Trail

Ref: DCNR Forbes State Forest
N

982   130   711   Rector   30
                    Laughlintown
70   381
31   Donegal
                          1
Jones
Mill   70
          711   2   76
                  3
Connellsville   711   31   Somerset
Normalville
            381
            Mill   653   New Centerville
            Run   653
119   Kingwood
40   4 MILES
Chalkhill   281
      Farmington   Confluence
381   Flat   53
        Rock   40   4   Salisbury
5   669
            P E N N S Y L V A N I A
W   V I R G I N I A   YOUGHIOGHENY   M A R Y L A N D   219
                        RIVER

Additionally, many of the trails are designated as multi-use. Mountain bikes, horses, snowmobiles, and cross-country skis are permitted on many of the trails.

One end of the 26-mile-long Lost Turkey Trail (*see* page 169) lies within the park. Since the trail rises in elevation as it approaches and enters the park, hikers are encouraged to begin their hike at the trailhead within the park and follow it downhill to the other end within the Babcock Picnic Area in the Gallitzin State Forest. To reach the trailhead follow Knob Road north from the park office to Tower Road, a distance of about 3 miles. Turn right onto Tower Road and drive approximately 0.7 mile and turn left. The trailhead is located at the end of the road. Hikers must register at the park office before setting off on the trail. A park map, which shows the location of all the trailheads, is available at the park office.

The northwest corner of the park is leased to a private corporation that operates Ski Blue Knob. The area's steep slopes, combined with an average 10 feet of snow each year, make Ski Blue Knob one of the most popular ski resorts in Pennsylvania, hosting more than 80,000 people annually. Ski Blue Knob has the highest vertical drop of any ski slope in the state and includes four chair lifts, a lodge, a restaurant, and a golf course. Only the ski slopes and lodge are located on parkland.

Directions: From the Pennsylvania Turnpike, Exit 11, follow PA Route 869 north for approximately 21 miles to the park office.

Activities: Hiking, camping, fishing, hunting, swimming, mountain biking, snowmobiling, cross-country skiing, horseback riding, picnicking.

Facilities: Multi-purpose trails, swimming pool, picnic areas, scenic vistas, campgrounds.

Dates: Open for day use year-round. Camping is open from the second Fri. in Apr. until the third Sun. in Oct.

Fees: There is a charge for camping.

Closest town: Pavia, adjacent.

For more information: Blue Knob State Park, RR 1, Box 449, Imler, PA 16655. Phone (814) 276-3576.

Forbes State Forest

Forbes State Forest encompasses 58,000 acres in Fayette, Somerset, and Westmoreland counties. Unlike many of Pennsylvania's state forests, which are comprised of large unbroken tracts of forest, Forbes is made up of 20 separate tracts of land interspersed with privately-owned land, state parks, and state game lands that are managed by the Pennsylvania Game Commission. Given its close proximity to Pittsburgh, the forest is heavily used during the summer months and hunting season, and snowmobile and cross-country ski use is heavy in the winter.

The forest is named after Brigadier General John Forbes who led the British attack on Fort Duquesne, the French stronghold at the confluence of the Ohio, Monongo-hela, and Allegheny rivers. After capturing the fort, which the French had abandoned and set on fire, he renamed it Fort Pitt. Unfortunately, Forbes did not live to see the city that he helped name. He died a year later after retiring from the military.

The forest is located on three mountains. The bulk of the forest is located on Laurel Ridge between Ligonier and PA Route 653. The southeastern portion of the forest is located on Negro Mountain and includes Mount Davis, which is the highest point in Pennsylvania. The southwestern corner of the forest is composed of various distinct tracts of land located along or just north of the Pennsylvania/West Virginia border on Chestnut Ridge.

The forest is an ecologically diverse area containing numerous cold-water streams, wetlands, and woodlands. Second- and third-growth hardwoods and oak dominate most of Forbes State Forest. Some of the valleys and lowlands contain small pockets of hemlock, but the vast stands of virgin conifers were cut long ago. This forest, like nearly all in Pennsylvania, was subjected to extensive clear-cutting early in the 1900s.

Wildflowers are common throughout the forest. One particularly good area to view them is located along Linn Run Road from the Linn Run State Park office to the foot of Fish Run Hill. Among the flowers found here are red trillium (*Trillium erectum*), white trillium (*Trillium grandiflorum*), cardinal flower (*Lobelia cardinalis*), bee-balm (*Monarda didyma*), and American bugbane (*Cimicifuga americana*). Because of its wildflower diversity, foresters plan to designate this area as a wildflower sanctuary.

The Forbes State Forest includes four special management areas. The Quebec Wild Area contains nearly 5,000 acres of forest along the eastern slope of Chestnut Ridge. The Mount Davis Natural Area is small in size with only 581 acres, but it is big in stature because it is the highest point in Pennsylvania at 3,213 feet above sea level. The Roaring Run Natural Area is considerably larger than the Mount Davis area, encompassing more than 3,000 acres along the western slope of Laurel Ridge. Numerous wetlands, including a bog, are found along the summit of Laurel Ridge in the Spruce Flats Wildlife Management Area.

There are numerous recreational opportunities within Forbes State Forest. Hiking trails, including much of the 70-mile-long Laurel Highlands Trail (*see* page 277), are located in all but the smallest of the 20 separate tracts that make up the forest. During the winter many of the trails are used for cross-country skiing. Among these are the North Woods Ski Touring Area, which lies along the summit of Laurel Ridge between PA Route 31 and the Pennsylvania Turnpike. To reach the North Woods Ski Touring Area follow PA Route 31 west from Somerset for about 10 miles. Turn right into Tunnel Road and travel 0.5 mile to the parking area on the left. The Laurel Highlands Ski Touring Area, located at the northern end of Forbes State Forest, also passes through a portion of Laurel Mountain State Park. Access to this ski area is from the parking area along Laurel Summit Road near the entrance of Laurel Mountain State Park, about 2 miles south of PA Route 30. The ski trails follow old logging roads and railroad grades as well as hiking trails and are marked with red paint blazes. Hiking trails are marked with blue blazes.

Another popular winter attraction is the Laurel Highlands Snowmobile Trail System. This extensive trail system extends from Laurel Hill State Park (*see* page 149) in the south, along the summit of Laurel Ridge, through the length of the northern portion of Forbes State Forest, and over the Pennsylvania Turnpike to just south of PA Route 30. While the trail has numerous side loops and spurs, making short and long trips possible, a round trip from one end of the system to the other is approximately 36 miles. There are numerous parking areas along the route, portions of which follow state forest roads. A good point of access is from the parking area just south of the access area for the Laurel Highlands Ski Touring Area. There are a total of 112 miles of trails in the forest.

Both hunters and fishermen heavily use Forbes State Forest. Deer, turkey, grouse, bear, and small game are common throughout the area. Trout, both native and stocked, are found in most of the streams. The most common native is the brook trout, but some of the streams also support populations of brown trout. Anglers should be aware that a 1.6-mile stretch of Indian Creek, just north of the intersection of PA Routes 31 and 381, is a delayed harvest area and therefore operates under a special set of regulations.

There are seven state parks located along Laurel Ridge in close proximity to Forbes State Forest. From north to south they are Laurel Ridge State Park, Laurel Mountain State Park, Laurel Summit State Park, Linn Run State Park, Kooser State Park, Laurel Hill State Park (*see* page 149), and Ohiopyle State Park (*see* page 143).

CARDINAL FLOWER
(*Lobelia cardinalis*)
A favorite stop for hummingbirds, this flower grows up to 5 feet tall.

Directions: To reach the Forbes State Forest headquarters follow PA Route 30 east from Ligonier to the village of Laughlintown. The headquarters (district office) is located 0.25 mile east of Laughlintown at the foot of Laurel Ridge. From Ligonier to the office is 3 miles.

Activities: Hiking, cross-country skiing, fishing, hunting, snowmobiling.

Facilities: Hiking trails, cross-country ski trails, snowmobile trails, picnic areas.

Dates: Open year-round.

Fees: None.

Closest town: Ligonier, 5.5 miles.

For more information: Forbes State Forest, PO Box 519, Laughlintown, PA 15655. Phone (724) 238-9533.

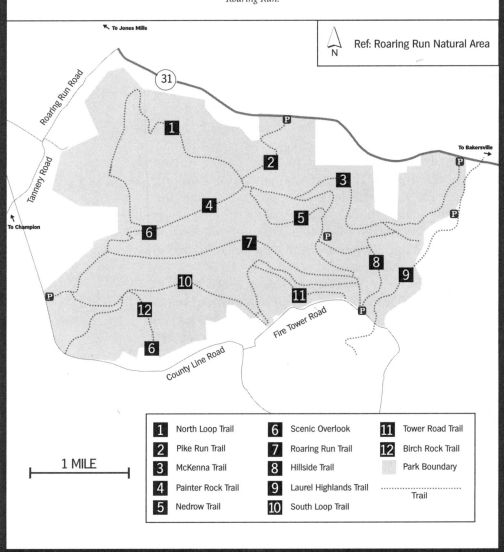

Roaring Run
Natural Area

*Roaring Run Natural Area encompasses the entire watershed of
Roaring Run.*

To Jones Mills

Ref: Roaring Run Natural Area

N

Roaring Run Road

31

To Bakersville

Tannery Road

To Champion

1   North Loop Trail

2   Pike Run Trail

3   McKenna Trail

4   Painter Rock Trail

5   Nedrow Trail

6   Scenic Overlook

7   Roaring Run Trail

8   Hillside Trail

9   Laurel Highlands Trail

10   South Loop Trail

11   Tower Road Trail

12   Birch Rock Trail

Park Boundary

Trail

Fire Tower Road

County Line Road

1 MILE

🏵 ROARING RUN NATURAL AREA

Situated on 3,070 acres of the western slope of Laurel Ridge, the Roaring Run Natural Area encompasses the entire watershed of Roaring Run. This stream is formed by the joining of numerous springs along the summit of Laurel Ridge, and it ends above the junction with Indian Creek. The stream has exceptional water quality and contains native brook trout.

The area has been logged several times in the past, including most recently in the 1960s. As a result, the area is an excellent example of ecological succession, the gradual evolution of one ecosystem into another over time. The most recently logged areas are now covered with blackberry thickets so dense a man can't walk through. Growing among these briars are the vanguard of the forest to come, seedlings of black cherry and maple.

Hardwoods and oaks today dominate those areas that haven't been logged as recently. The oaks—white (*Quercus alba*), black (*Quercus velutina*), and red (*Quercus rubra*)—are most commonly found on the southern and western portions of the ridge. Found on some of the rocky outcrops are old-growth chestnut oaks (*Quercus prinus*). They were left by loggers, along with black birch (*Betula lenta*) of similar age, because of their poor quality timber and remote location.

Hikers can visit any of the successional stages, or seres as they're called by ecologists, by exploring the numerous trails which run through the area. The trails provide access to nearly all of the natural area. Most of these trails are of moderate difficulty with occasional steeper slopes.

Roaring Run Trail: This 3.9-mile trail runs along an old logging railroad grade that parallels Roaring Run.

Painter Rock Trail: This trail, which is also 3.9 miles in length, offers several scenic views of the Roaring Run Valley and passes Painter Rock Hill, which is one of the highest points on Laurel Ridge at 2,920 feet.

North Loop Trail: This 2.7-mile trail connects with the Painter Rock Trail and varies in elevation from 1,820–2,760 feet.

South Loop Trail: This 3.7-mile trail, which connects with Roaring Run Trail, rises from a low point of 2,040 feet along Roaring Run to 2,580 feet along the ridge above the stream.

Birch Rock Trail: This is a short, 0.6-mile trail located in the southern end of the natural area that provides access to the Birch Rock Overlook.

All of these trails can be reached from the same trailhead. Follow County Line Road south from the town of Champion for 3 miles to the parking area on the left side of the road.

Some of these trails are suitable for cross-country skiing as well as hiking. Hiking trails are blazed with blue markers, and ski trails, also suitable for hiking, are marked with red markers. A portion of the 70-mile-long Laurel Highlands Trail (*see* page 277) passes through the eastern portion of the Roaring Run Natural Area, but it is not suitable for skiing. There are 9.7 miles of designated cross-country ski trails and 20.8 miles of designated hiking trails in the natural area.

Directions: From Donegal follow PA Route 31 east to Fire Tower Road, which is located near the summit of Laurel Ridge. Turn right onto Fire Tower Road, which marks the eastern boundary of the natural area. There are two parking areas on this road.

Activities: Hiking, cross-country skiing, fishing, hunting.

Facilities: Trails, parking areas.

Dates: Open year-round.

Fees: None.

Closest town: Jones Mill, 0.8 mile.

For more information: Forbes State Forest, PO Box 519, Laughlintown, PA 15655. Phone (724) 238-9533.

SPRUCE FLATS WILDLIFE MANAGEMENT AREA

The Spruce Flats Wildlife Management Area occupies 305 acres along the summit of Laurel Ridge a short distance north of the Pennsylvania Turnpike. While it may be small in size, it is easy to access, and its unique ecosystem makes it a popular spot with nature lovers.

The focal point of the area is a 28-acre bog. Bogs are acidic, nutrient-poor wetlands which are almost always formed by glaciers. Scientists have been able to accurately map the southern extent of the glaciers during the last ice age, and they stopped well north of this area.

This bog then, is a mystery. It may be a consequence of an earlier farther-reaching period of glaciation or of some unexplained change in stream drainage patterns, leaving an orphaned pocket of water.

When loggers first arrived in the area, they found a vast stand of hemlock that they mistakenly called spruce, thereby giving the area its inaccurate name. The area was not a bog, but rather a swampy woodland that may have started off as a bog centuries before. Once the loggers removed the trees, however, they reversed the ecological clock, and the area reverted to a wet, treeless bog.

The main trail within the area is the Wolf Rock Trail, which begins at the Laurel Summit

SCARLET TANAGER
(Piranga olivacea)
This bird has a distinctive "chick-kurr" call.

The Cranberry

Just about everyone has seen a cranberry in the store, but few have seen them growing along lakeshores, swamps, and bogs. Like other members of the heath family, which includes rhododendron and mountain laurel, it is evergreen and prefers acidic soil, making it an ideal bog dweller. The cranberry (*Vaccinium macrocarpon*), so named because its white flowers resemble cranes, is one of our more common bog plants and is often found growing in dense thickets.

Native Americans used the berries as a source of dye and also as a poultice for wounds. Today's commercially grown cranberries, most of which are produced in New England and New Jersey, were developed from native plants. As anyone who's had Thanksgiving dinner knows, the fruit is quite tasty, but you wouldn't want to pick a berry right off the bush and eat it, because they're very tart and need to be cooked first. Wildlife, on the other hand, relish the fresh berries.

State Park in the southern end of the Spruce Flats Wildlife Management Area and continues north out of the area. A short two-minute walk from the picnic area, visitors will find many of the unique plants found only in these unusual wetlands. Seeds left over from the early days of the bog germinated, producing cranberry bushes and cotton grass (*Eriophorum virginicum*). Carnivorous plants are found here as well. Sundew (*Drosers* sp.) were recently found growing in the bog, but it's not known if they're native or introduced. Pitcher plants (*Sarracenia* sp.), a common member of most northern bog communities, were introduced to the bog by the Westmoreland County Botanical Society.

The Spruce Flats Wildlife Management Area is managed specifically for wildlife. Trees have been removed from some small areas to create habitat for animals such as grouse and certain songbirds that require these openings. Likewise, the only trails created within the area are those used for wildlife viewing, and no motorized vehicles are allowed. The Audubon Society of Western Pennsylvania regularly conducts wildlife surveys including bird counts. The Society has identified 68 species of birds, including 13 different warblers.

Directions: From the village of Rector along PA Route 381 follow Linn Run Road through Linn Run State Park to the Laurel Summit State Park.

Activities: Hiking, wildlife watching, hunting.

Facilities: Trail, picnic area.

Dates: Open year-round.

Fees: None.

Closest town: Rector, 7 miles.

For more information: Forbes State Forest, PO Box 519, Laughlintown, PA 15655. Phone (724) 238-9533.

MOUNT DAVIS NATURAL AREA

Located on Negro Mountain at 3,213 feet above sea level is Mount Davis, the highest point in Pennsylvania. The area contains an observation tower and interpretive area built during the 1970s. The parking area serves as a good starting point for a visit to the Mount Davis Natural Area. The natural area encompasses 581 acres surrounding the 7-acre parcel on which the tower and parking area are built.

The Mount Davis Natural Area is part of the Tub Mill Run watershed that drains into the Casselman River. Like most of Pennsylvania the area has changed over the past 100 years as a result of extensive logging and subsequent forest fires. The area is once again forested, but the trees tend to be short and somewhat deformed, especially on the exposed ridgetops. This is because the climate is severe at this high altitude, with temperature extremes and high winds. The combination of a severe climate and nutrient-poor soil resulting from the fires produces a different looking forest than is seen in most other parts of the state.

The temperature extremes also result in frequent freezing and thawing of the soil, producing small mounds where the earth heaves as it freezes. Stones lying on top of the soil roll off of the mounds and collect at their base, forming the peculiar stone rings that are common on the top of the mountain.

There are three marked trails that begin near the observation tower and then pass through the natural area. The Shelter Rock Trail is 1.1 miles long and extends to Shelter Rock Road, which forms the eastern boundary of the Mount Davis Natural Area. Along the way it passes through a grove of pitch pine (*Pinus rigida*) and past a spring which feeds Tub Mill Run. The trail is rocky, it climbs a gradual slope, and it takes about 50 minutes to walk one-way.

The Mount Davis Trail is a short, difficult trail designed to give the hiker a feel for the ruggedness of the area. The rocky trail, which extends for 0.25 mile, is a good place to identify the most common trees and shrubs of the area including black birch, quaking aspen (*Populus tremuloides*), black gum (*Nyssa sylvatica*), and rhododendron. To reach the trail follow the Shelter Rock Trail for 250 feet. The Mount Davis Trail ends at the High Point Trail only 150 feet from the observation tower area.

In contrast to the Mount Davis Trail, the High Point Trail provides an easy hike along a grassy path. The trail ends at the Mount Davis State Forest Picnic Area about 1 mile from the observation tower. This relatively flat trail takes only 20 minutes to walk.

The Mount Davis State Forest Picnic Area was built by the CCC in the late 1930s. It lies along LR 55008 just outside the boundary of the natural area, but it serves as a good starting point for a hike into the natural area. The picnic area contains restrooms, picnic tables, and a shelter. In addition to the High Point Trail, the picnic area provides easy access to the Tub Mill Run Trail. This trail provides a much more strenuous hike than the other trails within the natural area. It is a steep, rocky trail that is 3 miles long. Along its course it passes through a mixed-oak forest with a dense undergrowth of rhododendron and parallels and then eventually crosses Tub Mill Run. This stream is strewn with sandstone boulders, producing numerous small but scenic waterfalls. The trail passes out of the natural area and runs along the east side of Negro Mountain. The total hiking time is about two hours one-way. The beginning of the trail is marked and is about a five-minute walk from the picnic area along the High Point Trail.

FLAME AZALEA
(Rhododendron calendulaceum)

Directions: From Salisbury follow PA Route 669 west. Turn right onto LR 55008 just after you cross the Casselman River. Follow LR 55008 approximately 6 miles to South Wolf Road. Turn left and drive about 0.75 mile to the parking area.

Activities: Hiking, hunting.

Facilities: Hiking trails, observation tower, restrooms, parking area.

Dates: Open year-round.

Fees: None.

Closest town: Salisbury, 6 miles.

For more information: Forbes State Forest, PO Box 519, Laughlintown, PA 15655. Phone (724) 238-9533.

QUEBEC RUN WILD AREA

The Quebec Run Wild Area is a massive woodland located along the eastern slope of Chestnut Ridge in southern Fayette County. The 4,765-acre area contains most of the Tebolt Run and Quebec Run watersheds. Additionally, Mill Run and Big Sandy Creek flow through the area. The latter, a tributary of the Cheat River, continues on into West Virginia.

The Forbes State Forest, like most of the forests of southwestern Pennsylvania, is a highly diverse assemblage of species known as a mixed-mesophytic forest. There are subtle variations in the species composition depending on the orientation of the slope. The woodlands on the north and east slopes receive less direct sunlight and wind and so are slightly wetter. Tulip poplars and red and sugar maples dominate these slopes. The drier south and west facing slopes are dominated by assorted species of oak. Most of the trees growing in the Quebec Run Wild Area are third-growth. In addition to being clear-cut from the late 1800s to the early 1900s, the area was logged in the late 1930s. The understory is dense and dominated by mountain laurel, rhododendron, and dogwood (*Cornus florida*).

The movement of water and the nature of the underlying rock have shaped the topography of the area. Sandstone outcrops are common along Chestnut Ridge, so hikers passing through the area will see numerous examples of the parent material of the forest soil. Numerous streams and brooks run through the area and have cut deep channels into the ridge. Fishermen will find native trout in portions of Quebec and Tebolt runs, and Big Sandy Creek and Mill Run are stocked by the Pennsylvania Fish and Boat Commission.

The Pennsylvania Bureau of Forestry has two management goals for the area: enhancement of wildlife habitat and providing opportunities for nonmotorized, low-density recreation. To increase wildlife diversity the bureau increases habitat diversity through selective cutting. Small areas of less than 5 acres are cut to create grassy openings. These openings support large insect communities that in turn provide food for birds that live in or on the edge of openings, such as tree swallows (*Iridoprocne bicolor*) and mourning warblers (*Oporornis philadelphia*). The bureau attempts to keep 2 percent to 5 percent of the wild area in this growth stage through periodic cutting.

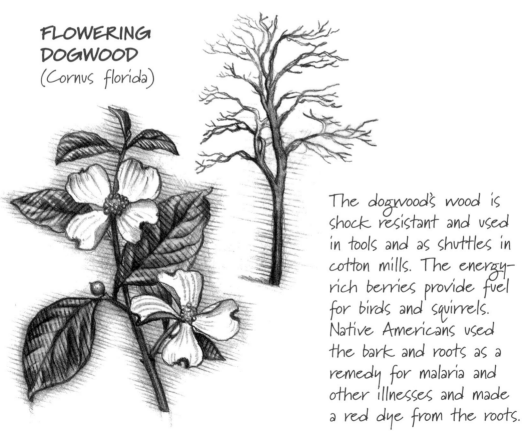

FLOWERING DOGWOOD
(Cornus florida)

The dogwood's wood is shock resistant and used in tools and as shuttles in cotton mills. The energy-rich berries provide fuel for birds and squirrels. Native Americans used the bark and roots as a remedy for malaria and other illnesses and made a red dye from the roots.

After a decade or so these clearings are no longer grasslands but are dominated by brush and saplings. The type of wildlife found here differs from that in both the openings and the more mature forest. The dense undergrowth provides excellent cover from predators.

Common here are ruffed grouse and yellow-breasted chats (*Icteria virens*). The bureau attempts to keep about 10 percent of the wild area in this growth stage.

Two species of game birds are highly desired in Pennsylvania—the turkey and the ruffed grouse. Keys to these birds' winter survival are the energy and nutrients contained in the dormant buds of the aspen tree. To encourage the growth of aspen the Bureau of Forestry selectively cuts the trees growing around the edges of existing aspen stands. This reduces the competition for nutrients, water, and sunlight between the aspen and the surrounding trees, thereby allowing the aspen stand to expand.

Not all of the forest management practices require cutting. All of the existing evergreens, which include pine, hemlock, and spruce, as well as mountain laurel and rhododendron, are protected. Likewise no cutting occurs along any streams or trails.

There are six maintained hiking trails within the area with a combined length of 14 miles. In addition to these trails, which are marked with blue paint blazes, there are numerous old logging roads and unmarked trails that are used by hikers. Also available are the 3-mile-long West Road and the 3.8-mile Quebec Road. These roads are closed to motor vehicles. When used in conjunction with the hiking trails they provide a wide variety of possible loops for the hiker.

Directions: From Uniontown follow PA Route 40 east to the top of Chestnut Ridge. After passing the Mount Summit Inn turn right onto Seaton Road and drive 6.5 miles to the intersection with Mud Pike. Follow Mud Pike approximately 1.25 miles east to the parking area. Parking is also available about 0.75 mile farther along Mud Pike, on Tebolt Road at the southern end of the Quebec Run Wild Area, along Skyline Drive at the western end of the area, and along the area's eastern boundary along Old Woods Road.

Activities: Hiking, hunting, fishing.
Facilities: Hiking trails.
Dates: Open year-round.
Fees: None.
Closest town: Elliotsville, 1 mile.
For more information: Forbes State Forest, PO Box 519, Laughlintown, PA 15655. Phone (724) 238-9533.

BLUEGILL

(Lepomis macrochirus)
Bluegills make nests on shallow sand and gravel bars in small to medium sized streams. They are popular stock fish for lakes and ponds.

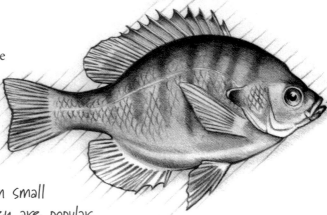

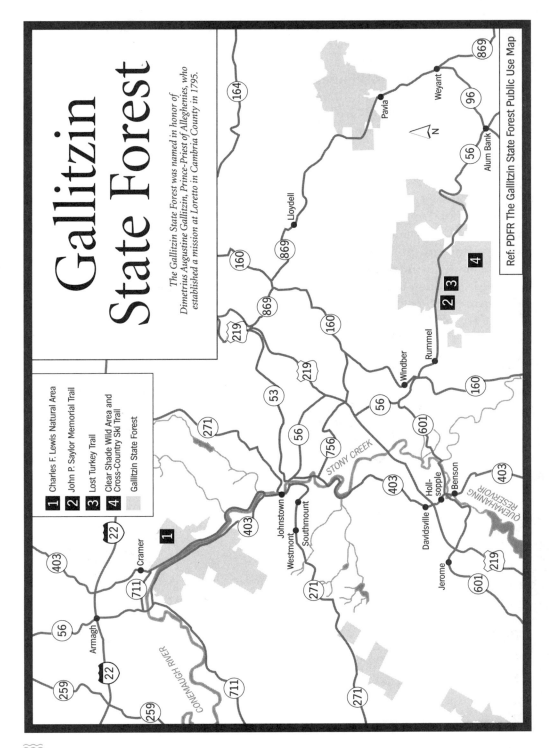

Gallitzin State Forest

The Gallitzin State Forest was named in honor of Dimetrius Augustine Gallitzin, Prince-Priest of Alleghenies, who established a mission at Loretto in Cambria County in 1795.

1 Charles F. Lewis Natural Area

2 John P. Saylor Memorial Trail

3 Lost Turkey Trail

4 Clear Shade Wild Area and Cross-Country Ski Trail

Gallitzin State Forest

Ref: PDFR The Gallitzin State Forest Public Use Map

Gallitzin State Forest

The Gallitzin State Forest is named after Dimetrius Augustine Gallitzin who established a mission in Cambria County in the late 1700s. Gallitzin is among the smallest of Pennsylvania's state forests, encompassing only 17,973 acres in two divisions. The larger of the two, the Babcock Division, is found in northern Somerset County and includes 16,473 acres. The smaller, the Rager Mountain Division, contains 1,503 acres in Cambria County and Indiana County across the Conemaugh River from Laurel Hill State Park.

The area was clear-cut from the late 1800s to 1914. Then, forest fires fueled by woody debris left on the ground spread over much of the area. The combination of scorched earth and lack of trees led to a buildup of water in the soil, resulting in the formation of wetlands that are still present today.

Coal mining has also shaped the area. Both deep mining, in which coal is removed from underground shafts, and strip mining, where the surface of the earth is peeled back to expose the coal deposits, still occur in the forest today.

Before it was clear-cut, the Babcock Division was the meeting place of two different forests. Here the northern forest, which was composed of hemlock, white pine, and northern hardwoods, met the mixed-mesophytic forest of the south. The mixed-mesophytic forest was very diverse. It contained yellow birch (*Betula lutea*), red maple, red oak, beech, sugar maple, ash (*Fraxinus* sp.), basswood (*Tilia americana*), black cherry, walnut (*Juglans nigra*), tulip poplar, and chestnut (*Castanea dentata*). Today the Babcock Division is a mixed-hardwood forest dominated by black cherry and maple.

There are two special protection areas within the Gallitzin State Forest. The Charles F. Lewis Natural Area is located in the Rager Mountain Division and includes the entire watershed of Clark Run. Located in the Babcock Division is the Clear Shade Wild Area, a vast undeveloped area encompassing 2,790 acres.

Directions: To reach the Babcock Division follow PA Route 56 from Windber approximately 5 miles east to the forest office. To reach the Rager Mountain Division follow PA Route 403 approximately 0.75 mile from Cramer to the Charles F. Lewis Natural Area parking lot.

Activities: Hiking, cross-country skiing, snowmobiling, hunting, fishing.

Facilities: Trails, picnic area in the Babcock Division.

Dates: Open year-round. Snowmobiling is allowed from the day following antlerless deer season to Mar. 31.

Fees: None.

Closest town: Rager Mountain Division: Cramer, 0.75 mile. Babcock Division: Ogletown, less than 0.5 mile.

For more information: Gallitzin State Forest, PO Box 506, 155 Hillcrest Drive, Ebensburg, PA 15931. Phone (814) 472-1862.

JOHN P. SAYLOR MEMORIAL TRAIL

John P. Saylor was a native of southwestern Pennsylvania and served in the U.S. House of Representatives for 24 years. In addition to helping convince the Commonwealth of Pennsylvania to purchase the land that is today the Gallitzin State Forest, he played a key role in the passage of the Wilderness Act. This act sets aside primitive areas within federally owned lands and treats them as natural areas where logging and motorized vehicles are prohibited. The John P. Saylor Memorial Trail is composed of two loops within the Babcock Division of the Gallitzin State Forest. The western loop is 12 miles long and lies to the west of Clear Shade Creek, while the eastern loop is 6 miles long and lies to the east of Clear Shade Creek within the Clear Shade Wild Area.

To reach the western loop follow PA Route 56 west from the state forest headquarters for about 2.5 miles. Turn left onto the dirt road. The trail begins at the Babcock Picnic Area on the left side of the road. The trail is relatively flat, but rocky in places, and makes for an easy hike through a mixed-hardwood forest. Several points of interest lie along the trail, including Wolf Rocks. The rocks are an outcrop of conglomerate formed when small rocks became imbedded in sediment and the two were fused over time and under pressure to form a new rock type.

Wolf Rocks mark the middle of the Bog Path, a spur trail that travels northeast and reconnects with the John P. Saylor Memorial Trail on the other side of the western loop. The path passes a boglike wetland formed as a result of poor drainage, fires, and the lack of trees-all a consequence of logging. It is an interpretive trail with 42 species of trees and shrubs marked with numbered green stakes. An interpretive guide is available from the state forest office. Hikers will also see decay-resistant hemlock stumps nearly a century old. Two types of forest management can be seen along the northern loop. One portion passes through an area that has been clear-cut and subsequently replanted by the Bureau of Forestry. The end result of this type of management will be a forest composed of trees of the same size and species, a so-called even-aged stand.

Along another portion of the trail is an area of selective cutting where some trees have been removed and others, including dead snags, have been left. This type of management results in a greater diversity of tree species and age classes, which in turn increases wildlife and plant diversity. The eastern loop is located within the Clear Shade Wild Area (*see* page 169) and is connected to the northern loop by an 80-foot swinging footbridge across Clear Shade Creek. This 6-mile trail passes through a hardwood forest utilized for recreation only. There is no trailhead and the only access is from the north loop of the John P. Saylor Memorial Trail.

Trail: Western loop, 12 miles. Eastern loop, 6 miles.

Elevation: 2,200–2,600 feet.

Degree of difficulty: Easy, rocky in some places.

Surface and blaze: John P. Saylor Memorial trail, orange blazes. Bog Path, yellow blazes.

For more information: Gallitzin State Forest, PO Box 506, 155 Hillcrest Drive, Ebensburg, PA 15931. Phone (814) 472-1862.

CLEAR SHADE WILD AREA AND CROSS-COUNTRY SKI TRAIL

The Clear Shade Wild Area is located in the southeast corner of the Babcock Division of Gallitzin State Forest in Somerset County. The area encompasses 2,790 acres, including much of the watershed of Clear Shade Creek, an Exceptional Value Stream. Like most of the state forest, the area is dominated by northern hardwoods. No development is permitted and logging is limited to salvage cuts (only dead and dying trees are removed) and cuts that are designed to improve wildlife habitat.

There are two major trails within the area: the eastern loop of the John P. Saylor Memorial Trail (*see* page 168) and the Babcock Ski Touring Trail. The ski trail was developed by the Bureau of Forestry, the Greater Johnstown Athletic Ski Club, and the Pennsylvania Conservation Corps. There are three loops to the ski trail, each beginning at the parking lot on Clear Shade Road.

Loop A, also called the Tenderfoot Trail, stretches for 1.7 miles, ranges in elevation from 2,500 feet to 2,580 feet, and lies to the west of Clear Shade Creek. Loop B, the Nordic Trail, is 4.4 miles in length, ranges in elevation from 2,300 feet to 2,540 feet, and parallels Clear Shade Creek along part of its course. The longest part of the trail is Loop C, or the Clear Shade Run Trail, which extends for 8 miles, much of it lying along an abandoned logging railroad grade along Clear Shade Creek. The elevational range is the same as the Nordic Trail. All trails are marked with blue paint blazes.

Directions: Follow PA Route 56 east from the forest headquarters to Shade Road, a distance of less than 0.5 mile. Turn right onto Shade Road, and there is a parking lot immediately adjacent.

Activities: Hiking, cross-country skiing, fishing, hunting.
Facilities: Trails.
Dates: Open year-round.
Fees: None.
Closest town: Ogletown, 1.5 miles.
For more information: Gallitzin State Forest, PO Box 506, 155 Hillcrest Drive, Ebensburg, PA 15931. Phone (814) 472-1862.

LOST TURKEY TRAIL

The Lost Turkey Trail extends 26 miles from the Babcock Picnic Area in Gallitzin State Forest to Blue Knob State Park. The trail follows old woods roads and abandoned railroad grades along much of its route. As the trail moves north from the state forest it crosses the Allegheny Front, a steep escarpment that is the dividing line between the Allegheny Plateau and Valley and Ridge provinces. The northern end of the trail is near Blue Knob, the second highest point in the state at 3,120 feet. The total elevational change along the trail is 1,360 feet.

The trail passes through second-growth, mixed-hardwood forests; oak forests; and stream valleys dominated by hemlock. Along the way hikers pass through not only state forest and state park land but also through private lands and state game land managed by the Pennsylvania Game Commission.

Among the points of interest along the trail are apple trees that mark the location of old logging camps and farms, old railroad grades and skid trails, scenic vistas, beaver dams at the headwaters of the Little Conemaugh River, and timber cuts. Cross-country skiers and snowmobilers also use much of the trail. Snowmobiles are limited to the portion of the trail marked with orange diamonds that extends from the midpoint of the trail to the Babcock Picnic Area. To reach the Babcock Picnic Area follow PA Route 56 west from the state forest headquarters for about 2.5 miles. Turn left onto the dirt road, and the picnic area on the left side of the road.

Trail: 26 miles one-way.

Elevation: 1,674–3,034 feet.

Degree of difficulty: Moderate.

Surface and blaze: Rectangular red paint blazes.

For more information: Gallitzen State Forest, PO Box 506, 155 Hillcrest Drive, Ebensburg, PA 15931. Phone (814) 472-1862.

CHARLES F. LEWIS NATURAL AREA

Tucked into the southeastern corner of Indiana County along PA Route 403 is the Charles F. Lewis Natural Area. While relatively small at 384 acres, the area includes the complete drainage basin of Clark Run, a tributary of the Conemaugh River.

The narrow, steep-sided ravine cut by Clark Run is biologically diverse and contains several different types of forest. The best way to explore the ravine is by hiking the Clark Run Trail, a loop that runs through the ravine. The trail is marked with rectangular yellow paint blazes.

The trail begins at a parking area near the mouth of Clark Run and proceeds along the bottom of the ravine. The soils here are rich and deep, having been deposited by the stream and washed from the hillsides. The forest is classified as a northern-hardwood cove forest and is dominated by yellow poplars (often called tulip trees), basswood, sugar maple, and yellow birch.

The trail soon begins to climb the south side of the ravine, rising 520 feet above the parking lot in less than 1 mile. In addition to providing a dramatic view of the stream below, the trail takes the hiker through a typical northern-hardwood forest containing black cherry, birch, maple, hemlock, and beech.

As the trail passes above the headwaters of the stream, it loops back along the north side of the ravine, and the forest changes again, this time to mixed oak. The soil here is poor because of severe wildfires that occurred between 1945 and 1950. Fire scars can be seen on some of the dead snags and the living sassafras (*Sassafras albidum*), black gum (*Nyssa sylvatica*), red oak, and chestnut oak.

A hike along the trail is more than good exercise; it's also educational. More than

83 species of trees, shrubs, and woody vines are marked with green numbered stakes. An inventory booklet, which identifies the plants by common and Latin name, is available from the forest office. Common species such as hemlock, staghorn sumac (*Rhus typhina*), and Virginia creeper (*Parthenocissus quinquefolia*), as well as the less common American elm (*Ulmus americana*), red-berried elder (*Sambucus racemosa*), and fox grape (*Vitis labrusca*) are identified.

The Clark Run Trail is a primitive, 1.8-mile trail that traverses steep, rocky terrain. Spring seeps, where groundwater percolates to the surface, combined with loose rocks make the trail challenging. These same conditions also make the ravine an especially good habitat for a wide variety of amphibians and reptiles. In fact, hikers are advised to watch for rattlesnakes and copperheads (*Agkistrodon contortrix*) as they hike the trail. The entire ravine has been designated a special protection area for reptiles and amphibians, so no hunting or removal of these animals is permitted.

Those who want to extend their hike should consider the Rager Mountain Trail. This 3-mile loop is attached to the Clark Run Trail and is marked with orange paint blazes. The trail's high point is 2,400 feet, 1,100 feet above the Clark Run Trail trailhead.

Directions: From the village of Cramer follow PA Route 403 southwest for 0.75 mile. There is a parking area and trailhead on the left side of the road.

Activities: Hiking, hunting.

Facilities: Trails.

Dates: Open year-round.

Fees: None.

Closest town: Cramer, 0.75 mile.

For more information: Gallitzin State Forest, PO Box 506, 155 Hillcrest Drive, Ebensburg, PA 15931. Phone (814) 472-1862.

VIRGINIA CREEPER
(Parthenocissus quinquefolia)
A cousin of grapes, the Virginia creeper climbs and sprawls as it grows up to 150 feet high. Leaves are green in summer and red in fall. The dark blue berries are poisonous to humans but are food for songbirds and other wildlife.

Private Lands

🌸 BEAR RUN NATURE RESERVE

Bear Run Nature Reserve is a 5,000-acre tract located on the west slope of Laurel Ridge in Fayette County. The Western Pennsylvania Conservancy, the largest private land conservation organization in Pennsylvania, owns the reserve.

The reserve contains most of the watershed of Bear Run and Beaver Run as well as part of Laurel Run. All three are tributaries of the Youghiogheny River. Like most of the Laurel Highlands, the area was clear-cut in the early part of this century and is today dominated by second-growth oak forests with scattered pine plantations and native hemlock.

This is one of only three locations in Pennsylvania where the endangered solitary pussytoes (*Antennaria solitaria*), a white wildflower belonging to the daisy family, is found. In addition, the Allegheny woodrat (*Neotoma magister*) is suspected to make its home here.

The area contains a 20-mile-long trail system composed of 16 named and marked trails. They range in length from the Saddle Trail, which extends for only 0.3 mile and is especially good for viewing wildflowers, to the Laurel Run Trail and Ridge Trail, which are the reserve's longest at 2.3 miles. In addition to hikers, the trails are also used by bikers and cross-country skiers during the winter. A trail brochure is available from the conservancy.

Hunting and fishing are allowed within the reserve. However, hunting is limited to turkey and deer, and fishing is only allowed upstream from the Route 381 bridge.

Adjacent to the Bear Run Nature Reserve is one of the most famous and unique homes ever built. In 1936 the Kaufmann family, owners of a large Pittsburgh-based department store chain which bears their name, commissioned world-renowned

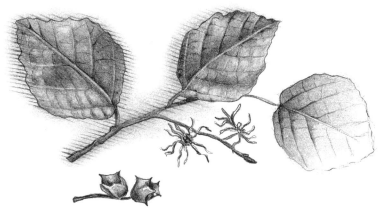

WITCH-HAZEL
(Hamamelis virginiana)
This plant blooms after its leaves fall in autumn. It is recognized by its spidery, yellow flowers.

Allegheny Woodrat

The Allegheny woodrat, the only member of the genus Neotoma found in the eastern U.S., is a cousin of the better-known pack rat. It shares its western counterpart's habit of collecting things. Eyeglasses, coins, bones, and feathers are just some of the items that have been found in woodrat nests.

The Allegheny woodrat, which is also known as the eastern woodrat and the cave rat, lives in rock piles on rocky mountaintops and slopes. These remote habitats combined with its nocturnal habits make this one of the most seldom seen mammals in the state.

Historically found throughout the Appalachian chain, the woodrat has begun to disappear from the northern end of its range. It's no longer found in New York or Connecticut, and it has nearly disappeared from eastern Pennsylvania. While no one really knows for sure, biologists believe that most of the woodrat colonies left in the state are found west of the Susquehanna. The cause of the population decline is unknown.

architect Frank Lloyd Wright to design a weekend home along a small waterfall on Bear Run. At the time the Kaufmanns owned much of the land that is today the Bear Run Nature Reserve.

The house that Wright designed was not built next to the waterfall but over it. Fallingwater, as the house came to be known, is made from concrete and sandstone quarried from the property. The house is cantilevered over the stream, making it seem as much a part of the surrounding ecosystem as the stream itself. In 1963 the Kaufmann family donated the home to the Western Pennsylvania Conservancy which then opened it to the public. Since 1964 more than 2.7 million people have toured the house.

Directions: Take PA Route 381 north 3.5-miles from the town of Ohiopyle to the Bear Run Visitor's Center. Trailheads are located at the visitor's center.

Activities: Hiking, cross-country skiing, biking, hunting, and fishing.

Facilities: Trails and Fallingwater.

Fallingwater: Apr. 1–mid-Nov. (reservations are recommended).

Dates: Open year-round.

Fees: There is a fee for touring Fallingwater.

Closest town: Ohiopyle, 3.5 miles.

For more information: Western Pennsylvania Conservancy, 209 Fourth Avenue, Pittsburgh, PA 15222. Phone (412) 288-2777.

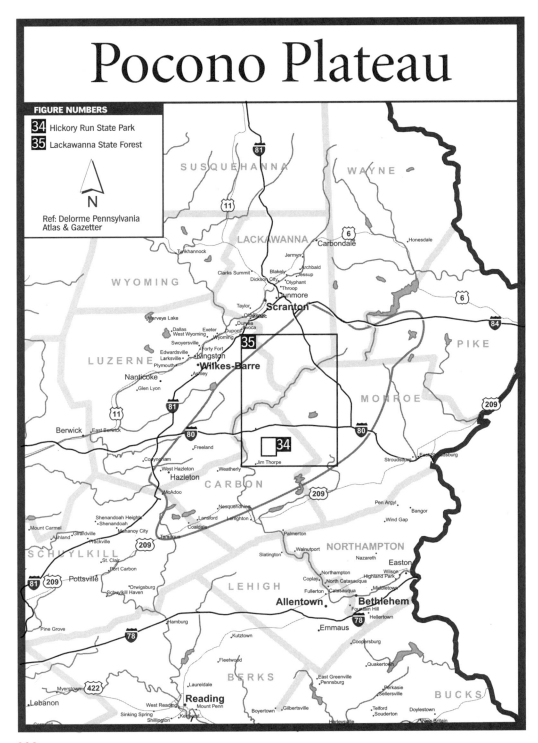

Pocono Plateau

FIGURE NUMBERS

34 Hickory Run State Park
35 Lackawanna State Forest

N

Ref: Delorme Pennsylvania
Atlas & Gazetter

Pocono Plateau

The Pocono Plateau Section is also known as the Pocono Mountain Section, although the former is a more accurate description because the area looks more like a plateau than a mountain range. The section doesn't contain any cities or towns with more than 5,000 inhabitants and is best known for its vacation and recreation areas. The Lackawanna State Forest and the Gouldsboro, Promised Land, and Hickory Run state parks are all located on the plateau. All or part of Pike, Monroe, Wayne, Lackawanna, and Luzerne counties are located in this section.

The Pocono Plateau is characterized by gently rolling hills ranging in elevation from 1,300 feet to 1,640 feet. The plateau contains numerous lakes, wetlands, and bogs, especially in the eastern portions, which were glaciated during the last ice age. A steep, 1,000-foot sandstone escarpment separates the plateau from the neighboring Valley and Ridge province to the west and south. To the north and east lies the Glaciated Low Plateau Section. The major east-west roadway is Interstate 80, and the major north-south roadways are Interstate 380 and PA Route 9.

🏞 HICKORY RUN STATE PARK

Hickory Run State Park is one of the largest in the Pennsylvania State Park system, encompassing 15,500 acres within Carbon County. Once called the Shades of Death because of the dense pine and hemlock forest that grew here, the park is located within the western foothills of the Pocono Mountains.

The land was acquired by the United States in a treaty with the Native Americans that inhabited the area in the late 1700s. To make sure the area was settled, the government granted ownership of 400-acre tracts, called warrants, to anyone willing to pay to have the land surveyed. The area remained relatively unchanged until the Lehigh Canal, which connected the area to Philadelphia and New York, was built. Logging companies began buying up the warrants and logging camps and sawmills quickly sprang up. Over the next 40 or so years the area was clear-cut.

Logging towns disappeared as rapidly as they appeared. One of them was the village of Hickory Run, located where the small creeks of Hickory Run and Sand Spring Run meet. The only thing left of the village today is a couple of buildings, including one that houses the park administration office.

In 1935 the area was acquired by the National Park Service and developed as a Recreational Demonstration Area to be utilized for low-cost outdoor activities. In 1946 ownership was transferred to the state, and Hickory Run State Park was born. Today the park is dominated by second-growth, mixed-oak forests; northern-hardwood forests; and white pine-hemlock forests. The understory contains dense stands of mountain laurel and rhododendron. As is the case throughout most of the Pocono region, wetlands are common due to past glacial activity. Swamps dominated by woody vegetation, bogs,

Hickory Run State Park

One of the largest state parks in the Pennsylvania state park system, Hickory Run is 15,500 acres in the western foothills of the Pocono Mountains.

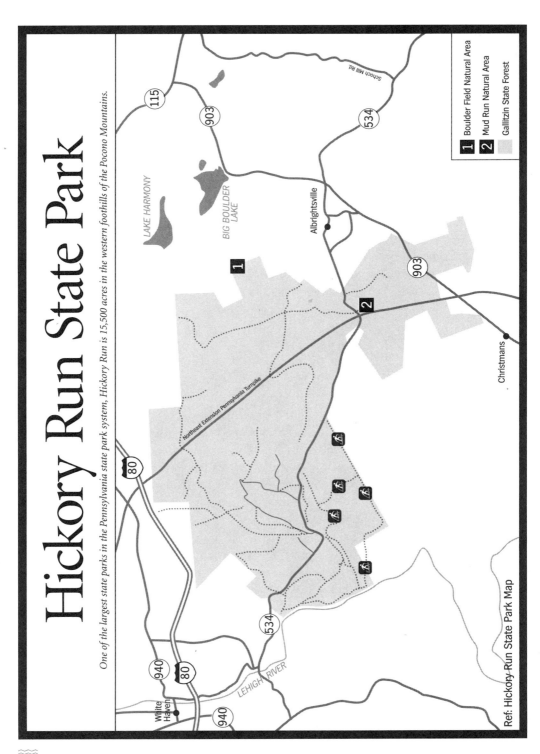

	Boulder Field Natural Area
1	
2	Mud Run Natural Area
	Galllitzin State Forest

Schoch Mill Rd.

115

903

534

LAKE HARMONY

BIG BOULDER LAKE

Albrightsville

903

Christmans

Northeast Extension Pennsylvania Turnpike

80

534

940

80

940

White Haven

LEHIGH RIVER

Ref: Hickory-Run State Park Map

vernal ponds that dry out in the summer, and wet meadows are all found here. Among the common species living here are impatiens (*Impatiens capensis*), soft rush (*Juncus effusus*), skunk cabbage (*Symplocarpus foetidus*), and highbush blueberry (*Vaccinium corymbosum*).

Also common in the Poconos are lakes, and Hickory Run State Park contains two. Hickory Run Lake covers 4 acres and can be reached by a short walk along the Lake Trail. The larger Sand Spring Lake, which encompasses 11 acres, is part of the Sand Springs Day Use Area. The area includes a concession stand, picnic area, guarded beach, and parking lot. To reach the lakes follow PA Route 534 east from the park office for about 0.5 mile to the road marked with the Sand Springs Day Use Area sign. Follow the road until it splits. To reach Sand Spring Lake bear to the right. To reach Hickory Lake bear left and follow the signs for the Boulder Field. The Lake Trail is down the road about 1 mile on the right.

For those interested in exploring the less developed areas of the park there is a 42-mile-long system of marked trails. Yellow blazes indicate hiking-only trails, blue blazes identify trails for hiking and cross-country skiing, and orange blazes mark trails designated for hiking and snowmobiling. A total of 21 miles of trails are designated for snowmobiles, and 13 miles are designated for cross-country skiing. A detailed trail guide is available at the park office.

Most of the park is open to hunting. Among the more commonly pursued species are white-tailed deer, gray squirrel (*Sciurus carolinensis*), and black bear. One of the park's most common game species, the snowshoe hare (*Lepus americanus*), is uncommon in Pennsylvania. Trout fishermen will find brook trout and brown trout stocked in Fourth Run, Sand Spring, and Mud Run. Trout and panfish are also found in the Lehigh River, which flows along the western side of the park.

SNOWSHOE HARE
(Lepus americanus)
A shy boreal species that is more active at night. Dark brown in summer, white in winter.

Directions: From Interstate 80 take Exit 41 (Hickory Run State Park Exit). Follow PA Route 534 South, which runs through the park, east for 6 miles.

Activities: Hiking, camping, swimming, cross-country skiing, snowmobiling, hunting, fishing, and environmental education programs.

Facilities: Hiking trails, snowmobile trails, cross-country ski trails, picnic areas, campgrounds, playground, guarded beach.

Dates: Open year-round.

Fees: Camping fees.

Closest town: White Haven, 3 miles.

For more information: Hickory Run State Park, RR 1, Box 81, White Haven, PA 18661. Phone (717) 443-0400.

BOULDER FIELD NATURAL AREA

Located in the northeastern corner of Hickory Run State Park is a geologic feature unique to North America. The Boulder Field Natural Area is a flat accumulation of boulders, most of them less than 4 feet in diameter, covering an area 400 feet by 1,800 feet. Surrounding the area are wooded slopes that gradually rise about 200 feet above the rock-strewn flat. A walk through the woods around the boulder field reveals a forest floor with protruding boulders similar to those found in the field. While it's obvious that the boulders must have come from the slopes, what's not so obvious is how they ended up in the boulder field. Boulder fields are not unknown in the Appalachian Mountains, but they're usually found in valleys at the base of slopes much steeper than this.

Geologists believe they know how the boulder field formed. It is a consequence of the geologic characteristics of the surrounding slopes and a climatic event that helped shape much of the northeastern United States, the Wisconsin glaciation.

The glaciers did not reach this far south, stopping about a mile northeast of Hickory Run State Park, but they came close enough to drastically change the climate. During the Wisconsin glaciation 15,000 years ago, the climate was much like that seen today near the ice cap in northern Greenland. The ground was permanently frozen, but the surface experienced frequent freezing and thawing during the summer months.

The rocks that underlie the slopes surrounding the boulder field are naturally fractured in a blocklike configuration. As water seeped into the cracks between the blocks and froze, the expanding water broke the blocks apart. As these blocks were loosened over time, they tumbled down the slopes into what is today the boulder field.

When the climate returned to preglacial conditions, the process came to an end. As the glacier melted, the water washed away all of the sediment and small gravel, leaving only the large immovable boulders. Today a stream flows about 4 to 6 feet below the boulders. It can be heard flowing below the boulders and seen 0.5 mile below the boulder field as it emerges from a rocky, wooded area, eventually flowing into Hickory Run Stream.

Visitors can walk across the boulder field but should be aware that some parts are harder to cross than others. Walking is easiest in the western end of the field because the boulders are smaller and more rounded. Toward the northeastern end of the field the boulders become larger, and more uneven in size, and the rocks teeter as you step on them. The most difficult area to cross is the eastern end where the largest blocks are found. While most of the boulder field is nearly flat, the boulders here are lying at different angles with large crevices in between. The elevation here varies 6 feet to 8 feet, so hikers do more jumping and climbing than walking.

Geologists have found a few boulder fields of similar size and formed by similar processes in Sweden and even larger ones in the Falkland Islands in the South Atlantic, but they have found nothing comparable anywhere else in North America. Because this boulder field is so unique, it was designated a National Natural Landmark by the U.S. Department of the Interior in 1967.

Two trails, both beginning at the Boulder Field parking area, are located within the Boulder Field Natural Area. The Stone Trail is an easy trail open to both hikers and snowmobilers that extends for 1.5 miles. It climbs the ridge above the boulder field and then follows the park boundary west, ending at the Fourth Run Trail. The Boulder Trail is a much more difficult hiking trail that extends 3.3 miles to PA Route 534, where there is a trailhead and parking area. The rocky trail passes through conifer and beech forests and crosses the Stage Trail at the halfway point.

Directions: From the park office follow PA Route 534 to the road marked with the Sand Springs Day Use Area sign. Follow this road until it splits and bear left. Follow the signs to the Boulder Field.

Activities: Hiking, snowmobiling, hunting.

Facilities: Trails.

Dates: Open for day use year-round. Camping is permitted from the second Friday in April until the day after anterless deer season.

Fees: None.

Closest town: Albrightsville, approximately 5 miles.

For more information: Hickory Run State Park, RR 1, PO Box 81, White Haven, PA 18661. Phone (717) 443-0400.

🏞 MUD RUN NATURAL AREA

The main feature of the Mud Run Natural Area is the Mud Run Gorge, a steep-sided stream valley containing numerous waterfalls. The largest is Hawk Falls, where Hawk Run drops 25 feet into Mud Run. Mixed hardwoods with a dense understory of rhododendron dominate the area. Mud Run is classified as a High Quality Stream and is well known for its native brown trout and brook trout. Fishing is permitted, but the stream has been designated a delayed harvest-artificial lure area only. The best way to reach the stream is by the 3.25-mile Hawk Falls Trail. The trail passes through a rhododendron thicket, down a hill, and across Hawk Run. To cross Hawk Run the hiker must use stepping stones which may be underwater if it has rained recently. The trail ends at Mud Run near Hawk Falls.

Directions: From the park office travel east along PA Route 534 for approximately 4.5 miles. A parking area and the Hawk Falls trailhead are on the south side of the road just after the road passes under the Pennsylvania Turnpike.

Activities: Hiking, hunting, fishing, swimming, snowmobiling, cross-country skiing, picnicking.

Facilities: Trail.

Dates: Open year-round.

Fees: None.

Closest town: Albrightsville, 1.5 miles.

For more information: Hickory Run State Park, RR 1, PO Box 81, White Haven, PA 18661. Phone (717) 443-0400.

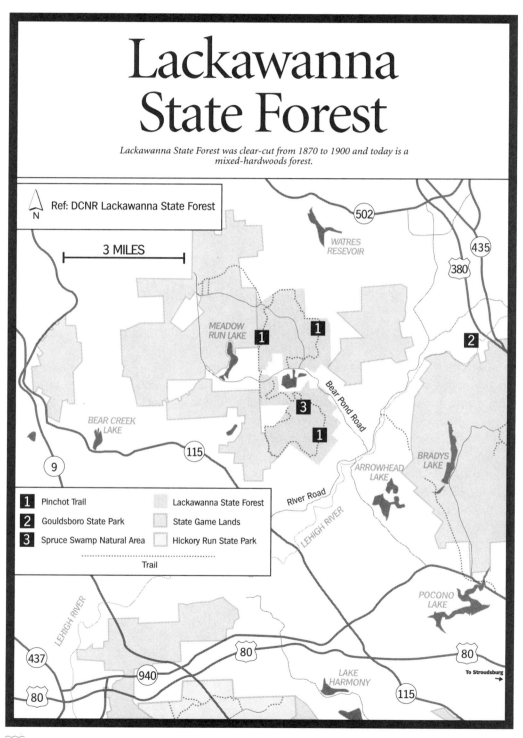

Lackawanna State Forest

Lackawanna State Forest was clear-cut from 1870 to 1900 and today is a mixed-hardwoods forest.

N

Ref: DCNR Lackawanna State Forest

3 MILES

WATRES RESEVOIR

502

435

380

MEADOW RUN LAKE **1**

1

2

3

1

BEAR CREEK LAKE

Bear Pond Road

BRADYS LAKE

ARROWHEAD LAKE

115

9

River Road

LEHIGH RIVER

1 Pinchot Trail

2 Gouldsboro State Park

3 Spruce Swamp Natural Area

Lackawanna State Forest

State Game Lands

Hickory Run State Park

Trail

LEHIGH RIVER

POCONO LAKE

437

80

940

80

LAKE HARMONY

115

80

To Stroudsburg

Lackawanna State Forest

The Lackawanna State Forest is composed of two separate tracts of land. The Thornhurst Tract encompasses 7,027 acres in Lackawanna County and is the more developed of the two. The West Nanticoke Tract is an undeveloped area of 1,404 acres located in Luzerne County. The entire forest was clear-cut from 1870 to 1900. The deadwood left behind then fueled wildfires that consumed many of the nutrients and organic material in the soil. Adding insult to injury, rain then washed away much of the depleted soil.

At one time the chestnut was one of the Lackawanna State Forest's most common trees. A fungus introduced from Asia in the late nineteenth century, however, wiped out nearly all of the chestnuts. Today only an occasional chestnut tree is found in the Lackawanna State Forest sprouting from the roots of a tree killed long ago by the chestnut blight. Currently, the area is primarily a mixed-hardwood forest that the Bureau of Forestry manages for forest recreation, wildlife habitat, and commercial timber sales. In addition to valuable hardwoods, wildflowers are common. They can be found just about anywhere in the forest, especially in the spring when there is abundant sunlight on the forest floor. Starflower (*Trientalis borealis*), painted trillium (*Trilium undulatum*), asters (*Aster* spp.), pink lady's-slipper (*Cypripedium acaule*), and goldthread (*Coptis groenlandica*) are just a few of the wildflowers found here.

One of the biggest threats to the Lackawanna State Forest is Pennsylvania's largest herbivore, the white-tailed deer. In areas where new trees are being planted, the seedlings are placed deep in opaque plastic tubes that let light in but keep deer out. In other areas electrified fences powered by solar-powered batteries are used to keep deer out. Deer populations are large throughout Pennsylvania but especially in the Poconos. Motorists should be on the lookout for herds of deer grazing along side of the road or walking across it at almost any time of day. Also common are wetlands, a consequence of glaciation during past ice ages. Three types of wetlands are found in the Lackawanna State Forest: natural ponds, glacial kettlehole bogs, and boreal-conifer swamps. The last type of swamp, dominated by balsam fir (*Abies balsamea*) and tamarack, is rarely found in Pennsylvania but is common in northern Quebec.

The bogs and swamps are home to many uncommon plants. Hartford fern (*Lygodium palmatum*), capitate spike rush (*Eleocharis caribaea*), creeping snowberry (*Gaultheria hispidula*), and small-floating manna grass (*Glyceria borealis*) are just some of the Species of Special Concern that occur within the wetlands of Lackawanna State Forest.

Of the two tracts that make up the Lackawanna State Forest, only one, the Thornhurst Tract, contains areas developed for recreation. Located in a conifer grove near the park office is a 30-acre picnic ground, known as the Manny Gordon Recreation Site, with tables, grills, and potable water. Also found within this tract is the 23-mile-long Pinchot Trail System (*see page 183*), a 24-mile-long trail system used by snowmobilers and cross-country skiers. Trout fishermen may want to use the Pinchot Trail to reach Choke Creek which contains native brook trout.

Directions: To reach the forest office follow Bear Pond Road north from Thornhurst for about 2.5 miles.

Activities: Hiking, picnicking, backpacking, hunting, snowmobiling, cross-country skiing, fishing, hunting.

Facilities: Hiking trails, cross-country ski/snowmobile trails, picnic ground, orienteering area.

Dates: Open year-round.

Closest town: Thornhurst, 2.5 miles.

For more information: Lackawanna State Forest, 401 Samter Building, 101 Penn Avenue, Scranton, PA 18503. Phone (717) 963-4561.

SPRUCE SWAMP NATURAL AREA

The Spruce Swamp Natural Area has been set aside to preserve a glacial kettlehole bog. This wetland is a remnant of the last ice age and contains many plants not commonly found in Pennsylvania, including Labrador tea (*Ledum groenlandicium*) and bog rosemary, a shrub of the genus *Andromeda*. The trees found here are also unusual. Scattered throughout the bog are black spruce, red spruce, balsam fir, and tamarack, which are more commonly found in the subarctic regions of Canada. This 87-acre natural area contains a wide variety of wildlife including bear, white-tailed deer, gray fox (*Urocyon cineroeargenteus*), and snowshoe hare.

Surrounding the bog is a mixed-hardwood forest containing a diversity of trees. Red oak, white oak (*Quercus alba*), chestnut oak (*Quercus prinus*), red maple, beech, white ash, gray birch (*Betula populifolia*), striped maple (*Acer pensylvanicum*), aspen, black birch (*Betula lenta*), yellow birch, black cherry, serviceberry (*Amelanchier* sp.), and even a few American chestnuts are found here as well as a few species of conifers. Rhododendron and mountain laurel dominate the understory, with highbush blueberry (*Vaccinium corymbosum*) common around the periphery of the bog.

The area is bounded on the south by Tannery Road, on the north by the Sunday Trail, on the east by the Birch Still Trail (both of these trails are part of the Pinchot Trail System, *see* page 183), and on the west by an old forest road that has been gated and planted with grasses such as alfalfa and clover to provide food for wildlife. There are no trails within the Spruce Swamp Natural Area.

Directions: Follow LR 2016 (a paved township road) west from Thornhurst for approximately 5 miles to Tannery Road. Follow Tannery Road southwest about 2.9 miles to Phelps Road. A small parking area and sign are located at the intersection.

Activities: Hiking, hunting.

Facilities: None.

Dates: Open year-round.

Closest town: Thornhurst, 3.2 miles.

For more information: Lackawanna State Forest, 401 Samters Building, 101 Penn

Avenue, Scranton, PA 18503. Phone (717) 963-4561.

PINCHOT TRAIL

The Pinchot Trail is a 23-mile-long trail system loop composed of numerous shorter trails. These trails, in combination with four connector trails, provide numerous short day hikes as well as longer overnight hikes. Overnight hikers can camp along the trail, but a permit is required from the Lackawanna State Forest.

The trail passes through a primarily mixed-hardwood forest and across several small streams. It also passes by several bogs including the Spruce Swamp Natural Area. The high points along the trail offer scenic vistas of the surrounding forest, while at lower elevations the trail follows hemlock-lined stream channels. An observation platform is situated on Pine Hill of the Thornhurst tract, and offers the visitor a magnificent panoramic view of the forested valleys and mountains of the region. There are two trailheads, one at the midpoint of the loop and another along the southern end of the loop. To reach the main trailhead near the middle of the loop follow LR 2016 (a paved township road) west from Thornhurst. A parking area and sign are located on the right about four miles down the road. The southern trailhead is marked with a sign for the Choke Creek Nature Trail, which is one of the Pinchot Trail system's connecting trails. It can be reached by following LR 2016 about 0.5 mile past the main trailhead and then turning left onto Tannery Road. A parking area is located about 2 miles down this road.

Trail: 23-mile loop.

Elevation: 1,640–2,180 feet.

Degree of difficulty: Moderate.

Surface and blaze: Unpaved. Blue blazes mark the main trail. Red blazes mark the connecting trails.

For more information: Lackawanna State Forest, 401 Samters Building, 101 Penn Avenue, Scranton, PA 18503. Phone (717) 963-4561.

Gifford Pinchot

Gifford Pinchot, whose family home was in Milford, Pennsylvania, is considered by many to be the father of conservationism and modern forestry in this country. He studied forestry in Europe and in the late 1800s served as the head of the Agriculture Department's Forestry Division where he oversaw the development of that agency into the U.S. Forest Service. Eventually he returned to Pennsylvania to become the Commissioner of the Pennsylvania Department of Forestry until he was elected Governor in 1922.

He is best known for pioneering the concept of sustained forestry. He believed forests could be managed indefinitely as commercial and natural resources if harvest and growth were balanced. This concept is the foundation of modern forestry and has eliminated the massive clear-cutting practices that led to the deforestation of Pennsylvania in the latter half of the nineteenth century.

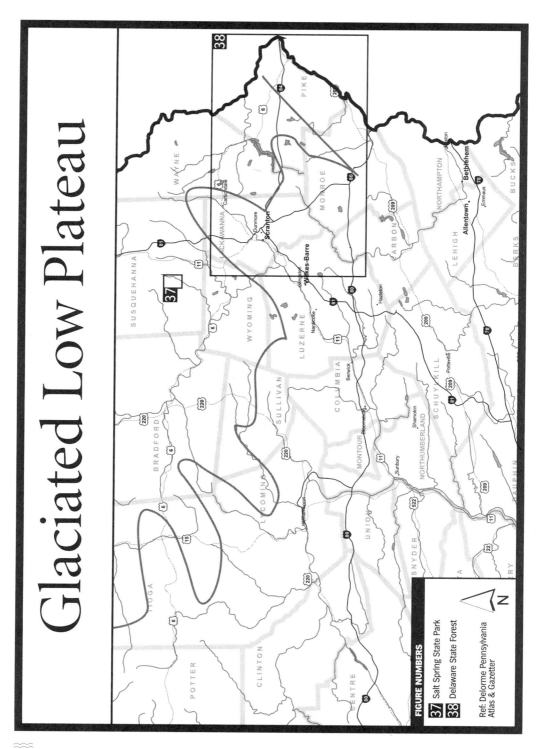

Glaciated Low Plateau

Glaciated Low Plateau

The Glaciated Low Plateau is a primarily wooded, topographically diverse area that has been shaped by glaciation. Swamps, bogs, and lakes, formed from glacial meltwater and glacial till (gravel and rock left behind during the last ice age) are common. All or part of Tioga, Bradford, Susquehanna, Wyoming, Wayne, Pike, Monroe, and Lackawanna counties are located within this section. The largest town is Sayre with a population of less than 10,000 people.

The plateau rises in elevation from 754 feet along the Susquehanna River in the west to 2,300 feet along the resistant sandstone ridges in the east. These ridges continue into New York as the Catskill Mountains. A portion of the plateau's eastern edge borders the Delaware River. Numerous waterfalls are found where streams flow from the plateau into the river.

Located within the Glaciated Low Plateau Section are Mount Pisgah, Hills Creek, Lackawanna, Frances Slocum, and Salt Spring state parks as well as the Delaware State Forest. The major east-west highways are Interstate 84 and US Route 6. The major north-south routes are Interstate 81, US Route 15, and US Route 220.

SALT SPRING STATE PARK

While it's among the smallest of Pennsylvania's state parks, Salt Spring State Park contains some of the most unique trails, most unusual geologic features, and rarest trees in the state. The park encompasses 400 acres of woodland along Fall Brook and Silver Creek in Susquehanna County.

Salt Spring State Park takes its name from a mineral spring that was a source of valuable salt from precolonial times up until the early part of the twentieth century. The Oneidas, a Native American tribe that inhabited the area up until the time of the first white settlers, gathered salt here as did the Europeans who succeeded them. In the 1920s, a 400-foot well was drilled to pump out the salt-laden water called brine. The hope was that commercial quantities of salt could be collected for the dairy industry, which uses salt to manufacture cheese. The venture did not yield enough salt to make the operation profitable and so ended the exploitation of the salt spring.

Located near the spring in the deep gorge cut by Fall Brook is a stand of virgin hemlocks. These trees, which probably escaped the logger's ax because of their inaccessibility, are estimated to be 600 to 700 years old. Because of the uniqueness of the spring and the rarity of the trees, the Nature Conservancy purchased the area in the 1960s from the Wheaton family, which had owned it since before the Civil War. The Nature Conservancy then sold the land to the state in 1973.

The park offers recreational opportunities for picnickers, hikers, fishermen, and hunters. A parking area and restrooms are located along Salt Spring Road near the point where Fall Brook flows into Silver Creek. A picnic area is located just across Fall

Salt Spring State Park

Salt Spring State Park is located in Susquehanna County 7 miles north of Montrose in northeastern Pennsylvania. The park was first conceived of during the 1960s when local conservation-oriented citizens learned that the property was for sale by James Wheaton whose family had owned the land since 1848.

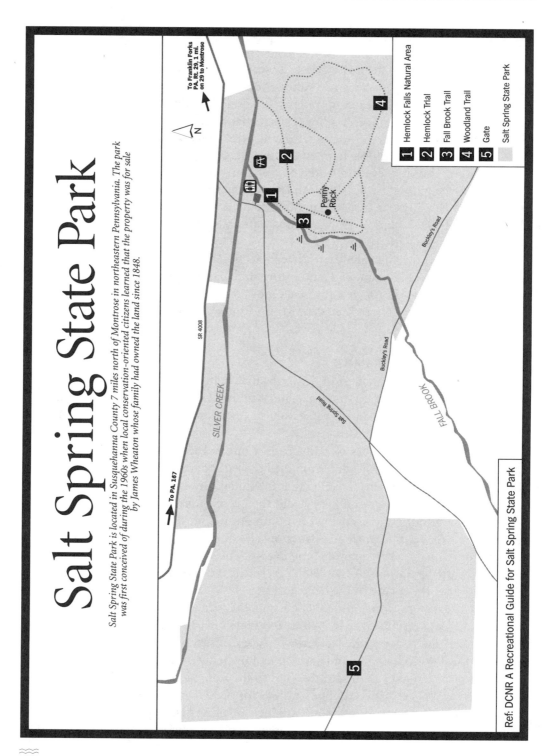

To Franklin Forks
PA, Rt. 29, 1 mL
on 29 to Montrose

N

To PA 167

SR 4008

SILVER CREEK

Salt Spring Road

Buckley's Road

Buckley's Road

FALL BROOK

Penny
Rock

1 Hemlock Falls Natural Area
2 Hemlock Trial
3 Fall Brook Trail
4 Woodland Trail
5 Gate
Salt Spring State Park

Ref: DCNR A Recreational Guide for Salt Spring State Park

Brook from the parking lot. Both of these areas provide easy access to the three trails that run through the park and the Hemlock/Falls Natural Area (*see* below).

Both Fall Brook and Silver Creek are stocked with trout. One of the most popular fishing spots is the picnic area, which is located where the two streams meet. Three hundred of the park's 400 acres are also open to hunting.

Directions: From Montrose follow PA Route 29 north for 7 miles. At Franklin Fork turn left onto SR 4008 and travel 1 mile to Salt Spring Road. Turn left onto Salt Spring Road, and the parking area is on the left just across the bridge over Silver Creek.

Activities: Hiking, hunting, fishing, picnicking.

Facilities: Trails, picnic area.

Dates: Open year-round.

Fees: None.

Closest town: Franklin Fork, 1 mile.

For more information: Salt Spring State Park, c/o Lackawanna State Park, RR 1, Box 230, Dalton, PA 18414. Phone (717) 945-3239.

⬚ HEMLOCK/FALLS NATURAL AREA

The Hemlock/Falls Natural Area encompasses 34 acres along Fall Brook and includes three waterfalls and a stand of old-growth hemlock. This is one of the state's newest natural areas, having been designated in 1996. There are three trails within the natural area.

The Fall Brook Trail begins at the bridge adjacent to the parking area and runs upstream past all three waterfalls. While the trail is only about 0.25 mile long, it provides a strenuous walk because of its unique construction. The trail is composed of steps cut into the rock alongside the stream and its waterfalls. Since the trail is literally part of the streambed, it is not passable during periods of high water. The trail rises approximately 300 feet and is marked.

The Hemlock Trail, which was built along an old logging road, begins at the terminus of the Fall Brook Trail. This trail runs northwest, paralleling the Fall Brook Trail, and passes through the old-growth hemlock, past the salt spring, and ends at Silver Creek. The trail is about 0.25 mile long and descends approximately 300 feet. Along the way it passes an outcrop of stratified rock. After thousands of years of weathering, the parallel layers that make up the rock have separated producing small cracks. For at least the past 100 years, people have placed pennies in the cracks and made wishes, giving this outcrop its name, Penny Rock. Visitors should be aware that the practice is discouraged by park managers so as to prevent damage to the rock.

Connecting to the Hemlock Trail at about the halfway point is the park's longest trail, the Woodland Trail. This trail is a 0.75-mile loop that passes through a predominantly mixed-hardwood forest, as well as a portion of the old-growth hemlock stand. The trail varies in elevation 400 feet.

Directions: From Montrose follow PA Route 29 north for 7 miles. At Franklin Fork turn left onto SR 4008 and travel 1 mile to Salt Spring Road. Turn left onto Salt Spring Road, the parking area is on the left just across the bridge over Silver Creek.

Activities: Hiking, fishing.

Facilities: Trails.

Dates: Open year-round.

Fees: None.

Closest town: Franklin Fork, 1 mile.

For more information: Salt Spring State Park, c/o Lackawanna State Park, RR 1, PO Box 230, Dalton, PA 18414. Phone (717) 945-3239.

PROMISED LAND STATE PARK

The area today known as Promised Land State Park once served as hunting grounds for the Delaware Indians. The Indians hunted on this part of the Pocono Plateau because of the abundant game, but they lived and farmed along the Delaware River, 30 miles to the east, because the park's soil is rocky and thin. During the late 1800s, however, a religious group called the Shakers moved in with the intention of farming the area. It didn't take them long to learn that they couldn't live off of the land, and they subsequently sold it to a lumber company. Before they moved, they sarcastically named it the "promised land."

Once the lumber companies were done with the area, the pine and hemlock forests were gone, and the slash left behind fueled wildfires that prevented the forest from reestablishing itself. In the early 1900s the Pennsylvania Department of Forestry bought the land and began planting hundreds of thousands of white pine, Norway spruce, sugar maple, and red oak. Slowly a forest began to reappear. Then in the 1930s the Civilian Conservation Corps began to build and develop recreational facilities including cabins, trails, and roads. The CCC officer's quarters still stands and is today a museum that contains a blacksmith shop, wildlife dioramas, artifacts from the CCC period, and a mounted 500-pound black bear.

Promised Land State Park encompasses nearly 3,000 acres of Pike County within the Pocono Mountains. The park lies within the Delaware State Forest, but it is very accessible because PA Route 30 runs through the middle of the park. Promised

HIGHBUSH BLUEBERRY
(Vaccinium corymbosum)

Land receives about 0.5 million visitors each year, making it one of the five most heavily used state parks in Pennsylvania.

The park is so popular because it offers a wide range of recreational activities and facilities, primarily focused around two man-made lakes. The larger of the two lakes is 422-acre Promised Land Lake, which was built in the 1850s. Lower Lake, which lies just to the west of Promised Land Lake and flows into it, was built in 1959. It was built to aid with flood control in response to the extensive flooding that occurred in nearby Greentown during Hurricane Diane in 1955.

Both lakes are popular with fishermen year-round. Warm-water gamefish such as bass, northern pike, and tiger muskie, as well as panfish are found in both lakes. Additionally, Lower Lake is stocked by the Pennsylvania Fish and Boat Commission with trout. Nonmotorized boats are permitted on both lakes (electric motors are allowed), and there are four boat launches on Promised Land Lake and one on Lower Lake. For those who don't have their own boat, a rental concession is located on Promised Land Lake.

For those who want to enjoy the water but don't want to fish, there are two guarded beaches. The main beach is located along the north shore of Promised Land Lake, just east of the inlet with Lower Lake. The beach is open from Memorial Day to Labor Day and has a concession area. The other swimming area is located on the southern shore of Promised Land Lake on a small peninsula called Pickerel Point. The small beach, which is used primarily by campers at the adjacent campground, is open from Memorial Day to Labor Day on weekends only.

Surrounding the two lakes is a forest dominated by beech, oak, maple, and hemlock, a much different forest than occurred here before the logging of the late 1800s. The forest contains a dense undergrowth of rhododendrons, and like most of the Pocono Plateau, it is sprinkled with a generous helping of wetlands. Wildlife thrives in this park perched at 1,800 feet above sea level. The lakes attract waterfowl and even an occasional bald eagle, while the wetlands and forests are home to many of the state's best-known game species, including white-tailed deer, turkey, and ruffed grouse. The wetlands are also home to black bears, which feed here during the summer and hibernate here during the winter. The bears are not an uncommon site in the campgrounds during the early morning hours in spring and summer and are not adverse to an occasional picnic lunch, so campers be aware.

The park has a wide variety of environmental education programs throughout the summer, including guided hikes, canoe trips, arts and crafts programs, and the very popular campfire programs. The latter are held every Friday and Saturday evening and feature park personnel and guest speakers covering everything from wildlife to wetlands.

For those who want a more self-directed approach to environmental education, there is Conservation Island. The island is located along the western shore of Promised Land Lake on Park Avenue about 0.75 mile south of the intersection with PA

Route 390. A 1-mile-long self-guided nature trail encircles the island, taking the hiker past beaver lodges, a wide variety of wildflowers, and often deer. Since the trail is short, easy, and offers a lot to see, it is often very crowded.

There are 30 miles of hiking trails within the park, many of which connect with trails in the Delaware State Forest, including those running through the Bruce Lake Natural Area (*see* page 197). Bruce Lake Natural Area lies just north of the state park. Most of these trails are moderately challenging and rocky.

One of the more picturesque trails within the park is the Little Falls Trail, which parallels Little Falls Creek, a native trout stream. This 3-mile loop follows the creek from its mouth on Lower Lake north for 1.5 miles, then crosses the creek and follows it back along the other side. The trail passes through a hemlock-white pine forest and presents a moderate degree of difficulty. To reach the trail follow Lower Lake Road north from the park office for about 1.5 miles to the trailhead, which is on the left.

Many of the trails within the park are multi-use trails. In addition to hiking, some also permit horseback riding, cross-country skiing, and snowmobiling. For bikers, Park Avenue and North Shore Road form a 6.5-mile loop around Promised Land Lake.

Directions: From the town of Canadensis, follow PA Route 390 north for 10 miles to the park office, which is located on the left.

Activities: Hiking, hunting, fishing, camping, swimming, biking, horseback riding, boating (nonmotorized), cross-country skiing, snowmobiling.

Facilities: Multiple-use trails, guarded beaches, campgrounds, picnic areas.

Dates: Open year-round

Fees: There is a charge for camping.

Closest town: Promised Land, adjacent.

For more information: Promised Land State Park, RR 1, Box 96, Greentown, PA 18426. Phone (717) 676-3428.

BIG POCONO STATE PARK

Big Pocono State Park encompasses 1,306 acres of mountaintop in Monroe County. The park covers the summit and slopes of Camelback Mountain, which at 2,133 feet above sea level is one of the highest points on the Pocono Plateau. The wind almost always blows, and it's almost always colder than at lower elevations, with snow and frost still common when warm temperatures have led to lush growth lower on the slopes and in the valleys. Additionally, the soil, if there is any, is thin, rocky, and low in nutrients. Consequently, the forest that grows here is much different from the forests seen elsewhere in Pennsylvania's mountains.

Unlike most of the Pocono Plateau, which is rich in wetlands thanks to its glacial heritage, Big Pocono State Park is a very dry place because of its altitude, wind, and steepness. Big Pocono State Park contains a pine-oak barren forest, dominated by jack pine (*Pinus banksiana*) and scrub oak. The jack pine is common in areas that have been logged, especially those that have been subjected to wildfires, because pine cones require the heat of fire to open up and release their seeds. Scrub oak is relatively small as oaks go, rarely growing more than 20 feet high or more than 0.5 foot in diameter. Mountain laurel, blueberry, and sheep laurel dominate the understory of this short forest.

The focal point of the park is a day-use recreation area that lies at the summit of the mountain. From the summit you can see not only Pennsylvania, but also New York and New Jersey. This high perspective and commanding view give the park an important role in monitoring and controlling forest fires on the Pocono Plateau. The park has a fire tower, which is used to watch for fires, and a heliport used by fire-fighting aircraft.

Reaching the summit requires a very steep drive up a mountain road that serves as the access point to both state game lands and the park. The road is steep enough that visitors pulling trailers are discouraged from attempting the ascent. Once at the top the driver is rewarded with a 1.4-mile drive along Rim Road, which forms a loop around the summit and offers a commanding view. Located along the road are picnic areas, scenic overlooks, restrooms, parking areas, and trailheads.

While park visitors can enjoy the dramatic scenery from the road or from the picnic areas, those who venture into the forest along the trails will be rewarded with more scenic overlooks and can experience the oak-pine barrens first hand. There are three trails within the park. The longest of these is the yellow-blazed South Trail, a 3-mile-long hiking and bridle trail that begins near the park entrance and extends to the Indian Trail. It is the most level of the park's trails and provides a moderately challenging hike through the oak-pine barren forest. The trailhead is located on the right side of the road near the park entrance.

More challenging is the North Trail, which begins at a trailhead located near the center of the circle within Rim Road. This 1-mile-long red-blazed trail is steep and rocky, making for a difficult hike. For those willing to tackle it, however, there are numerous scenic vistas along the trail. The trail is not a loop, but it terminates at the Indian Trail, making a loop hike possible by hiking back along the Indian Trail. The Indian Trail is 1.3 miles long and is the most difficult one in the park. The trail begins at the North Trail about 0.3 mile from the trailhead. As it runs east it descends Camelback Mountain becoming progressively steeper. The end of the trail is so steep that it becomes nearly impassable. On the return trip hikers have to climb back up hand-over-fist. Unlike the North Trail, the Indian Trail lies deep within the oak-pine barren and offers no scenic vistas.

Adjacent to the park, also lying along the summit of the mountain, is Ski Camelback, one of the biggest and busiest ski resorts in Pennsylvania. During the winter the resort makes snow to supplement the abundant naturally occurring snow. Because of its proximity to Big Pocono and the prevailing wind direction, the man-made snow covers not only the ski slopes but the entrance road to the park as well. Since the entrance road is not maintained during the winter, the park is closed from 7 days after the close of antlerless deer season in December until the spring.

Directions: From Exit 45 of Interstate 80 follow PA Route 715 north for about 0.25 mile to Camelback Road. Turn left and follow Camelback Road for 1.3 miles to the road leading to the park and Camelback Mountain.

Activities: Hiking, hunting, horseback riding.

Facilities: Hiking trails, bridle trail, picnic areas, scenic vistas.

Dates: Open for day use from spring when the weather improves until a week after the close of antlerless deer season in December.

Fees: None.

Closest town: Tannersville, 3 miles.

For more information: Big Pocono State Park, c/o Tobyhanna State Park, Box 387, Tobyhanna, PA 18466. Phone (717) 894-8336.

TOBYHANNA STATE PARK

Tobyhanna State Park has one of the most interesting histories of all of Pennsylvania's 116 state parks. From 1912 to 1931, Tobyhanna was an artillery and tank training center. During this time thousands of rounds of artillery shells were fired in the park, most of them by cadets from West Point. Some of the shells didn't detonate and remained buried, and explosive, for more than 85 years. Beginning in early 1998 the park was closed in order for explosives experts to locate and destroy the buried ordinance. Now that the operation has been completed and the park reopened, it is unlikely that visitors will encounter these dangerous vestiges from the First World War.

Besides being a military installation, the park was an important source of ice during the first part of the twentieth century. From 1900 to 1936, ice was harvested from Tobyhanna Lake, which lies at the southern end of the park. During the summer, blocks of ice that were previously cut from the lake's surface and stored in icehouses were loaded into rail cars and shipped to eastern cities for use in ice boxes. Ice was also added to railcars containing fresh produce and meat, thereby allowing the food to be shipped greater distances.

In 1949 the 5,440-acre Tobyhanna State Park opened. The park is located on the Pocono Plateau in Monroe and Wayne counties, and it sits 2,000 feet above sea level. Like much of the plateau, a significant part of the park's acreage is covered with wetlands. Most of the north-central part of the park is dominated by an acidic scrub wetland, which was officially designated as one of the state's newest natural areas during the first half of 1998.

The Black Bear/Bender Swamp Natural Area contains boglike habitats more commonly found farther north in Canada. Common here are plants that are adapted to growing in acidic conditions where nutrients are in short supply. Carnivorous sundew plants carpet parts of the area, providing a breathtaking groundcover when they are in bloom. Also common here is Labrador tea, a short evergreen shrub so named because it can be used to make tea. The natural area is so named because the park contains a large population of black bears, which spend most of their time in the swamp.

There is only one trail passing through the natural area. The Yellow Trail extends 2.75 miles from the playground north of the lake to PA Route 196, which runs along the eastern boundary of the park. The trail can be hiked, out and back, in about 3 hours, but it is a demanding hike. Since it passes along the periphery of the natural area's wetlands, hikers should expect wet feet. Also located within the natural area are other relics of past glacial activity, boulderfields. Walking across these rock-strewn areas is less like walking than it is like hopping. The Yellow Trail passes through several boulderfields, so hikers should be prepared and wear the appropriate footwear.

A similarly challenging trail lies along the southwestern boundary of the natural area. The Frank Gantz Trail, which passes along wetlands and through boulderfields, is marked with red blazes and stretches 3.2 miles from Tobyhanna to the adjacent Gouldsboro State Park. The trail begins at the Lakeside Trail just south of the Black Bear/Bender Swamp Natural Area, then extends westward across PA Route 4013, around the southern end of Gouldsboro Lake, and finally terminates at the parking area in Gouldsboro State Park.

For those looking for an easier, less remote hike, the Lakeside Trail is probably a better choice. The trail has a hardened base covered with gravel and can be comfortably tackled by hikers, bikers, and even baby strollers. This blue-blazed trail makes a 5-mile loop around Tobyhanna Lake, crossing several streams along the way. The northern part of the trail passes just south of the natural area and serves as a connection between the Yellow Trail and the Frank Gantz Trail. The trail passes by nearly all of the park's recreational facilities including a playground, swimming beach, restrooms, and boat launch. Snowmobilers and cross-country skiers also use this trail during the winter.

Tobyhanna Lake is the center of the park's recreational activities. The 170-acre lake contains warm-water gamefish, panfish, and trout. Additionally, all of the streams leading into the lake contain native trout. Anglers can pursue the fish from the shoreline or from nonmotorized boats, which can be launched from the east side of the lake. There is also a boat rental concession available, where visitors can rent rowboats, canoes, and sailboats. There is a small guarded swimming beach that is open from Memorial Day to Labor Day. During the winter ice fishing and ice skating are popular here.

While the park is relatively flat and a significant portion of it is covered with wetlands, there are second-growth northern hardwood forests as well. Common here

Fig. 38: Delaware State Forest

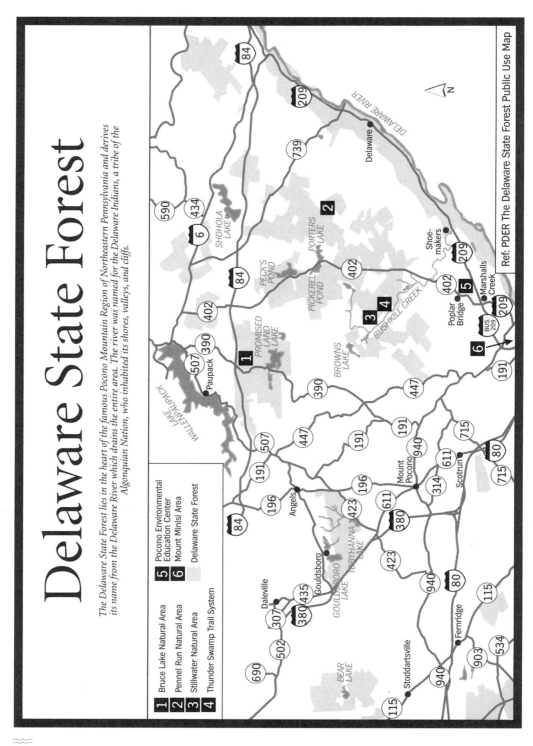

Delaware State Forest

The Delaware State Forest lies in the heart of the famous Pocono Mountain Region of Northeastern Pennsylvania and derives its name from the Delaware River which drains the entire area. The river was named for the Delaware Indians, a tribe of the Algonquian Nation, who inhabited its shores, valleys, and cliffs.

1. Bruce Lake Natural Area
2. Pennel Run Natural Area
3. Stillwater Natural Area
4. Thunder Swamp Trail System
5. Pocono Environmental Education Center
6. Mount Minisi Area
   Delaware State Forest

Ref: PDER The Delaware State Forest Public Use Map

are beech, birch, and maple, the successors of the white pine-hemlock forest that stood before the great logging era. The combination of woods and water provide ideal habitat for a number of wildlife species. The most unusual of these is the river otter. Otters are occasionally seen at the north end of the lake where Tobyhanna Creek flows into Tobyhanna Lake. As many as six otters have been seen at the same time near the inlet.

Directions: From the village of Tobyhanna follow PA Route 423 north for about 1 mile into the park.

Activities: Hiking, biking, hunting, fishing, boating, camping, swimming, ice skating, cross-country skiing, snowmobiling, ice fishing.

Facilities: Multi-use trails, campgrounds, picnic areas, guarded beach, boat launch, boat rental, playground.

Dates: Open year-round.

Fees: There is a charge for camping.

Closest town: Tobyhanna, less than 1 mile.

For more information: Tobyhanna State Park, PO Box 867, Tobyhanna, PA 18466. Phone (717) 894-8336.

Delaware State Forest

The Delaware State Forest and the river it drains into were named after the Delaware Indians, a tribe of the Algonquin Nation. The forest is a sprawling public land encompassing more than 80,000 acres in 14 separate tracts. The forest is so large that portions of it are located on the Pocono Plateau, the Valley and Ridge province, and the Glaciated Low Plateau.

The forest is spread across parts of Pike, Monroe, Northampton, and Carbon counties.

While this is a sparsely populated part of the state, it is within a two-hour drive of New York City and Philadelphia, so the Delaware State Forest is heavily used.

Logging began in 1820, and by the turn of the century, the forest had been completely cut. Today there are two forest ecosystems present, one dominated by oak and one dominated by a mixture of northern hardwoods, white pine, and hemlock. There are also a few areas dominated by scrub oak (*Quercus ilicifolia*), a shrublike tree that usually follows after forest fires and grows in rocky soil. This oak is commonly found growing in areas that have been logged before the larger species of oak move in.

Wildlife is plentiful in the Delaware State Forest making it a popular hunting area. White-tailed deer, turkey, and black bear are among the most common quarry. Bear are particularly plentiful; in fact Pike County has one of the largest bear populations in the state. Consequently, state biologists use the Delaware State Forest as a black bear research area.

About 20 percent of the Delaware State Forest is covered by wetlands, including six glacial lakes. There are also four man-made lakes. The lakes support warm-water species of fish such as bass and panfish, while the streams that feed the lakes contain trout.

The most ecologically significant wetlands form the nucleus of six natural areas encompassing more than 6,000 acres. Some of the natural areas are small and relatively inaccessible, while others are large and contain numerous trails. The Little Mud Swamp Natural Area measures only 182 acres but contains rare carnivorous plants including pitcher plants and sundews. Smaller yet is the 67-acre Pine Lake Natural Area. This natural area has a lake and a 10-acre bog that also contains pitcher plants and sundews. Neither one of these natural areas contains any trails or facilities.

AMERICAN TOAD
(Bufo americanus)
Despite popular myth, toads do
not cause warts.

Larger in size but no more accessible is the Buckhorn Natural Area, which has been set aside to preserve a mountain swamp. This area is 1 mile south of the Delaware River where it flows between Pennsylvania and New York. The Bruce Lake Natural Area (*see* page 197), Pennel Run Natural Area (*see* page 199), and Stillwater Natural Area (*see* page 200) are the largest natural areas in the Delaware State Forest and each contains trails.

Recreational opportunities abound in the Delaware State Forest. Visitors can hike, go cross-country skiing, or ride a mountain bike, snowmobile, ATV, or horse. For those who want to extend their visit, camping is allowed in most parts of the forest with a free permit from the state forest. The forest also contains more than 700 cabins permanently leased to regular forest visitors.

There are two state forest picnic areas within the Delaware State Forest. Located in the southern end of the forest is the Snow Hill State Forest Picnic Area. In addition to picnic tables, grills, and latrines, the picnic area has a small lake suitable for fishing. Farther north, near the center of the forest, is Pecks Pond State Forest Picnic Area. This area offers picnic facilities, fishing, and boating on the 2-mile-long Pecks Pond.

The Delaware State Forest contains miles of trails designated for specific activities. There are 180 miles of hiking trails, including 6 miles of the Appalachian Trail, 21 miles of ATV trails, 13 miles of cross-country ski trails, 31 miles of mountain bike trails, and more than 15 miles of equestrian trails. There is also a 90-mile-long snowmobile trail system. A machine similar to that used on downhill ski slopes grooms the 35-mile segment around Pecks Pond. Many of these activities are also permitted on the 55 miles of state forest roads as well as on the designated trails.

There are four state parks and numerous state game lands near the Delaware State Forest, and many of the trails continue into these public lands. Tobyhanna, Gouldsboro, and Big Pocono state parks are all located near the Delaware State Forest. Promised Land State Park, which is totally contained within one of the forest's tracts, is located near the Bruce Lake Natural Area (*see* below). Together the two form one of the state forest's major recreation areas.

Delaware State Forest public use and trail maps are available at the state forest office, Promised Land State Park office, and at parking lots throughout the forest.

Directions: To reach Pecks Pond State Forest Picnic Area, which is near the center of the forest, take Exit 8 off of I-84 and follow PA Route 402 south for approximately 7 miles. Turn left onto Brewster Road and then left onto the first dirt road, a distance of less than 0.25 mile. The picnic area is at the end of the dirt road.

Activities: Hiking, mountain biking, camping, fishing, hunting, snowmobiling, horseback riding, ATV riding, cross-country skiing.

Facilities: Hiking trails, mountain bike trails, cross-country ski trails, snowmobile trails, equestrian trails, ATV trails, picnic areas.

Dates: Open year-round, activities permitted depends on season.

Fees: None.

Closest town: Edgemere, 7 miles.

For more information: Delaware State Forest, HC1, Box 95A, Swiftwater, PA 18370. Phone (717) 895-4000.

BRUCE LAKE NATURAL AREA

The Bruce Lake Natural Area is large, encompassing 2,712 acres in Pike County. The two dominant physical features are Bruce Lake and Egypt Meadow Lake. Bruce Lake is a spring-fed, 48-acre lake formed during the last ice age. Egypt Meadow Lake, on the other hand, was constructed by the Civilian Conservation Corps in 1935 and covers an area of 60 acres. Glacial wetlands, containing pitcher plants and sundews, are also common here.

Up until the late nineteenth century, a hemlock-white pine forest blanketed the area. However, clear-cutting and subsequent wildfires have drastically changed the area, and today it is a mixed-hardwood forest with a dense understory of rhododendron and mountain laurel.

There are several trails passing through the Bruce Lake Natural Area. Most of these trails connect to Bruce Lake Road, which runs from the southernmost parking area along PA Route 390 to Bruce Lake, a distance of approximately 2.5 miles. The road is not open to motorized vehicle traffic, so it is both a good hiking trail and a good point of access to the other trails in the natural area. As it crosses the natural area, the road passes immediately south of Panther Swamp near the parking area. It then crosses Egypt Meadow Lake about halfway along its course, ending at the Bruce Lake Trail.

MAYAPPLE
(Podophyllum peltatum)
Growing to 20 inches tall, the mayapple produces a lemon-yellow fruit that is poisonous when immature. Mature fruit are used in jellies.

The Bruce Lake Trail is composed of two branches. The main branch, which is about 1.5 miles long, extends from Bruce Lake Road, along the east side of Bruce Lake, to its ending at the Rock Ridge Trail. The Rock Ridge Trail extends southward into Promised Land State Park. The West Branch Trail runs from Bruce Lake Road, along the west side of Bruce Lake, to its ending at the main branch of the trail, a distance of about 0.8 mile.

Egypt Meadow Lake is only a 0.5-mile walk down the Egypt Meadow Trail from the northern parking lot along PA Route 390 just south of the I-84 interchange. Two trails connect the Egypt Lake Trail with Bruce Lake Road. The Snowshoe Trail is a little over 1 mile long, passes through Panther Swamp, and meets the road near the southernmost parking area. The Panther Swamp Trail begins near Egypt Meadow Lake, is about 0.5 mile long, and meets Bruce Lake Road about 0.5 mile from the southernmost parking area.

In combination, these trails provide access to most of the natural area and both of the lakes. The Egypt Meadow Trail, Snowshoe Trail, and Panther Swamp Trail are also suitable for cross-country skiing.

Directions: From Interstate 84 take Exit 7. There are two parking areas along the left side of PA Route 390. One is just south of the exit, while the southernmost is about 1.5 miles south of the exit.

Activities: Hiking, hunting, fishing, mountain biking, cross-country skiing.

Facilities: Trails.

Dates: Open year-round.

Fees: None.

Closest town: Blooming Grove, 4 miles.

For more information: Delaware State Forest, HC1, Box 95A, Swiftwater, PA 18370. Phone (717) 895-4000.

🪨 PENNEL RUN NATURAL AREA

The Pennel Run Natural Area encompasses 936 acres of forest and wetland in western Pike County. Elevations range from 1,100 feet to 1,300 feet, with swamps and streams in the lowlands and woodlands on the high ground. The forested areas contain stands of scrub oak, aspen, gray birch (*Betula populifolia*), and mixed oaks. A portion of Utts Swamp is located on the western side of the natural area. This forested wetland is the headwaters of Utts Run, a tributary of Big Bushkill Creek.

The only trail within the Pennel Run Natural Area is a side trail of the Thunder Swamp Trail System (*see* page 201). The trail is composed of a 0.5-mile spur off of the main trail connected to a loop that is 2 miles to 2.5 miles long. The trail rises and falls over an elevational range of 200 feet, crosses a tributary of Big Bushkill Creek, and passes along the periphery of Utts Swamp. To reach the trail, follow the Thunder Swamp Trail System north for about 1.4 miles from the parking area along Snow Hill Road.

Directions: From I-84, Exit 8, follow PA Route 402 south to Snow Hill Road, approximately 14 miles. Follow Snow Hill Road southwest 2 to 2.5 miles to the Thunder Swamp Trail System parking area.

Activities: Hiking, hunting.

Facilities: Trail.

Dates: Open year-round.

Fees: None

Closest town: Marshalls Creek.

For more information: Delaware State Forest, HC1, Box 95A, Swiftwater, PA 18370. Phone (717) 895-4000.

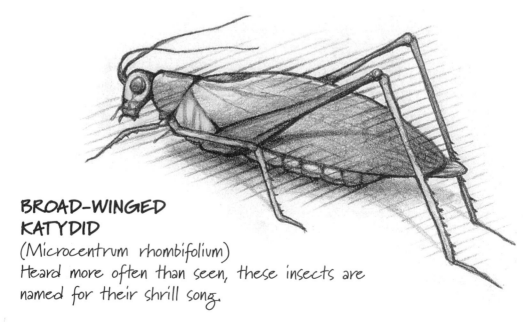

BROAD-WINGED
KATYDID
(Microcentrum rhombifolium)
Heard more often than seen, these insects are
named for their shrill song.

STILLWATER NATURAL AREA

The Stillwater Natural Area takes its name from the placid headwaters of Little Bushkill Creek. One mile of these slow moving waters is located here. The natural area is an irregularly shaped parcel encompassing 1,931 acres, much of it wetland.

The forested areas contain primarily mixed hardwoods, but stands of conifers can be found in the wet areas.

The biggest wetland within the Stillwater Natural Area is Big Bear Swamp. The swamp is actually a boreal bog that contains rare plants such as sundew and pitcher plants. Hikers have good access to the swamp. The Thunder Swamp Trail System (*see* page 201) ends in a 4.2-mile-long loop that encircles the swamp. A 3.7-mile side loop of the trail also passes through the northern end of the natural area, paralleling Little Bushkill Creek along part of its course.

There's an interesting history surrounding the swamps of the Stillwater Natural Area. The area's remoteness and dense vegetation make it a good place for a man to hide, and during the Civil War many draft dodgers did just that. They built cabins in the dense thickets around the edges of the swamps and on the islands in the middle. Remnants of some of the cabins' foundations can still be found today.

Directions: From the Delaware State Forest headquarters in Edgemere follow Silver Lake Road west for about 0.75 mile to Flat Ridge Road. Turn left on Flat Ridge Road and drive 1.7 miles to the Thunder Swamp Trail System parking area on the left-hand side of the road. Hike the Thunder Swamp Trail System side trail for 1.3 miles to the Stillwater Natural Area.

Activities: Hiking, hunting.

SWEET JOE-PYE-WEED
(Eupatorium purpureum)
Joe-pye-weeds are named after an Indian healer who used the plant to treat ailments.

Facilities: Trails.
Dates: Open year-round.
Fees: None.
Closest town: Marshalls Creek.
For more information: Delaware State Forest, HC1, Box 95A, Swiftwater, PA 18370. Phone (717) 895-4000.

▓ THUNDER SWAMP TRAIL SYSTEM

The Thunder Swamp Trail System is one of the most popular hiking destinations in the area. It is designated a state hiking trail, which means no biking, horseback riding, or other activities other than hiking are allowed.

The Thunder Swamp Trail System is composed of a 30-mile-long main trail with 15 miles of side trails. Camping is permitted along the trail, thereby allowing overnight expeditions. The side trails, most of which are relatively short loops, are great for shorter day hikes.

This trail system gives the hiker a good feel for the typical habitats found on the Glaciated Low Plateau. It crosses numerous mountain streams; passes along many swamps, forested wetlands, and bogs; and climbs ridges and descends into stream valleys. The trail system also provides the only access to the Pennel Run Natural Area (*see* page 199) and the Stillwater Natural Area (*see* page 200).

The main trailhead lies along PA Route 402 just north of the border between Pike and Monroe counties. From the village of Marshalls Creek follow PA Route 402 north for 7.6 miles to the trailhead and parking area on the right. In addition to the parking area at the trailhead, there are five other parking areas distributed along the length of the trail, making any portion available for dayhikes. An excellent topographic trail map that indicates the length of each of the individual segments is available from the Delaware State Forest.

Trail: 30-mile main trail with 15 miles of side trails.

Elevation: 960–1,400 feet.

Degree of difficulty: Moderate.

Surface and blaze: Unpaved. Main trail has blue blazes. Side trails have red blazes.

For more information: Delaware State Forest, HC1, Box 95A, Swiftwater, PA 18370. Phone (717) 895-4000.

BROWNHEADED
COWBIRD
(Molothrus ater)
The cowbird lays its eggs
in the nests of other birds
that feed the newly
hatched intruder until it
can fly.

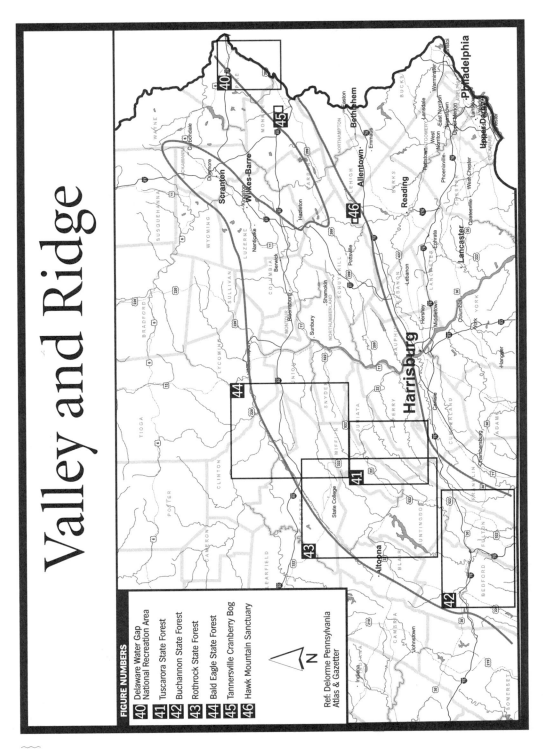

Valley and Ridge

FIGURE NUMBERS

40 Delaware Water Gap National Recreation Area
41 Tuscarora State Forest
42 Buchannon State Forest
43 Rothrock State Forest
44 Bald Eagle State Forest
45 Tannersville Cranberry Bog
46 Hawk Mountain Sanctuary

N

Ref: Delorme Pennsylvania Atlas & Gazetter

Pennsylvania's
Valley & Ridge Province

T he Valley and Ridge province provides some of the most dramatic scenery and
topography in Pennsylvania. The province is composed of a series of parallel
ridges that form an arc running from the Maryland border in south-central
Pennsylvania to the New Jersey border in the eastern part of the state. Approximately
25 percent of the state, including all or part of 27 counties, are located within the
Valley and Ridge province.

The province is broken up into two sections, the Appalachian Mountain section
and the Great Valley. As their names indicate, one is mountainous and the other
relatively flat; consequently, the Great Valley section is not covered in this book.

The well-defined ridges of the Appalachian Mountain section are composed of
resistant sandstone, while the valleys are composed of more easily eroded shale and
limestone. Water flowing off of the hillsides has eroded deeply into the softer valley

[*Above:* Delaware Water Gap]

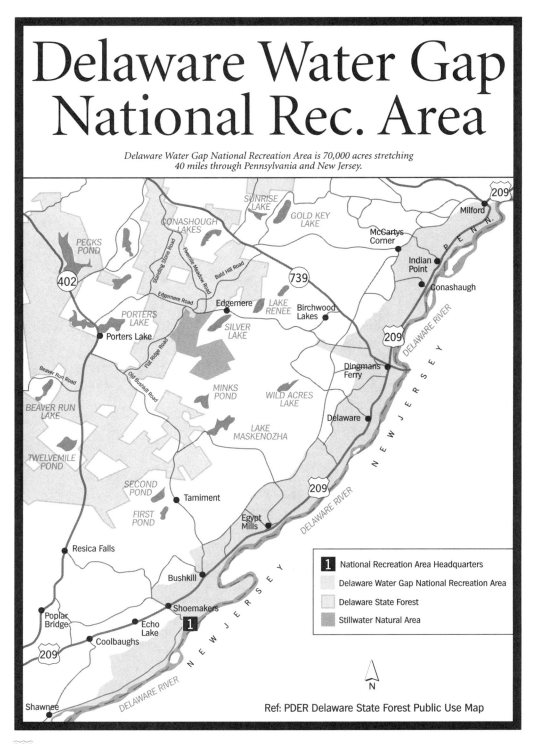

Delaware Water Gap National Rec. Area

Delaware Water Gap National Recreation Area is 70,000 acres stretching 40 miles through Pennsylvania and New Jersey.

Ref: PDER Delaware State Forest Public Use Map

rocks creating topographic relief that varies from several hundred feet to 1,000 feet. The ridges are generally blanketed with dry, rocky soil, if any soil at all, while the valleys are carpeted with rich, fertile soil.

While most of the streams flow through the valleys, rivers have sliced their own paths through the sandstone ridges creating deep, scenic water gaps. The largest of these rivers is the Susquehanna, which drains most of the area with the assistance of its major tributary, the Juniata River. The Delaware River and its tributaries, the Lehigh and Schuykill rivers, drain the eastern portion of the Appalachian Mountain section. There is also a small portion of the Potomac River basin within the Valley and Ridge province.

The Appalachian Mountain section is separated from the Appalachian Plateau, which lies to the north and west, by a steep escarpment called the Allegheny Front. The rocks that underlie both areas are the same, yet the topography of the two is dramatically different. The reason is that the Appalachian Mountain section experienced tremendous pressure and deformation because it was closer to the continental collision that produced the Appalachian Mountain chain.

To the south of the Appalachian Mountain section lies the Great Valley. The southern boundary of this section is a ridge that extends from Maryland to the Delaware River, rising more than 900 feet above the valley floor. The ridge is known by several names: Blue Mountain, Kittatinny Mountain, and First Mountain. Much of the Pennsylvania portion of the Appalachian Trail follows this ridge, allowing hikers to experience the Appalachian Mountains and giving them a spectacular view of Pennsylvania's primary agricultural area.

Located within this section are the major urban centers of Williamsport, Altoona, State College, Wilkes-Barre, and Scranton. These cities are well connected by the major east/west routes of Interstate 76 (better known as the Pennsylvania Turnpike), Interstate 80, and PA Route 322. The major north/south routes are Interstates 81, 180, and 70, and PA Routes 11 and 15.

There are a significant number of public lands within the Appalachian Mountain section. Found here are five state forests, more than 30 state parks, and the Delaware Water Gap National Recreation Area.

National Lands

🏛 DELAWARE WATER GAP NATIONAL RECREATION AREA

[Fig. 40] While mountains and the rock from which they are made seem indestructible, given time and persistence something as innocuous as water can wear them down. Throughout Pennsylvania are places where powerful rivers have sliced through mountains and ridges creating gaps. These water gaps provide some of the most dramatic scenery in the commonwealth. One of the state's best-known water gaps was created by the Delaware River where it cut through Kittatinny Ridge.

During the nineteenth century, the water gap was a popular vacation destination for city-dwellers from New York and Philadelphia. There were numerous large hotels in the area that catered to people looking to escape the heat and congestion of the city. The resorts are gone now, but this is still a popular vacation getaway, receiving 4 million visitors a year looking for an outdoor experience.

The Delaware River drains portions of New York and Delaware and forms the boundary between New Jersey and Pennsylvania. A 40-mile stretch of the river, from the water gap north to the town of Milford and the adjacent shores of New Jersey and Pennsylvania, has been designated the Delaware Water Gap National Recreation Area by the National Park Service. The area encompasses 70,000 acres of land within two states and includes portions of both the Valley and Ridge province and Pocono Plateau in Pennsylvania. Also included in the area are 21 islands ranging in size from diminutive Quicks Island to 435-acre Minisink Island.

The river is generally slow moving and shallow within the recreation area and is a popular spot for canoeing and water tubing. This stretch of the river has also been officially designated as the Middle Delaware Scenic and Recreational River because of its high water quality and because it is one of the few free-flowing major rivers within the eastern U.S.

The river's clean water supports a diverse and healthy fish community. Common within the river are shad,

BALD EAGLE
(Haliaeetus leucocephalus)
It is believed that bald eagles mate for life. The 40-inch-long bird, which can have a 7½-foot wingspan, builds a large nest in trees, cliffs, or on the ground that can weigh up to 1,000 pounds. Eagles eat carrion, fish, and waterfowl.

walleye, muskellunge, bass, eel, and catfish. Additionally, trout are found within the 40 or so tributaries located within the area. An agreement between the states of New Jersey and Pennsylvania allows sportsmen to fish from either shore, on the river itself, or from its islands, with a fishing license from either state.

Humans aren't the only fishermen on the river. The piscivorous bald eagle fishes here as well. Bald eagles migrate from points north to the Delaware Water Gap National Recreation Area to spend the winter feeding on the river's open waters. During the months of January and February, visitors have a reasonably good chance of seeing the feeding eagles. By using their cars as blinds (eagles recognize people as something to fear but not their machines), visitors are most likely to see the birds during mid-morning or late afternoon. In addition to being a place to see wintering eagles, the recreation area is a good spot to watch the fall raptor migration.

The Delaware Water Gap National Recreation Area is diverse in both ecosystems and plant and animal life. In addition to the riverine island ecosystems, the park contains fens, talus slopes, hemlock ravines, shale cliffs, mixed-hardwood forests, cobble beaches, and even rocky cactus barrens. Within the national recreation area are 12 rare plant communities and more than 100 Species of Special Concern.

Among the more common plants in the recreation area are the rhododendron. This evergreen shrub blooms in early July and makes a walk through the forests a real treat. Unfortunately, also common here are poison ivy and ticks. Consequently, visitors are encouraged to wear long pants and long-sleeve shirts when venturing into any of the woods or fields.

The Pennsylvania side of the recreation area includes portions of Monroe, Northampton, and Pike counties. Within the recreation area, there are three toll bridges crossing the river. One bridge is located at the north end of the area on US Route 206 south of Milford Beach. Another bridge connects PA Route 739 with NJ Route 560 near Dingmans Ferry. The third bridge is located at the southern end of the area near the gap in Kittatinny Mountain and carries Interstate 80 over the river. Also passing through the area from north to south is PA Route 209.

This is a major recreation area. On the Pennsylvania side are nine developed recreation sites. At the north end of the Delaware Water Gap National Recreation Area is Milford Beach, one of two bathing beaches on the Pennsylvania side of the river. The access road to the beach is located just south of Milford on US Route 209. In addition to swimming there is a picnic area and boat launch.

Many of the streams that flow through the recreation area pass over waterfalls on their journey to the Delaware River. A good place to see an example is at the George Childs Recreation Site. There is a 1.8-mile loop trail that passes Factory Falls, Fulmer Falls, and Deer Leap Falls, and crosses Dingmans Creek. The trail includes wooden stairs and boardwalks and is a moderately challenging hike. To reach the area follow PA Route 739 west from the town of Dingmans Ferry for about 1.3 miles to Silver Lake Road and turn left. Follow the signs to the recreation site.

Located along Bushkill Creek about 11 miles south of Dingmans Ferry on US Route 209 is the Bushkill Visitor Center. Here visitors can learn about the Delaware Water Gap National Recreation Area from displays and programs held at the center, which is open from April to late October.

About 6.2 miles south of the Bushkill Visitor Center is Smithfield Beach. In addition to swimming, the beach has a boat launch and picnic area. The area is also used during the winter by snowmobilers. There is a 3-mile-long trail that passes through fields and a 6-mile loop that runs across a wooded ridge. To reach Smithfield Beach follow US Route 209 south from Bushkill for 1.8 miles and turn left onto River Road. Follow this road for about 4 miles, going past the park headquarters to the beach.

In addition to the many hiking trails, there is an equestrian trail on the Pennsylvania side of the recreation area. The Conashaugh View Trail is 9 miles long and includes a 5-mile loop. Adjacent to the trailhead parking area is a visitors center. The trailhead is located about 5 miles south of Milford on Conashaugh Road off of Old Milford Road.

All of the facilities within the Delaware Water Gap National Recreation Area are for day use only. Camping is only permitted within designated campgrounds, along the Appalachian Trail, and on selected designated river islands. Island camping is only available to boaters whose trip can't be completed in a day.

Directions: To reach the Delaware Water Gap National Recreation Area take the Delaware Water Gap Exit off of Interstate 80. PA Route 209 and River Road can be used to travel through the recreation area.

Activities: Hiking, camping, fishing, hunting, snowmobiling, cross-country skiing, swimming, canoeing, boating, ice fishing, ice boating, ice climbing, horseback riding.

Facilities: Hiking trails, equestrian trail, snowmobile trails, boat launches, campgrounds, picnic areas, beaches, visitor centers.

Dates: Most facilities open year-round. Some visitor centers closed Nov.–Apr.

Fees: None.

Closest town: Dingmans Ferry, located within the Delaware Water Gap National Recreation Area.

For more information: Delaware Water Gap National Recreation Area, Bushkill, PA 18324. Phone (717) 588-2415.

PAWPAW
(Asimina triloba)
The fruit of the pawpaw is an ingredient for breads and ice cream.

▓ MOUNT MINISI AREA

[Fig. 38(6)] Mount Minisi is located at the southern end of the Delaware Water Gap National Recreation Area. It sits atop Kittatinny Ridge above the water gap and, at an elevation of 1,463 feet, offers a spectacular view of the river. From here the dominance of water over rock is evident.

Visitors to the area can enjoy the spectacular view from their car or by taking one of several hikes up Kittatinny Ridge. Those who don't want to hike can make the 5.5-mile drive along PA Route 611 from the town of Delaware Water Gap to Portland. Along the way is Resort Point Overlook, Point of Gap Overlook, and Arrow Island Overlook. Each of these overlooks has a roadside parking area.

For those who want to get a little exercise with their scenery, several trails lead to the top of Kittatinny Ridge and Mount Minisi. One of these is the Appalachian Trail, which enters the southern end of the recreation area along the peak of Kittatinny Ridge and leads to the town of Delaware Water Gap. It continues north on the New Jersey side of the river at the Kittatinny Point Visitor Center.

A trailhead is located just south of the town of Delaware Water Gap. The trail, which is marked with white blazes, begins at the Lake Lenape parking area just south of PA Route 611 on Mountain Road. The Mount Minisi overlook is about a 2-mile hike from the trailhead. The hike can be made a 3.5-mile loop by returning on the Mount Minisi Fire Road.

An alternate access to the Appalachian Trail is from the Resort Point Overlook. A blue-blazed trail about 0.25 mile long begins at the parking lot. A short distance from the trailhead the trail splits. The right fork leads to Lake Lenape and the Appalachian Trail north, and the left fork leads to a scenic overlook and the Appalachian Trail south. In addition to these trails, there are several shorter spurs and connecting trails adjacent to the Appalachian Trail and Mount Minisi Fire Road.

Directions: From Interstate 80 take the Delaware Water Gap Exit to the town of Delaware Water Gap.

Activities: Hiking, scenic driving.

Facilities: Hiking trails, scenic overlooks.

Dates: Open year-round.

Fees: None.

Closest town: Delaware Water Gap.

For more information: Delaware Water Gap National Recreation Area, Bushkill, PA 18324. Phone (717) 588-2951.

COMMON FOXGLOVE
(Digitalis purpurea) This is the source of digitalis, a drug used to treat heart disease. Its medicinal effects were discovered in 1775 by English physician William Withering, who learned of its effects from an old woman.

POCONO ENVIRONMENTAL EDUCATION CENTER

[Fig. 38(5)] The Pocono Environmental Education Center, or PEEC as it's usually called, is a private, nonprofit, residential education center operated in conjunction with the National Park Service. PEEC is located in Dingmans Ferry in a former Pocono honeymoon resort and is the largest residential environmental education center in the Western Hemisphere. The center's mission is to "advance environmental awareness, knowledge, and skills through education in order that people may better understand the complexities of earth systems."

PEEC has programs ranging in length from one day to an entire week. Programs are available for families, school groups, church groups, and scout groups, and there are even several elderhostels held each year. The programs are designed to allow groups time to explore and enjoy the area on their own in addition to the structured group activities.

There are several programs of interest to teachers. Teachers can come here to learn about environmental education along with their peers, or they can bring their students and team-teach with PEEC staff. Students and teachers can learn firsthand about tracking and stalking, orienteering, forest biology, field ornithology, and other areas of natural history.

The PEEC complex is large enough that it also offers conference and retreat facilities for up to 400 people.

Visitors to the center don't have to stay overnight or participate in scheduled programs. They can just come and hike the trails. PEEC has six loop trails covering 12 miles. The trails run through several different habitats and vary in difficulty and length. The trails are listed below from the shortest to the longest.

Sensory Trail: This 0.25-mile trail is unique in that the hiker does it blindfolded. After picking a blindfold up from the visitor education center, the hiker follows the guide rope along the trail, experiencing the area using senses other than sight.

Two Ponds Trail: This trail provides an easy, one-hour hike that extends 1.5 miles. The trail passes through a pine plantation, crosses a small stream, passes two ponds, and has a blind for observing birds.

Fossil Trail: This moderately challenging trail is 1.25 miles in length and takes about one hour to hike. The trail descends an escarpment and passes a rocky outcrop containing fossils of marine organisms that inhabited the area long ago. The National Park Service, however, prohibits fossil collecting.

Scenic Gorge Trail: This 2-mile trail provides an easy hike that takes about one hour. The trail follows a stream through a hemlock ravine. During rainy periods the trail can be muddy so dress appropriately.

Tumbling Waters Trail: This is a moderately challenging trail that extends for 3 miles and takes two to three hours to hike. The trail offers a scenic view of Kittatinny Ridge and the Delaware River Valley and passes through a hemlock ravine with two waterfalls.

Sunrise Trail: This is the longest trail at PEEC, extending for 5 miles. The trail passes through a variety of habitats including an oak-hickory forest, a field, and a hemlock ravine. The trail is moderately challenging and takes about three hours to hike. One portion is steep enough that guide cables are used to help with the descent.

All of the trails are blazed and accessible from the visitors center.

Directions: From Exit 52 off Interstate 80, follow PA Route 209 north to Marshall's Creek. At the stoplight in Marshall's Creek turn right and continue on Route 209 to the sign marking the entrance road to PEEC.

Activities: Hiking, educational programs.

Facilities: Hiking trails, residence areas, conference and retreat facilities.

Dates: Open year-round.

Fees: There is a charge for education programs.

Closest town: Dingmans Ferry, 5 miles.

For more information: Pocono Environmental Education Center, RR 2, PO Box 1010, Dingmans Ferry, PA 18328. Phone (717) 828-2319.

STEAMTOWN NATIONAL HISTORIC SITE

[Fig. 3(30)] Railroads played an important role in the development patterns not only of northeastern Pennsylvania but also of the United States. In Scranton, the National Park Service operates its only park dedicated to telling the story of steam railroading and the people who made it possible. Steamtown National Historic Site offers visitors a unique look at a working steam rail yard in its historic urban setting.

The steam locomotive was invented in England in 1804, but railroad investment didn't begin in earnest in the U.S. until after 1830. As the country expanded, railroads were used to transform the U.S. from an agricultural to a manufacturing nation. They moved goods and people much faster than stagecoaches, wagons, steamboats, or canal packets. After World War I, the railroad industry faced increasing competition from automobiles and trucks, and in 1925, the diesel-electric engine was introduced. Within 15 years, steam locomotives were replaced by less labor-intensive, cleaner, and more flexible diesel locomotives.

Scranton once served as the headquarters for the Delaware, Lackawanna, and Western Railroad, which during the last quarter of the nineteenth century and the first quarter of the twentieth century was a major carrier of anthracite. This hard, clean-burning coal was found in abundance in northeastern Pennsylvania, especially in the Lackawanna Valley where Scranton is located, a region that was once considered the anthracite capital of the world.

Today, the Steamtown National Historic Site features coal-fired steam locomotives, restored cabooses, freight cars and railroad coaches, museums, and a fully operational roundhouse and turntable. Start your visit at the visitor center where you can receive an orientation to the park and its facilities and attractions. The heart of the park is the Steamhouse Collection, a large collection of standard-gauge steam locomotives and

Steamtown National Historic Site is popular with tourists interested in the history of Pennsylvania's steam-powered railroad industry.

freight and passenger cars that F. Nelson Blount, a New England seafood processor, assembled in the 1950s and 1960s. The oldest locomotive in the collection is a freight engine built in 1903 for the Chicago Union Transfer Railway Company.

Park rangers offer daily educational tours of the yard, roundhouse, and locomotive repair shops, and on certain days, rail excursions are offered. Seating on the excursions is limited, and reservations are recommended. Two of the park's annual special events attract visitors from across the country. During Memorial Day weekend, Steamtown kicks off its rail excursion season with an event to recognize U.S. military service members and their relationship with the railroad. The Rail Expo is held annually during Labor Day weekend and features visiting state-of-the-art railroad equipment and historic steam and vintage diesel locomotives.

Directions: Steamtown is located in Scranton. Take I-81 to Exit 53 (Central Scranton Expressway), then follow the signs past the Mall at Steamtown to the park's main entrance at Lackawanna and Cliff avenues.

Activities: Touring museums and other historic exhibits, train excursions.

Facilities: Visitor center, museum store, 52-acre working railroad park, 250-seat theater.

Dates: Open daily, except Thanksgiving Day, Christmas Day, and New Years Day.

Fees: There is a charge for the museum and rail excursions.

For more information: Steamtown National Historic Site, 150 South Washington Avenue, Scranton, PA 18503-2018. Phone (717) 340-5200 or (888) 693-9391. Web site: www.nps.gov/stea.

State Parks

▨ LITTLE BUFFALO STATE PARK

[Fig. 3(26)] Little Buffalo State Park, opened in 1972, is among the youngest of Pennsylvania's state parks. The park offers something for everyone, from strenuous backwoods hiking, to swimming and exercising, to learning about the history of Perry County. The 830-acre park is centered around Holman Lake.

The lake was constructed in 1971 as a recreational facility, but it also serves as a flood control device during heavy rain. Holman Lake is fed and also drained by Little Buffalo Creek. Both are stocked with trout, and warm-water game fish and panfish are found in the lake as well. Fishermen can take advantage of the lake either from shore or on the water. Although no boats with internal combustion engines are allowed on the lake, those powered by people or electric motors are permitted. For visitors who lack the means to venture onto the lake to fish or enjoy the scenery, there is a boat rental concession where rowboats, canoes, and paddleboats are available. Two boat launches, one at the eastern end and the other at the western end of the lake, are available. At the northeastern corner of the lake, near where it drains into Little Buffalo Creek, there is a handicapped-accessible fishing pier.

Holman Lake isn't just a summer resource. During the winter the lake freezes over, presenting a whole new range of recreational opportunities. At the east end of the lake, near the main boat launch, is a 1-acre, lighted ice skating area. Skating is permitted during the day and night, weather and ice conditions permitting, and a warming area and heated restrooms are available. The rest of the lake is used by ice fishermen, who should be cautious, however, because the park does not monitor the ice conditions.

There are two main picnic areas in the park connected by the Fisherman's Trail. The trail is about 1 mile long and provides an easy, level hike through a cool hemlock forest. One of the picnic areas is located along the south shore of the lake. In addition to the many picnic tables, there is a large parking area, picnic pavilions, a playground, and a 0.5-acre swimming pool. The pool, which is guarded, is open from Memorial Day to Labor Day and is available for a small fee. A shower house and food concession is also located nearby.

The other picnic area is located at the eastern end of Holman Lake. In addition to a picnic pavilion, restrooms, and ample parking, several of the park's historical features are found here. Shoaff's Mill is a completely restored and functional eighteenth-century gristmill powered by a water wheel. The mill is open on Saturday and Sunday afternoons from mid-May to mid-October. Visitors can see the 2,700-pound grindstones pulverize corn into birdseed and corn meal, both of which are offered for sale. The mill closes out its season in the third week of October by using the grindstones to make apple cider. Located not far from the mill is the Moore Pavilion. This pavilion is used throughout the summer months for band concerts. It's also the focal point for a popular arts and crafts festival held every year during the third week in September.

Another popular attraction in the park is the Blue Ball Tavern. The historical structure began operating as a tavern in the 1790s, however, spirits are no longer served here. Today it is home to a museum and library operated by the Perry County Historical Society. The tavern contains a wide assortment of artifacts from Perry County history, including Indian artifacts, blacksmithing tools, and military uniforms from World Wars I and II. The tavern is open on Sunday afternoons from Memorial Day to Labor Day, and admission is free. The tavern is located along a small tributary of Little Buffalo Creek. Just a short distance north along the tributary is Sulphur Springs Cemetery. The cemetery contains graves dating back to 1780, and among those buried here are the owners of the tavern. Most of the gravestones are still readable and have been recently covered with a coating to protect them from the effects of acid rain.

In addition to the recreational and historical features of the park, there are also 7 miles of trails. Among the more unusual of these is the Exercise Trail, which is heavily used by local residents during the evening. This 1.2-mile loop is a grass trail with exercise stations located along the route. The stations include chin-up bars, places to do sit-ups, and even a balance beam. The trailhead and parking area are located along New Bloomfield Road just south of the park office and north of Little Buffalo Creek.

If you're more interested in a nature walk than a fitness walk, there are several trails of varying difficulty available. For a short, easy hike consider the Mill Race Trail. This 0.5-mile loop begins at Shoaf's Mill and follows the canal that supplies water to the mill. The trail continues on to the dam that backs up water to provide a continuous flow to the mill. The canal lies in a small, scenic valley made even more picturesque by the 6-foot waterfall created by water flowing over the dam.

For a hike with a little more environmental education value take the Buffalo Ridge Trail. This self-guided interpretive trail stretches 1.5 miles from the main picnic area at the eastern end of the lake to the parking area near the other picnic area on the south side. Much of this trail is rocky and steep. By using the guide available from the park office, the hiker can learn about 25 natural features along the trail. Among the more interesting things found along the trail are large blackened areas. These are the remnants of charcoal mounds from the 1840s. Large piles of wood were carefully constructed and then burned very slowly. All of the water and volatile gases were driven off, leaving behind pure carbon, better known as charcoal. The charcoal was then used in the nearby iron furnaces to help convert iron ore to cast iron.

Just before the Buffalo Ridge Trail reaches the parking area south of the lake it intersects with the Little Buffalo Creek Trail. This trail is about 1-mile long and is relatively easy to hike. It follows Little Buffalo Creek upstream from the lake and is an especially good trail for birding. The trail ends at the western end of the park's most difficult trail, the Middle Ridge Trail. The Middle Ridge Trail runs along the northern side of the lake, extending 3 miles to the parking area at the east end of the lake and sharing a small portion of its route with the Exercise Trail. The trail rises and falls as it passes through ravines and across streams. Because it is difficult, it is not heavily used. The chances of seeing wildlife, such as deer and turkey, are very good. While the trail seems remote and secluded, it is only a few hundred yards from PA Route 4010, which runs through the park from east to west, just north of the lake.

In addition to the hiking trails there is a 2-mile-long cross-country ski loop. The trail begins at the intersection of the Little Buffalo Creek and Buffalo Ridge trails, follows the Little Buffalo Creek Trail, and then turns south following an old railroad bed back to the beginning. In addition to this trail, some of the park's other trails and roads are open to cross-country skiing, providing a total of 7 miles of cross-country ski trails.

Directions: From Newport follow PA Route 4010 west for about 2 miles. The park office is located at the intersection with New Bloomfield Road.

Activities: Hiking, fishing, hunting, electric boating (no gas), swimming, picnicking, cross-country skiing, sledding, environmental education programs, festivals, summer programs.

Facilities: Picnic shelters, museum, hiking trails, cross-country ski trails, boat rental, boat launch, swimming pool, visitor center, grist mill, band shell.

Dates: Park open year-round. Some facilities only open from mid-May to mid-Oct.

Fees: There is a charge for the swimming pool and boat rentals.

Closest town: Newport, 2 miles.

For more information: Little Buffalo State Park, RR 2, Box 256A, Newport, PA 17074. Phone (717) 567-9255.

COLONEL DENNING STATE PARK

[Fig. 3(27)] William Denning, after whom Colonel Denning State Park is named, was a Revolutionary War veteran who was really a sergeant and not a colonel. Denning lived in nearby Newville, but served out the war near Carlisle at the Washingtonburg Forge. There he built a lighter, more reliable cannon than had been previously available. Cannons were traditionally made from cast iron, but Denning's cannons were made by welding strips of wrought iron together in layers. None of the cannons survive today, and all that is known about them comes from documents of the period.

Colonel Denning State Park is located in an area known as Doubling Gap because Blue Mountain, one of the highest ridges within the Valley and Ridge province, doubles back on itself forming an S. The park encompasses 273 acres of hilly forest and is readily accessible from PA Route 233, which forms its western border. The southern portion of the park contains a small parcel of land that is separated from the rest of the park. Located here is a parking area and trailhead for the 105-mile-long Tuscarora Trail (*see* page 279). The trailhead is about 19 miles west of the intersection of the Tuscarora and Appalachian trails. To reach the parking area follow PA Route 233 north from Newville for about 9.5 miles. The parking area is on the right.

The main natural feature of the park is the 3.5-acre, manmade Doubling Gap Lake, which was formed by damming Doubling Gap Run. Both the stream and lake are stocked with trout, and warm-water gamefish and panfish can be caught in the lake as well. Also on the lake is a small guarded beach that is open from Memorial Day to Labor Day. During the winter a portion of the lake is open to ice skating, with lighted night skating available.

The park contains a 52-site campground that can accommodate tents and trailers. Since the park is nearly surrounded by the Tuscarora State Forest (*see* page 229), and many of the park's trails connect with state forest trails, the park is a good base camp for exploring the state forest, including the nearby Hemlocks Natural Area (*see* page 230).

There are several trails within the park. The Doubling Gap Nature Trail is a 1.5-mile loop that begins near the dam and follows Doubling Gap Run upstream from the lake. Visitors can pick up a pamphlet from the park office or nature center to help them identify highlights along this self-guided interpretive trail. Wood ducks, turkey, and sometimes even bear can be seen along the trail as it winds through woodlands and extensive stretches of marsh. Also found within the stream is the hellbender (*Cryptobranchus alleganiensis*), one of the biggest salamanders in the world, which sometimes reaches more than 2 feet in length.

The Rattlesnake Trail, which also begins near the dam, is a 1.15-mile loop that runs through the foothills of Blue Mountain. With the exception of one rocky section that is about 0.4 mile in length, the trail is relatively easy. The trail gives the hiker a good look at the mixed oak forest and old logging roads, some of which it traverses. The trail is named after the timber rattlesnake, which is relatively common in the park.

The Flat Rock Trail begins within Colonel Denning State Park, but most of the trail lies within the Tuscarora State Forest. The trail is 2.5 miles long and climbs the mountain to Flat Rock, where the hiker is rewarded with a dramatic panoramic view of the Cumberland Valley. The trail is moderately challenging because it is rocky and somewhat steep, and hikers are discouraged from leaving the trail to avoid unwanted encounters with rattlesnakes.

A park map, which shows the location of all the trailheads, is available at the park office.

Directions: From Landisburg follow PA Route 233 south for about 8.4 miles to the park road, which is on the left.

Activities: Hiking, camping, fishing, hunting, picnicking, swimming, ice skating.

Facilities: Hiking trails, visitors center, lake, swimming beach, picnic areas, playground, campground.

Eastern Hellbender

It's big, it's ugly, it's slimy, and it hides under rocks. It is the Eastern hellbender (*Cryptobranchus allegoniensis*). There are two common misconceptions surrounding this aquatic salamander: it inflicts a poisonous bite and it spreads a slime on fishing lines that drives away fish. Both are untrue but have led to nicknames such as devil dog and Allegheny alligator.

The hellbender is the only member of the giant salamander family found in North America. These salamanders like to live in clear, clean, fast-moving streams with rocky bottoms, and in Pennsylvania they're found in the Allegheny River and Ohio River drainage basins. They are primarily nocturnal and spend most of their day hiding under logs or rocks. It's here that unsuspecting fishermen sometimes find them while collecting bait. At night the salamander emerges to forage for food. Its favorite dinner items are snails and crayfish, but they won't turn their nose up at worms either, leading to more unsuspected encounters with anglers.

The hellbender's reproductive process is also unique. Late in the summer the male digs a shallow nest in the stream bottom beneath a log or rock. A female then deposits up to 500 eggs in the nest as the male releases sperm into the water to fertilize them. The hellbender is the only Pennsylvania salamander that fertilizes its eggs externally. The male then does his fatherly duty and guards the nest for two to three months until the young hatch and make their way into the world.

Dates: Open year-round.
Fees: There is a charge for camping.
Closest town: Landisburg, 8.4 miles.
For more information: Colonel Denning State Park, 1599 Doubling Gap Road, Newville, PA 17241. Phone (717) 776-5272.

COWANS GAP STATE PARK

[Fig. 3(11)] Cowans Gap State Park is probably the only Pennsylvania state park with a romantic story attached to its name. Major Samuel Cowan was a British officer that fought in the Revolutionary War. While in the colonies he fell in love with a Boston girl, but he had to return to England alone because his love's father forbade her to see him. He eventually returned to the U.S. and the two eloped and settled down in Chambersburg, Pennsylvania. After a few years, the couple decided to move to Kentucky and packed their belongings onto a wagon and headed west. They got no farther than Tuscarora Mountain when their wagon broke as they were passing through a wind gap in the mountain. They traded their wagon to the Indian chief that ruled the area in exchange for the land and lived out their lives in what is today Cowans Gap State Park.

Cowans Gap encompasses 1,085 acres within the Tuscarora Mountain area of the Valley and Ridge province in Fulton County. The stream that cut the mountain gap in which the park lies has since disappeared, having been pirated by another stream that crossed its course, thereby robbing it of its water. Dry mountain gaps such as these are known as wind gaps, and the park's visitor center has displays that illustrate and explain this unusual process.

Cowans Gap is a forested park dominated by oaks and chestnuts. Little Aughwick Creek flows through the park, and other than small streamside wetlands, there are no significant wetland areas. The only endangered species within the park is the glade spurge (*Euphorbia purpurea*). This purple-flowered wetland plant is known to occur in only a dozen or so locations in Pennsylvania.

Located near the center of the park is Cowans Gap Lake, which was constructed by the Civilian Conservation Corps (CCC) in the 1930s by building a dam across Little Aughwick Creek. This 42-acre lake contains trout, panfish, perch, and bass and is the primary focus of most of the park's recreational activity. There is a small, guarded swimming beach, two boat launches, picnic facilities, and a wheelchair-accessible fishing pier. During the winter a portion of the lake is maintained for ice skating, while the balance is open to ice fishermen.

The CCC also built 10 rustic cabins that are still in use today. Visitors can rent the cabins, which sleep four and have a refrigerator, stove, and fireplace but no indoor plumbing. The cabins have been placed on the National Registry of Historic Places because they are a prime example of the hand-built wooden structures constructed by the CCC during its short-lived existence. For campers who bring their own tents or campers, the park has two large campgrounds with 233 campsites. The campgrounds are open from the second Friday of April until the end of antlerless deer season.

Hiking is a popular park activity. One of the more heavily used trails is the Lakeside Trail, which

GREAT HORNED OWL
(Bubo virginianus)
This owl, growing to two feet in height, will prey on medium sized mammals or birds, including waterfowl, grouse, skunks and porcupines. It is distinguished from other owls by its ear tufts and "hoo, hoo-hoo, hooo-hoo" call.

encircles Cowans Gap Lake. The 1.3-mile loop is an easy hike and offers a scenic view of Tuscarora Mountain to the east. The trail can be accessed from nearly anywhere along the edge of the lake. Most of the park's other trails are more challenging. The Plessinger Trail is a 1-mile-long, moderately challenging trail that runs alongside Aughwick Creek. Beginning near the stream's inlet into the lake and extending to the park's southern boundary, the trail takes the hiker through the oak-hickory forest. Among the more difficult trails in the park is the Horseshoe Trail, which runs along the park's northern boundary. As the trail ascends the hillside along the park's western edge it becomes more of a climb than a hike. At the end of the trail lies a scenic vista that looks out over the lake. A similarly impressive view can be enjoyed by hiking up Knobsville Road, a gated woods road that now serves as a relatively easy hiking trail. Also running through the park is a section of the 248-mile Tuscarora Trail (*see* page 279). This section of the trail contains a number of very large rocks, making the trail difficult. There are signs along the park roads directing hikers to each of the trails.

Directions: From the Pennsylvania Turnpike take Exit 13, Fort Littleton, and follow US Route 522 north for about 5.5 miles to Burnt Cabins and then follow the signs to the park.

Activities: Hiking, camping, hunting, fishing, swimming, ice skating.

Facilities: Hiking trails, campground, cabins, guarded beach, interpretive center.

Dates: Open year-round.

Fees: There is a charge for camping.

Closest town: McConnellsburg, 11 miles.

For more information: Cowans Gap State Park, HC 17266, Fort Loudon, PA 17224. Phone (717) 485-3948.

🏞 GREENWOOD FURNACE STATE PARK

[Fig. 3(8)] To look at this small 423-acre state park today, it's hard to imagine that it was once a bustling industrial area with more than 100 buildings. For 70 years, from 1834 to 1904, iron furnaces ran day and night, providing as many as 300 employees and their families a way of life. Because of its rich historical heritage, the National Park Service has designated the park the Greenwood Furnace National Historic District. Several of the original structures still stand, including the ironmasters mansion, the church, the blacksmith and wagon shop (which is now the visitors center), and the cemetery.

The community of Greenwood Furnace and the iron company, Greenwood Works, are the primary focuses of the park's educational programs. From April through November the park sponsors guided walks, living history exhibits, films, and programs about the history and culture of the area. The visitor center, which is open during the summer and on weekends during the spring and fall, shows visitors what it was like to live in a nineteenth-century iron town. There's also an Old Home Days heritage festival in August.

A great way to learn about the Greenwood Furnace ironworks is to pick up an interpretive brochure from the park office and walk the historic trail. This 60-minute tour, which begins at the park office, highlights both the iron industry and the community that grew up around it. The blacksmith shop, meat house, cemetery, and Methodist Episcopal Church are among the sites along the route.

The center of the park's recreational facilities also dates back to the industrial period. Greenwood Lake encompasses 6 acres and was built to supply water to the iron furnaces. The lake, which is cold and relatively deep, flows into the East Branch Stone Creek, and both are stocked with trout every year. A small guarded beach is located on the east side of the lake and is open from Memorial Day to Labor Day. Also located nearby are picnic facilities, a concession stand, and a handicapped-accessible fishing pier. The Lakeview Trail provides an easy, 0.6-mile hike around the lake and offers access to most of the facilities. During the winter, ice skating is popular on the lake.

Greenwood Furnace State Park is a popular point of departure for snowmobilers, hikers, and horseback riders planning an excursion into the adjacent Rothrock State Forest. Located within 11 miles of the park are the Alan Seeger Natural Area (*see* page 243), Detweiler Run Natural Area (*see* page 240), Bear Meadows Natural Area (*see* page 242), and Big Flat Laurel Natural Area.

One of the trails leading into the state forest is the Greenwood Spur to the Mid State Trail (*see* page 275). This 7-mile spur, which begins near the eastern side of the park, runs through Rothrock State Forest passing a fire tower, charcoal hearths (where wood was converted to charcoal for the iron furnaces), and through the Alan Seeger Natural Area. The blue-blazed trail provides a strenuous, difficult hike. Another difficult trail, which begins at the park boundary near the church, is the Link Trail. This trail extends 68 miles to Cowans Gap State Park (*see* page 217) and connects with the Tuscarora Trail (*see* page 279) about 2 miles before entering Cowans Gap.

For those wanting a shorter, easier hike there are several trails within the park boundaries. One option is the moderately challenging ore mine loop, which is 5.2 miles long. The loop uses the Brush Ridge, Tramway, and Chestnut Spring trails to take the hiker along an old wagon road and a portion of the iron furnace's tramway. The tramway was a type of railroad on which iron ore was transported to the furnace, but rather than a steam engine, mules pulled the cars.

The tramway passed a small group of homes where some of the ironworkers lived. Each time the mules came by, the ironworkers' dogs came out and barked at them, giving the area the name Dogtown. Passing by here today is the Dogtown Trail, a 1.5-mile, moderately challenging trail that is also used by cross-country skiers and snowmobilers during the winter. A map that shows the locations of all of the trailheads is available at the park office.

Directions: From Belleville follow PA Route 305 west for about 5 miles into the park.

Activities: Hiking, hunting, fishing, swimming, ice skating, snowmobiling, cross-country skiing, camping.

Facilities: Picnic areas, guarded beach, visitor center, trails, historic structures, campground, handicapped-accessible fishing pier.

Dates: Open for day use year-round. Camping is open from second Friday in Apr. until mid-Dec. Beach is open from Memorial Day-Labor Day.

Fees: There is a charge for camping.

Closest town: Belleville, 5 miles.

For more information: Greenwood Furnace State Park, RR2, Box 118, Huntingdon, PA 16652. Phone (814) 667-1800.

▓ TROUGH CREEK STATE PARK

[Fig. 3(9)] The area today known as Trough Creek State Park was initially a part of the Rothrock State Forest (*see* page 239), which surrounds the park. The park lies within the gorge cut through Terrace Mountain by Great Trough Creek as it winds its way to Raystown Lake. Elevations in the park range from 879 feet along Trough Creek, to 1,480 feet at the park's northeastern corner.

The park is about 80 percent forested, most of it mixed hardwoods and oak, with some hemlock found along the stream. There are three main tributaries to Great Trough Creek: Abbott Run (which spills into the creek over Rainbow Falls), Laurel Run, and Tar Kiln Run.

Two Species of Special Concern are found within the park. Golden Club (*Orontium aquaticum*) is a wetland plant whose tiny yellow flowers grow along an unusual spikelike structure called a spadix. This member of the arum family is considered rare in Pennsylvania and is found along the banks of Trough Creek. Also found here is the Allegheny woodrat (*see* page 173). This relative of the packrat was just discovered here in 1997 near two of the park's well-known geologic features, Balanced Rock and the ice mine.

Because of its unique geology, the Trough Creek gorge was set apart from the state forest, and the Civilian Conservation Corps built trails and other facilities to produce a popular recreational facility. The park lies along one of the coves of Raystown Lake, which is the largest inland lake in Pennsylvania. Shad from the lake migrate up Trough Creek to spawn and can be netted within the park. Fishermen will also find trout, panfish, and bass in the creek.

Before it was state property, the park housed an iron furnace and, like most of the state, was logged. The Paradise Furnace produced cast iron during the middle part of the nineteenth century, and remnants of the furnace stack, the ironmaster's mansion, and a log home, which today houses the visitor center, still remain. Today the mansion is used as a lodge and rented to park visitors year-round.

The park is a popular point of departure for visitors to the Rothrock State Forest. Hikers, snowmobilers, hunters, and cross-country skiers can all find trails that extend into the state forest. Additionally, there is a campground that can accommodate both tents and trailers for visitors wishing to use the park as a base camp.

There are 16 miles of trails within the park giving visitors access to most of the unique geologic features, scenic vistas, and historic sites. Many of the trails rise up the side of the gorge and follow narrow ledges, so visitors should wear the appropriate hiking shoes and exercise caution, particularly when it's wet or icy. Signs marking the trailheads are located along Trough Creek Drive, which winds its way through the park alongside the creek.

The Rhododendron Trail is about 0.6 mile long and is a popular way to reach Balanced Rock, a sandstone boulder about 12 feet long and 6 feet wide that is poised at a 45-degree angle on the edge of the gorge. The rocks around it have gradually eroded away through a process called block weathering, in which water seeps into cracks in the rock, freezes, and then expands, breaking the rock apart. The Rhododendron Trail is very scenic, crossing Great Trough Creek on a suspension bridge, following the edge of the creek, and then climbing a set of stone steps past Rainbow Falls to Balanced Rock. Just across the road from the trailhead on the hillside is an area called Copperas Rock. The area takes its name from the yellow-green crust that forms on the surface of the rocks. Cooperas, as the crust is called, is hydrated ferrous sulfate and was collected in the past and used to set the dye in cloth.

Near the northern end of the park, not far from Raystown Lake, is the Ice Mine Trail. This trail is about 1.2 miles long and runs from the ice mine eastward into Rothrock State Forest and then back into the park ending at a parking area along Trough Creek Drive. The ice mine is a man-made depression at the base of a cliff that acts as a sort of cold air duct. The hillside above is littered with sandstone boulders that trap cold air. The air flows down the hillside and accumulates in the depression. It's so cold that ice can be found here as late as June. Historians believe the ice mine was built by workers from the iron furnace to keep their lunches cold.

One of the easiest trails within the park is the Terrace Mountain Trail. This level trail runs along one of the small coves of Raystown Lake and passes an old stone dam. Only about 1 mile of the trail lies within the park. The trail then extends another 14 miles or so into the Raystown Lake area, which is managed by the U.S. Army Corps of Engineers, and then into the Rothrock State Forest.

Directions: From Huntingdon follow PA Route 26 south for 15 miles to PA Route 994. Follow PA Route 994 east for 5 miles to the sign marking the park entrance road, which is on the left.

Activities: Hiking, camping, hunting, fishing, snowmobiling, cross-country skiing.

Facilities: Hiking trails, snowmobile trial, cross-country ski trail, lodge, campsite, picnic grounds, playgrounds.

Dates: Open year-round.

Fees: There is a charge for campsites.

Closest town: Newburg, 5 miles.

For more information: Trough Creek State Park, RR1, Box 211, James Creek, PA 16657. Phone (814) 658-3847.

REEDS GAP STATE PARK

[Fig. 3(25)] Reeds Gap State Park was a popular recreation spot long before it became a state park in 1938. As far back as the 1700s, settlers in the area gathered here for homecomings, social events, church services, or just for camaraderie. This part of the New Lancaster Valley sits within a water gap cut by Honey Creek into Thick Mountain. Most of the park is a pine and hemlock forest, with many of the trees reaching well over 100 feet tall. A mixed hardwood forest that includes oaks, maples, ash, hickory, tulip poplar, and dogwood dominates the northern third of the park, which lies along the mountainside. Also common throughout the park are rhododendron and mountain laurel.

During the mid-1800s, Edward Reed, the park's namesake, built a sawmill near the park's western boundary along Honey Creek. The water-powered mill needed a steady source of water to operate, so a dam was built across the creek. Remnants of the dam are still visible along the Honey Creek Trail. Eventually the entire forest in the area was clear-cut, and the barren land was purchased by the state in 1904. During the 1930s, the Civilian Conservation Corps built many of the recreational facilities that are found in the park today including picnic areas, stone fireplaces, playgrounds, and waterlines. Many of these facilities were upgraded during the 1960s, and two swimming pools were also constructed.

Reeds Gap is a small park encompassing only 220 acres, but it is a popular recreation area. Most of the facilities are located along State Park Road, which runs along the north side of the creek. Reeds Gap is primarily a day-use area since there are only 14 campsites in the park, and unlike most state park campgrounds, Reeds Gap can accommodate only tents and not trailers. Campsites are available from the second Friday in April until the third Sunday in October.

There are several hiking trails within the park, some of which continue into Bald Eagle State Forest, which lies both north and south of the park. One of the more popular of these is the self-guided interpretive trail. This easy trail extends for about 1 mile and runs along both sides of Honey Creek. Metal signs along the path describe significant natural features. The interpretive trail uses portions of two other popular trails. The Honey Creek Trail extends for 1.8 miles along the creek and takes the hiker through an extensive stand of large pine and hemlock. The Blue Jay Trail is a 1.3-mile loop that also passes through an extensive stand of conifers, as well as through the center of the park's recreational area. A park map,

COMMON JUNIPER
(Juniperus communis)
Also known as dwarf juniper, the common juniper produces berries that are used as flavoring in gin.

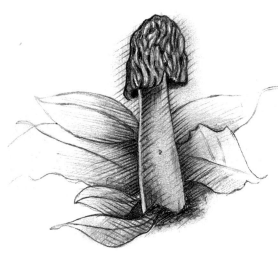

EARLY MOREL
(Verpa bohemica)
Growing up to 4 inches tall, this morel is identified by a yellow-brown, bell-shaped cap atop a hollow, light-colored stem. It grows in wet areas.

which shows the location of all the trailheads, is available at the park office.

The most difficult trail within the park is the Reeds Gap Trail, which runs along Reeds Gap Run, a tributary of Honey Creek. The trail begins at a parking area along New Lancaster Valley Road, which runs through the center of the park, and extends northward all the way to Poe Valley State Park, a distance of 18 miles. Before exiting Reeds Gap State Park the trail passes a designated sledding area near Reeds Gap Run. The trail offers some dramatic scenery, but it climbs three mountain ridges on its way to Poe Valley and is rocky, steep, and quite rugged. Approximately 0.4 mile of the trail lies within the park. Fishermen frequent the trail because Reeds Gap Run contains native and stocked trout, as does Honey Creek. A small portion of the park, 96 acres, is also open to hunting.

Directions: From PA Route 322 in Milroy follow the signs north for 7 miles.

Activities: Hiking, hunting, fishing, camping, swimming, cross-country skiing, sledding, picnicking.

Facilities: Hiking trails, picnic areas, campground, playground, swimming pools, concession stand, designated sledding area.

Dates: Open year-round.

Fees: There is a charge for camping.

Closest town: Milroy, 6 miles.

For more information: Reeds Gap State Park, 1405 New Lancaster Valley Road, Milroy, PA 17063. Phone (717) 667-3622.

R.B. WINTER STATE PARK

[Fig. 3(24)] R.B. Winter State Park lies within the narrow Brush Valley in the Bald Eagle State Forest (*see* page 245). The valley was once a major transportation route for produce, which was transported from the fertile agricultural areas of Centre County in the west, to the Susquehanna River in the east where it was loaded onto barges. Near the halfway point of their journey, the teamsters hauling the produce would stop at a tavern called the Halfway House to feed their horses and spend the night. That tavern stood near what is today Halfway Dam near the center of R.B. Winter State Park. The road used by the teamsters, Narrows Road, was built in the

White-tailed Deer

No animal, other than man, has had a bigger influence on Pennsylvania's forests than the white-tailed deer (*Odocoileus virginianus*), the official state mammal. Deer have always lived in the state's mountains, but there are more today than ever. That's because, contrary to popular belief, deer don't thrive in the deep woods but rather around woodland edges. As a result of agriculture, roads, and utility rights-of-way, ideal deer habitat abounds throughout the state.

Another contributing factor is the lack of a significant numbers of predators. The deer has only two predators in Pennsylvania, the coyote and man. While the number of deer killed by coyotes is probably not significant, the number taken by hunters is. In 1997, hunters culled nearly 400,000 deer from the state's deer herd. Nevertheless, the state's deer population has remained high and their appetite has taken its toll on the forest.

Deer will eat nearly any type of plant material, and when the population is high, that includes ornamental shrubs and trees in residential areas and endangered plants and tree seedlings in forested areas. There are, however, two things they won't eat—black cherry seedlings and ferns. That's why a walk through many of Pennsylvania's forests today reveals nearly pure stands of black cherry towering above a vast carpet of ferns.

1700s. While the original road is gone, Sand Mountain Road, which runs through the center of the park, follows approximately the same path.

During the late 1800s, logging began in this area and a sawmill and timber dam were built. Eventually the 200-foot-tall white pine that grew in the valley were all cut, and all that remains of them today are stumps in Pine Swamp. By 1910 the entire area was treeless and the log dam had nearly disintegrated. In 1933 the Civilian Conservation Corps began making improvements in several parts of the Bald Eagle State Forest, including this area, which at the time was called the Halfway Dam State Forest Park. In addition to clearing brush and stumps left behind by the logging and subsequent fires, they built parking areas, stone fireplaces, and picnic tables and installed water lines. Perhaps most significant of all, however, they built a dam. A cement and sandstone dam, the first structure of its type ever built by the CCC, replaced the old log structure. Behind the dam, which was built across Rapid Run, 7-acre Halfway Lake was formed.

Today the park is named after Raymond B. Winter who oversaw much of the work in the park from 1910, just five years after it was purchased by the state, until 1955. The park encompasses 695 acres of forest and wetland, one-third of it in the valley and the rest on the adjacent hillsides and ridges. The valley is dominated by white pine and hemlock with a dense understory of rhododendron and mountain laurel, while oak forests dominate the ridges and slopes along the edge of the park. Scattered

RACCOON (*Procyon lotor*)
The raccoon often appears to wash its food, resulting in its Latin name, "lotor," meaning "a washer."

throughout the valley along the streams are small wetlands that can best be described as forested marshes. Rather than the more typical open marsh that is dominated by rushes and sedges, these are dominated by sphagnum moss.

A small, 34-acre section of the valley has been designated as the Rapid Run Natural Area. The area was so desig-nated because it contains a pristine stand of second-growth white pine and hemlock, very reminiscent of what grew here before the loggers moved in. Running through the natural area is the Rapid Run Nature Trail. This 1-mile-long loop provides an easy hike through the pine-hemlock forest, paralleling and crossing Rapid Run along the way. Cross-country skiers also use the trail. Hikers can pick up a brochure at the park office that will help them identify some of the highlights of the natural area.

Two streams, Rapid Run and Halfway Run, flow through the park and into Halfway Lake. Fishermen will find brown trout and brook trout in Rapid Run as well as the lake. The streams are often tea-colored, a result of tannic acid produced during the decomposition of sphagnum moss and pine and hemlock needles. In addition to fishermen, swimmers also use the lake. There is a small guarded beach available and a nearby concession area. No boats, including canoes, are permitted on the lake.

Of the park's nearly 700 acres, 400 are open to hunting. Among the game species found here are small game including squirrel, woodcock, and grouse, and larger species including turkey, white-tailed deer, and bear.

There is a campground that can accommodate both tents and trailers, which is open from the second Friday in April until the end of antlerless deer season in December. For those who want a more civilized camping experience, there is a lodge available at the park. The two-story log home has appliances, four bedrooms, and even wall-to-wall carpeting. Advanced registration is required.

The park has a well-developed trail system that includes 6 miles of hiking trails and 5 miles of cross-country ski trails, and many of the park roads are open to snowmobiles. Many of these trails connect with trails in the surrounding Bald Eagle State Forest, providing hikers, skiers, and snowmobilers with a wide variety of long-distance treks. As a result, R.B. Winter State Park is a favorite point of departure for many outdoors enthusiasts utilizing the state forest. A word of caution for cross-country skiers: Most of the trails within the park are rocky and contain some steep sections. Consequently, most of the trails are not recommended for novice skiers and shouldn't be attempted until the trails are covered with at least 8 to 10 inches of snow.

The Old Boundary Trail extends about 0.5 mile from Sand Mountain Road in the valley south to the top of Bake Oven Knob, one of the ridges within the park. The first three-quarters of the trail is relatively easy, but as the trail climbs the ridge it becomes difficult. At the top of the ridge the trail connects with the Mid State Trail (*see* page 275), which continues on into the state forest. This trail can also be accessed from the campground. A short spur trail connects the Old Boundary Trail with the campground, about halfway between Sand Mountain Road and the Mid State Trail.

The Brush Hollow Trail is about 0.75 mile long and provides a moderately challenging hike up to a ridge along the park's southern boundary, sharing part of its route with the Mid State Trail. When combined with the West Boundary Trail, at which it ends, a 1.5-mile loop is possible. The West Boundary Trail, which is difficult in spots, begins along the ridge in the oak forest, but then descends into the valley and into the pine/hemlock forest. The loop formed by these two trails provides an excellent look at the contrasts between the dry, oak forest on the ridges and the moist, pine-hemlock forest and associated wetlands in the stream bottom.

One of the longest trails in the park is the Boiling Springs Trail. The trail follows the route of the water line, installed by the CCC in the 1930s, from the park office in the valley up to the boiling springs along a ridgetop in the northern edge of the park. The 1.5-mile trail provides a moderate hike and is also a popular route for mountain bikers riding into the Bald Eagle State Forest.

The most difficult trail in the park, although short at only 0.25 mile long, is the Overlook Trail. So named because it provides a panoramic view of the park and lake from atop the ridge, the trail is a steep and rocky switchback route terminating at the Boiling Springs Trail.

A park map, which shows the location of all the trailheads, is available at the park office.

Directions: From Lewisburg follow PA Route 192 west for about 16 miles into the park.

Activities: Hiking, biking, cross-country skiing, snowmobiling, hunting, fishing, camping, swimming, mountain biking, environmental learning seminars.

Facilities: Visitor center, guarded beach, trails, campground, playgrounds, picnic areas, lodge.

Dates: Open year-round.

Fees: There is a charge for camping in cabins.

Closest town: Lewisburg, 16 miles.

For more information: R.B. Winter State Park, RR 2, Box 314, Mifflinburg, PA 17844. Phone (717) 966-1455.

Tuscarora State Forest

The Tuscarora State Forest derives its name from the Tuscarora Mountain which passes through this region. The mountain was named for the Tuscarora Indians, a tribe adopted by the Iroquois Nation and allowed to migrate to this region around 1714.

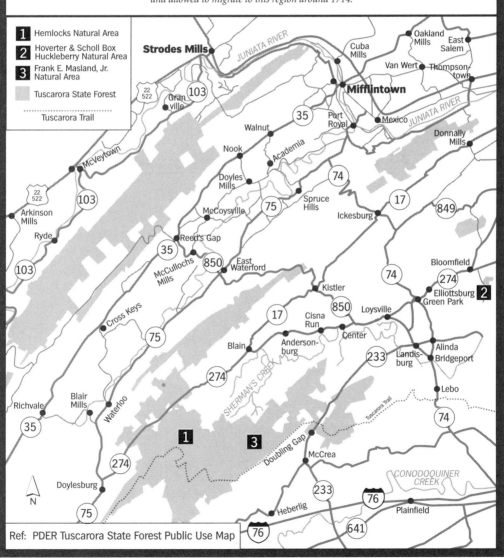

1 Hemlocks Natural Area

2 Hoverter & Scholl Box Huckleberry Natural Area

3 Frank E. Masland, Jr. Natural Area

Tuscarora State Forest

Tuscarora Trail

Ref: PDER Tuscarora State Forest Public Use Map

State Forests

Tuscarora State Forest

[Fig. 41] Lying between the Pennsylvania Turnpike and the Juniata River, not far from the state capitol at Harrisburg, is the Tuscarora State Forest, which occupies several ridges and valleys within the Valley and Ridge province. In addition to Tuscarora Mountain, portions of Shade Mountain, Kittatinny Mountain, Blue Mountain, and others are located within the forest. Tuscarora encompasses more than 91,000 acres in Huntingdon, Cumberland, Franklin, Juniata, Mifflin, and Perry counties.

The forest is broken up into two large tracts, one small tract, and one minuscule 10-acre parcel. A good way to get a flavor for the area is to take the Tuscarora State Forest Auto Tour. A map available from the state forest office outlines a 26-mile-long route through the forest's main southern tract. The route passes Big Spring State Park, several trailheads, Fowler Hollow State Forest Picnic Area, Hickory Ridge Vista, and the Hemlocks Natural Area.

There are four state parks located within or in close proximity to the Tuscarora State Forest. Big Spring State Park is located a couple of miles west of the Hemlocks Natural Area (see page 230). Colonel Denning State Park is located in the southeastern portion of the forest along PA Route 233. Little Buffalo State Park is located east of the major tracts of state forest land but only about 2.5 miles north of the Hoverterer & Scholl Box Huckleberry Natural Area (see page 231). Fowlers Hollow State Park is located about 7 miles south of Blain near the Fowler Hollow State Forest Picnic Area.

Before the forest was clear-cut from 1901 to 1930, hemlocks dominated the stream valleys, and oaks and American chestnut were common along the slopes and ridge-tops. The chestnut accounted for nearly half of the trees growing here, but those that survived the logging were killed off by the chestnut blight.

There are several special protection areas within the Tuscarora State Forest. The largest of these is the Tuscarora Wild Area. This 5,382-acre parcel straddles the border between Perry County and Juniata County atop Tuscarora Mountain. The wild area is an isolated tract of land along the southern edge of the Juniata River, about 9 miles northeast of the rest of the forest. While there are no developed trails or facilities within the wild area, primitive backpack camping is permitted. In addition to the wild area, there are three natural areas within the forest, the Hemlocks Natural Area (see page 230), the Hoverter & Scholl Box Huckleberry Natural Area (see page 231), and the Frank E. Masland, Jr. Natural Area (see page 232).

In addition to the many shorter hiking trails that pass through the forest, a 22-mile stretch of the Tuscarora Trail passes through the forest. This 220-mile-long trail is a side loop of the Appalachian Trail that begins in Virginia and ends in Pennsylvania. It follows the crest of Tuscarora Mountain along most of its length.

Fishing and hunting are among the most popular recreational activities within the forest. Deer and turkey are plentiful here, and there are 48 miles of major trout streams as well.

Directions: To reach the Tuscarora State Forest Headquarters within the forest's southern tract follow PA Route 274 west from Blain for about 5 miles.

Activities: Hiking, fishing, hunting, snowmobiling, camping, horseback riding, cross-country skiing.

Facilities: Hiking trails, snowmobile trails, equestrian trails, cross-country ski trails, state forest picnic area, campgrounds.

Dates: Open year-round.

Fees: None.

Closest town: Blain, 5 miles.

For more information: Tuscarora State Forest, RD 1, PO Box 42A, Blain, PA 17006. Phone (717) 536-3191.

☙ HEMLOCKS NATURAL AREA

[Fig. 41(1)] About 10 miles west of Blain, near Big Spring State Park, is a narrow ravine containing 300- to 500-year-old hemlocks. These trees didn't succumb to the logger's ax because the area was too remote. Today the Hemlocks Natural Area remains as an example of the native forests of Pennsylvania and consequently has been designated a National Natural Landmark.

The natural area encompasses 131 acres of forest along Hemlock Road and contains yellow birch, black birch, red oak, red maple, and chestnut oak, in addition to hemlock. There are 3 miles of hiking trails running along either side of the stream. The Hemlock Trail runs along both sides of Patterson Run, crossing back and forth across five wooden footbridges. Higher up on the ravine slope is the Rim Trail. Portions of this slope were logged, and charred stumps and snags, remnants of the wildfires that occurred after the loggers left, remain. Hikers can learn more about these two trails as well as the Patterson Run Trail, which forms the northern boundary of the natural area, and the Laurel Trail, which is especially beautiful in late May and early June when the mountain laurel is in bloom, by picking up an informational brochure at the trailhead.

Directions: From Blain follow PA Route 274 south about 8 miles to the intersection with Hemlock Road in Big Spring State Park. Turn onto Hemlock Road and drive about 3.5 miles to Hemlocks Natural Area parking lot and trailhead.

Activities: Hiking, fishing.

Facilities: Trails.

Dates: Open year-round.

Fees: None.

Closest town: Blain, 10 miles.

For more information: Tuscarora State Forest, PO Box 67, Blain, PA 17006. Phone (717) 536-3191.

HOVERTER & SCHOLL BOX HUCKLEBERRY NATURAL AREA

[Fig. 41(2)] About 1,300 years ago, a tiny box huckleberry (*Gaylussacia brachycera*) seed was germinating in eastern Perry County. This diminutive member of the heath family, standing only a couple of inches high, began to spread across the forest floor, and it's still spreading today.

The plant was first discovered in 1845, but it wasn't until 1929 that the area was acquired by the state, thereby ensuring its preservation. The ground appears to be covered with thousands of huckleberry plants, but they are really just sprouts of one individual plant. The box huckleberry spreads by producing runners that grow about 6 inches a year. Now that it covers 10 acres, it is estimated to be the oldest known plant in the Northern Hemisphere, and until an even older king's holly plant was discovered in Tasmania recently, it was thought to be the oldest plant in the world.

The 10-acre Hoverter & Scholl Box Huckleberry Natural Area seems as small in comparison to the rest of the Tuscarora State Forest as the huckleberry seems in comparison to the hemlocks, white pines, and hardwoods that tower above it. The natural area is a completely separate tract of land located 6 miles east of the rest of the forest. It contains a 0.25-mile interpretive trail that identifies the huckleberry,

Eastern Spadefoot Toad

The Eastern spadefoot toad (*Scaphiopus holbrookii*) is one of seven North American members of the spadefoot toad family and the only one found east of the Mississippi. The toad takes its name from a horny spade-shaped structure found on the inner surface of each hind leg, which it uses to dig the burrow in which it spends most of its time. If you want to tell a spadefoot toad from the more common toads, and you don't want to look at its back feet, look it in the eye. The spadefoot is the only Pennsylvania toad with vertical pupils.

In Pennsylvania the Eastern spadefoot is found in two locations. In the central part of the state it is found within the Susquehanna River valley, and in the eastern part of the state it's found in the Delaware River valley as far north as Monroe County. The nocturnal toads spend most of their time either in or very near their burrow eating insects and spiders. One thing does draw them away, however. After a heavy rain during the spring, the male travels to a nearby puddle or pool of water and begins calling for a mate. Once a receptive female arrives she lays 2,000 eggs, he fertilizes them, and they both return to their burrows, never knowing the outcome of their reproductive attempt. Because the pools are temporary, the eggs must develop quickly. It's not unheard of for young toads to emerge from the pool just two weeks after the eggs were laid.

trees, and other species of plants growing within the natural area.

Directions: Follow PA Route 34 south from New Bloomfield for 1.5 miles. Turn right onto Huckleberry Road. The natural area is about 0.5 mile down the road on the left. A small sign on the hillside marks the area, and a very small parking area is located along the side of the road.

Activities: Hiking.

Facilities: Hiking trail.

Dates: Open year-round.

Fees: None.

Closest town: New Bloomfield, 1.5 miles.

For more information: Tuscarora State Forest, PO Box 67, Blain, PA 17006. Phone (717) 536-3191.

FRANK E. MASLAND, JR. NATURAL AREA

[Fig. 41(3)] This 1,270-acre natural area surrounds a 2-mile section of North Branch Laurel Run, a Wilderness Trout Stream containing native brook trout. Rising above the stream, which lies at 1,150 feet above sea level, are Bowers Mountain at 1,921 feet and Middle Ridge at 1,700 feet. The natural area is named after a native Pennsylvanian who was involved in conservation projects around the world.

This tract of land has been designated a natural area because it contains the oldest stand of second-growth oak forest within the Pennsylvania state forest system. While most of the area is dominated by oaks, there are also assorted hardwoods, pitch pine, hemlock, and even some old-growth trees scattered throughout the area. Many of the trees along the lower slopes are more than 100 feet high and are more than 40 inches in diameter. The trees living on the ridgetops are just as old but only half as large because of the more severe climate. The understory shrubs are typical for this part of the state. Rhododendrons are found on the lower slopes, while mountain laurel and huckleberry occupy the upper slopes and ridgetops.

An interesting feature of the ridgetops is rock-covered slopes called talus slopes. These rocky outcrops are thought to have formed when repeated freezing and thawing fractured the sandstone into chunks during the Pleistocene Age. Many of the talus slopes are devoid of vegetation, while others contain trees but no understory plants.

There are three trails within the Frank E. Masland, Jr. Natural Area. The Masland Trail is the longest and runs alongside Laurel Run. This 1.5-mile trail extends from Laurel Run Road, along the southern end of the natural area, to the pipeline

TIMBER RATTLESNAKE
(Crotalus horridus)

Timber Rattlesnake

The timber rattlesnake (*Crotalus horridus*) is the largest of Pennsylvania's venomous snakes, reaching up to 4.5 feet long. It's a shy animal that usually flees when confronted by man, but when it doesn't see an opportunity to escape it stands its ground. Contrary to popular belief it doesn't always rattle its tail before making a defensive strike.

While the timber rattler is found throughout the mountains of Pennsylvania, the species is considered vulnerable due to habitat loss and organized snake hunts. Additionally, they're slow to mature (they don't reach breeding age until they're five years old) and have a low reproductive potential. Its favorite habitat is second-growth woodlands (because they have high populations of small rodents) on hillsides that have rocky outcrops for basking in the sun. Timber rattlers tend to be homebodies, spending their entire lives, which can be as long as 50 years, within a few miles of the same spot. In fact, they return to the same hibernation den, generally in a deep, rocky crevice, every year, often sharing it with other rattlers.

The snakes mate during the summer, and the female doesn't give birth to her 5- to 17-inch-long young until a year later. Because the 12-month gestation period takes so much out of her body, the female rattler can only mate every two years. While not much is known about these shy creatures, scientists believe that the female fasts during her entire pregnancy.

right-of-way that forms its northern boundary. Two other trails extend from Boiler Road to the Masland Trail. The Deer Hollow Trail is approximately 0.75 mile long, and the Turbett Trail is about 1 mile long. Both of these trails drop about 250 feet as they descend from the trailhead to the stream. Combining the Masland Trail with one of the other two trails allows for loop hikes that pass through a variety of upland and bottomland habitats of varying lengths.

In addition to receiving the special protection granted by its natural area status, this has also been designated a special protection area for reptiles and amphibians. The area is home to six species of salamanders and assorted species of frogs, toads, newts, and reptiles, including the timber rattlesnake.

Directions: From Landisburg follow PA Route 233 south 4 miles to Laurel Run Road. Follow Laurel Run Road south for 10 miles to the Masland Trail trailhead.

Activities: Hiking.

Facilities: Hiking trails.

Dates: Open year-round.

Fees: None.

Closest town: Landisburg, 14 miles.

For more information: Tuscarora State Forest, PO Box 67, Blain, PA 17006. Phone (717) 536-3191.

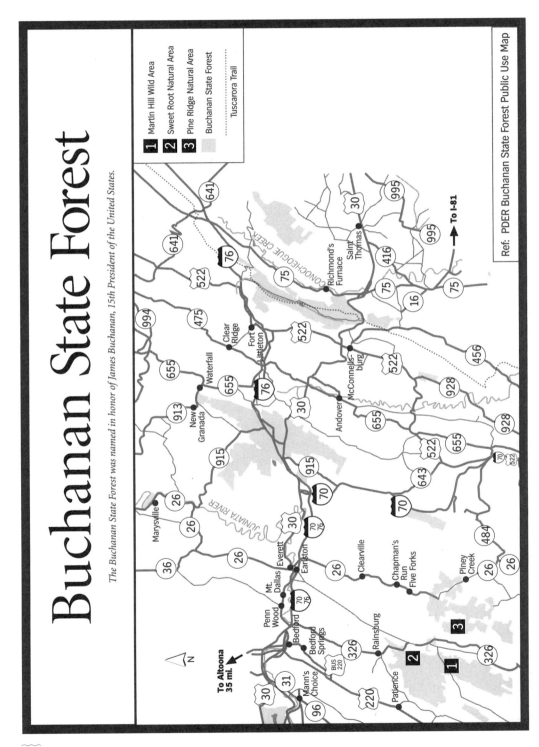

Buchanan State Forest

The Buchanan State Forest was named in honor of James Buchanan, 15th President of the United States.

1 Martin Hill Wild Area
2 Sweet Root Natural Area
3 Pine Ridge Natural Area
Buchanan State Forest
Tuscarora Trail

Ref: PDER Buchanan State Forest Public Use Map

Buchanan State Forest

[Fig. 42] The Buchanan State Forest occupies 70,000 acres in Bedford, Fulton, and Franklin counties. Like many of Pennsylvania's forests, it is not one contiguous tract of land but is fragmented, consisting of five major tracts and six smaller isolated parcels. While Buchanan is located within the Valley and Ridge province, nearly all of the forest lies on the mountaintops, including portions of Tussey Mountain, Tuscarora Mountain, Broad Mountain, Town Hill, and Sideling Hill.

The forest is named after James Buchanan who was born near the village of Cove Gap, Franklin County, in 1791. Buchanan went on to become the fifteenth President of the United States. Today his birthplace is marked with a monument surrounded by 3,000 Norway spruce trees (*Picea abies*). To reach the monument and adjacent picnic area follow PA Route 16 northwest from Mercersburg to Cove Gap, a distance of about 4 miles.

Earlier in the 1700s, before Buchanan was born, a well-known road passed through the forest. Forbes Road was a supply route which ran from the city of Carlisle in south-central Pennsylvania to what is today Pittsburgh. The road was used by the British to supply the frontier outposts of Fort Duquesne and Fort Pitt.

By the early part of the twentieth century, Buchanan State Forest had been clear-cut. Since the land was of no value to the logging companies after the trees were gone, much of the land was purchased by the state for only $2 per acre. The forest has since grown back and today is comprised of second- and third-growth trees.

While clear-cutting is no longer practiced here, the forest now faces different threats. During the early 1980s, gypsy moths defoliated vast stretches of the forest, killing many of the trees. The Buchanan State Forest probably suffered more tree mortality than any other state forest in Pennsylvania. More recently, a larger, more attractive pest has assailed the forest. White-tailed deer are eating the vast majority of tree seedlings and other plants, leaving only unpalatable black cherry seedlings and ferns.

Many of the developed facilities in the Tuscarora State Forest were constructed by the Civilian Conservation Corps during the late 1930s and early 1940s. When the CCC program came to an end at the beginning of World War II, one of the camps built to house the workers was put to a different use. The camp located near the base of the west slope of Sideling Hill was used to house conscientious objectors, draftees who were excused from bearing arms. During the later stages of the war, however, the conscientious objectors were replaced by German prisoners-of-war captured in Europe.

The Tuscarora State Forest provides numerous recreational opportunities. In addition to hunting, fishing, hiking, cross-country skiing, and snowmobiling, the forest also permits hang-gliding. There are two designated hang-gliding launch sites within the forest, but given the dangerous nature of this sport, participants are required to have written permission from the Bureau of Forestry.

In addition to numerous short trails, 39 miles of the Tuscarora Trail (*see* page 279) pass through the forest. This trail is a side loop of the Appalachian Trail that enters Pennsylvania from Maryland, connecting with the Appalachian Trail northeast of the Tuscarora State Forest. The trail passes several scenic vistas and rocky outcrops as it winds through the forest, and it varies in elevation from 1,310 feet to 2,460 feet.

Directions: To reach the forest headquarters building follow PA Route 30 east from Breezewood for about 4 miles.

Activities: Hiking, hunting, fishing, camping, cross-country skiing, snowmobiling, and hang-gliding.

Facilities: Hiking trails, snowmobile trails, cross-country ski trails, picnic areas, hang-gliding launch sites.

Dates: Open year-round.

Fees: None.

Closest town: Breezewood, 4 miles.

For more information: Buchanan State Forest, RR 2, PO Box 3, McConnellsburg, PA 17233. Phone (717) 485-3148.

MARTIN HILL WILD AREA

[Fig. 42(1)] Sportsmen looking for an area to hunt with little competition should consider the Martin Hill Wild Area, a vast expanse of remote woodland sitting atop Tussey Mountain in southern Bedford County. The area extends from the Pennsylvania/Maryland border 9 miles north to Evitts Mountain. The streams within this 11,500-acre wild area drain into Town Creek, which is a tributary of the Potomac River. While the area was clear-cut near the turn of the century, there are a few areas near the Maryland border where some old-growth Virginia pine (*Pinus virginiana*) can still be found. White-tailed deer and turkey are both common. Also found here, but less often seen, are black bears, bobcats, and rattlesnakes.

The primary access into the southern and largest portion of the wild area lies at the intersection of Martin Hill and Beans Cove roads. There is a sign, parking area, and trailhead leading to Tussey Mountain Road, an old woods road that is closed to motor vehicle traffic. By hiking this road, which extends nearly all the way to the Maryland border, visitors can gain access to numerous side trails that run down the slopes of Tussey Mountain. Running parallel to this road along the eastern slope of the mountain is the Gap Trail. By combining Tussey Mountain Road, the Gap Trail, and the side trails, numerous loop hikes of varying lengths are possible.

The northern portion of the Martin Hill Wild Area is accessible from four trailheads along Evitts Mountain Road. Each of these provides access to old woods roads that intersect hiking trails.

Directions: To reach the southern portion of the Martin Hill Wild Area follow Beans Cove Road north for about 2.5 miles from the village of Beans Cove. A trailhead and parking area are located near the intersection with Martin Hill Road. To reach the northern part of the wild area turn left onto Martin Hill Road and follow it about 1 mile to Tower Road and turn left. Follow Tower Road to Evitts Mountain Road. There are four gated old woods roads along Evitts Mountain Road that lead into the wild area.

Activities: Hiking, hunting, fishing.

Facilities: Hiking trails.

Dates: Open year-round.

Fees: None.

Closest town: Beans Cove, 2 miles.

For more information: Buchanan State Forest, RR 2, PO Box 3, McConnellsburg, PA 17233. Phone (717) 485-3148.

SWEET ROOT NATURAL AREA

[Fig. 42(2)] The Sweet Root Natural Area is located adjacent to and just north of the Martin Hill Wild Area. The focal point of the area is a deep, narrow gorge cut by Sweet Root Run through Tussey Mountain. Located along Sweet Root Run is a 69-acre stand of virgin hemlock. The slopes above the stream are dominated by oaks, while the ridgetops are covered with oaks and hard pines. The pines include Virginia pine, table mountain pine (*Pinus pungens*), which is found only in the Appalachian Mountains, and pitch pine. The early colonists used the latter as a source of tar and turpentine.

Just north of the gap cut by Sweet Root Run through Tussey Mountain is a cave containing a natural form of potassium nitrate. Colonists used the cave during the Revolution to collect the chemical, commonly called saltpeter, that is a critical ingredient in the manufacture of gunpowder.

Located just to the east of the Sweet Root Natural Area is the Sweet Root Picnic Area. This serves as a good entry point to the natural area. Leading from the picnic area, through the water gap, and into the heart of the natural area is the Tarkiln Trail. The trail ends at Blankfield Road along the natural area's western boundary. This 3-mile trail also provides access to several other shorter trails that pass through the area.

The natural area has been designated a special protection area for reptiles and amphibians, thereby prohibiting all hunting or removal of these animals.

Directions: From the Buchanan State Forest headquarters in Chaneysville follow PA Route 326 north less than 1 mile to the Sweet Root Picnic Area.

Activities: Hiking, fishing, hunting.

Facilities: Hiking trails.

Dates: Open year-round.

Fees: None.

Closest town: Chaneysville, 1 mile.

For more information: Buchanan State Forest, RR 2, PO Box 3, McConnellsburg, PA 17233. Phone (717) 485-3148.

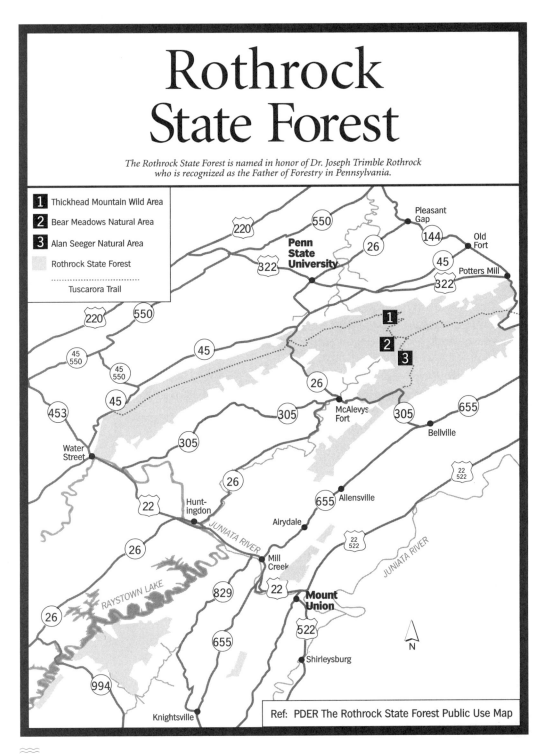

Rothrock State Forest

*The Rothrock State Forest is named in honor of Dr. Joseph Trimble Rothrock
who is recognized as the Father of Forestry in Pennsylvania.*

1 Thickhead Mountain Wild Area

2 Bear Meadows Natural Area

3 Alan Seeger Natural Area

Rothrock State Forest

Tuscarora Trail

Ref: PDER The Rothrock State Forest Public Use Map

🌲 PINE RIDGE NATURAL AREA

[Fig. 42(3)] Located 1 mile south of Chaneysville in southern Bedford County is an area known as the Resettlement Lands. At one time farms operated on the rocky, marginally productive soil. During the Great Depression of the 1930s, the U.S. purchased the land and relocated the farmers to more fertile fields. Part of the land eventually came under the jurisdiction of the Pennsylvania Bureau of Forestry and is today the 568-acre Pine Ridge Natural Area. It has been designated a natural area because of a unique combination of trees. Pines planted by the Bureau of Forestry have been joined by native Virginia pine and hickory, creating the only forest of its kind in Pennsylvania. The parts of the area that were not previously farmland are dominated by mixed oaks.

Directions: From the state forest headquarters along PA Route 326, drive 0.3 mile and bear right at the village of Chaneysville. Follow this unnamed paved road for 1.5 to 2 miles and the Pine Ridge Natural Area, which is marked with a sign, is on the right.

Activities: Hiking, horseback riding.

Facilities: Hiking and equestrian trails.

Dates: Open year-round.

Fees: None.

Closest town: Chaneysville, 1 mile.

For more information: Buchanan State Forest, RR 2, PO Box 3, McConnellsburg, PA 17233. Phone (717) 485-3148.

Rothrock State Forest

[Fig. 43] The 94,264-acre Rothrock State Forest is named after Dr. Joseph Rothrock, the father of forestry in Pennsylvania. Dr. Rothrock, a professor at the University of Pennsylvania, was one of the first people in the U.S. to begin lecturing about the problems resulting from uncontrolled clear-cutting. In addition to lecturing at the University, he also spoke to the general public and many of the prominent citizens of Philadelphia. This lead to the formation of the Pennsylvania Forestry Association, of which he was elected the first president. Rothrock played a key role in the development of Pennsylvania's public ownership of forests. In 1895 he wrote: "The conviction is fast growing that it is unwise in a state or government to allow all lands to pass out of its possession. There are certain surface functions depending on the configuration and character of the highlands, for example, which concern the whole people, and for this reason should be under control of the public rather than the private citizen."

The forest is located in Huntingdon, Mifflin, and Centre counties and is divided into two main tracts. The bulk of the forest, 79,468 acres, is contained in the northern tract called the Seven Mountains Area. Farther south, along the eastern side of Raystown Lake, is the 10,910-acre Broad Top Mountain Area.

While the forest lies within the Valley and Ridge province, which is characterized by parallel ridges separated by broad valleys, the ridges here are more complex and not parallel to one another. This is especially true in the Seven Mountains Area, which contains numerous mountain peaks separated by narrow, meandering stream valleys.

Logging first began in the forest in 1840 when the iron furnaces began operating. The furnaces, which produced cast iron, required charcoal, which was produced by heating wood to very high temperatures, thereby driving off all of the water, gases, and impurities and leaving behind nearly pure carbon. Logging was limited to the areas surrounding the furnaces and not all trees were used. Hickory and oak were preferred.

Greenwood Furnace State Park is built on the site of the Greenwood Iron Works and is a good place to learn more about this historical legacy. The entrance to the park is located on PA Route 305, 15 minutes west of Belleville. In addition to Greenwood Furnace, there are three other state parks within the forest: Whipple Dam State Park, Penn Roosevelt State Park, and Trough Creek State Park.

Eventually, the large logging companies moved in and clear-cut nearly all of the Rothrock State Forest. Mixed oaks have since replaced the white pine and hemlock forests that blanketed the area. Flowing through this second-growth forest are Spruce Creek, Shaver Creek, Standing Stone Creek, and Furnace Run, all of which are classified as high quality waters. Many of the streams contain native brook trout, while others are stalked annually. Nearly the entire forest lies within the Juniata River watershed.

There are seven special protection areas within the Rothrock State Forest. Located in the Broad Top Mountain Area is the Trough Creek Wild Area. This 1,701-acre wilderness is composed of three narrow parcels along the west slope of Terrace Mountain. The wild area borders on Raystown Lake, the largest inland lake in Pennsylvania.

The Thickhead Mountain Wild Area (*see* page 241) encompasses nearly 5,000 acres in the Seven Mountains Area and includes the Bear Meadows Natural Area (*see* page 242), the Detweiler Run Natural Area, and the Big Flat Laurel Natural Area. Located near the southern end of the Seven Mountains Area is the Little Juniata Natural Area, which surrounds a water gap cut through Short Mountain by the Little Juniata River. For reasons not completely understood, the river makes a 90-degree turn here. Exposed within the walls of the water gap is a 132-foot high section of white Tuscarora sandstone, one of the primary rock types underlying the Appalachian Mountains. The river here contains a large trout population, making it a popular fishing area.

The forest contains nearly 200 miles of snowmobile trails, most of them in the Seven Mountains Area, 40 miles of cross-country ski trails, and many miles of hiking trails. The longest of these is the Mid State Trail (*see* page 275). Beginning at the Colerain State Forest Picnic Area, just north of the village of Colerain along PA Route 45, this 189-mile-long trail passes through the Seven Mountains Area and then into the Bald Eagle State Forest. The main trail is marked with orange blazes, and the side spur trails are marked with blue blazes.

Directions: Located near the center of Rothrock State Forest is Whipple Dam State Park. To reach the park follow PA Route 26 north from McAlveys Fort for about 4 miles. A sign and entry road are on the right.

Activities: Hiking, hunting, fishing, snowmobiling, cross-country skiing.

Facilities: Hiking trails, snowmobile trails, cross-country ski trails, picnic areas.

Dates: Open year-round.

Fees: None.

Closest town: McAlveys Fort, 4 miles.

For more information: Rothrock State Forest, PO Box 403, Rothrock Lane, Huntingdon, PA 17120. Phone (814) 643-2340.

THICKHEAD MOUNTAIN WILD AREA

[Fig. 43(1)] The Thickhead Mountain Wild Area is a sprawling 4,886-acre tract of land within the Seven Mountains Area of the Rothrock State Forest. The area contains a series of low ridges dominated by mixed oaks with ravines lined with white pine and hemlock in between. This portion of the Rothrock State Forest was designated as a wild area because of its vast undeveloped nature. Unlike most of Pennsylvania's state forest wild areas, however, it contains three areas that have been further protected by being designated natural areas.

Located near the western boundary of the Thickhead Mountain Wild Area is the Big Flat Laurel Natural Area. This 60-acre parcel is a high mountain plateau covered with Pennsylvania's state flower, the mountain laurel. Late May and early July, when these shrubs are in bloom, is the best time to visit the site. There are no developed trails within the area, but both Bear Gap Road and Gettis Ridge Road pass through it. To reach the area follow Greenlee Road north from Whipple Dam State Park for about 6 miles. The road intersects with Gettis Ridge Road and then becomes Bear Gap Road within the natural area.

Located just a short distance to the east of Big Flat Laurel Natural Area, over the crest of Thickhead Mountain, is the Detweiler Run Natural Area. The area has two notable features. One is a 45-acre stand of virgin white pine and hemlock. Unlike most old-growth stands in Pennsylvania, which survived logging because they were inaccessible, this stand survived because of a land dispute between two rival logging companies. The other notable feature is an almost impenetrable stand of rhododendron. The area is remote and contains no developed trails. It can be reached by hiking the Greenwood Spur of the Mid State Trail (*see* page 275) north for 2.5 miles from the Alan Seeger State Forest Picnic Area (*see* page 243).

The Bear Meadows Natural Area (*see* page 242) is a bog containing carnivorous plants and other plants not normally found this far south.

Directions: To reach the forest headquarters office, follow PA Route 305 north from Petersburg for 0.7 mile. Turn left onto Diamond Valley Road and drive about 2 miles to the office on the left.

Activities: Hiking, hunting, fishing.

Facilities: Trails.

Dates: Open year-round.

Fees: None.

Closest town: State College, 8 miles.

For more information: Rothrock State Forest, PO Box 403, Rothrock Lane, Huntingdon, PA 17120. Phone (814) 643-2340.

BEAR MEADOWS NATURAL AREA

[Fig. 43(2)] Located about 8 miles southeast of State College is an unusual wetland habitat known as the Bear Meadows Natural Area. Bear Meadows encompasses about 880 acres, the focal point of which is a 325-acre bog. The bog's origins are something of a mystery because it lies well south of the point where the glaciers stopped during the last ice age. Nearly all bogs are formed as a result of glacial activity.

The bog sits within a depression about 0.5 mile wide and 1.25 miles long, and it is surrounded by ridges 400 to 600 feet high. Lying beneath the bog is impermeable sandstone that traps the groundwater flowing into the depression and the precipitation running off of the hillsides. This water eventually flows out of the bog through Sinking Creek, which is sometimes called Coffee Creek because the water is stained brown by decomposing moss. The climate in the bog is unusually cool because of the cold air flowing down the hillsides.

About 10,000 years ago this bog was a lake. Over time, sphagnum moss began to grow around the edges and eventually spread across the entire surface forming a floating mat. Today the bog exhibits all of the stages of bog succession, from open sunny areas with wildflowers and carnivorous plants, to dense thickets of highbush blueberry and swamp laurel. The oldest parts of the bog contain northern species of trees including black spruce, red spruce, and balsam fir. This model of bog succession has been designated a National Natural Landmark and is used extensively by the faculty and students from nearby Penn State University as a study area.

The bog is home to a number of unusual species. Found here are the twayblade (*Listera cordata*), a small orchid with purple flowers, and the yellow-fringed orchid (*Habenaria ciliaris*). Numerous amphibians call this bog home, including the red-spotted newt (*Notophthalmus viridescens*) and spring peeper (*Hyla crucifer*), the first frog that's heard in the spring, as well as 58 species of dragonflies, half of which are rare. Larger animals are found here, too. Bears come to feed on the blueberries, hence the name Bear Meadows.

Encircling the bog is the 3.5-mile Bear Meadows Trail, a flat trail that provides an easy hike through the natural area. A portion of this trail forms part of the Mid State Trail (*see* page 275). Visitors are asked to remain on the foot trails and not venture into the bog.

Directions: Travel east on PA Route 322 from State College. Turn right at the sign for Skiemont Lodge, across from the Elks Country Club. Follow the road and the signs for 9 miles to the Bears Meadows Natural Area.

Activities: Hiking.

Facilities: Hiking trail.

Dates: Open year-round.

Fees: None.

Closest town: State College, 8 miles.

For more information: Rothrock State Forest, PO Box 403, Rothrock Lane, Huntingdon, PA 17120. Phone (814) 643-2340.

ALAN SEEGER NATURAL AREA

[Fig. 43(3)] The Alan Seeger Natural Area is named after a young poet killed during World War I. Seeger was born in New York City, but grew up in Mexico. After graduating from Harvard University in 1910, he moved to Paris and began establishing himself as a talented poet. With the outbreak of World War I, he joined the French Foreign Legion, earning the Croix de Guerre and Me Daille Militaire medals. Sadly, he was killed on July 4, 1916 during an attack on the town of Bellory-en-Santerre, fulfilling the prediction he made in his poem "I Have a Rendezvous With Death."

The area encompasses 368 acres of stream bottom and adjacent hillside along Standing Stone Creek, and has been designated a natural area because it contains 118 acres of old-growth trees. Along the bottom of the ravine are hemlock and white pine measuring up to 4 feet in diameter, while old-growth oaks are found on the hillside. The understory contains equally impressive rhododendrons measuring 15 to 20 feet high.

The only trail within the natural area is the Alan Seeger Trail, which is a short, easy trail that can be hiked in 15 minutes. The trailhead can be reached from the Alan Seeger State Forest Picnic Area, which is adjacent to the natural area.

Directions: To reach the Alan Seeger State Forest Picnic Area follow SR 1023 north from McAlveys Fort to Black Lick Road, a distance of about 2.5 miles. Turn left onto Black Lick Road and drive about 3 miles to the picnic area.

Activities: Hiking, fishing.

Facilities: Hiking trail.

Dates: Open year-round.

Fees: None.

Closest town: McAlveys Fort, 5.5 miles.

For more information: Rothrock State Forest, PO Box 403, Rothrock Lane, Huntingdon, PA 17120. Phone (814) 643-2340.

BLACK BEAR
(Ursus americanus)

Bald Eagle
State Forest

The Bald Eagle State Forest was named for the famous Indian Chief "Bald Eagle." It is located in Snyder, Union, and parts of Centre, Mifflin, and Clinton Counties and comprises 195,624 acres of State Forest land.

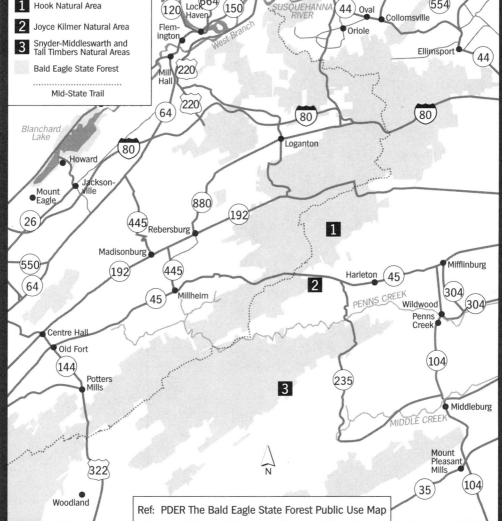

1 Hook Natural Area

2 Joyce Kilmer Natural Area

3 Snyder-Middleswarth and Tall Timbers Natural Areas

Bald Eagle State Forest

Mid-State Trail

Ref: PDER The Bald Eagle State Forest Public Use Map

Bald Eagle State Forest

[Fig. 44] The Bald Eagle State Forest is named after a Chief of the Delaware Indian tribe that once lived here. Located within Snyder, Union, Centre, Mifflin, and Clinton counties in central Pennsylvania, the forest lies atop a series of sandstone ridges within the Valley and Ridge province. Parts of Bald Eagle Mountain, Strong Mountain, Sand Mountain and Long Mountain are located in the 195,624-acre forest. Within the forest, there are numerous streams, 47 miles of which are stocked with trout, that are all part of the Susquehanna River drainage basin.

The forest was clear-cut from 1880 to 1914 when logging companies removed the native white pines for their wood and the native hemlocks for the chemicals contained in their bark. Once the trees were gone, the logging companies no longer had a use for the land. Since it was a tax liability, they sold much of the land to the state for only $1 per acre.

There are eight special protection areas within the Bald Eagle State Forest. The most accessible of these are the Hook Natural Area (*see* page 246), the Joyce Kilmer Natural Area (*see* page 247), and the Snyder-Middleswarth Natural Area (*see* page 247). Less accessible is the White Mountain Wild Area, which encompasses more than 3,500 acres of remote woodland atop White Mountain. Both the wild area and the mountain got their name from the talus slopes, areas covered with loose chunks of sandstone bleached white by the sun, common on the hillside. An access point into the wild area can be reached by the Tram Trail. To reach the trail follow Weikert Road south from the town of Weikert to Weikert Run Road, a distance of about 1 mile. Turn right onto Weikert Run Road, which forms the southern boundary of the wild area, and drive to the first bridge, where there is parking and a sign marking the trail. The Tram Trail connects with the White Mountain Trail.

Located atop Mount Logan, at an altitude of 2,108 feet is the Mount Logan Natural Area, so designated because of a stand of old-growth hemlock near the top of the mountain on the north side. There is only one trail into this 512-acre area, and it can only be reached by taking a four-wheel-drive vehicle down a series of old woods roads that are impassable during times of wet or wintry weather.

The Rosencrans Bog Natural Area encompasses 152 acres of high mountain bog north of Logantown in Clinton County. The bog, which is surrounded by mountain holly and highbush blueberry, contains no trails and is relatively inaccessible. To visit, from Route 80 take Exit 27 to Route 477 North to the village of Rosencrans. Turn right onto Pine Mountain Road and travel approximately 1 mile. Then turn right onto Cranberry Road. Go 1 mile and reach Rosencrans Bog Natural Area.

There are numerous recreational opportunities in the Bald Eagle State Forest. While the forest is massive and much of it remote, there is an extensive series of trails designated for specific uses. There are more than 300 miles of snowmobile trails and 48 miles of mountain bike trails. Each of these trail systems is made even larger by the extensive system of forest roads. Additionally, there are trails designated for all terrain vehicles and dirt motorcycles.

The most popular trails, however, are the forest's hiking trails, which vary from easy to difficult. The longest continuous trail is the Mid State Trail (*see* page 275), which enters the Bald Eagle State Forest from the Rothrock State Forest along PA Route 322. It then runs through the center of the forest, ending at the small town of McElhattan along the West Branch of the Susquehanna River. Along its route it crosses Penns Creek, runs along the edge of Poe Valley State Park, Harry Johns State Forest Picnic Area, Poe Paddy State Park, and Hook Natural Area, and passes through R.B. Winter State Park and Ravensburg State Park. The main trail is marked with orange paint blazes, while side branches are marked with blue blazes. The trail is relatively rugged and much of it remote, so hikers should be in good condition and well prepared for a wilderness hike.

Directions: The district office is located 9 miles west of Mifflinburg on Route 45.

Activities: Hiking, hunting, fishing, camping, snowmobiling, cross-country skiing, ATV riding, dirt motorcycle riding, mountain biking.

Facilities: Hiking trails, biking trails, snowmobile trails, cross-country ski trails, ATV trails, dirt motorcycle trails, picnic areas.

Dates: Open year-round.

Fees: None.

Closest town: Eastville, 0.5 mile.

For more information: Bald Eagle State Forest, PO Box 147, Laurelton, PA 17845. Phone (717) 922-3344.

▨ HOOK NATURAL AREA

[Fig. 44(1)] The Hook Natural Area is among the biggest state forest natural areas within Pennsylvania, encompassing 5,119 acres in Union and Centre counties. The area includes the entire watershed of the North Branch of Buffalo Creek.

At the time the first Europeans arrived, the entire parcel was blanketed with white pine, white oak, and hemlock. During the 1890s, however, logging companies moved into the area and clear-cut the forest. That forest has since been replaced by one with a much greater diversity of species. Found here are black oak, chestnut oak, scarlet oak, red oak, white oak, hemlock, white pine, red maple, and black, yellow, and white birches. The understory is dominated by rhododendron, dogwood, mountain laurel, and ferns.

The focal point of the Hook Natural Area is the North Branch of Buffalo Creek and its tributaries. The stream is sometimes stained brown from decomposing plant material, but the water is of very high quality. It's clean enough, in fact, to support native brook trout.

There are several rugged foot trails within the area but a limited number of trailheads. A good starting point for a trip into the Hook Natural Area is via the

Molasses Gap Trail along Jones Mountain Road. This trail, which is blazed but very rocky, meets with several other trails within the natural area.

Directions: Follow PA Route 192 west from Lewisburg to Forest House Hotel. Turn southwest onto Jones Mountain Road and travel about 5 miles to the Molasses Gap Trail. There is a parking area and sign marking the entrance to the trail.

Activities: Hiking, hunting, fishing.

Facilities: Trails.

Dates: Open year-round.

Fees: None.

Closest town: Pleasant Grove, 2 miles.

For more information: Bald Eagle State Forest, PO Box 147, Laurelton, PA 17845. Phone (717) 922-3344.

JOYCE KILMER NATURAL AREA

[Fig. 44(2)] Joyce Kilmer died long ago during World War I, but his poem "Trees" embodies for many the essence of nature. Located on the north slope of Paddy Mountain is a small 77-acre natural area dedicated to Kilmer's memory. The focal point of the natural area is a 21-acre stand of virgin white pine and hemlock that was inaccessible to loggers clear-cutting the area during the early part of the twentieth century.

The Joyce Kilmer Trail is the only point of access to the Joyce Kilmer Natural Area. The trail begins along Bear Run Road, and, while not marked, the trail is obvious. At the trailhead is a sign with Kilmer's famous poem on it. From there the trail crosses Laurel Run and enters the natural area, climbing 0.75 mile up the side of Paddy Mountain. The trail ends at a natural amphitheater of flat boulders lying in a semi-circle beneath the old-growth hemlocks.

Directions: From the Forest District Office in Laurelton Center follow PA Route 45 west about 3 miles to Bear Run Road. Turn left onto Bear Run Road and travel about 0.2 mile. There is a parking area and sign marking the trailhead on the left side of the road.

Activities: Hiking.

Facilities: Hiking trail.

Dates: Open year-round.

Fees: None.

Closest town: Laurelton, 3 miles.

For more information: Bald Eagle State Forest, PO Box 147, Laurelton, PA 17845. Phone (717) 922-3344.

SYNDER-MIDDLESWARTH NATURAL AREA AND TALL TIMBERS NATURAL AREA

[Fig. 44(3)] The Snyder-Middleswarth and Tall Timbers natural areas are adjacent woodlands that together encompass more than 1,100 acres of the Swift Run watershed on Thick Mountain. The natural areas are located 5 miles west of Troxelville in Snyder County near the southern end of Bald Eagle State Forest.

The Snyder-Middleswarth Natural Area is named after Simon Snyder, the third governor of Pennsylvania, and Captain Ner Middleswarth, an officer who served during the War of 1812. The distinguishing feature of this natural area is 250 acres of virgin stream bottom forest along Swift Run. The hemlock, white pine, and pitch pine that grow here comprise one of the largest stands of old-growth forest within the Pennsylvania state forest system, and escaped the logger's axe due to its inaccessibility. Because of the significance of this old-growth stand the area has also been designated a National Natural Landmark.

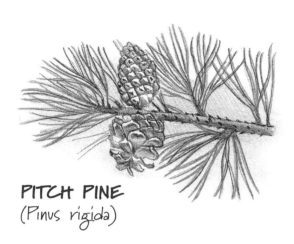

PITCH PINE
(Pinus rigida)

Adjacent to the natural area is the Snyder-Middleswarth State Forest Picnic Area. Leading from the picnic area is the Swift Run Trail, which follows Swift Run through the old-growth forest in the Snyder-Middleswarth Natural Area and into the Tall Timbers Natural Area. Within the Tall Timbers Natural Area the trail connects with the Tower Trail, which climbs to the top of Thick Mountain, ending on Swift Run Road. By then walking back along the road, the hiker can form a 6-mile loop that passes through a stream bottom forest with trees greater than 150-feet high, climbs a mountain slope dominated by oaks and hard pines, and traverses one of the ridges of the Valley and Ridge province.

Directions: To reach the Swift Run State Forest Picnic Area follow Brieninger Road northwest from the village of Troxelville to Swift Run Road, a distance of about 2 miles. Turn left onto Swift Run Road, and the picnic area is about 2 miles down the road on the right.

Activities: Hiking, hunting, fishing.

Facilities: Hiking trails.

Dates: Open year-round.

Fees: None.

Closest town: Troxelville, 4 miles.

For more information: Bald Eagle State Forest, PO Box 147, Laurelton, PA 17845. Phone (717) 922-3344.

Private Lands

▨ TANNERSVILLE CRANBERRY BOG PRESERVE

[Fig. 45] The Tannersville Cranberry Bog is a privately owned nature preserve managed by The Nature Conservancy. The preserve encompasses more than 1,000 acres of mixed-oak forest and boreal bog. The bog has been designated a National Natural Landmark because it is the southernmost, low altitude, boreal bog on the Eastern seaboard. It is a habitat that normally occurs either farther north or at much higher altitudes.

There are three trails that wind through the preserve, but the general public may only walk them with a tour guide. Call the Monroe County Conservation District for more information.

Like almost all habitats, a bog changes as it grows older. This bog started off as a pool of glacial meltwater 13,000 years ago and today is maturing into a bog forest. The Tannersville Cranberry Bog is considered a model of bog succession and so is currently being studied by researchers.

As hikers follow the boardwalk, they pass through open sunny areas containing carnivorous plants such as sundew and pitcher plants, the rare yellow-eyed grass (*Xyris* sp.), and assorted species of orchids, including the grass-pink orchid (*Calopogon pulchessus*), white-fringed orchid (*Habenaria blephariglottis*), rose pogonia (*Pogonia ophioglossoides*), and the yellow lady slipper (*Cypripedium calceolus*). These are the youngest parts of the bog's ecosystem. At one time the entire bog was an open, sunny, sphagnum mat such as this.

Some portions of the boardwalk pass through dense thickets containing highbush blueberry, cranberry, leatherleaf, and swamp azalea (*Rhododendron viscosum*). These bushes are all members of the heath family, which thrives in the low-nutrient, acidic conditions. They are the next stage in bog succession, replacing the smaller sun-loving plants.

The final stage of bog succession is marked by the infiltration of trees. As the sphagnum mat thickens, black spruce and American larch, also called tamarack, grow on the hummocks. Because of the harsh conditions, these trees, which are near the southern edge of their range, grow slowly, and 300-year-old trees may be only 40 feet tall. Some of the spruce here also look deformed, their branches sending off numerous side shoots called witches brooms. The cause is a very rare parasitic plant called the dwarf mistletoe which is only found in bogs.

Visitors who want to hike the boardwalk trail must contact the preserve office. Access is limited to scheduled, guided walks that generally occur once a month on the weekends from May to October and once a week from June through September.

In addition to rare and unusual plants, the bog is also home to two rare animals, the bog turtle (*Clemmys muhlenbergii*) and the bog copper (*Lycaena epixanthe*). The

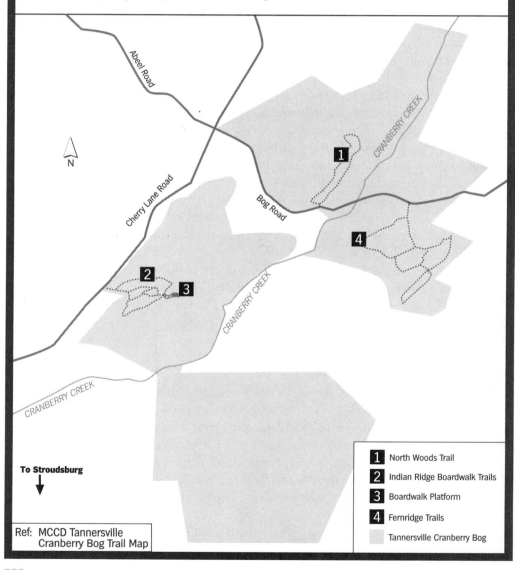

Tannersville Cranberry Bog

Created by the action of glaciers thousands of years ago, the Tannersville Cranberry bog is a 150-acre wetland and relict boreal bog owned by the Nature Conservancy and dedicated as a National Natural Landmark.

N

Abeel Road

Cherry Lane Road

Bog Road

CRANBERRY CREEK

CRANBERRY CREEK

CRANBERRY CREEK

To Stroudsburg

1 North Woods Trail
2 Indian Ridge Boardwalk Trails
3 Boardwalk Platform
4 Fernridge Trails
Tannersville Cranberry Bog

Ref: MCCD Tannersville Cranberry Bog Trail Map

latter, a butterfly, is restricted in Pennsylvania to bogs because the caterpillars feed only on cranberry plants. Also found here are species normally found farther north, where this type of wetland is common. These include birds such as the brown creeper (*Certhia familiaris*), Nashville warbler (*Vermivora rucficapilla*), and Canada warbler.

More common species of wildlife are also found in the preserve. White-tailed deer, turkey, bear, and coyote are frequently seen. Visitors to the preserve have a reasonably good chance of seeing some of these animals while hiking the preserve's other two trails. The North Woods Trail [Fig. 45(1)] is a 0.75-mile loop that passes through a mixed-oak forest. This self-guided interpretive trail contains some large oaks and white pines and is an easy hike. The Fernridge Trails [Fig. 45(4)] are a series of loops 0.75 mile in length that pass through similar forest habitat. Cross-country skiers also use this trail system during the winter.

Both of these trails border on wetlands, where hikers will be able to see skunk cabbage, marsh marigold (*Caltha palustris*) (also called cowslips), and goldthread. Both trails are blazed, but neither is heavily used, so the chances of seeing wildlife are good. Cranberry Creek, which passes between the two trails and along the eastern edge of the bog, contains river otters, but only the luckiest of visitors will get a glimpse of these secretive and uncommon fish-loving weasels.

Directions: From the intersection of PA Routes 611 and 715 in Tannersville, follow PA Route 611 south for 1 mile and turn left onto Cherry Lane. Travel 2.7 miles to Bog Road and turn right. The North Wood Trail is 0.3 mile on the left and the Fern Ridge Trails are 0.6 mile on the right.

Activities: Hiking, cross-country skiing.

Facilities: Trails.

Dates: Open year-round, but access to the Indian Ridge Boardwalk Trail is limited to scheduled, guided walks.

Fees: None.

Closest town: Tannersville, 3 miles.

For more information: Monroe County Conservation District, 8050 Running Valley Road, Stroudsburg, PA 18360. Phone (717) 629-3061.

SKUNK CABBAGE
(Symplocarpus foetidus)
Flies and gnats are attracted to the plant's odor, helping to pollinate its tiny flowers located on the spadix. The heat generated within the developing floral sheath is so intense that it will melt a circle in the snow.

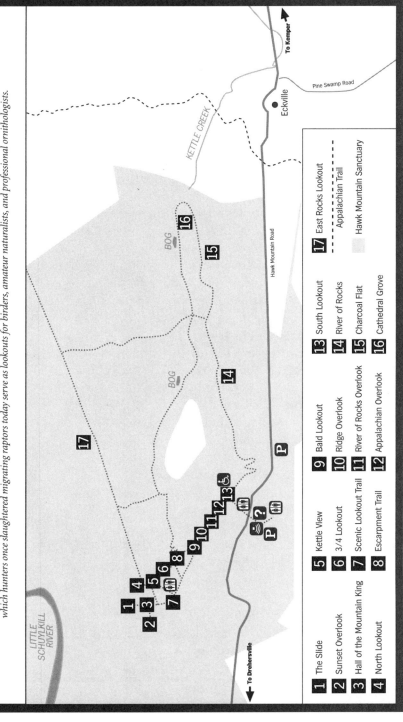

Hawk Mountain Sanctuary

In 1934, before raptors were given federal protection, Rosalie Edge founded the Hawk Mountain Sanctuary to stop the mass slaughter of raptors along this part of Kittatinny Ridge. The Sanctuary encompasses 2,380 acres of Kittatinny Ridge. The rocky outcroppings from which hunters once slaughtered migrating raptors today serve as lookouts for birders, amateur naturalists, and professional ornithologists.

Legend:

1 The Slide
2 Sunset Overlook
3 Hall of the Mountain King
4 North Lookout
5 Kettle View
6 3/4 Lookout
7 Scenic Lookout Trail
8 Escarpment Trail
9 Bald Lookout
10 Ridge Overlook
11 River of Rocks Overlook
12 Appalachian Overlook
13 South Lookout
14 River of Rocks
15 Charcoal Flat
16 Cathedral Grove
17 East Rocks Lookout

- - - Appalachian Trail
Hawk Mountain Sanctuary

HAWK MOUNTAIN SANCTUARY

[Fig. 46] Birds-of-prey, or raptors as they're often called, are easily identified in flight by the way they fly. They're soaring birds. Unlike smaller birds that flap their wings to create lift, raptors operate more like a sailplane, using their broad wings to catch rising currents of air and letting the winds carry them.

In the Valley and Ridge province of central Pennsylvania, the prevailing wind is from the northwest. When the wind strikes the parallel ridges that cross the province from southwest to northeast, it's deflected upward, creating significant updrafts along the length of the ridges. These updrafts are used by migrating raptors to rise into the upper-level winds that carry them south.

Kittatinny Ridge is the southernmost ridge in the province and borders on a broad flatland known as the Great Valley. Raptors gather above this ridge in great numbers, spiraling skyward in the updraft and gaining the height they need to cross the southern part of the state. The result is a dramatic concentration of birds of prey during the fall migration.

While the thought of shooting an eagle, hawk, or falcon today is unimaginable, it was standard practice during the late nineteenth and early twentieth centuries. They were considered vermin that competed with man for game and therefore should be eliminated. Hunters would shoot birds of prey by the hundreds each day, and one of their favorite spots to hunt was along the part of Kittatinny Ridge now occupied by Hawk Mountain Sanctuary. Today it is a violation of federal law to shoot a raptor anywhere in the U.S.

In 1934, before raptors were given federal protection, Rosalie Edge founded the Hawk Mountain Sanctuary to stop the mass slaughter of these birds along this part of Kittatinny Ridge. The sanctuary was the first refuge in the world founded to protect birds of prey. Today it is internationally known as the best place in North America and perhaps the world to view migrating raptors and also as a research facility for the study of raptor migration and Appalachian ecosystems.

The number and diversity of birds of prey that pass above the sanctuary is phenomenal. Regularly seen are the northern goshawk (*Accipiter gentilis*), Cooper's hawk (*Accipiter cooperii*), sharp-shinned hawk (*Accipiter striatus*), red-tailed hawk (*Buteo jamaicensis*), red-shouldered hawk (*Buteo lineatus*), broad-winged hawk (*Buteo platypterus*), rough-legged hawk (*Buteo lagopus*), golden eagle (*Aquila chrysaetos*), bald eagle (*Haliaeetus leucocephalus*), northern harrier (*Circus cyaneus*), osprey (*Pandion haliaetus*), peregrine falcon (*Faleo peregrinus*), merlin (*Falco columbarius*), and American kestrel (*Falco sparverius*). These birds don't all pass through at the same time, however. Bald eagle and osprey are among the early migrants that pass through in late August and September. The later migrants include the golden eagle and goshawk, which cross the ridge in November.

Beginning on August 15 and continuing for four months, the number and species of raptors passing over the ridge are documented. This census began in 1934 and is

RED-TAILED HAWK

(Buteo jamaicensis)
This hawk hunts for small animals from the air or from exposed perches.

the longest running record of raptor migration in the world. The number of individuals for each species seen varies dramatically. In 1997, for example, 5,519 broad-winged hawks were counted, but only five rough-legged hawks were seen. A sizable number of eagles, 130 bald eagles and 101 golden eagles, were also seen.

Hawk Mountain Sanctuary encompasses 2,380 acres of Kittatinny Ridge. The rocky outcroppings from which hunters once slaughtered migrating raptors today serve as lookouts for birders, amateur naturalists, and professional ornithologists. Trails crisscross the area providing access to the ridge as well as the valley below. There is also an impressive visitors center that contains a raptor museum, a gift shop with a wide variety of natural history books, and an art gallery.

The ecological significance of this area combined with the breathtaking scenery, superb trail system, and first class visitors center have made it a very popular attraction during the fall. During the peak of the migration in October, the parking lots are usually full by 10 a.m. Since the sanctuary sits atop the ridge, there is no access once the lot is full. If you plan on visiting at this time of year, try arriving before 10 a.m. or after 3 p.m.

Visit the sanctuary on a nice October day, and you'll be amazed at the different languages and accents you hear while sitting at one of the lookouts. Hawk Mountain Sanctuary receives about 80,000 visitors a year, and since many are from overseas, it is sometimes referred to as the Crossroads of Naturalists.

Located along the ridge are numerous rocky outcrops that serve as lookouts. Visitors can hike to one of the eight outlooks, climb onto a comfortable boulder, and begin hawk watching. The most popular lookout is North Lookout, where the official raptor migration counts are conducted. This lookout is located at an elevation of 1,521 feet and sits at the end of a gap in the ridge. As a result, there is a panoramic view stretching for 70 miles across the Valley and Ridge province. Hundreds of raptors a day pass at close range and at eye level during the fall migration. Since it is so popular, hundreds of people gather here on nice fall days and it can be difficult to find a place to sit.

The North Lookout [Fig. 46(4)] lies at the end of Lookout Trail, which is about 1 mile from the parking area and visitors center. This trail, which is marked with orange blazes, is rocky and difficult in places. On busy days, or if the rocky trails present a problem, visitors should consider the South Lookout. This lookout is only 300 yards from the trailhead, and the portion of the Lookout Trail leading up to it is accessible to handicapped visitors.

There are several other trails within the sanctuary worth exploring. About halfway along the Lookout Trail is a shortcut to the North Lookout. The Escarpment Trail [Fig. 46(8)] runs along the very edge of the ridge and is a difficult hike, but it provides a dramatic view of the valley below. Beyond the North Lookout is the Skyline Trail. It crosses the gap in Kittatinny Ridge, which requires the hiker to begin by making a 10-foot vertical descent and then follows the peak of the ridge 2.5 miles to the Appalachian Trail. This trail, which is marked with blue blazes, provides access to the remote East Rocks Lookout [Fig. 46(17)], but it is a very difficult trail and should be attempted only by seasoned hikers.

Hawk Mountain Sanctuary also encompasses part of the valley below the ridge. Located here are a couple of small bogs and the River of Rocks [Fig. 46(14)], a boulder field left behind during the last ice age about 13,000 years ago. The River of Rocks Trail descends from the South Outlook and loops around the boulder field, eventually rising back up the ridge and intersecting with the Escarpment Trail. The River of Rocks Trail, which is marked with red blazes, is difficult and rocky. Hikers attempting this 4-mile trail should allow three to four hours for the hike.

Among the most difficult and steepest trails in the sanctuary is the Golden Eagle Trail. This trail, which is marked with yellow blazes, is a 4-mile loop that connects the River of Rocks Trail with the Skyline Trail. When taken in combination, these trails provide a variety of possible loops of varying length, but most of them are relatively difficult and designed for the experienced and fit hiker.

Directions: From the intersection of PA Routes 61 and 895 near the town of Molino, follow PA Route 895 east for 2 miles to the Hawk Mountain sign at Drehersville. Turn right onto Hawk Mountain Road and drive 2 miles up the mountain to the parking lot on the right.

Activities: Hiking, bird watching.

Facilities: Trails, visitors center.

Dates: Trails are open dawn to dusk. Hours vary seasonally.

Fees: There is a charge for admission.

Closest town: Drehersville, 2 miles.

For more information: Hawk Mountain Sanctuary Association, 1700 Hawk Mountain Road, Kempton, PA 19529. Phone (610) 756-6961.

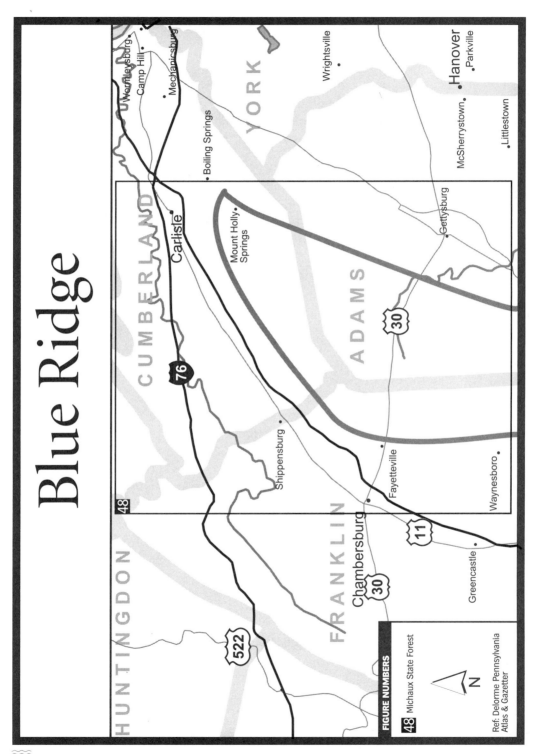

Pennsylvania's Blue Ridge Province

T he Blue Ridge physiographic province is one of the smallest in Pennsylvania, extending only about 40 miles from the Maryland border north to just south of the town of Carlisle. While the Pennsylvania portion of the province is small, the bulk of the Blue Ridge is found in Maryland, where it is known as the Catoctin Mountains, and in Virginia, where it is known as the Blue Ridge Mountains. In Pennsylvania the Blue Ridge province is better known as South Mountain.

South Mountain is composed of a series of flat-topped ridges separated by narrow stream valleys as much as 600 feet deep. The mountain, which ranges from 800 to 1,800 feet above sea level, is only about 10 miles wide and is bordered on the west by the Cumberland Valley of the Valley and Ridge province and on the east by the Triassic Lowlands of the Piedmont province. At the core of the mountain are Precambrian metamorphic rocks, the oldest rocks in Pennsylvania.

[*Above:* Red fox kits emerge from their den in the Blue Ridge]

Also found on the mountain are iron ore and limestone, two of the principal ingredients in the manufacture of iron. South Mountain was a major center of iron production during the eighteenth and nineteenth centuries. The furnaces that operated here were charcoal-fired blast furnaces that required tremendous amounts of wood. Consequently, the area was clear-cut numerous times, and the remnants of the old furnaces and charcoal hearths are still evident. While iron ore is no longer mined here, another mineral resource is still extracted. Quartzite is quarried at several locations on the mountain and crushed to form masonry sand.

Originally this area contained an oak-chestnut forest. Today, as a consequence of logging and the chestnut blight, a mixture of oak species dominates most of the forest. Scattered throughout, however, are small enclaves dominated by as many as five different species of pine, and there is one small area similar to a northern hardwood forest.

Because South Mountain is a forested, wilderness oasis surrounded by fertile agricultural valleys that is in close proximity to the major metropolitan areas of Harrisburg, Baltimore, and Washington, it is a heavily used recreation and wilderness area. Nearly the entire mountain is contained within the Michaux State Forest (*see* page 265) and the much smaller Pine Grove Furnace (*see* page 262), Caledonia, Kings Gap (*see* below), and Mont Alto state parks.

There are only three major roads on the mountain: PA Route 30, which runs from east to west connecting Gettysburg and Chambersburg, PA Route 16, which also runs east to west along the Maryland border, and PA Route 233, which runs from north to south near the summit of the mountain. Interstates 81 and 83 run just to the west and east of the mountain respectively.

State Parks

KINGS GAP ENVIRONMENTAL EDUCATION AND TRAINING CENTER

[Fig. 3(28)] Kings Gap Environmental Education and Training Center encompasses 1,443 acres of varied habitat on South Mountain in Cumberland County. The center, as its name implies, is a state park dedicated solely to educating visitors about the natural world and environmental issues. The park is a day-use only area.

The park has an interesting history. During the 1700s and 1800s, iron furnaces dominated the area surrounding Kings Gap. The furnaces, which converted iron ore to cast iron at very high temperatures, were fired with charcoal. It was charcoal, which is nothing more than wood with the water removed, that was produced in Kings Gap during much of the eighteenth and nineteenth centuries. So voracious were the appetites of the iron furnaces, some consuming an acre of trees each day, that the park was clear-cut numerous times during this period.

Men called colliers, who carefully piled logs in large conical piles, produced the charcoal. The piles were carefully set on fire and tended so that they slowly smoldered for 10 to 14 days, producing a form of pure carbon known as charcoal. The remains of the charcoal hearths can still be seen throughout the park. They are large circular areas 30 feet to 50 feet in diameter that are free of vegetation.

HIGHBUSH BLACKBERRY
(*Rubus allegheniensis*)
This bramble produces a delectable fruit that is popular food for wildlife.

After the charcoal industry ended its work, Kings Gap was successively owned by two wealthy families from the early 1900s up until 1973. In 1973, Kings Gap was purchased by the state with the help of The Nature Conservancy. During the time the park was privately owned, many of the buildings, and even some of the habitats, including the mansion, ice house, carriage house, pond, and pine plantation were constructed.

Today, the centers of activity within the park are its three day-use areas: the Mansion Day Use Area, the Pine Plantation Day Use Area, and the Pond Day Use Area. The Mansion Day Use Area sits atop South Mountain and offers a commanding view of the Cumberland Valley to the west. The mansion, which was built of Antietam quartzite from a nearby quarry, is used today as a meeting facility by state agencies. Near the mansion is a garden that was once used to grow vegetables, but today it is used to teach the beneficial uses of plants. The garden is divided into four separate areas. One part of the garden is devoted exclusively to plants used by butterflies, another contains herbs used for healing and cooking, another native plants used by wildlife, and yet another demonstrates garden composting methods.

The forest surrounding the Mansion Day Use Area is dominated by chestnut oak with an understory of blueberries, huckleberries, and mountain laurel. Among the more interesting species of wildlife found here is the five-lined skink (*Eumeces fasciatus*), one of Pennsylvania's few lizards, and two venomous snakes, the copperhead (*Agkistrodon contortrix*) and timber rattlesnake (*Crotalus horridus*). Both of these snakes are routinely seen in the park and have even been seen hunting rodents in the garden and on the patio of the mansion. The snakes are shy by nature, so visitors should consider themselves lucky to see one.

Within the Mansion Day Use Area there are five trailheads, all of which are located near the mansion. The Scenic Vista Trail is a 2.5-mile-long trail that begins near the mansion and runs south, ending at the parking area in the Pond Day Use Area. The trail offers some very nice views of the adjacent Michaux State Forest and is relatively easy to hike. It is marked with orange blazes and has benches scattered along its course. For those who want a more challenging hike there is the Ridge Overlook Trail. This rocky, somewhat difficult trail is 0.8-mile long and runs along the ridgetop near the northern end of the Mansion Day Use Area. The Forest Heritage Trail, which is marked with lime green blazes, is a good choice for hikers who want to see the remnants of the old charcoal hearths. This moderately challenging trail is a 1.6-mile loop that passes by several of the hearths, which today are nothing more than bare spots on the ground. The Maple Hollow Trail is a study in forest contrasts. The first part of the trail passes through a maple forest growing on rich, moist soils. Farther on it moves into a drier woodland dominated by chestnut oak, a much more common type of forest within Kings Gap. This loop trail is relatively easy to hike, yellow-blazed, and 1.3 miles long. The Woodland Ecology Trail is an easy, short (0.6-mile) hike through the chestnut–oak forest. Along the path are signs explaining various aspects of the ecology of this type of forest.

The Pond Day Use Area is located south of the Mansion Day Use Area and contains a deciduous forest, Kings Gap Hollow Run, wetlands, and a man-made pond. Because of the wide variety of habitats and associated plants and wildlife, including ferns, sphagnum moss, skunk cabbage, impatiens, assorted turtles, frogs, and even spotted salamanders (*Ambystoma maculatum*), this part of the park is heavily used for environmental education. There are also several trails worth investigating. The Watershed Trail is a 1.8-mile loop that follows Kings Gap Hollow Run upstream to its source. The trail is a relatively easy hike and is a good place to see colonies of Allegheny mound-building ants whose ant hills can be several feet high. The Boundary Trail is a 1.5-mile long trail that runs through an oak-pitch pine forest along the park's western boundary. The trail is relatively easy and is marked with lime green blazes. Perhaps the most unique trail within this area is the White Oaks Trail. This 0.3-mile-long, paved interpretive trail passes through a white oak forest and has signs explaining the ecology of the forest in both script and Braille.

The Pine Plantation Day Use Area is centered around a pine plantation that was planted in the 1950s and contains white pine, larch, and Douglas fir. The habitat here is quite different from the rest of the park. This area contains wildlife species, such as red squirrels (*Tamiascirus hudsonicus*) and red-headed woodpeckers (*Melanerpes erythrocephalus*), adapted to coniferous rather than deciduous forests. Also

RUBY-THROATED HUMMINGBIRD (*Archilochus colubris*) Hummingbirds have the unique ability among birds to fly backwards or straight up or down.

found here are a number of vernal ponds. These ephemeral wetlands are among the most ecologically valuable of all wetlands, yet their temporary nature has made them one of the wetland types most commonly destroyed by development. These wetlands are small, shallow pools that fill with groundwater, meltwater, and precipitation in the spring, just when many species of amphibians are laying their eggs. By summer they have completely dried up, but not before another generation of tree frogs, spring peepers, and spotted salamanders have been born. Also found here is a small clearing where a re-creation of a log farmhouse from the 1850s has been built. The house is used as the focal point for many of the park's historical education programs.

For a short but educational hike through the pine plantation try the Whispering Pines Trail. The trail is paved, 0.3 mile long, and has interpretive signs printed in both script and Braille. About twice as long, but still an easy hike, is the Pine Plantation Trail. This trail, which is orange blazed, gives the hiker a good view of the plantation and some of the tree-thinning management practices that are used to guarantee the stand's long-term survival. For those who want a longer, more strenuous hike there is the Rock Scree Trail. This 1.9-mile trail, which is moderately challenging and blazed with red, begins in the Pine Plantation Day Use Area and rises up the mountain to the mansion. Along the way it passes the quarry where the stone to build the mansion was collected.

Directions: From I-81 take Exit 11 and travel south on PA Route 233 for about 2.5 miles. Turn left onto Pine Road and travel approximately 2.3 miles to the park entrance on the right.

Activities: Hiking, orienteering, environmental education.

Facilities: Hiking trails, orienteering course.

Dates: Open year-round.

Fees: None.

Closest town: Mount Holly Springs, 5 miles.

For more information: Kings Gap Environmental Education and Training Center, 500 Kings Gap Road, Carlisle, PA 17013. Phone (717) 486-5031.

Spotted Salamander

One of Pennsylvania's most beautiful salamanders is also one of its most common and yet least frequently seen. The spotted salamander (*Ambystoma maculatum*) isn't commonly seen because it's a member of the mole salamander family, whose members spend most of their time in underground burrows. They only venture out at night to feed on insects, spiders, slugs, and any other bite-sized invertebrate they happen to come across. The salamander takes its name from the two rows of bright yellow spots that run the length of its body, standing out in stark contrast to its blue-black colored skin. The spotted salamander is found across the state, but its preferred habitat is hardwood forests that contain wetlands.

▓ PINE GROVE FURNACE STATE PARK

[Fig. 3(29)] The land on which Pine Grove Furnace State Park now sits was once home to a small but prosperous community of ironworkers. Located here, in the heart of the Michaux State Forest, were two things that, 200 years ago, were critical to the manufacture of iron. One was the metallic ore from which the iron was made, and the other was wood, which was converted to charcoal, a necessary component of the early iron-making process. From 1764 to 1897 the Pine Grove Iron Furnace produced cast iron stoves, kettles, and military supplies. Surrounding the furnace were stables, residences, shops, and even a mansion. All of these still stand today within a National Historic Area that is the focal point of the park.

Today, the mansion that was once home to the ironmaster is an American Youth Hostel used by hikers following the Appalachian Trail. Also located within the historic area are the park office and a historic/interpretive center where visitors can learn about the park and the iron community that once flourished here. To view all of the historical sites within the area hike the self-guided historical trail. This 1.25-mile-long trail runs throughout the old iron works and takes about 1.5 hours to complete. One of the highlights of the trail, and one of the park's most conspicuous structures, is the well-preserved cold-blast furnace stack. For more than 100 years ironworkers poured charcoal, limestone, and iron ore in the top of the stack and molten cast iron poured out of channels in the bottom. The trail begins just across the street from the park office.

A small lake, measuring only 1.7 acres, is also located within the historic area of the park. Fuller Lake is the pit from which the iron ore was removed during the 1700s and 1800s. It has since filled with groundwater and today is a popular swimming spot. The beach is guarded, but because the lake is very deep and cold, swimmers should exercise caution. Fishermen use the lake as well, pursuing cold-water species such as pickerel, perch, and trout that are stocked by the Pennsylvania Fish and Boat Commission. Boats are not permitted on the lake.

Pine Grove Furnace is a long, thin park stretching from west to east and occupying 696 acres within Cumberland County. The largest body of water within the park is 25-acre Laurel Lake, which is located at the eastern end of the park. The lake has a guarded beach and is a popular fishing area. There is a boat launch and boat rental facility located on the northern shore of the lake about 1.7 miles east of the park office along Pine Grove Road. Only nonmotorized boats are permitted on the lake. Laurel Lake also has a historical tie to the iron industry. It served as a water source for Laurel Forge, which took the cast iron produced in the Pine Grove Furnace, heated it, and then made it into wrought iron, blacksmith tools, and other iron implements. In addition to summer recreation, the lake is used during the winter. A small portion of the lake is maintained for ice skating once the ice thickness is at least 4 inches. The remainder of the lake is open to ice fishing.

A nice way to see much of the park is by bicycle. There is a bike trail that follows an old railroad bed from the historic area to Laurel Lake. This relatively level trail is 3 miles long and passes Mountain Creek, which is stocked with trout, and Fuller Lake within the historic area. The trailhead is about 500 feet east of the old furnace stack on Quarry Road. For visitors who didn't bring bikes, rentals are available at the boat rental concession on Laurel Lake. The same path used by bikers during the spring, summer, and fall, is used by cross-country skiers in the winter. While there are no specifically designated ski trails within the park, this trail and others are suitable when there is enough snow.

There are a number of short trails within the park. Located near the campground is the Creek Trail. This 0.5-mile-long trail passes through an area of white pines and vernal ponds—transient wetlands that are flooded in the spring and often dry during the summer. The trailhead is located at the amphitheater, which is about 0.6 mile south of the historic/interpretive center on Bendersville Road. Shorter yet is the Swamp Trail. This 0.25-mile-long trail passes through a forested swamp near the middle of the park just east of the National Historic Area. The trail branches off of the bike trail about 0.4 mile east of the trailhead and is marked with a sign. Those wanting a longer hike should consider the Koppenhaver Trail, which is a 1-mile loop. The trail begins and ends at the Fuller ballfield just north of Fuller Lake and passes through stands of white pine and hemlock while passing along and across Toms Run.

Also passing through the park is a portion of the Appalachian Trail (*see* page 273). Approximately 1 mile of the white-blazed, 2,000-mile-long trail is located within the park. The portion within the park makes for a nice day hike and takes the hiker along portions of several of the park's other trails. The trailhead is located at the beginning of the bike path. Pine Grove Furnace State Park marks the halfway point of the Appalachian Trail as it journeys from Georgia to Maine.

The Pole Steeple Trail trailhead is located at a parking area on the south shore of Laurel Lake along Railroad Bed Road. The trail runs south from the park into the Michaux State Forest. While this blue-blazed trail is only 0.75 mile long, it is steep and difficult. It climbs Piney Mountain, ending at an outcropping of quartzite called Pole Steeple Overlook. From this overlook hikers are rewarded with a view of the entire Pine Furnace State Park. To reach the trailhead, follow Pine Grove Road east from the park administration building for about 2.2 miles. Turn right onto Railroad Bed Road and the parking area is about 0.5 mile down the road on the right.

Directions: From Interstate 81 take Exit 11 and follow PA Route 233 south for 8.5 miles. The park office and historical area are located at the intersection with Pine Grove Road.

Activities: Hiking, hunting, fishing, camping, swimming, boating, ice skating, picnicking.

Facilities: Historic/interpretive center, campgrounds, picnic grounds, swimming beach, hiking trails, biking trail, boat and bike rental concession, historic sites, youth hostel.

Dates: Open year round.

Fees: There is a charge for camping.

Closest town: Mount Holly Springs, 8 miles.

For more information: Pine Grove Furnace State Park, 1100 Pine Grove Road, Gardners, PA 17324. Phone (717) 486-7174.

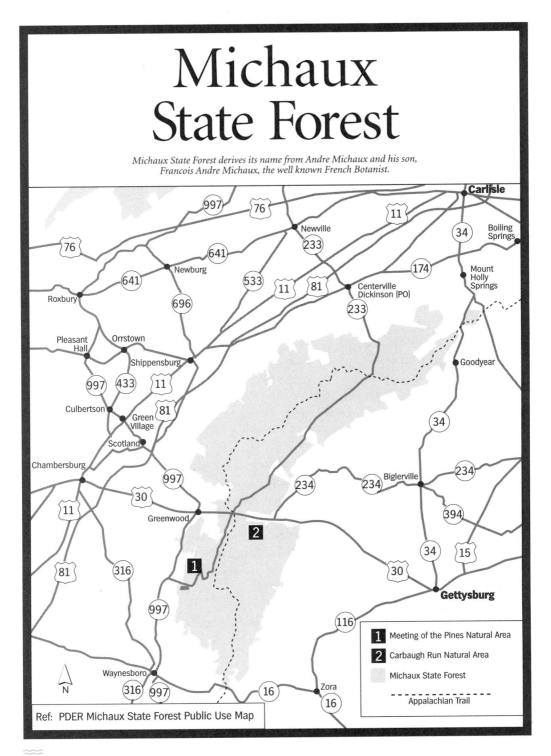

Michaux State Forest

Michaux State Forest derives its name from Andre Michaux and his son, Francois Andre Michaux, the well known French Botanist.

Ref: PDER Michaux State Forest Public Use Map

Michaux State Forest

[Fig. 48] The Michaux State Forest encompasses 84,369 acres within Adams, Franklin, and Cumberland counties in south-central Pennsylvania. The forest lies on South Mountain, which is flanked on the east by the Cumberland Valley and on the west by the Buchanan Valley. The mountain itself is composed of individual ridges separated by narrow valleys. Elevations within the forest vary from 2,100 feet on Big Pine Flat Ridge, to 675 feet near the town of Scotland.

The forest lies within two watersheds: the southern half eventually drains into the Potomac River, and the northern half drains into the Susquehanna River. There are more than 50 miles of trout streams within the Michaux State Forest, some of them containing native brook trout and most of them stocked as well. Wildlife is plentiful throughout the forest. Among the rarer species found here are the bog turtle (*see* page 266), bald eagle, pygmy shrew (*Microsorex hoyi*), and spadefoot toad (*Scaphiopus holbrooki*).

Located within the forest's boundaries are three state parks. Mont Alto State Park, while diminutive in size at only 36 acres, has the distinction of being Pennsylvania's oldest state park. Pine Grove Furnace State Park (*see* page 262) is located near the northern end of the forest and contains the remnants of an old iron furnace. Located near the center of the forest is Caledonia State Park. The state parks and the surrounding state forest are heavily used because of their proximity to large urban areas and a surrounding network of Interstate and state highways. Because the forest is less than a two-hour drive from Baltimore, Washington DC, and Harrisburg, it receives more than 1 million visitors each year.

The area was clear-cut repeatedly during the eighteenth and nineteenth century to supply charcoal for the iron industry. In fact, most of the land that today makes up the Michaux State Forest was owned by iron companies up until the early part of the twentieth century. The voracious charcoal appetite of the iron furnaces was characterized this way in an early Bureau of Forestry report: "The original timber had all been removed between 1870 and 1886, and the young second growth was cut as soon as it became large enough to make a stick."

When the first European settlers came to this area, it contained a deciduous forest dominated by oaks and chestnut. Since that time the forest has changed considerably. The clear-cutting and subsequent wildfires, which were common during the late nineteenth and early twentieth centuries, encouraged the growth of scrub oak. Then came the chestnut blight, which permanently eliminated the chestnut. As a result, the forest is now dominated by mixed-oaks and oak-hard pine forests. Unfortunately, the high density of oaks makes the forest especially vulnerable to the oak-loving gypsy moth, and the forest has experienced periodic widespread defoliation.

At one time there was a hospital, devoted exclusively to the treatment of tuberculosis, located 3 miles east of Mont Alto. The hospital was built in 1902 under the direction of Dr. Joseph Rothrock, who was the director of the Department of Forestry. Eventually it

Bog Turtle

Wetlands play a key role in the lives of many North American animal species. Since more than half of our wetlands have been lost since the Europeans arrived, it's not surprising that more than half of our endangered species call wetlands home for at least part of their life cycle. Among these is the bog turtle (*Clemmys muhlenbergii*).

The bog turtle has probably always been rare and rarely seen (because of its habit of burrowing into the mud when it feels threatened), but in recent years it has declined significantly because of wetland loss and collecting by turtle fanciers. Collectors like the turtle because it is among the smallest turtles in North America at only 4.5 inches long, and because it's a very beautiful reptile. It's dark brown shell, which often has faint yellow or red markings, is set off by its most distinguishing characteristic, a large, bright yellow or red spot behind each eye. This spot makes the bog turtle one of the easiest of all turtles to identify.

Like most turtles, the bog turtle likes to spend its day sunning itself. The turtle may be found sitting on a tussock of wetland plants in swamps, marshes, and bogs, the three most likely places to find them. They've also been known to show up in wet cow pastures on occasion. These reptiles aren't fussy about their diet and are known to eat just about anything, including insects, worms, plant material, and even carrion.

Today the bog turtle is only known to occur in parts of southeastern Pennsylvania in Michaux State Forest, the southern part of the Valley and Ridge province, and in parts of the Pocono Plateau.

was turned over to the Department of Health, which operated it until 1967. Today it is a geriatric facility known as the South Mountain Restoration Center. Another remnant of the hospital still exists. A golf course, built for the medical staff, is still used today.

The Appalachian Trail enters the southern end of the Michaux State Forest, follows the crest of South Mountain for about 40 miles, and passes out of the forest's northern end. The Potomac Trail Club, which maintains the Appalachian Trail, has developed several side trails within the forest so hikers can visit some of the dramatic rock outcroppings on South Mountain. The halfway point of the Appalachian Trail lies within the forest, very near the southern boundary of Pine Grove Furnace State Park (*see* page 262). Within the park is a youth hostel that is used by trail hikers. Tradition holds that those hiking the complete length of the trail, from Georgia to Maine, eat a half-gallon of ice cream within a half a hour once they reach the halfway point.

There are also many state forest trails winding through Michaux. In addition to hiking, many of the trails are also open to horseback riding. One of the forest's hiking trails is the Rocky Knob Trail. This 4.2-mile loop crosses the Appalachian Trail and winds its way back and forth across the boundary between Cumberland and Adams counties. By using an interpretive guide that is available at the forest headquarters, hikers can learn about the boulderfields, Allegheny mound-building ants, and scenic vistas they'll come across. To reach the trailhead follow PA Route 233 north 1.8 miles from the intersection with US Route 30. Turn left on Milesburg Road and follow it about 4 miles to Ridge Road. The trail is about 1 mile down Ridge Road on the right.

For those who want to see the forest from the comfort of their car, there is a self-guided automobile tour. Pick up a tour guide from the park office and use it to navigate a 19-mile trek through the forest. Along the route there are markers indicating various natural and man-made features including dark, moist cove forests, dry, scrubby oak forests along the peak of the mountain, a fire tower, and the Appalachian Trail. The tour, which begins at the forest headquarters on US Route 30, uses some old woods roads that can be a little rough in places.

There are four designated natural areas within the Michaux State Forest: the Meeting of the Pines Natural Area (*see* page 268), Carbaugh Run Natural Area (*see* page 269), Cydonia Ponds Natural Area, and Beartown Woods Natural Area. The Cydonia Ponds Natural Area is located along the western edge of the forest just south of US Route 30. This 183-acre area contains 60 small ponds within the English Valley between Mount Cydonia and Little Mountain. What makes the ponds unique is their age. It was once thought that the ponds might be man-made, artifacts of the iron industry. Scientists studying pollen in the sediments of some of the ponds, however, have found profiles similar to ponds known to be 11,000 years old. Consequently, the ponds are believed to be natural and, given their great age, are now protected from development and logging within the natural area. There is one trail within the area, the Muck Pond Trail, which begins on Irishtown Road. The trail is not marked, however, and is nearly impossible to find.

The Beartown Woods Natural Area is a diminutive 27-acre wood lot located at the very southern tip of the forest just north of the Maryland border. Beartown Woods has been designated a natural area because it contains an assemblage of tree species more typical of a northern hardwood forest rather than the oak-hickory forest common on South Mountain. Found here are beech, sugar maple, basswood, and yellow birch. In addition to a small stretch of the Appalachian Trail, there is one interpretive trail within the natural area. The Bicentennial Trail is a .15-mile trail with signs identifying tree species and their link to U.S. history. To reach the natural area and trailhead follow PA Route 16 east from Waynesboro for about 4.6 miles to the sign located on the right side of the road.

BOG TURTLE
(*Clemmys muhlenbergi*)
This turtle is only 4 inches long.

Directions: From Chambersburg follow US Route 30 east for about 4.6 miles to the forest office, which is located on the left side of the road.

Activities: Hiking, hunting, fishing, snowmobiling,

picnicking, horseback riding, cross-country skiing.

Facilities: Trails, picnic areas, golf course.

Dates: Open year-round.

Closest town: Fayetteville, 4.6 miles.

For more information: Michaux State Forest, RD 2, Fayetteville, PA 17222. Phone (717) 352-2211.

🌲 MEETING OF THE PINES NATURAL AREA

[Fig. 48(1)] Most of the designated natural areas within Pennsylvania's state forest system were granted their status because they contain an uncommon natural habitat, a rare or endangered species, or have some other significant geologic or natural feature. In the case of the Meeting of the Pines Natural Area, the habitat is unique, but not natural. It is a consequence of man's past activity.

The forest found here today is dominated by oaks, but scattered throughout are white, pitch, table mountain, Virginia, and shortleaf pines. All five of these pines are native to Pennsylvania, but this one location on South Mountain is one of the few places where they grow together in significant numbers.

After this part of the forest was clear-cut during the eighteenth and nineteenth centuries to produce charcoal, wildfires frequently swept through the area. These conditions, combined with the elimination of the chestnut tree, prevented the re-establishment of the oak forest, thereby allowing the pines to move in. Forest fires are no longer a common occurrence and the oaks have again regained their dominant role. But this unique assemblage of pine species remains. The trees can be found growing alone, in small groups, and in stands more than 10 acres in size.

The Meeting of the Pines Natural Area is located on the western slope of South Mountain, at the southern end of the state forest, near the Mont Alto Campus of Penn State University. The area encompasses 811 acres and is accessible by foot only. There is only one trail leading into the natural area. The Bricker's Clearing Trail (a gated four-wheel-drive road open only to authorized vehicles) runs from Penn State's Mont Alto campus at the south end of the natural area to White Rocks Road at the northern end. There is also a fire trail that runs along the eastern border of the area near the top of the ridge, but this trail is not readily accessible.

Directions: From the town of Mont Alto follow PA Route 233 about 1 mile east to the Penn State campus. Turn left into the school and follow the road to a stop sign near the administration building. Turn right and drive to the parking area behind Conklin Hall next to the soccer field. Bricker's Clearing Trail is a closed dirt road and begins at the yellow and black gate.

Activities: Hiking, hunting.

Facilities: Hiking trail.

Dates: Open year-round.

Closest town: Mont Alto, 1 mile.

For more information: Michaux State Forest, RD 2, Fayetteville, PA 17222. Phone (717) 352-2211.

CARBAUGH RUN NATURAL AREA

[Fig. 48(2)] The Carbaugh Run Natural Area contains a stream valley lined with a pine-hemlock forest with a dense rhododendron understory. The stream valley is surrounded by steep, rocky slopes that are much drier and are dominated by mixed oaks. Carbaugh Run is a pristine headwater stream that contains native trout and has been designated as both a Wilderness Trout Stream and an Exceptional Value Stream. Because of its size and pristine nature, the natural area has also been designated a Reptile and Amphibian Protection Area.

This 780-acre area was afforded protection not because of its natural characteristics but because it is archaeologically significant. South Mountain is composed of Precambrian metamorphic rocks, which at 600 million years old are the oldest rocks in Pennsylvania. Within the natural area there are outcrops where these rocks are exposed. Rhyolite, a hard rock that can be easily chipped and fractured into tools and sharp points, is found in these outcrops. It is believed that Carbaugh Run Natural Area was used first by prehistoric man, as long ago as 8000 B.C., and then by Native Americans as recently as 1500 A.D., to make projectile points and tools from the rhyolite. The projectiles made here were of such high quality that they were used in bartering. Archaeologists believe that rhyolite projectile points made in Carbaugh Run have been found as far away as Canada and Florida.

As many as 50 shallow quarries have been found so far, but the archeological sites within the natural area have been studied only minimally and research is currently underway. These sites are listed on the National Registry of Historic Places, but their exact location remains a secret.

There is only one trail running through the natural area. Carbaugh Run Trail is approximately 1 mile long and is moderately challenging because it is relatively steep and rocky as it descends into Carbaugh Run Gorge.

Directions: From the Michaux State Forest headquarters follow US Route 30 west for about 0.5 mile and turn left onto PA Route 233. Follow PA Route 233 south for 1.7 miles and turn left onto District Road. Follow this narrow dirt road for about 2.1 miles to the access trail, which is marked with a small sign.

Activities: Hiking, hunting, fishing.

Facilities: Hiking trail.

Dates: Open year-round.

Closest town: Fayetteville, 8 miles.

For more information: Michaux State Forest, RD 2, Fayetteville, PA 17222. Phone (717) 352-2211.

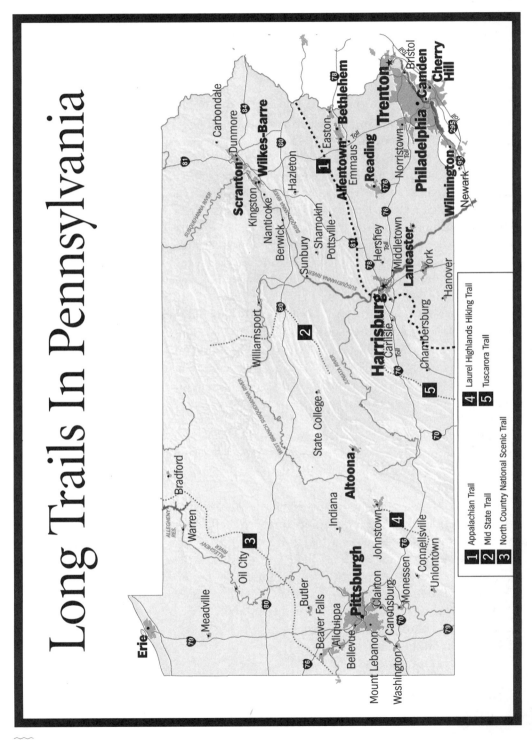

Long Trails In Pennsylvania

Legend:
1 Appalachian Trail
2 Mid State Trail
3 North Country National Scenic Trail
4 Laurel Highlands Hiking Trail
5 Tuscarora Trail

Long Trails

Pennsylvania is blessed with five excellent long trails: The Appalachian Trail, the Mid State Trail, the North Country National Scenic Trail, the Laurel Highlands Hiking Trail, and the Tuscarora Trail.

The Appalachian Trail is perhaps the most famous hiking trail in the world, stretching from Georgia to Maine. The Mid State Trail slices 189 miles across the center of the state through the heart of Pennsylvania's mountains. The North Country National Scenic Trail is scheduled to go from New York's Adirondacks to North Dakota. It is not completed yet, but portions of the trail in Pennsylvania can be hiked. The 70-mile long eponymously named Laurel Highlands Trail is found in Pennsylvania's Laurel Highlands. The Tuscarora Trail is a 248-mile loop off the Appalachian Trail.

[*Above:* Pennsylvania has many long trails for more serious hikers]

Appalachian Trail

The Appalachian Trail is over 2,100 miles long and stretches from Springer Mountain in Georgia to Mount Katahdin in Maine.

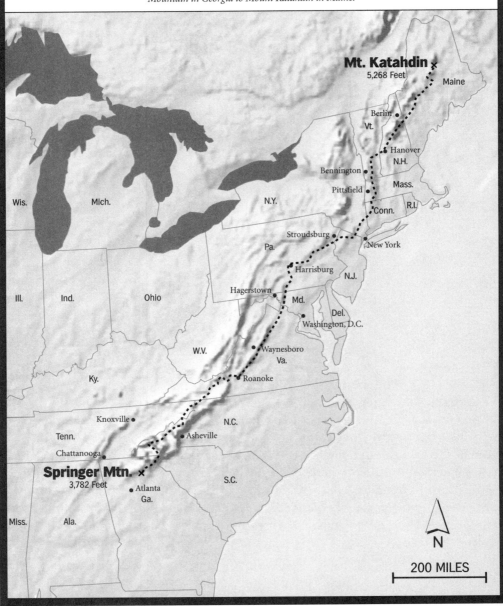

Mt. Katahdin
5,268 Feet
Maine

Berlin

Vt.

Hanover
N.H.

Bennington

Pittsfield

Mass.

Conn.

R.I.

Wis.

Mich.

N.Y.

Stroudsburg

New York

Pa.

Harrisburg

N.J.

Hagerstown

Md.

Ill.

Ind.

Ohio

Del.
Washington, D.C.

W.V.

Waynesboro
Va.

Ky.

Roanoke

Knoxville

N.C.

Asheville

Tenn.

Chattanooga

Springer Mtn.
3,782 Feet

S.C.

Atlanta
Ga.

Miss.

Ala.

N

200 MILES

The Appalachian Trail

[Fig. 49(1), Fig. 50, Fig. 51] The Appalachian Trail is a 2,159-mile-long trail that follows the Appalachian Mountain chain from Maine to Georgia. Trail construction began in 1921 and was finished in 1937. Today the trail is managed by the National Park Service and is actually designated a linear national park and is part of the National Trail System. The Appalachian Trail Conference, a federation of hiking clubs, maintains the trail.

The Pennsylvania portion of the trail, which is 232-miles long, includes the halfway-point on the AT. The Pennsylvania portion extends from the Maryland border, not far from Gettysburg, northeast across the Valley and Ridge province to the Delaware Water Gap National Recreation Area (*see* page 205) along the Delaware River across from New Jersey. In Maryland, the AT covers 39.8 miles, from the Pennsylvania line at Pen Mar to the Potomac River. In Pennsylvania, the trail traverses Cove Mountain and South Mountain west of the Susquehanna River, and Blue Mountain and Peters Mountain east of it.

A hike through Pennsylvania on the Appalachian Trail provides a look at the biological, geological, and cultural diversity that characterizes the Valley and Ridge province. Along the ridgetops are dense, remote woodlands with thick understories of mountain laurel and rhododendron. The trail is rocky, narrow, and sometimes steep. Where the trail crosses the valleys it is flat and wide, and in many places it runs along side roads. Rather than woods, it passes farms and pastures where evidence of man is abundant.

The trail passes through several public lands. The Michaux State Forest (*see* page 265), located in Franklin, Cumberland, and Adams counties is the only state forest along the trail's route. The trail also passes through Pine Grove Furnace State Park (*see* page 262), Caledonia State Park, Swatara State Park, and the Delaware Water Gap National Recreation Area (*see* page 205). Along its route the trail crosses numerous small streams and two major rivers, the Lehigh River and the Susquehanna River.

There are innumerable scenic vistas and overlooks along the trail. Among the more spectacular is Bake Oven Knob, located on Blue Mountain about 45 miles south of the Delaware Water Gap National Recreation Area. The overlook provides a dramatic view of the Great Valley that lies to the south of the Appalachian Mountains. It is also an exceptional place to view the annual fall migration of hawks and eagles. These birds rise on the updrafts along the mountain in order to reach the upper level winds that carry them across the Great Valley. About 15 miles farther south on the trail is an even better area for watching hawks, the Hawk Mountain Wildlife Sanctuary (*see* page 253), which is widely considered the best place in the world to watch raptor migrations. One of the sanctuary's trails, the Skyline Trail, intersects the Appalachian Trail.

Primitive backpack camping is permitted along the Appalachian Trail. Campers are asked to camp off of the side of the trail, making sure that they are still on public

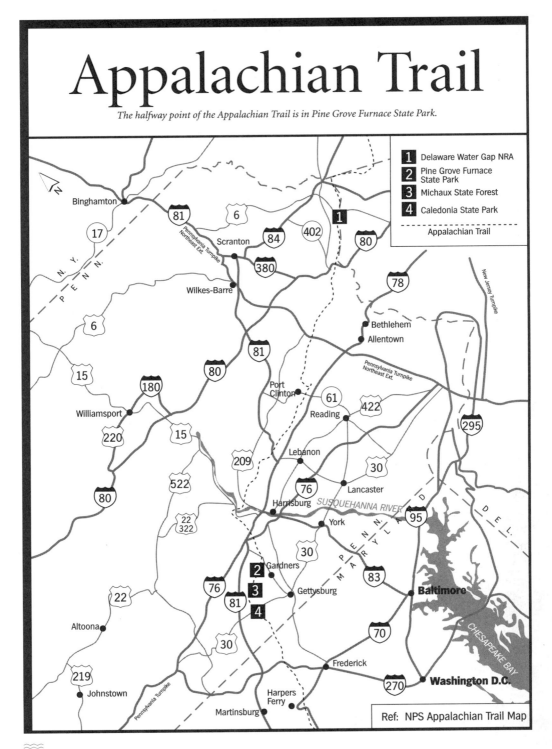

Appalachian Trail

The halfway point of the Appalachian Trail is in Pine Grove Furnace State Park.

land. Additionally, open fires are prohibited and hikers are advised not to bathe in or drink from any of the streams along the trail. There are primitive shelters located every 10 miles or so, but these shelters are heavily used, so hikers should not depend on them. There is also a youth hostel in Pine Grove Furnace State Park near the southern end of the trail for those who want more civilized amenities.

The Appalachian Trail is marked with white blazes. There are also many side trails that lead into state parks, state forests, and other public lands. The longest of these is the Tuscarora Trail (*see* page 279), a 248-mile loop that runs from Pennsylvania to Virginia. Most of the spur trails are marked with blue blazes. The best guide to the AT in Pennsylvania is published by the Appalachian Trail Conference and is titled the *Appalachian Trail Guide to Pennsylvania*.

For more information: The Keystone Trails Association maintains the Appalachian Trail in Pennsylvania. Guide maps and trail information can be obtained from them at PO Box 251, Dept. WWW, Cogan Station, PA 17728.

Mid State Trail

[Fig. 49(2)] The Mid State Trail is a 189-mile-long trail slicing through the heart of Pennsylvania's Mountains. The state's mountains, and the ecosystems that grow upon them, are quite varied, and hikers who follow this trail from the southern end in the Valley and Ridge province to the northern end on the Allegheny High Plateau will experience that variety firsthand.

Almost the entire length of the trail is on public land. It passes through Rothrock State Forest (*see* page 239), Bald Eagle State Forest (*see* page 66), Tiadaghton State Forest (*see* page 123), Tioga State Forest (*see* page 115), and Buchanan State Forest (*see* page 235). The Mid State Trail connects with many of the trails that pass through the state forests, providing an almost unlimited number of side trips. These state forest trails also serve as points of access to hikers not intending to follow the complete length of the Mid State Trail.

The trail also passes through 10 state parks. Seven of them, Greenwood Furnace (*see* page 219), Penn Roosevelt, Poe Valley, Reeds Gap (*see* page 223), Poe Paddy, R.B. Winter (*see* page 224), and Little Pine (*see* page 71), have camping facilities and potable water. Here again, the Mid State Trail connects with many of the state park trails, expanding the hiking opportunities. Primitive backpack camping is also allowed on state forest land, as long as it's not along a stretch of the trail passing through a designated natural area. While camping on state forest land requires a free permit, there is a fee for camping in state parks, and reservations may be necessary. Call the individual park for details.

The Mid State Trail runs from the Little Juniata Natural Area, a part of the Rothrock State Forest in Bedford County, north to PA Route 414 near the town of

Blackwell in Tioga County. In addition to offering an opportunity to experience mountain ecosystems such as mixed-oak forests, mixed-hardwood forests, and talus slopes, the trail offers some dramatic views from the ridgetops. As it traverses Tussey Mountain, for example, hikers are treated to a panoramic view of Happy Valley and the town of State College, the home of Penn State University. The trail also passes along what is arguably the most dramatic natural feature in the state, the Pine Creek Gorge, or the grand canyon of Pennsylvania as its often called.

Generally speaking the Mid State Trail is a challenging footpath that varies from easy to difficult. As it passes through the Valley and Ridge province, it traverses the ridges, occasionally dipping into the valleys below. In one case, however, it passes through the mountain. Instead of crossing over Paddy Mountain, the trail uses an old Penn Central Railroad Tunnel to take the hiker through it. Another portion of the trail utilizes the Great Island Indian Path, reportedly a footpath that has been in use since before Europeans came to Pennsylvania.

Hikers in need of some warm clothing might want to stop at the Woolrich Outlet Store, which lies near the trail, just a short distance north of the point where the trail crosses the West Branch of the Susquehanna River. This portion of the trail lies on land owned by the Woolrich Woolen Mills Company.

While the trail provides a remote backwoods hiking experience, no part is more than a half-hour walk from the nearest road, thereby providing numerous points of access. Where the trail crosses roads, there are usually trail signs.

The trail is marked with orange rectangles, while connecting side trails are marked with blue rectangles. Elevations range from 550 feet in the valleys to 2,400 feet along the highest ridgetops. No motorized vehicles of any kind are permitted, so hikers need not worry about having the peace and solitude disturbed. The trail is maintained by the Mid State Trail Association, which has also produced a series of maps of the trail.

For more information: Mid State Trail Association, PO Box 167, Boalsburg, PA 16827.

North Country National Scenic Trail

[Fig. 49(3)] Not as well known as Pennsylvania's only other national scenic trail, the Appalachian Trail, the North Country National Scenic Trail passes through the northwestern corner of the state. From end to end the trail stretches 4,400 miles, beginning in the Adirondack Mountains of New York and ending in the plains of North Dakota. Designated portions of the trail are open to mountain biking, cross-country skiing, and horseback riding, as well as hiking.

The trail was founded in 1980 and is managed by the National Park Service. It is far from complete, with only 1,300 miles currently certified as meeting the standards of the

National Trail System. However, about 3,000 miles of the system are usable.

Unlike the Appalachian Trail, which follows a prominent geologic feature, the North Country Trail simply meanders through seven northern states. The trail passes through many different ecosystems, including mountains, hardwood forests, tallgrass prairies, and even rocky shores and sand dunes along Lake Superior. Just as diverse are the historical and cultural features along the trail, which passes lighthouses, forts, and mills and runs along old logging railroad grades and near innumerable small towns.

In Pennsylvania the trail enters the northern tier of the state from Allegany State Park in New York. It then passes through 95 miles of the Allegheny National Forest, where it connects with several other trails, including the Tanbark Trail that gives the hiker access to the Hearts Content Recreation Area (see page 47) and the Hickory Creek Wilderness (see page 37). The trail passes through the Tionesta Scenic Area (see page 45), where hikers will see the remnants of the devastation caused by the 1985 tornadoes, and an area with 400-year-old hemlock trees. Several portions of the trail within the Allegheny National Forest are also suitable for cross-country skiing.

South of the Allegheny National Forest (see page 29) the trail intersects with the Baker Trail, which passes through Cook Forest State Park (see page 55). The trail then parallels portions of the Clarion and Allegheny rivers as it passes southwest towards Ohio. Before exiting Pennsylvania, the trail passes through Morraine State Park, named after the geologic formation left by the ice sheet during the last ice age, and across Slippery Rock Creek in McConnells Mill State Park. This park is located along one of the most scenic stream gorges in the western part of the state and contains a restored grist mill.

For more information: North Country Trail Association, 49 Monroe Center, Suite 200B, Grand Rapids, MI 49503. Phone (616) 454-5506.

Laurel Highlands Hiking Trail

[Fig. 49(4)] Stretching from the Youghiogheny River gorge at Ohiopyle to the Conemaugh River gorge near Johnstown, is the 70-mile-long Laurel Highlands Hiking Trail. The trail runs along Laurel Ridge and provides an excellent opportunity to see one of the most beautiful mountainous areas in Pennsylvania, the Allegheny Mountains' Laurel Highlands.

The Laurel Highlands are characterized by dense forests containing beech, oak, maple, tulip poplar, and other trees above a dense understory of rhododendron and mountain laurel. The deep, narrow ravines cut by mountain streams are lined with hemlock. Also scattered along the trail are scrub ecosystems, wildflower meadows, and rocky outcrops where the sandstone and limestone normally hidden beneath the surface of Laurel Ridge has been exposed.

The trail offers many scenic vistas and overlooks, especially at the northern and southern ends. The trail climbs Laurel Ridge from the southern trailhead in the town

Pygmy Shrew

Weighing no more than a dime, the pygmy shrew (*Microsorex hoyi*) is not just the smallest land mammal in Pennsylvania, it's the smallest land mammal in the world. It's so small that it often travels in the same tunnels dug by beetles and earthworms. This little insectivore can be found living in almost any habitat, from wetlands to forests to urban areas. Surprisingly, the pygmy shrew wasn't discovered in Pennsylvania until 1984.

The shrew, like all mammals, maintains its constant body temperature using internal metabolic heat. Its small body has a high surface area to volume ratio, which means it looses heat much more quickly than larger mammals and has a nonstop, high metabolic rate. The pygmy shrew eats twice its weight in food every day, including insect larvae, worms, slugs, and other invertebrates. This high metabolism and incessant need for food leads to an unusual lifestyle. The shrew alternates eating with short periods of sleep. This eat-sleep cycle continues day and night, year-round.

of Ohiopyle. Once they reach the summit of the ridge, hikers have a dramatic view of the Youghiogheny River and its rapids down below. As the trail proceeds north, it passes waterfalls and crosses the old Forbes Road, which was used by the British during the French and Indian War to move troops and supplies to the present-day city of Pittsburgh.

In Somerset County the trail passes through Seven Springs Resort, which is the highest point on the trail at 2,950 feet. The trail crosses the resort's famous ski slopes and continues its journey northward towards Johnstown. As the trail reaches the northern trailhead near the Conemaugh River gorge it provides an outstanding view of the river 1,000 feet below.

The trail is very accessible and accommodating to hikers. In addition to the trailheads at either end, there are four other access points in between, each of which is well marked and has a large parking area. Along the trail are eight overnight camping areas with restrooms, potable water, tent pads, and shelters. Hikers should plan ahead, however, because reservations are required and there is a fee. To make reservations phone (724) 455-3744.

The trail is marked with yellow blazes. For maps and a guidebook for the Laurel Highlands Hiking Trail contact the Sierra Club of Pittsburgh.

For more information: Sierra Club of Pittsburgh, 80 Rose Leaf Road, Pittsburgh, PA 15220.

Tuscarora Trail

[Fig. 49(5)] The Tuscarora Trail is a 248-mile-long side loop off of the Appalachian National Scenic Trail. The southern end of the trail splits off from the Appalachian Trail in Virginia. It then passes north through West Virginia and Maryland, reconnecting with the Appalachian Trail in Pennsylvania, northwest of Harrisburg in Perry County.

The trail was built in the late 1960s because there was concern that development in Virginia would eliminate a portion of the Appalachian Trail. Even though the Appalachian Trail is still intact, the Tuscarora Trail remains and has become a popular hiking trail.

In Pennsylvania, the Tuscarora Trail lies completely within the Valley and Ridge province, following the summit of Tuscarora Mountain along much of its 106-mile course. Portions of the trail also cross valleys and Rising Mountain and Blue Mountain. The mountainous portions of the trail pass through mixed-oak forests and mixed-hardwood forests. Much of the forested portions of the trail, particularly along the southern end, were heavily damaged by gypsy moths. The increased amount of sunlight reaching the ground through the leafless canopy allowed briars and thick underbrush to grow and make portions of the trail impassable. Today the canopy is once again full and lush, and volunteer organizations have cleared the trail.

In addition to State Game Lands managed by the Pennsylvania Game Commission, the trail passes through several state parks and forests. The southern end of the trail passes through Buchanan State Forest (*see* page 235), passing near the birthplace of President James Buchanan. The trail also crosses the old Forbes Road, a supply route used by the British during the French and Indian War. As it passes through Colonel Denning State Park (*see* page 215) on Blue Mountain, the trail passes Flat Rock, a scenic vista offering a dramatic view of the Cumberland Valley. Also lying along the trail in Pennsylvania are the Tuscarora State Forest (*see* page 229) and Cowans Gap State Park (*see* page 217).

The Keystone Trails Association

EASTERN MOLE
(Scalopus aquaticus)
Spending most of its life underground, the mole feeds on earthworms and insect larvae in its passageway of tunnels 10 inches below the surface. It is identified by a pink snout, hairless tail, and furry body that grows to 6 inches.

maintains the trail in Pennsylvania. Guide maps and trail information can be obtained from them.

For more information: Keystone Trails Association, PO Box 251, Dept. WWW, Cogan Station, PA 17728.

QUEEN ANNE'S LACE
(Daucus carota)
A very common wildflower found across North America from Alaska to Mexico. Growing to five feet tall, the flowers are creamy white with a single dark flower in the center.

Appendixes

A. Books and References

A Geography of Pennsylvania by E. Willard Miller, Editor, Penn State Press, University Park, PA, 1995.

Appalachian Autumn by Marcia Bonta, University of Pittsburgh Press, Pittsburgh, PA, 1994.

Appalachian Spring by Marcia Bonta, University of Pittsburgh Press, Pittsburgh, PA, 1991.

Atlas of Breeding Birds in Pennsylvania by Daniel W. Brauning, Editor, University of Pittsburgh Press, Pittsburgh, PA, 1992.

A Viewer's Guide Pennsylvania Wildlife by Kathy & Hal Korber, Northwoods Publications, Inc., Lemoyne, PA, 1994.

Birders Guide to Pennsylvania by Paula Ford, Gulf Publishing, Houston, TX, 1995.

Endangered and Threatened Species of Pennsylvania by Frank Felbaum, Editor, Pennsylvania Wild Resource Conservation Fund, Harrisburg, PA, 1995.

50 Hikes in Central Pennsylvania by Tom Thwaites, Backcountry Publications, Woodstock, VT, 1985.

50 Hikes in Eastern Pennsylvania by Tom Thwaites, Backcountry Publications, Woodstock, VT, 1997.

Hiking Pennsylvania by Rhonda and George Ostertag, Falcon Publishing Co., Inc., Helena, MT, 1998.

More Outbound Journeys in Pennsylvania: A Guide to Natural Places for Individual and Group Outings by Marcia Bonta, University of Pittsburgh Press, Pittsburgh, PA, 1995.

Mountains of the Heart: A Natural History of the Appalachians by Scott Weidensaul, Fulcrum Publishing, Golden, CO, 1994.

Outbound Journeys in Pennsylvania by Marcia Bonta, University of Pittsburgh Press, Pittsburgh, PA, 1991.

Pennsylvania by H. Mark Weidman, Graphic Arts Center Publishing Company, Portland, OR, 1994.

Pennsylvania Almanac by Jere Martin, Stackpole Books, Mechanicsburg, PA, 1997.

Pennsylvania One-Day Trip Book by Jane Ockershausen, EPM Publication, McLean, VA, 1995.

Pennsylvania State Parks: A Complete Recreation Guide by Bill Bailey, Glovebox Guidebooks of America, Saginaw, MI, 1996.

Pennsylvania Trout Streams and Their Hatches by Charles Meck, Backcountry Publications, Woodstock, VT, 1993.

Roadside Geology of Pennsylvania by Bradford B. Van Diver, Mountain Press Publishing Company, Missoula, MT, 1990.

Susquehanna: River of Dreams by Susan Q. Stranahan, John Hopkins University Press, Baltimore, MD, 1993.

The Allegheny River: Watershed of a Nation by Jim Schafer and Mike Sajna, Penn State Press, University Park, PA, 1992.

The Cook Forest by Anthony E. Cook, Falcon Publishing Co., Inc., Helena, MT, 1997.

The Crown Jewel of Pennsylvania: The State Forest System by R.R. Thorpe, Pennsylvania Department of Conservation and Natural Resources, Harrisburg, PA, 1997.

B. Chambers of Commerce and Tourist Promotion Agencies

ALTOONA-BLAIR COUNTY CHAMBER OF COMMERCE
1212 12th Avenue
Altoona, PA 16601-3493
Phone (814) 943-8151

BEDFORD COUNTY CHAMBER OF COMMERCE
137 East Pitt Street
Bedford, PA 15522
Phone (814) 623-2233

BELLEFONTE AREA CHAMBER OF COMMERCE
Train Station, West High Street
Bellefonte, PA 18623
Phone (814) 355-2917

BRADFORD AREA CHAMBER OF COMMERCE
10 Main Street, On the Square
PO Box 135
Bradford, PA 16701
Phone (814) 368-7115

CENTRAL BRADFORD COUNTY CHAMBER OF COMMERCE
PO Box 146
Towanda, PA 18848
Phone (717) 265-8106

CLARION AREA CHAMBER OF COMMERCE
41 South Fifth Avenue
Clarion, PA 16214
Phone (814) 226-9161

DUBOIS AREA CHAMBER OF COMMERCE
33 N. Brady Street
DuBois, PA 15801
Phone (814) 371-5010

EMPORIUM-CAMERON COUNTY CHAMBER OF COMMERCE
33 East Fourth Street
Emporium, PA 15834
Phone (814) 486-4314

FULTON COUNTY CHAMBER OF COMMERCE
PO Box 141
112 North Second Street
McConnellsburg, PA 17233
Phone (717) 485-4064

GREATER MANSFIELD AREA CHAMBER OF COMMERCE
14 South Main Street
Suite 206
Mansfield, PA 16933
Phone (717) 662-3442

HAWLEY-LAKE WALLENPAUPACK CHAMBER OF COMMERCE
PO Box 150, Route 6
Hawley, PA 18428
Phone (717) 226-3191

INDIANA COUNTY CHAMBER OF COMMERCE
1019 Philadelphia Street
Indiana, PA 15701
Phone (412) 465-2511

JUNIATA VALLEY AREA CHAMBER OF COMMERCE

3 W. Monument Square, Suite 204
Lewistown, PA 17044
Phone (717) 248-6713

LAUREL HIGHLANDS VISITORS BUREAU

120 E. Main Street
Ligonier, PA 15658
Phone (412) 238-5661

LIGONIER VALLEY CHAMBER OF COMMERCE

120 East Main Street
Ligonier, PA 15658
Phone (412) 238-4200

MIFFLIN & JUNIATA COUNTIES TOURIST PROMOTION AGENCY

3 W. Monument Square
Lewistown, PA 17044
Phone (717) 248-6713.

PIKE COUNTY CHAMBER OF COMMERCE

305 Broad Street, PO Box 883
Milford, PA 18337
Phone (717) 296-8700

POCONO MOUNTAINS CHAMBER OF COMMERCE

556 Main Street
Stroudsburg, PA 18360
Phone (717) 421-4433

POCONO MOUNTAINS VACATION BUREAU, INC.

1004 Main Street
Stroudsburg, PA 18360-1695
Phone (717) 424-6050 or (800) POCONOS

PORT ALLEGANY CHAMBER OF COMMERCE

22 Church Street
Port Allegany, PA 16743-1136
Phone (814) 642-9555

RIDGWAY-ELK COUNTY CHAMBER OF COMMERCE

231 Main Street, PO Box 357
Ridgway, PA 15853-0357
Phone (814) 776-1424

SHIPPENSBURG AREA CHAMBER OF COMMERCE

75 West King Street
Shippensburg, PA 17257
Phone (717) 532-5509

SOMERSET COUNTY CHAMBER OF COMMERCE

601 N. Center Avenue
Somerset, PA 15501
Phone (814) 445-6431

ST. MARYS AREA CHAMBER OF COMMERCE

126 Center Street
St. Marys, PA 15857
Phone (814) 781-3804

SUSQUEHANNA VALLEY VISITORS BUREAU

RR 3, 219-D Hafer Road
Lewisburg, PA 17837
Phone (717) 524-7234

UNION COUNTY CHAMBER OF COMMERCE

219 D. Hafer Road
Lewisburg, PA 17837
Phone (717) 524-2815

WARREN COUNTY CHAMBER OF COMMERCE
> PO Box 942
> 315 Second Avenue, Suite 409
> Warren, PA 16365
> Phone (814) 723-3050

WAYNE COUNTY CHAMBER OF COMMERCE
> 742 Main Street
> Honesdale, PA 18431
> Phone (717) 253-1960

C. Conservation Organizations and Government Agencies

Appalachian Mountain Club-Delaware Valley Chapter, 183 Baldwin Street, Philadelphia, PA 19127. Phone (215) 751-2576.

Allegheny National Forest, 222 Liberty Street, Warren, PA 16365. Phone (814) 723-5150.

Appalachian Trail Conference-Mid-Atlantic Regional Office, PO Box 381, Boiling Springs, PA 17113. Phone (717) 258-5771.

Audubon Council of Pennsylvania, 1104 Fernwood Avenue, Suite 300, Camp Hill, PA 17011. Phone (717) 763-4985.

Berks County Conservancy, 960 Old Mill Road, Wyomissing, PA 19610. Phone (610) 372-4992.

Botanical Society of Western Pennsylvania, 3333 Fifth Avenue, Pittsburgh, PA 15213. Phone (412) 578-6175.

Central Pennsylvania Conservancy, 17 North Front Street, 3rd Floor, PO Box 587, Harrisburg, PA 17108-0587. Phone (717) 233-0221.

Coalition of Concerned Pennsylvania Anglers, 3519 Ada Drive, Mechanicsburg, PA 17055. Phone (717) 732-5050.

Conemaugh Valley Conservancy, PO Box 907, Johnstown, PA 15907-0907. Phone (814) 536-6615.

Ducks Unlimited-Western Pennsylvania, 217 Pflugh Road, Butler, PA 16001. Phone (412) 865-2422.

French Creek Project, Box 172, Allegheny College, Meadville, PA 16335. Phone (814) 332-2946.

Friends of Salt Springs Park, Inc., RR3, Box 130 B, Montrose, PA 18801. Phone (717) 967-2437.

Heritage Conservancy, 85 Dublin Pike, Doylestown, PA 18901. Phone (215) 345-7020.

Keystone Trails Association, PO Box 251, Cogan Station, PA 17728-0251.

National Park Service, Philadelphia Support Office, Customs House, 3rd Fl., 200 Chestnut Street, Philadelphia, PA 19106. Phone (215) 597-7018.

National Wildlife Federation, 70 Concord Creek Road, Glen Mills, PA 19342.

Natural Land Trust, Inc., Hildacy Farm, 1031 Palmers Mill Road, Media, PA 19063. Phone (610) 353-5587.

Northcentral Pennsylvania Conservancy, 320 East Third Street, Second Floor, Williamsport, PA 17701. Phone (717) 323-6222.

Northern Allegheny Conservation Association, PO Box 661, Warren, PA 16365. Phone (814) 723-5872.

Pennsylvania Alliance for Environmental Education, 225 Pine Street, Harrisburg, PA 17101. Phone (610) 967-7233.

Pennsylvania Association of Conservation Districts (PACD), 225 Pine Street, Harrisburg, PA 17019. Phone (717) 236-1006.

Pennsylvania Boating Association, 313 Runny Mede Avenue, Jenkintown, PA 19046. Phone (215) 887-0150.

Pennsylvania Bureau of Forestry, PO Box 8552, Harrisburg, PA 17105-8552. Phone (717) 783-7941.

Pennsylvania Bureau of State Parks, PO Box 8551, Harrisburg, PA 17105-8551. Phone (888) PA-PARKS.

Pennsylvania Department of Community and Economic Development: Travel, Tourism, and Film Promotion, Room 404, Forum Building, Harrisburg, PA 17120. Phone (717) 787-5453.

Pennsylvania Department of Environmental Protection, Rachel Carson State Office Building, 400 Market Street, Harrisburg, PA 17105. Phone (717) 783-2300.

Pennsylvania Environmental Council-Headquarters, 1211 Chestnut Street, Suite 900, Philadelphia, PA 19107. Phone (215) 563-0250.

Pennsylvania Environmental Defense Fund, RD 5, Box, 354, Muncy, PA 17756-8660. Phone (717) 326-1551.

Pennsylvania Environmental Network (PEN), PO Box 92, Fombell, PA 16123. Phone (717) 786-2184.

Pennsylvania Federation of Sportsmen's Clubs (1), 2426 North Second Street, Harrisburg, PA 17110. Phone (717) 232-3480.

Pennsylvania Fish and Boat Commission, PO Box 67000, Harrisburg, PA 17106-7000. Phone (717) 657-4518.

Pennsylvania Game Commission, Dept. MS, 2001 Elmerton Avenue, Harrisburg, PA 17110-9797. Phone (717) 783-7507.

Pennsylvania Wildlife Federation, 2426 North Second Street, Harrisburg, PA 17110. Phone (717) 232-3480.

Pennsylvania Wild Resource Conservation Fund, Evangelical Press Building, 3rd & Reily Streets, PO Box 8764, Harrisburg, PA 17105-8764. Phone (717) 783-1639.

Pine Creek Preservation Association, PO Box 110, Slate Run, PA 17769. Phone (717) 753-8700.

Rails-to-Trails Conservancy-Pennsylvania Chapter, 105 Locust Street, Harrisburg, PA 17101. Phone (717) 238-1717.

Rocky Mountain Elk Foundation, 198 Bennett Road, Julian, PA 16844.

Sierra Club-Pennsylvania Chapter, PO Box 606, Harrisburg, PA 17108. Phone (717) 232-0101.

Southern Alleghenies Conservancy, 702 West Pitt Street, Suite 8, Fairlawn Court, Bedford, PA 15522. Phone (814) 623-7900.

Susquehanna Appalachian Trail Club, PO Box 399, Boiling Springs, PA 17007. Phone (717) 258-5261.

Tannersville Cranberry Bog Preserve Committee, 8050 Running Valley Road, Stroudsburg, PA 18360. Phone (717) 629-3061.

The Nature Conservancy, 1211 Chestnut Street, 12th Floor, Philadelphia, PA 19107-4122. Phone (215) 963-1400.

Trout Unlimited-Pennsylvania Council, 300 South Hanover Street, Carlisle, PA 17013. Phone (717) 249-1646.

U.S. Fish and Wildlife Service, National Wildlife Refuge System (NWR), Erie NWR, phone (814) 789-3585. John Heinz NWR at Tinicum, phone (610) 521-0662.

Western Pennsylvania Conservancy, 316 Fourth Avenue, Pittsburgh, PA 15222-2075. Phone (412) 288-2777.

D. Outdoor Guide Services

Whitewater Rafting Adventures, Inc./Biking Adventures. Guided tours, kayak clinics, and weekend tours. Route 534, Box 88, Albrightsville, PA 18210. Phone (717) 722-0285 or (800) 876-0285.

Ridge & Valley Outings Co-op. Plans local hiking trips/environmental outings. 227 Kimport Avenue, Boalsburg, PA 16827. Phone (814) 446-9260 or (814) 692-8223.

Water Gap Trolley. Located at Exit 53 off I-80. PO Box 159, Main Street, Route 611, Delaware Water Gap, PA 18327. Phone (717) 476-9766.

Kittatinny Canoes. Canoeing, tubing, kayaking, whitewater rafting, camping, guided tours, and an introduction to whitewater canoeing and learn to kayak days. Located at Dingman Bridge, Dingmans Ferry, PA 18328. Phone (717) 828-2338 or (800) FLOAT-KC.

Grayline Tours of the Poconos. Fully guided tours and tour guide services. 1200 Conroy Place, Easton, PA 18040. Phone (610) 253-4055.

Mountain Top Outfitters. Hunting and fishing guides. PO Box 201, Emporium, PA. Phone (814) 486-0363.

Pocono Bicycle Tours, Inc. PO Box 114, Hawley, PA 18428. Phone (717) 226-7303.

Stourbridge Line Rail Excursions. Train excursions. 742 Main Street, Honesdale, PA 18431. Phone (717) 253-1960.

Triple W Riding Stable, Inc. Group trips. RR 2, Box 1543, Honesdale, PA 18431-9643. Phone (717) 226-2620 or (800) 540-2620.

Jim Thorpe River Adventures, Inc. Whitewater rafting and guided tours. 1 Adventure Lane, Jim Thorpe, PA 18229. Phone (717) 325-2570 or (717) 325-4960.

Pocono Whitewater Adventures. Whitewater rafting. HC 2, Box 2245, Jim Thorpe, PA 18229. Phone (800) WHITEWATER.

Pocono Whitewater Bike Tours. Bike on a scenic trail tour. HC-2, Box 2245, Route 903, Jim Thorpe, PA 18229. Phone (717) 325-8430 or (800) GRAB-FUN.

Rail Tours, Inc. Rail excursions. PO Box 285, Jim Thorpe, PA 18229. Phone (717) 325-4606.

Bill Albright Fishing Guide Service. Box 256, Lake Ariel, PA 18436. Phone (717) 698-6035 or (717) 347-4484.

Nittany Mountain Trailrides. Featuring hayrides. RD #6, Box 383G, Lewistown, PA 17044. Phone (717) 248-2120 or (717) 234-1300.

Adventure Sports Canoe & Raft Trips. Canoe and raft trips on the Delaware River. Route 209 (2 miles north of I-80 Exit 52), Marshalls Creek, PA 18335. Phone (717) 223-0505 or (800) 487-2628.

Chamberlain Canoes, Rafts, Tubes. Canoe, raft, and tube trips on the Delaware River. PO Box 155, River Road, Minisink Acres Mall, Minisink Hills, PA 18341. Phone (717) 422-6631 or (717) 421-0180.

Moyer Aviation Inc. Guided tours. Pocono Mts. Airport, Mount Pocono, PA 18344. Phone (717) 839-7161 or (800) 321-5890.

Allegheny Valleys Bicycle Tours. Scenic bike tours. 1508 Wolfe Avenue, North Braddock, PA 15104-3066. Phone (412) 824-3844.

Laurel Highlands River Tours. Guided whitewater rafting tours. Box 107, Ohiopyle, PA 15470. Phone (412) 329-8531 or (800) 4-RAFTIN.

Mountain Streams & Trails. Guided rafting. Box 106, Ohiopyle, PA 15470. Phone (412) 329-8810 or (800) RAFT NOW.

Whitewater Adventurers. Guided raft trips. Box 31, Ohiopyle, PA 15470. Phone (412) 329-8850 or (800) WWA-RAFT.

Wilderness Voyageurs Inc. Guided trips on the Youghiogheny. Box 97, Ohiopyle, PA 15470. Phone (412) 329-5517 or (800) 272-4141.

Wallenpaupack Scenic Boat Tour. PO Box 326, Paupack, PA 18451. Phone (717) 226-0640 or (717) 226-6211.

Shawnee River Adventures. Rafts, tubing, and canoeing. Box 189, Shawnee-on-Delaware, PA 18356. Phone (717) 421-1500 or (800) SHAWNEE, Ext. 1850.

Appalachian Ski & Outdoors. Hikes, wildlife viewing, and guided mountain biking expeditions. 324 West College Avenue, State College, PA 16801. Phone (814) 234-4284 or (800) 690-5220.

Allegheny Outfitters. Canoe trips and overnight island camping. PO Box 1681, Warren, PA 16365. Phone (814) 723-4868.

Headwaters and Backwoods Guide Service. Day fishing trips. 444 Conewango Avenue, Warren, PA 16365. Phone (814) 726-0426.

Kinzua Boat Rentals & Marina. Excursion rides. Route 59 (10 miles east of Warren), PO Box 825, Warren, PA 16365. Phone (814) 726-1650.

Kinzua Fly Fishing Camp. Introduction to fly fishing, fly tying, and fly casting techniques. 44 Parkview Avenue, Bradford, PA 16701. Phone (814) 368-5814.

Lehigh Rafting Rentals, Inc. Self-guided float trips on the Lehigh River. PO Box 296, White Haven, PA 18661. Phone (717) 443-4441 or (800) 291-7238.

Whitewater Challengers, Inc. Guided raft tours. 4480 State Street, Route 940, White Haven, PA 18661. Phone (717) 443-9532 or (800) 443-8554.

E. Special Events, Fairs, and Festivals

JANUARY
   Pennsylvania Learn to Ski Day—Held at area ski resorts in the Pocono Mountains. Special discounts on lessons and rentals. Reservations are required. Pocono Mountains Vacation Bureau, Inc., phone (717) 424-6050.

FEBRUARY
   Annual Ice Tee Golf Tournament—Held at Lake Wallenpaupack in Hawley. Play nine holes of golf atop frozen Lake Wallenpaupack. Refreshments and prizes are offered. Hawley-Lake Wallenpaupack Chamber of Commerce, phone (717) 226-3191.

MARCH
   Spring Whitewater Rafting—Held throughout March in the Pocono Mountains. Melting snow and spring rain make for a wild ride on the Lehigh River. Pocono Mountains Vacation Bureau, Inc., phone (717) 424-6050.

APRIL
   Pennsylvania Maple Festival—Held in Meyersdale in Somerset County. Learn about the maple industry and sample its products. Enjoy tours, bands, crafts, and more. Phone (814) 634-0213.

MAY
   Laurel Festival of the Arts—Held in Jim Thorpe in Carbon County. Musical event of the Pocono Mountains. Gallery tours, children's programs, poetry reading, sculpture, and dance performances. Carbon County/Jim Thorpe Tourist Promotion Agency, phone (717) 325-3673.
   Upper Delaware Shad Fest—Held in Pike County at Fireman's Field, Lackawaxen. Shad fishing tournament featuring vendors, crafts, quilt making, blacksmithing, silk making, and seminars on archery and black powder shooting. Phone (717) 685-2010.

JUNE
   Allegheny National Forest "Forest Fest"—Held in Northwest Pennsylvania throughout the Allegheny National Forest. Third weekend in June. An opportunity to discover natural treasures of the forest, interpretive programs and discounts to the museums and fish hatchery. Phone (814) 362-4613.
   Lehigh Legacy Sojourn—Begins in White Haven in Luzerne County. A six-day rafting, biking, canoeing trip down the Lehigh River. The Wildlands Conservancy, phone (610) 965-4397.

Laurel Blossom Festival—Held at the railroad station in Jim Thorpe, Carbon County. Arts, crafts, entertainment, train rides, and more. Carbon County/Jim Thorpe Tourist Promotion Agency, phone (717) 325-3673.

Dam Release Weekend—Held along the Lehigh River below the dam. The Army Corps of Engineers pops the dam open for a burst of fun, creating whitewater excitement. Pocono Mountains Vacation Bureau, phone (717) 424-6050.

Annual Mountain Bike Weekend—Held in Jim Thorpe in Carbon County. One of the largest noncompetitive gatherings of off-road bicyclists. Group camping, organized trail rides for all levels of ability, entertainment, seminars, swap meet, prizes and awards. For information send a self-addressed stamped envelope to MBW, 634 S. Spruce Street, Lititz, PA 17543.

Annual Sportsman's Quest National Walleye Tournament—Held at the Kinzua/Wolf Run Marina, Allegheny Reservoir, Warren. Two days of great fishing. Requires a two person team and an entry fee. Prizes awarded both days. For information contact the Northern Alleghenies office of tourism, phone (800) 624-7802. To register contact Sportsman's Quest, phone (800) 224-4990.

JULY

Revolutionary War Days—Held in Blair County at Fort Roberdeau National Historic Landmark, 8 miles northeast of Altoona. Re-enactments and games. Phone (814) 946-0048.

Woodcarving Competition & All Wood Festival—Held in Cook Forest, at the Sawmill Center for the Arts. Second weekend in June. Woodcarving competition with awards. Theme oriented craft show and sale. Phone (814) 927-6655.

Black Moshannon Summer Festival—Held at Black Moshannon State Park in Philipsburg. Third weekend in July. Two-day chicken barbecue, crafts and concessions. Volleyball tournament and beach party with free weiner roast on the last night. Log splitting and axe throwing competitions and demonstrations. Phone (814) 342-5960.

AUGUST

Old Home Days—Held at Greenwood Furnace State Park in Huntingdon County. Heritage festival, re-enactments and crafts. Phone (814) 667-1805.

Crook Farm Country Fair—Held in Bradford in McKean County. The weekend before Labor Day weekend. Arts, crafts, demonstrations of old-time crafts, chair caning, entertainment, and food. Phone (814) 966-3880.

Corn Festival—Held on the main street of Shippensburg in Franklin County. The last Saturday in August. A huge market of over 300 arts, crafts, and food vendors. Shippensburg Area Chamber of Commerce, phone (717) 532-5509.

SEPTEMBER

Bucktail Regiment—Held in Leonard Harrison State Park. Third weekend of September. Living history encampment and re-enactment. Phone (717) 724-3061.

Mountain Craft Days—Held in Somerset in Somerset County. Weekend following Labor Day. Craft demonstrations and food. Phone (814) 445-6077.

Pennsylvania State Fishing Tournament—Held in Tidioute in Warren County. Anglers event, town festival, and carnival. Phone (800) 624-7802.

Celebration of the Arts—Held in Delaware Water Gap. Annual three-day jazz festival, musicians, art exhibits, arts, crafts, and food. Phone (717) 424-2210.

Fall Whitewater Dam Release—Held along the Lehigh River. Dam releases create whitewater and exciting rapids. Pocono Mountains Vacation Bureau (717) 424-6050.

Annual Wild Wind Folk Art & Craft Festival—Held at the Pittsfield Fairgrounds in Warren County. Second weekend in September. Juried arts and crafts, live entertainment, demonstrations, and live animal displays. Northern Alleghenies office of tourism, phone (814) 726-1222 or (800) 624-7802.

Tall Oaks Annual Autumn Fest—Held in Sheffield on Route 666 in Warren County. Begins the second weekend in September and continues every weekend of September and October. Large autumn and Christmas craft event, food and live entertainment. Northern Alleghenies office of tourism (814) 726-1222 or (800) 624-7802.

OCTOBER

Annual Fall Foliage Festival—Held in Bedford. Crafts, parades, food, and carriage rides. Phone (800) 765-3331.

Harvest Festival—Held in Stroudsburg in Monroe County at Quiet Valley Living Historical Farm. Learn how farm living was back in the 19th century, basket-making, black smithing, bee keeping, colonial ale brewing, flax processing, and more. Phone (717) 992-6161.

Lumberjack Festival—Held at Shawnee Place and Shawnee Mountain in Shawnee on Delaware. Non-stop entertainment, competitions, log rolling, pole climbing, hayrides, buffet, arts & crafts, chairlift rides, and more. Phone (717) 421-7231.

Annual Shawnee Fall Foliage Balloon Festival—Held at the Shawnee Inn in Shawnee on Delaware. Hot air balloon rides, circus, entertainment, arts and crafts, skydiving, food, and more. Phone 1-800-SHAWNEE.

F. Websites

Adventure Sports Canoe & Raft Trips—http://www.poconomall.com/adventuressports
Allegheny National Forest—http://warren.penn.com/~anf
Allegheny Outfitters—http://members.tripod.com/~AlleghenyOutfitter/canoe.html
Delaware Water Gap National Recreation Area Home Page—http://www.nps.gov/dewa/
Hawk Mountain Sanctuary—http://www.hawkmountain.org
Keystone Trails Association—http://www.reston.com/kta/kta.html
Laurel Highlands River Tours—http://www.laurelhighlands.com
Laurel Highlands Visitors Bureau—http://www.laurelhighlands.org
Mountain Streams & Trails—http://www.mtstreams.com
National Park Service—http://www.nps.gov
Pedal Pennsylvania—http://www.pedal-pa.com
Pennsylvania Bureau of Forestry—http://www.dcnr.state.pa.us
Pennsylvania Bureau of State Parks—http://www.dcnr.state.pa.us
Pennsylvania Department of Environmental Protection—http://www.dep.state.pa.us
Pennsylvania Fish and Boat Commission—http://www.fish.state.pa.us
Pennsylvania Game Commission—http://www.state.pa.us/pa-exec/pgc
Pennsylvania Visitor's Guide—http://www.state.pa.us/visit
Pocono Mountains Vacation Bureau, Inc.—http://www.poconos.org
Potomac Appalachian Travel Club—http://www.patc.simplenet.com
The Nature Conservancy—http://www.tnc.org/
U.S. Fish and Wildlife Service—http://www.fws.gov
Western Pennsylvania Conservancy—http://www.paconserve.org/
Whitewater Adventures—http://www.waaraft.com
Whitewater Challengers, Inc.—http://www.wcrafting.com
Wilderness Voyageurs, Inc.—http://www.wilderness-voyageurs.com

G. Glossary

Anticline—Arching rock fold that is closed at the top and open at bottom. Oldest formation occurs in the center of an anticline.

Basement—Complex of igneous and metamorphic rock that underlies the sedimentary rocks of a region.

Biotic—Pertaining to plants and animals.

Boreal—Relating to the northern biotic area characterized by the dominance of coniferous forests.

Carbonate rock—Collective term including limestone and dolomite.

Coniferous—Describing the cone-bearing trees of the pine family; usually evergreen.

Continental drift—Theory that the continental land masses drift across the earth as the earth's plates move and interact in a process called plate tectonics.

Deciduous—Plants that shed their leaves seasonally and are leafless for part of the year.

Endemic—Having originated in and being restricted to one particular environment.

Escarpment—Cliff or steep rock face formed by faulting that separates two comparatively level land surfaces.

Extinct—No longer existing.

Extirpated—Extinct in a particular area.

Feldspar—Complex of silicates that make up bulk of the earth's crust.

Fold—Warped rock including synclines and anticlines.

Gneiss—Metamorphic granitelike rock showing layers.

Granite—Igneous rock composed predominantly of visible grains of feldspar and quartz. Used in building.

Igneous—Rock formed by cooled and hardened magma within the crust or lava on the surface.

Karst—Area of land lying over limestone and characterized by sinkholes, caves, and sinking streams.

Lava—Magma which reaches the surface of the earth.

Magma—Molten rock within the earth's crust.

Metamorphic—Rock which has been changed into present state after being subjected to heat and pressure from the crust, or chemical alteration.

Monadnock—Land that contains more erosion-resistant rock than surrounding area and therefore is higher.

Orogeny—A geologic process which results in the formation of mountain belts.

Outcrop—Exposed bedrock.

Overthrust belt—An area where older rock has been thrust over younger rock.

Rapids—Fast-moving water that flows around rocks and boulders in rivers; classified from I to VI according to degree of difficulty navigating.

Schist—Flaky, metamorphic rock containing parallel layers of minerals such as mica.

Sedimentary—Rocks formed by the accumulation of sediments (sandstone, shale) or the remains of products of animals or plants (limestone, coal).

Shale—Sedimentary rock composed of clay, mud, and silt grains which easily splits into layers.

Syncline—A rock fold shaped like a U that is closed at the bottom and open at the top. The youngest rock is at the center of a syncline.

Talus—Rock debris and boulders that accumulate at the base of a cliff.

Watershed—The area drained by a river and all its tributaries.

Index